Provincial
Development in RUSSIA

Provincial
Development in RUSSIA

CATHERINE II and JAKOB SIEVERS

Robert E. Jones

RUTGERS UNIVERSITY PRESS
New Brunswick, New Jersey

Library of Congress Cataloging in Publication Data

Jones, Robert E., 1942–
    Provincial development in Russia.

    Bibliography: p.
    Includes index.
    1. Soviet Union—Politics and government—1689–1800.
2. Catherine II, Empress of Russia, 1729–1796. 3. Sivers,
IAkov Efimovich, graf, 1731–1808. 4. Novgorod Region
(R.S.F.S.R.)—Economic conditions. I. Title.
DK180.J66 1984   947'.063   83–13947
ISBN 0–8135–1026–0

Contents

Maps and Tables

Acknowledgments

I AM INDEBTED TO MANY PEOPLE and institutions for assistance in researching and writing this book. A Fullbright-Hays Grant from the U.S. Office of Education and participation in the exchange of scholars administered by the International Research and Exchanges Board enabled me to carry out essential research in the archives and libraries of the Soviet Union. A grant from the Research Council of the University of Massachusetts, Amherst, allowed me to collect and photocopy important research materials.

I sincerely appreciate the cooperation and assistance given me by the archivists of the Central State Archive of Ancient Acts (TsGADA) in Moscow, especially S. R. Dolgova and A. V. Mushtafarov, and by those of the Central State Historical Archive (TsGIA) in Leningrad, especially S. G. Sakharova. I am equally indebted to the staffs and librarians at the Lenin State Library in Moscow, the Leningrad Public Library, the library of the Academy of Sciences in Leningrad, and the library of the University of Massachusetts, Amherst (particularly those in charge of inter-library loan).

I am especially grateful to Professors Marc Raeff, Walter Pintner, and Edward C. Thaden for their support and encouragement and to Professor Raeff and the late Professor S. M. Troitskii of the Soviet Academy of Sciences for their comments and suggestions on my work. I also wish to thank Professor M. T. Beliavskii of Moscow State University for the personal kindness and professional assistance extended to me while I was working in Moscow.

Finally I want to thank my wife, Maxine, for all of the help and support she has given me over the years.

Note on Style and Usage

THE TRANSLITERATION OF RUSSIAN NAMES and terms in this book follows the modified Library of Congress system, except that no indication has been given of a soft sign at the end of proper nouns (for example, Tver rather than Tver' and Kazan rather than Kazan'). When a Russian first name has a common English equivalent, the equivalent has been used instead of a transliteration (Catherine instead of Ekaterina and Paul rather than Pavel). Titles of prerevolutionary works have been transliterated according to the original spelling without modernization (*razskaz* rather than *rasskaz* and *ago* rather than *ogo* in the genative singular of masculine and neuter adjectives). Frequently used Russian terms have been treated as English words and given English plurals (guberniias rather than *gubernii* and pomeshchiks rather than *pomeshchiki*). This last practice may seem awkward at first, but it avoids the confusion of using imprecise English equivalents and the need for excessive use of italics. It follows the precedents established by other Russian specialists in writing of boyars, soviets, komissars, and oblasts.

All dates in this book have been given in accordance with the Julian calendar, which ran eleven days behind the Gregorian calendar in the eighteenth century and twelve days behind it in the nineteenth.

Provincial
Development in RUSSIA

Introduction

THE SUBJECT OF THIS BOOK is the attempt by the government of Catherine II to apply eighteenth-century ideas of progress and development to the provinces of the Russian Empire. In 1762 Russia's withdrawal from the Seven Years War, the financial crisis created by that war, and the accession of Catherine II to the Russian throne announced the beginning of a new era in the autocracy's treatment of the provinces. By adapting contemporary models and theories of development to Russian conditions, Catherine's government sought to increase the wealth and power of the Russian state by actively promoting the development of its long-neglected provinces. Although some of the measures introduced by Catherine's government had been suggested by statesmen associated with previous regimes, and although some had even been attempted by Peter the Great, the scope and consistency of Catherine's effort to develop the provinces had no precedent in Russian history. The aim of this book is to describe and analyze that effort in terms of the practical considerations confronting the empress and her officials.

Some definitions and explanations are in order. To designate the goal of Catherine's policy toward the provinces, the word "development" will be used throughout this book without reference to any specific theory or concept associated with modern social science. Instead that term will be used here simply to signify an increase in prosperity, productivity, and "happiness" (as that word was understood in the eighteenth century). Educated Russians of Catherine's time were familiar with the notion of development intended here: They knew that the level of prosperity, productivity, and happiness were higher in some countries than in others, and they believed that it could be raised (or lowered) by public policies and the actions of the state. In expressing that idea, however, they wrote and spoke not of a society's "development" (*razvitie*) but of its "enlightenment" (*prosveshchenie*), a term that implicitly attributed progress to ideas and understandings that could be transferred from one society to another. For example, Prince M. M. Shcherbatov attempted to calculate "in how much time, under the most favorable circumstances, Russia by itself, without the autocracy of Peter the Great, could have arrived at the condition in which it is in regard to enlightenment and glory."[1]

Understood in the contemporary sense, Shcherbatov's association of enlightenment with the autocracy of Peter I is less paradoxical that it would otherwise seem to a modern reader accustomed to thinking of enlightenment and of *the* Enlightenment in terms of intellectual and political freedom and the ideology of nineteenth-century liberalism.[2] If the Enlightenment in its broadest sense may be defined as the use of ideas to promote the advancement of society, then it clearly had different implications for societies at different levels of development. For Russia, as for other less developed states in southern, central, and eastern Europe, its immediate promise was not the intellectual or political liberation of the individual but the moral and material uplifting of the whole society.[3]

Because the government of Catherine II included many individuals with different outlooks and ideas, I shall try whenever possible to attribute specific ideas, policies, and programs to the person most directly responsible for them. In some cases that person was Catherine herself, but often it was a statesman with important but less than sovereign authority. Because Catherine tolerated and even encouraged differences over policy among her officials, members of her regime frequently engaged in struggles for predominance that made the policy of the government as a whole unclear. On another level, however, Catherine retained and exercised ultimate responsibility for choosing among the different courses of action advocated by her advisors. One of the subsidiary aims of this book, therefore, will be to describe some of the ways in which Catherine's government formulated policy and reached decisions on major issues affecting the provinces.

Ideas of development and political rivalries constituted only two of the important forces shaping the autocracy's policies toward the provinces. Other major determinants of those policies included the administrative capabilities of the Russian state and the current condition of the provinces. For all their interest in progress, Catherine and her officials understood that their dreams and schemes meant nothing if they exceeded the state's ability to implement them or if they failed to take the realities of provincial life into account. While striving to increase the size and efficiency of the state administration, Catherine's government collected vast amounts of detailed information about conditions within the empire. Because the knowledge and understanding of provincial Russia based on that information played a major role in determining what Catherine's government would try to accomplish in the provinces and how it would go about reform, any assessment of her government's efforts to promote the development of the provinces should also examine the objects of those efforts.

Since provincial Russia comprised too large and diverse an area to consider in the detail required by my purposes, I have focused this study on the guberniia of Novgorod. In 1762 Novgorod Guberniia embraced almost the entire northwestern corner of the Great Russian heartland, the territory between Poland and the Baltic provinces to the west, the Gulf of Finland and the guberniias of St. Petersburg and Arkhangel to the north, and the guberniias of Arkhangel, Moscow, and Smolensk to the east and south. With minor gains and loses, that territory would be redivided after 1775 to form the four guberniias of Pskov, Novgorod, Tver, and Olonets.

This area of northwestern Russia had three characteristics that make it especially relevant to a study of Catherine's efforts to promote the development of provincial Russia. First, it was a region of the Great Russian heartland. Siberia, the Volga Valley, New Russia, Little Russia, White Russia, and the Baltic provinces all presented the imperial government with problems, conditions, and opportunities that differed both in degree and in kind from those of the Great Russian heartland. Second, the territory lay between the imperial capitals of St. Petersburg and Moscow, where it was more likely than most provincial regions to be affected by the economy and culture of those cities and where it could receive more attention from the eye and the hand of the imperial government. Third, the chief administrator of that territory from 1764 to 1781 was Jakob Sievers, a purposeful and energetic statesman who regarded the development of the provinces as a moral duty. Sievers became one of Catherine's closest collaborators on provincial affairs, and his territories often served as a laboratory for experiments whose successes and failures helped to shape the programs and policies of Catherine's regime.

The principal concern of this book will be the connections and interactions among these three subjects: the enlightened policies of Catherine's government, Sievers's role in Catherine's government, and the conditions in northwestern Russia in the last third of the eighteenth century. By presenting them in such a context, I hope to show all three subjects more realistically than they would appear in isolation from each other. I intend to examine Catherine's regime in its natural environment in order to show how and why it behaved as it did. Similarly, by treating Sievers as one part of a regime that generally shared his aspirations but also had other concerns and priorities, I hope to modify Karl Blum's portrayal of Sievers as a solitary German *Kulturträger* surrounded by venal and unenlightened Russians.[4] In the same manner I shall treat the conditions in northwestern Russia as the given reality with which the imperial government and Sievers had to contend. Rather than describe those conditions for their own sake, I shall atempt to show how they affected efforts to promote progress and development and how they in turn were affected by those efforts. In doing so, I shall use Sievers's career in northwestern Russia as a bridge between intellectual and political history on the one hand and social and economic history and historical geography on the other. As governor and then as governor-general of northwestern Russia, Sievers had to deal simultaneously with the ideas of the European enlightenment, the policies and politics of the imperial government, and the hard realities of the territories he governed. His attempts to relate those subjects to one another and his successes and failures in doing so constitute an important chapter in the history of enlightened absolutism in provincial Russia.

My principal primary sources are the reports of the governors and governors-general of northwestern Russia to the Senate and the empress, letters from Sievers to Catherine and other correspondents, and the archival collections of central agencies (the Senate, the Commission on Commerce, the Legislative Commission) that dealt with subjects related to the development of the provinces. Inevitably, these sources convey official perceptions of provincial reality, but those perceptions are varied and illuminating, and it was on the basis of such perceptions rather than on reality itself that the government formulated its policies and made its decisions. I have used nonofficial primary sources whenever possible, but it seems safe to say that most of what we will ever know about provincial Russia in the eighteenth century will have to be based on government documents.

My use of the correspondence of governors and governors-general with central administrative agencies and of central agency files on provincial matters reflects my concern with the interaction between the central agencies of the absolutist state and the officials who were directly responsible for promoting development in the provinces. However, I regret that the constraints of time and the limitations of the cultural exchange between the United States and the Soviet Union prevented me from consulting provincial archives in northwestern Russia and examining the records of lower agencies of administration. I have tried to compensate for that loss by relying on the works of Soviet historians Kh. D. Sorina and E. G. Istomina. The former has written several articles on the towns in the region that became Tver Guberniia after 1776, and the latter has written a dissertation (unpublished), a book, and several articles on northwestern Russia that contain a wealth of detailed information.

For additional information on Sievers and his concerns I have had to rely on Blum's exhaustive, if antiquated, biography. With the cooperation of Sievers's daughter, Blum examined Sievers's personal papers and quoted extensively from letters that neither I nor any other historian has seen. In addition, Blum read and then reproduced many quotations from an auto-biographical memorandum that Sievers composed for the Ministry of the Interior in 1804. A copy of that memorandum once belonged to the Imperial Russian Historical Society, but it has since been lost, and neither I nor the Soviet archivists I consulted have been able to locate it. I may disagree with Blum's interpretation of many issues, but in every case in which we have used the same unpublished document, I have found his quotations to be accurate and reliable. For that reason I am willing to trust the accuracy of his quotations from documents that I have not seen. Among the sources I did not or could not use in this study for one reason or another, the one I regret most profoundly is the collection of more than three hundred letters from Catherine that Sievers reportedly destroyed before his death in 1808.[5]

In its outlook and concerns this book represents recent historiographical trends in Western writings on the reign of Catherine II. Through the first half of the twentieth century most studies of the reign of Catherine continued to reflect the interpretations formulated in the late tsarist period in Russia by liberal and populist historians interested primarily in civil liberties, self-government, and the legal status of social classes, especially the peasantry. Finding it incomprehensible that a professed adherent of the Enlightenment could have preserved both autocracy and serfdom, liberal and populist historians of Catherine's reign characterized the empress and most of her policies as exploitative, hypocritical, or foolish.[6] Such a negative assessment was all the more convincing because it drew upon and was reinforced by criticisms directed at Catherine by some of her own contemporaries.[7] Developed by some of Russia's most famous and influential historians, the received historiographic tradition that portrayed Catherine as a hypocritical and/or naive admirer of the philosophes was readily accepted by most historians in the West and intensified by those in the Soviet Union.

In the West the historiography on the reign of Catherine II began to change dramatically in the 1960s. By then the general collapse of the Whig interpretation of history, which assumed that history is the story of the expansion of toleration, civil liberties, and representative government, had begun to affect the study of Russian history and to make the Cadet variant of that historiographical tradition look increasingly old-fashioned and irrelevant. Inspired by the example of the *Annales* school, by the relativist reaction to Whig historiography, and by a contemporary concern with management and problem solving, historians began to ask different questions about Catherine's reign and to place a much greater emphasis on the actual conditions that prevailed in Russia during the second half of the eighteenth century. Coincidentally, the signing of cultural exchange agreements between Western nations and the Soviet Union made it possible for Western historians to pursue those new lines of inquiry in the archives and libraries of the USSR. The resulting outpouring of dissertations, articles, and monographs has made it increasingly possible to measure Catherine and her government not by the standards of liberal or socialist ideology but by their ability to cope with the problems they confronted.[8]

The same liberal and populist historians who disparaged Catherine's government in general had little sympathy for Catherine's efforts to promote the development of the provinces. Except in a few specific areas, such as education, their ideology led them to believe that the state should not try to mold society to conform to its wishes but should act instead to give Russians greater freedom to use their individual and collective talents in ways that would contribute to the real development of Russia. For them, state-directed development was a mistake ipso facto.

In the Soviet Union, Marxist historians concerned with the transition from feudalism to capitalism have devoted much attention to the development of the Russian economy in the second half of the eighteenth century. Yet, ironically, they have generally regarded state policy as little more than a passive, sometimes grudging response to the autonomous development of the national economy and the rise of bourgeois relationships within society. In the West, on the other hand, the prevalence of state-directed development throughout much of the world in the second half of the twentieth century has led some historians to a more sophisticated and somewhat more sympathetic consideration of the autocracy's attempts to cope with the underdevelopment of the Russian Empire in the nineteenth and early twentieth centuries.[9] In this book I shall attempt to push such considerations backward in time to the second half of the eighteenth century and to expose the structural similarities between the developmental policies of Catherine's time and those of later eras in Russian history. After a false start under Peter I, the autocracy's efforts to promote the development of provincial Russia with active government and deliberate policy had their real beginning in the reign of Catherine II, and in many respects Catherine's government established the basic patterns that would be followed by successive regimes.

I

Ideas of Development and Their Application to Russia

HEN SHE SEIZED THE RUSSIAN THRONE in a coup d'état on
June 28, 1762, Catherine II assumed responsibility for resolving a cri-
sis that threatened the solvency and security of the state. In order to finance its participation in the Seven Years War the Russian government
had raised taxes, debased the coinage, and borrowed heavily abroad. But
its last attempt to float a foreign loan had failed, and by June 1762 the
Russian army in Germany had gone six months without pay. Behind the
fiscal crisis in St. Petersburg lay an economic and administrative crisis in
the provinces. Despite Empress Elizabeth's desire for a quick, crushing victory over the Prussian armies, her government had been obliged to keep a
sizable part of the Russian army in the interior provinces to collect taxes
and military recruits and to suppress increasingly frequent disorders
among its overburdened subjects. During the first half of 1762 a crop
failure in central Russia and Peter III's decree on the secularization of ecclesiastical estates turned a serious problem into a genuine crisis: Many of
the ecclesiastical and factory serfs refused to pay their taxes or obey their
masters, and their insubordination had begun to affect the serfs of the
nobility.[1] Recalling the conditions she encountered at the time of her accession, Catherine later wrote that she had resolved then and there to
reorganize the Russian government.[2] The immediate task, of course, was

to restore order and solvency, but the more fundamental undertaking would be to improve Russia's internal condition and enhance its productive capacity.

The idea that governments could and should strive to increase the prosperity of their lands was already well established in Russia by 1762. In the first quarter of the eighteenth century Peter the Great assigned high priority to the development of Russia's resources and the expansion of its economy. His successors abandoned some of Peter's projects and curtailed others in order to bring their commitments into balance with their capabilities, but they never forsook the belief that better, more intelligent policies could enhance the national welfare and increase the power and the revenues of the autocracy. In the interval between Peter's death in 1725 and Catherine's accession in 1762, the imperial government considered scores of schemes for accomplishing those ends. Authored or sponsored by such high-ranking statesmen as V. N. Tatishchev, P. I. Shuvalov, R. L. Vorontsov, and D. V. Volkov, a number of these proposals anticipated the ideas expressed by Catherine and her advisors after 1762,[3] as did some of the discussions of the legislative commission that had been laboring since 1754 to codify and revise the laws of the Russian Empire.[4]

Since 1725 the Russian government had done relatively little to promote the development of the national economy and even less to increase the productive capacity of the provinces. In the 1750s P. I. Shuvalov had encouraged economic expansion by eliminating internal tariffs and by opening a bank to provide credit to the great landowners, but he had also constricted the economy and shortchanged the treasury by handing out lucrative contracts and monopolies to his clients and political allies. Thanks to the activities of some private entrepreneurs and the international demand for Russia's exports, the Russian economy continued to expand between 1725 and 1762, but no one attributed that expansion to the intelligence and efficacy of the government's policy. On the contrary, Catherine and her collaborators believed that their predecessors had behaved irresponsibly toward the national interest. In a memorandum on Russia's economy and commerce Nikita Panin, one of the most important figures in the new regime, blamed the crisis of the early 1760s on "the cupidity and avarice of ministers" and "the neglect of certain rulers."[5] Although Panin refrained from naming her, his description certainly applied to the reign of Elizabeth (1741–1761), whose indolence and indecision had frustrated the desire for change. After her death on December 25, 1762, the government of Peter II introduced a number of important measures aimed at revitalizing the government, the economy, and the social order, but Catherine and her associates considered those measures poorly prepared, arbitrary, and destabilizing.

With the cooperation of Panin and his ally G. N. Teplov, Catherine intended to put a stop to the mismanagement that she associated with previous regimes. In notes and memoranda written well before the coup d'é-

8

tat of June 28, Catherine expressed her conviction that governments should work to promote the prosperity and well-being of their states. Her frequent references to "the general happiness" or "the public good" (*le bien publique, vseobshchoe blago*) were commonly understood to include internal and external security, the development of economic resources, the maintenance of a favorable balance of trade, and the provision of a wide range of social services.[6] But the new empress had not yet committed herself to a specific program for attaining those goals. Her most explicit statements concerned the need to increase the population.[7] Under the influence of populationist theories current throughout contemporary Europe, Catherine pointed to a rapidly increasing population as both a source of national strength and greatness and an indication or measure of a country's internal health. In both of these senses demographic increase held the same importance for Catherine that an increase in the gross national product would hold for her twentieth-century counterparts. Before becoming empress she had written: "We need people. Make, if possible, the wilderness to swarm like a beehive."[8] Several years later, in Chapter Twenty-five of her *Instruction* to the Legislative Commission of 1767, Catherine would expound her conviction that demographic increase is a function of prosperity and happiness and that those ideals in turn are functions of law and public policy.[9]

A survey of postwar reform in other European states provides a necessary perspective on the problems facing Catherine's government. By 1762 all of the governments engaged in the Seven Years War were experiencing financial difficulties that hastened the return of peace and ushered in an era dedicated to balancing budgets and strengthening the bases of government finance. Although Catherine and educated Russians of her time understood that foreigners provided them with no ready-made solutions for Russia's problems, they were eager to profit from the experience of other countries, and they continued to look abroad for examples and ideas that might be adapted to their own situation.[10]

The governments of England and France operated in a political and economic context fundamentally different from that of Prussia, Austria, and Russia. The relatively well-developed economies of the Atlantic powers produced a comparative abundance of wealth, but their governments could claim only a small portion of that wealth for the royal treasury in the form of taxes. For those governments, the answer to their financial problems lay in controlling their expenses and/or in raising taxes in the face of legal and political obstacles. By directing their efforts at Britain's overseas colonies, the ministers of George III sought to minimize their political problems at home. In the process, however, they set in motion the chain of events that led directly to the American War of Independence. In France, meanwhile, the ministers of Louis XV and Louis XVI struggled to reform the system of taxation and thereby provoked a reaction that led eventually to the political crisis of 1788–1789. In both countries the ensuing conflicts intensified the ongoing debates over royal authority, legality, economic policy, and the wealth of nations. Catherine and her advisers followed those discussions with great interest, but their vastly different situations made the policies of the French and British governments irrelevant to Russia. Having no parliament or parlement to contend with, the Russian government could raise taxes at will and did so by 180 percent between 1724 and 1769.[11] Nevertheless, it still could not extract enough revenue from its underdeveloped economy to satisfy its needs and ambitions.

For Prussia and Austria, as for Russia, the greatest constraint on the government's ability to increase its revenues was the weakness of the national economy. Joseph II of Austria described their common situation during a postwar crisis when he observed: "Our provinces are impoverished and cannot afford to maintain the present military establishment . . . only the improvement of our agriculture, industry, trade, and finance will make possible the upkeep and expansion of our military forces to meet future eventualities."[12] In the 1760s Frederick II and Maria Theresa would both pursue those goals by resuming the programs of development they had carried on before the war. Lacking the economic and social resources of the Atlantic powers, they turned to agencies of the state to increase the taxable wealth of the nation.

Prussia's achievements in that undertaking made it a model of the statist approach to economic development. Claiming to be all-knowing, all-powerful, and all-caring in its supervision of the country and its people, the Prussian monarchy created a bureaucracy that combined elements of military discipline, efficiency, and technical expertise and used it to manage and develop the country's resources. From one of the poorer regions of Germany it extracted more public revenue in 1762 than the Russian government could extract from an empire containing five times the population and more than one hundred times the area of Prussia.[13]

Responsibility for managing and developing Prussia's resources rested with the provincial chambers (*Kammern*) and their executive functionaries (the *Landrat, Steurrat,* and *Amptmann*). From the 1760s on, those posts would be filled by officials who had studied cameralistic science (*Kammeralwissenschaft*) at a university, served an apprenticeship on a royal farm, and passed an entrance examination on economics, jurisprudence, and public administration. Adapting their efforts to local conditions, the chambers led the way in opening mines, expanding fisheries, draining swamps, colonizing wastelands, improving towns, establishing schools, constructing roads and canals, and teaching farmers how to improve crop yields.[14] As an agent of progress, the Prussian bureaucracy embodied the aims and the ideology of paternalistic absolutism more successfully than any other adminstrative agency in Europe. Even though its performance often fell short of Frederick's expectations, not to mention the ideals of cameralism, its accomplishments attracted the attention of other absolutist regimes. Writing about Prussia in the 1760s, the comte de Mirabeau observed: "The government of Prussia has become for the science of despotism what Egypt was for ancients in search of knowledge."[15]

By 1762, having fought Prussia on the battlefield for fifteen of the past twenty-three years and expecting to do so again in the future, the Austrian government had learned the advantages of the Prussian system. In 1749, at the end of the previous war, Maria Theresa had reformed the government's methods of recruiting and financing the army and created a rationalized system of local and provincial administration based on the *Kreisehauptmann* and supervised by the Directorum Publicis et Cameralibus in Vienna. To staff the expanded civil service and mollify the nobles, Maria Theresa took pains to attract young noblemen into the bureaucracy. To help train them, she followed the Prussian example of creating chairs of political science and natural law at the universities.

In the 1760s Maria Theresa and her ministers Kaunitz and Cobenzl extended and revised the reforms of the 1750s. They reorganized the agencies of the central administration, undertook new efforts to improve agriculture and industry, opened village schools in Bohemia, established a school of commerce in Vienna, and appointed Joseph Sonnenfels, who would soon become the leading cameralist scholar of his day, to the newly created chair of administration and commerce at the University of Vienna. On a more limited scale the empress and her ministers also initiated efforts to end the ruinous exploitation of peasants by their landlords and to weaken the cultural dominance of the Catholic church, policies that her son Joseph would push to extremes after her death in 1780. Austria continued to lag behind Prussia in the development of its administration and economy, but at the end of the Seven Years War Frederick II himself acknowledged his enemy's accomplishments in those areas and its emergence as a modern state. Austria's achievements also suggested that the Prussian model of development could be applied successfully to other lands.

Although Russia had not gone very far in adopting Prussian methods of administration by 1762, it had already committed itself to the political ideology from which those methods derived. Disregarding the religious theories with which his Moscovite predecessors had justified their authority, Peter I adopted the statist doctrines formulated in Lutheran Germany during the seventeenth and eighteenth centuries by Leibniz, Puffendorff, and Wolff. Combining Cartesian rationalism and natural law with Lutheran notions of duty and responsibility, those doctrines made no distinction between the state and the society as a whole: Subjects had no rights against their sovereign, only duties to him; sovereigns, conversely, bore the responsibility for promoting the welfare of their subjects. In Russia that ideology provided a satisfying justification for the power of the ruling elite by portraying the monarch and his agents as the protectors, benefactors, tutors, and guardians of the state and its people. It soon won the universal acceptance of educated Russians and excluded ideas based on other premises.[16]

At the same time, this ideology helped to hold Russia within the intellectual orbit of northern Germany, where statism had reduced the study of politics to a concern with methodology and technique characteristic of the Prussian administration and the cameralist school of political science. A majority of the foreign legal and administrative terms incorporated into the Russian language during the Petrine era came directly from new High German.[17] To spur Russia's intellectual development, Peter also turned to Leibniz and Wolff for help in staffing the Academy of Sciences, where German influence would predominate throughout the remainder of the century.[18] In the 1750s and 1760s German professors came to Russia to occupy virtually all of the chairs at the University of Moscow, and most of the textbooks studied there in the 1760s had been written by German scholars.[19] Natural law and political theory as formulated by Grotius, Puffendorff, and Wolff were taught as required courses in all the secular and ecclesiastical schools of eighteenth-century Russia, and at major institutions like Moscow University, the Cadet Corps, and the gymnasium of the Academy of Sciences the teachers themselves were Germans, with names such as Gross, Pflug, Langer, and Dilthey. The great majority of Russians who went abroad to study also enrolled in German universities, especially those at Halle, Marburg, Leipzig, Jena, and Tübingen, where the pupils and disciples of Christian Wolff continued to dominate the intellectual climate.[20] In the fourth decade of the eighteenth century French culture had begun to exert a dominant influence on the art, manners, clothing, cuisine, architecture, and belles-lettres of Russia (and most of the rest of Europe), but in serious matters Russians continued to look to Germany for guidance and inspiration.[21]

For all that, the autocracy's ideological reach exceeded its administrative grasp. Catherine's government could not follow the lead of the central European powers in seeking a cameralistic, bureaucratic solution to the problem of underdevelopment because its own system of internal administration would not permit it. In spite of its ideological conversion to German theories of absolutism, the Russian monarchy continued to collect money and services over a vast but thinly administered territory. The roots of that system can be traced back at least as far as the Muscovite princes of the fifteenth and sixteenth centuries, and some historians even see it as a direct continuation of the system of tribute collection imposed on Russia by the Tatars in the thirteenth century.[22] Peter I tried to reform Russia's internal administration along the lines of German political theory and administrative practice, but although he increased expenditures on provincial administration by some 500 to 600 percent, his reforms met with little success. In the so-called counter-reforms of 1726–1727 Peter's successor rescinded his programs for governing and administering the provinces, and the autocracy reverted to its centuries-old policy of exploiting the provinces at the lowest possible cost.[23] The imperial government reduced Peter's expenditures on roads, canals, schools, and local government, but it made no corresponding reduction in its demands on the provinces. The money saved was not left in the provinces for consumption or investment; it was brought to St. Petersburg to meet needs that the government considered more important, the foremost of which were the upkeep of the court and the maintenance of the largest standing army in Europe.[24]

A brief comparison of Russia's civil administration with those of Prussia and Austria reveals its most obvious shortcomings. Whereas Prussia employed 14,000 civil servants to govern 4,500,000 subjects, Russia stretched approximately the same number to govern 23,000,000 subjects inhabiting a much larger territory.[25] Similarly, Austria devoted one-third of the government's annual outlays to internal administration; the comparable figure in Russia was one-fifth.[26] The education and training of Russia's civil servants, moreover, was decidedly inferior to that of their central European counterpart. As of the 1750s only 20 percent of Russia's civilian officials had received a formal education in a state institution of any kind, and even at the highest levels of government the majority of officials obtained their only professional training in the army or the fleet.[27] In Prussia, by contrast, retired army officers could enter the civil service only as provincial subalterns, a grade of officials whom Frederick II eventually banned from promotion to higher offices.

Such general comparisons conceal the full dimensions of Russia's administrative weakness. More than half of Russia's administrators, including a disproportionate number of the most able and best educated, worked in the offices of the central government in St. Petersburg or Moscow. Outside the capitals, the civil administration of the Russian Empire in 1763 consisted of fewer than five thousand officials, most of whom were either low-ranking clerks and scribes or retired army officers performing duties that were often quasi-military in character.[28] Unable to live off their meager salaries, provincial officials in Russia were expected to support themselves with "gifts" acquired in the conduct of official business.[29]

Even more serious, officials were spread too thinly throughout the provinces. In 1763 the Russian Empire, exclusive of the Baltic provinces and some of the Ukraine, was divided into only twelve guberniias. Those guberniias were subdivided into thirty-four provintsiias, which were subdivided in turn into 165 uezds (see Table 1). That meant that each unit normally comprised an enormous expanse of territory. Thus, even though an uezd, as the basic level of administration, was functionally equivalent to an Austrian or Prussian *kreis*, it normally encompassed as much territory as an entire Austrian or Prussian province. Yet its administration consisted of only fifteen civilian officials and twenty-nine soldiers (see Table 2). Several Russian guberniias and even some provintsiias embraced an area greater than the entire kingdom of Prussia, even though a guberniia employed

TABLE 1. COSTS OF PROVINCIAL ADMINISTRATION BEFORE
AND AFTER THE REFORM OF 1768

Unit	No. in 1763	Cost in rubles	Abolished	Created	No. in 1768	Cost in rubles
Guberniia	12	120,085	0	1[a]	13	129,700
Provintsiia	34	131,028	3[b]	3	34	131,028
Gorod[c]	165	281,140	44	12	133	226,616
Prigorodok[d]	13	7,982	3	30	40	24,560

[a]Irkutsk.

[b]Including Irkutsk.

[c]These data refer not to urban administration per se but to the administration of the entire uezd centered on the gorod.

[d]This was a branch office of uezd administration.

Source: "Doklad Senata o preobrazobaniiakh gubernskikh i uezdnykh pristustvennykh mest," January 19, 1768. TsGADA, f. 248, d. 3716, pp. 521–522.

Note: Although the doklad includes Siberia, it does not include St. Petersburg, the Ukraine, or the Baltic provinces.

only forty-seven officials and a provintsiia only twenty-five (see Tables 3 and 4). Russia's physical dimensions challenged the basic cameralistic assumption that the sovereign could supervise officials who in turn could supervise the people. The rulers of Prussia and Austria found it difficult enough to supervise their officials;[30] Russian distances raised that problem to a new order of magnitude.

Given the inadequate size and training of Russia's provincial bureaucracy, one might ask how it managed to govern so many people and so much territory. The simple answer is that for the most part it could not and did not govern them. To deal with its millions of subjects, the imperial government relied on the serfowners and the class organizations of privileged orders like the merchants and Cossacks to act as intermediaries. These unsalaried and unofficial agents of the crown delivered most of the taxes and services owed to the state, and tax farmers and the army collected the remainder.

Under these circumstances, the principal duties of provincial administrators were to receive and record deliveries of taxes and military recruits to the towns that served as the outposts of the imperial government. Although other duties were occasionally demanded of them, provincial officials lacked both the capacity and the desire to perform at more than minimum levels.[31] If the local populace failed to fulfill its assigned obligations, if some elements of it became too disorderly, or if some emergency arose that required the government to act, the normal recourse of provincial officials was to notify their superiors and turn to the local garrison or the imperial army for assistance. Under such conditions initiative and responsibility for constructive action rested almost entirely with the government in St. Petersburg rather than, as in Prussia, with provincial officials. When the central government wanted to undertake some action outside the normal administrative routine, it frequently acted through some agency external to the regular civil administration, such as the army. For example, when it wanted to repair the road between St. Petersburg and Moscow or improve navigation on the waterways that connected the Volga with St. Petersburg, the imperial government sent General Fermor and General Murav'ev into the provinces at the head of specially commissioned *ekspeditsii* (special offices or agencies).

Unlike Frederick II or Maria Theresa, therefore, Catherine II could not simply *resume* a program of state-directed development that presupposed a fairly large and decently competent bureaucracy. If she were to try to follow their lead, she would have to *initiate* such a program by creating

TABLE 2. UEZD ADMINISTRATION IN 1763

| | Official or rank | | |
Civil Administration	Number needed	Salary	Cost (in rubles)
voevoda	1	375	375
tovarishch	1	250	250
registrator	1	200	200
kantseliarist	3	60	180
podkantseliarist	4	40	120
kopiist	4	30	120
storozh	1	18	18
na kantseliariia raskhody			50
Subtotal	15		1,353
	Garrison		
podporutchik	1	126.38	
serzhant	1	15.00	15.00
kapral	2	11.00	22.00
riadovye	24	7.50	180.00
barabanchik	1	7.50	7.50
Subtotal	29		350.88
TOTAL COST			1,703.88 per uezd

Source: Table included in Senate report on the establishment of four new towns in Novgorod Guberniia. TsGADA, f. 248 (*Zhurnal Senata*), d. 3823, p. 111. The report itself is dated July 17, 1770.

Note: The total cost of the civil administration and the garrison equals the total cost per uezd shown in Table 1 rounded off to the nearest kopeck (281,140 ÷ 165 = 1,703.88).

TABLE 3. PROVINTSIIA ADMINISTRATION IN
1763 (CIVILIAN ONLY)

Official	Number Needed	Salary	Cost
voevoda	1	600	600
tovarishch	1	375	375
prokuror	1	375	375
sekretar	2	225	450
protokolist	1	150	150
registrator	1	130	130
kantseliarist	4	100	400
podkantseliarist	5	60	300
kopiist	5	40	200
perepletchik	1	25	25
storozh	2	18	36
palach	1	18	18
expenses			200
TOTAL	25		3,259

Source: Kniga Shtatov, PSZ no. 11991 (Dec. 15, 1763,
Table VII).

a bureaucracy similar to theirs but on a much larger scale. Such an undertaking might justify itself in the long run, but it was certain to be difficult,
expensive, and slow to produce results. In 1762–1763, however, the new
empress and her advisers were seeking a course of action that would be
comparatively easy, cheap, and quick. Those constraints helped to offset
Catherine's predilection for the well-regulated or policed state of contemporary theory and practice and to encourage her interest in the liberal notions of politics and political economy that had arisen in England and
France during the preceding century.

England provided Catherine's contemporaries with an effective coun-
ter-example to the Prussian model of development. John Locke's defense
of the Glorious Revolution, his arguments on behalf of liberty and property, and his assertion that the public welfare required the limitation of
royal power had gained increasing credibility from England's economic,
commercial, and military achievements in the eighteenth century. England
and the Netherlands had demonstrated that nations could be prosperous,
productive, and "happy" without an absolute monarch to supervise and
regulate the affairs of their people, and until the 1770s at least, Catherine
believed that England had the best government in Europe.[32] Impressed by
the favorable discussions of England she encountered in the writings of
Voltaire and Montesquieu, Catherine read a French translation of Blackstone's *Commentaries* and subsequently tried to incorporate some of what
she learned from him into her own legal and administrative reforms.[33]

Two of her most important advisers on those subjects had a much more intimate knowledge of England: S. E. Desnitskii had studied under Adam Smith at Edinburgh University, and Jakob Sievers had spent seven years at the Russian embassy in London. Admiration for England was particularly strong among young aristocrats, including the brothers S. R. and A. R. Vorontsov. In 1766 A. R. Vorontsov sent Catherine a disquisition on the laws of Alfred the Great, who, in Vorontsov's words, "had laid the foundation of that powerful monarchy." In particular, Vorontsov praised the Anglo-Saxon king for defending liberty and property, for protecting the legal rights of his subjects, and for encouraging agriculture, promoting commerce, and building roads.[34]

Despite Catherine's admiration for it, England's example could hardly be applied to the problems confronting her government. In a letter written to his brother from London in 1796 S. R. Vorontsov explained the major obstacle: "The English government, he wrote, while perfect for an island, would not suffice for an immense continental country surrounded by neighbors who would be able to weaken it if it were not governed by a

TABLE 4. GUBERNIIA ADMINISTRATION IN
1763 (CIVILIAN ONLY)

Official	Number Needed	Salary	Cost
gubernator	1	1,875	1,875
tovarishch	2	600	1,200
prokuror	1	450	450
sekretar	3	300	900
protokolist	1	200	200
registrator	1	150	150
arkhivarius	1	150	150
kantseliarist	8	130	1,040
podkantseliarist	10	100	1,000
kopiist	10	60	600
perepletchik	1	25	25
uchenik	1	18	18
strozh	3	18	54
palach	1	12	12
perevodchik inovercheskikh iazykov	1	150	150
tolmach	2	30	60
expenses			400
TOTAL	47		8,284

Source: Kniga Shtatov, PSZ no. 11991 (Dec. 15, 1763, Table VI).

monarchy that was most vigorous in its administration."[35] Vorontsov had gone to the heart of the matter. Geography had done for England what absolute monarchs and their standing armies professed to do for the continental powers—protect them from their hostile neighbors. A serious effort to imitate the British pattern of development would require the Russian government to cut back drastically on its armed forces in order to put more money into the hands of investors and consumers, and that was out of the question. Catherine may have taken a few ideas directly from Blackstone, but in most cases the British influences that helped to shape Catherine's policies and legislation had already been adapted to Continental conditions by French and German thinkers.

England's example reinforced the criticisms that French intellectuals directed to their own government. In the 1690s Fénelon, Boisguilbert, Bellebat, and others attacked Louis XIV and Colbert for damaging the prosperity and well-being of France with religious persecution, needless wars, ruinous taxation, and excessive interference in the natural workings of the economy.[36] Fed by the failures and frustrations of Louis's last years, those arguments against the excesses and abuses of royal power and its attendant mercantilism swelled into a major current of eighteenth-century European thought. In one form or another they dominated the discussion of politics and political economy in France and influenced thinkers and statesmen beyond that country's frontiers.

By treating those arguments as constructive criticisms, Catherine and other influential Russians could incorporate them into their own notions of absolute monarchy. Following Montesquieu, Catherine emphasized the distinction between tyranny, which knows no restraint, and true monarchy, which governs through established laws and institutions. Nikita Panin shared Catherine's disdain for tyranny and added a lawful monarch's reliance on professional statesmen and advisers to the list of safeguards against it.[37] The opposition to needless and aggressive wars that had developed in France under Louis XIV also found a receptive audience among Russians who had been appalled by the cost and futility of their country's participation in the Seven Years War. In the 1760s Catherine's desire for peace sprang largely from her appraisal of the current situation; Panin's was more principled and more enduring. More ideological still were the antiwar sentiments of intellectuals like Sumarokov, Fonvizin, Bogdanovich, and Domashnev, who saw warfare and the national welfare as polar opposites.[38] Opponents of mercantilism and other forms of economic regulation found a sympathizer in G. N. Teplov, an ally of Panin and a major figure in the new regime, who doubed the state's ability to prescribe and enforce an economic order that did not correspond to physical and human nature.[39]

The doctrines of the French physiocrats in particular contained several elements that were especially attractive to Catherine and her advisers. One was Quesney's basic premise that agriculture and other extractive occupations constituted the ultimate source of all wealth. Russia, after all, was an overwhelmingly agricultural country, where the landowning class was even more important than in France and where all of the powerful people from the monarch on down derived the bulk of their income from the land. Another attraction of physiocratic theories was their assertion that in some respects governments could actually do more to promote prosperity by doing less to interfere with the natural functioning of the economy. Catherine and her senior officials took an understandable interest in a doctrine that made a virtue of their inability to direct the development of the Russian economy and suggested ways of working around that handicap. Still another attraction of physiocratic doctrines was their proponents' defense of absolute monarchy—of a sort. In opposition to Montesquieu, the physiocrats argued that abuses of royal power could best be eliminated by the monarch's own wisdom and self-interest rather than by external legal and institutional checks. On that basis Du Pont de Nemours distinguished between what he termed "legal despotism," which respected laws and property, and "arbitrary despotism," which did not. Asserting that nature was itself despotic, he and Mercier de la Rivière maintained that wise monarchs did not impose laws on the basis of arbitrary whims but simply made manifest what was already inherent in the laws of nature.[40] To "legal despots" the physiocrats assigned a limited but active role in economic development: While leaving primary economic decisions to their subjects, governments should create favorable conditions for economic activity by preserving order, simplifying weights and measures, providing effective means of transportation and communication, and eliminating barriers to commerce.[41] In its particulars, the program advocated by the physiocrats had a number of points in common with the proposals that Panin and Teplov recommended for improving Russia's commerce by making it easier for private individuals to carry on their self-interested economic activities. Like the physiocrats, those statesmen argued that the state should promote economic development by providing better roads, canals, and credit facilities for its subjects.[42]

For the most part, however, the very real differences between Russia and France limited the applicability of physiocratic theories and of French liberal thought in general. Although educated Russians and French intellectuals employed the same political vocabulary, they did so in different contexts. Differences that could be overlooked or ignored from a distance became all too apparent on closer contact. On their visits to Russia Mercier de la Rivière and, to a lesser degree, Senac de Meihan provoked their Russian hosts to anger and disdain. Diderot's visit to St. Petersburg in 1773–1774 was saved from a similar fate by the personal affection and mutual respect that existed between him and Catherine, but it forced both the empress and the philosophe to recognize the contextual incompatibility of their views. After leaving Russia, Diderot wrote Madame Meeker that Frenchmen only talked about despotism in a conventional, stylized way that bore little resemblance to the real thing.[43] Later Catherine confided to Segur that she had found Diderot's advice impractical and his manner patronizing, and to Baron Grimm she wrote that "had my instruction been to Diderot's liking, it would have turned Russia upside down."[44]

Russia's social realities joined its political ideology in limiting the applicability of French and British ideas. Political ideology denied the basic assumption that the state should serve the interests of individuals, and social realities confuted the assumption that undirected activities of self-interested individuals could modernize and expand an economy. In comparison with Britons and Frenchmen, the great majority of Russians in all classes of society lacked what Nikita Panin once termed "the spirit of enterprise." Some of the great landowners knew how to make the most of their economic resources, but most noblemen were strangers to commercial values. The great majority of them spent most of their lives in the army or the bureaucracy, in jobs that kept them away from their estates; unlike the great magnates, they had neither the capital nor the education needed to improve the productivity of their estates. After 1762 many noblemen began to search for means of increasing their incomes, but, having been trained to give and take orders, they possessed little aptitude for economic analysis and decision making and even less initiative. While Catherine's government had little choice but to look to the landlords for help in expanding the national economy, most landowners were looking to the state for help in improving their standard of living.[45]

The values of the marketplace exerted even less influence on the primary producers of the national wealth, the peasants. With limited opportunities for consumption and relatively simple wants, the peasants had little incentive to expand their production voluntarily. What usually prompted them to produce more than they needed for their own survival was compulsion in the form of taxes, serf dues, and conscription (which they could escape by purchasing substitutes).[46] Any reduction in those exploitative demands was likely to result in reduced output, the opposite of the government's goal. What, then, was the Russian government to make of the physiocrats' contention that taxes should be assessed not according to the needs of the state but according to the "natural" production of its subjects?[47] Like the nobles and the state, Russian peasants usually resorted to extensive rather than intensive means of increasing their incomes.[48]

Nor could Catherine's government expect Russia's merchants to perform the functions of the French bourgeoisie. Catherine and her officials regretted the absence of a "third estate" in Russia and considered it a handicap to the nation's development.[49] In the discussions of the Commission on Commerce, Teplov observed that merchants constituted the smallest category of the Russian population according to the most recent revision of the tax rolls and that many persons registered in that category were merchants in name only. According to Teplov, even those merchants who really did engage in commerce as opposed to handicrafts or manual labor lacked the experience, the knowledge, and the capital that a genuine bourgeoisie ought to possess.[50] The information collected by that commission and cited in its report, "On the Condition of the Merchantry in the Whole of the Russian State," supported Teplov's observations. And when merchants and townsmen were given the opportunity to inform the government of their needs and desires, they expressed little interest in the growth of trade or the expansion of commerce but requested, on the contrary, that the government protect their markets and eliminate competition through tighter regulation of economic activity.[51]

The limited applicability of all western models, whether practical or theoretical, accounts in part for the eclecticism and syncretism that scholars have noticed in Catherine's writings, in the policies of her government, and in the projects that various individuals submitted to government agencies in the 1760s.[52] Since no preformulated solution was entirely appropriate to their country's conditions or its problems, educated Russians tended to treat foreign models and theories as inspirations rather than as final answers. Quite often they borrowed ideas piecemeal, combined them with ideas from very different sources, and then tried to adapt the resulting mixture to Russian conditions as they understood them.

Another reason for the eclecticism and syncretism with which educated Russians treated western ideas was the prevalence of those same characteristics in the political and economic thought of mid-eighteenth-century Europe. Because the intellectual currents that circulated through the European world had already mingled before they ever reached St. Petersburg, Catherine and her officials rarely if ever found themselves in the position of having to choose between two discrete and easily distinguishable systems of thought, one liberal, primarily French, and specifically physiocratic and the other statist, primarily German, and specifically cameralist. For one thing, Catherine read and used some works that clearly defied such typology, including Lamare's *Traité de Police*, an older French treatise that was thoroughly statist in its approach to progress. For another, Catherine and her advisers were far more likely to be aware of explicit intranational disputes, such as that between Montesquieu and the physiocrats or between Montesquieu and Voltaire, than they were of implicit international differences. Most important of all, French and German theorists of the 1750s and 1760s were themselves combining such seemingly irreconcilable notions as absolute monarchy and individual liberty to produce the synthetic formulation that historians have identified with "enlightened despotism" or "enlightened absolutism." While French physiocrats were defining despotism in ways that were compatible with their belief in liberty and property, the heirs of the German cameralist tradition were incorporating French and even English notions of liberty and governmental restraint into their theories of absolute monarchy. Where the former began with the proposition that strong, purposeful government could benefit society and the individual, the latter began with the proposition that private initiative could serve the state and its monarch. Yet their specific recommendations were often indistinguishable. As Joseph Sonnenfels, the last of the great cameralist theoreticians, put it: "The welfare of the parts is based upon the welfare of the whole, but at the same time, the welfare of the whole springs only from the welfare of the parts."[53]

By incorporating liberal ideas into the statist outlook of cameralism, several German writers made them more accessible and more amenable to Russian readers. Johann Heinrich von Justi, a follower of Wolff and the most influential cameralist of the 1750s and 1760s, openly acknowledged his philosophical debt to Montesquieu and endorsed Abbé Coyer's arguments that commerce should be augmented—even at the expense of tradition, state regulation, and the hierarchical ordering of society—by allowing noblemen to engage in trade.[54] Justi called his formulation of enlightened absolutism *Policey*, which he defined as "all the measures in the internal affairs of a country through which the general means of the state may be more permanently founded and increased, the energies of the state better used, and the happiness of the community in general promoted. In the narrower sense we understand by *Policey* everything that is requisite for the good ordering of civil life and especially the maintenance of good discipline and order."[55] Justi advised monarchs and statesmen to use the apparatus and resources of the state to attain those goals, but he also urged them to encourage the initiative and responsibilities of individuals as well as the corporate orders of society. In much the same vein, Baron J. F. Bielfeld, in his *Institutions politiques* of 1760, combined a forceful defense of absolutism and the existing social hierarchy with an appeal to the enlightened self-interest of governments to be more flexible and more progressive in their treatment of society and their management of the national economy. According to Bielfeld, monarchs who pursued more active and more intelligent policies toward banking, commerce, agriculture, and education would succeed in benefiting their countries, their subjects, and themselves.[56] While Adam Smith's entrepreneur was to promote the general welfare by pursuing his own individual benefit, Bielfeld's monarch was to produce the same felicitous combination of public and private good by by reversing ends and means. In 1765 Joseph Sonnenfels continued the blending of liberalism with statism in his *Grundsätze der Policey, Handlung und Finanz,* in which he stated that most of his advice to monarchs could be summed up by the English phrase "Liberty and Property."[57]

Catherine and her advisers took a keen interest in the writings of Justi, Bielfeld, and Sonnenfels. Justi's *Grundfeste zu der Macht und Glückseligkeit,* published in 1760 and 1761, did not appear in a Russian translation until 1772–1778, but two of his articles on factories and manufacturing were published in Russian in 1756 and 1763, and in 1765 Panin's secretary, Denis Fonvizin, published his own translation of Justi's *Der handelnde Adel.* In that same year Catherine wrote a personal letter of thanks to Baron Bielfeld for sending her the first volume of his *Institutions politiques*.[58] A Russian translation of that volume appeared in 1768 over the name of F. I. Shakhovskoi, but V. E. Adadurov, the curator of Moscow University and Catherine's first tutor in the Russian language, confided in a letter to Academician C. F. Muller: "There is much of Her Majesty's personal labor in the translation of Bielfeld."[59] Together with the writings of Wolff, Montesquieu, and Beccaria (an Italian professor of *scienze camerali*), the works of Justi, Bielfeld, and, with less certainty, Sonnenfels provided many of the ideas that Catherine would incorporate into her *Instruction to the Commission of a New Code of Laws* issued in 1767.[60]

The sources from which Catherine and her advisers sought inspiration on matters of economics and statecraft often gave conflicting advice on specific issues, but on the broad outlines of governmental policy they presented a discernible consensus. They opposed unnecessary, shortsighted restraints on private initiative, and they counseled governments to design a framework of laws that would not only liberate private initiative but also channel it into constructive paths. To promote the development of the economy, they urged governments to create an infrastructure of works and services that included transportation, credit, education, and police. Theorists differed on where to strike a proper balance between the responsibilities of the state and the role of private initiative, but from one country to another the government's assignment tended to be inversely proportional to the level of development that had already been attained. Generally speaking, theorists in France assigned the government a greater role than did those in England, and those in Prussia and Austria assigned it an even greater role than did their counterparts in France.

For Catherine and her advisers, contemporary ideas for encouraging progress and stimulating development were as appealing in principle as they were difficult to implement in practice. Representing the wisdom of some of the best minds in the most advanced countries on earth, they offered the Russian government a long-range strategy for coping with budget deficits, poverty, and discontent, and they offered Catherine herself a path to glory as a great lawgiver and benefactress to her people. But to embrace a program based on such ideas would require the government to begin a vast undertaking with inadequate means. In order to formulate laws in accordance with the realities of nature and society, the autocracy would have to acquire a detailed knowledge of the *terra incognita* that lay outside the immediate environs of St. Petersburg and Moscow. Then it would have to design laws to improve those conditions without distorting them. At the same time, it would have to begin the task of providing the provinces with roads, canals, banks, schools, police, and other aids to progress. And all along it would have to reconcile governmental tutelage with individual liberty in a situation where neither the government nor most individuals were prepared to play the roles expected of them.

II

The New Regime

RUSSIA'S NEW EMPRESS HAD NO INTENTION of plunging ahead with a crash program to transform the provinces. Although she considered their development a necessary, worthwhile undertaking, Catherine knew that her government lacked both the knowledge and the means to deal effectively with the provinces, and she abhorred government actions that had not been carefully prepared.[1] For the first several years of her reign the government's most pressing concerns would be to stabilize its own position, put its affairs in order, and sort out its problems. During that time it preferred to take only those steps that it considered inescapable, inexpensive, or relatively easy to supervise and control. The rapid development of the provinces failed to meet those criteria.

With very few exceptions, the new government refrained from trying to make significant changes in the provinces until it had collected the information and created the institutions it would need to act effectively. The most glaring exception to this policy, the secularization of ecclesiastical estates, served to prove the wisdom of the rule. To put an end to decades of mismanagement by the church, Peter III had proclaimed an immediate and drastic change in the administration of ecclesiastical estates, but the government's inability to take over the management of those estates provoked the peasants to take matters into their own hands. Whatever the intention of Peter's precipitous reform, its most obvious consequence was chaos and rebellion. For Catherine and her associates, Peter's decrees on ecclesiastical estates provided an impressive lesson in how *not* to deal with sensitive issues,[2] but they saw no alternative to secularization. In 1764 the former estates of the Orthodox church and their 1,300,000 inhabitants were transferred to the civil authority of the College of Economy. Despite the acclaim accorded that decision by Voltaire and others, its consequences, in the short run at least, were discouraging. The College of Economy proved no more capable of governing large areas and great numbers of people than any other agency of the imperial government.[3]

Having observed that "often it is better to inspire a reform than to enforce it," Catherine sought to promote progress throughout her reign by disseminating enlightened ideas and practical knowledge among her subjects. Eventually her efforts would include a nationwide system of public schools, but that was far too ambitious an undertaking for the 1760s. In Moscow and St. Petersburg, where the government could initiate and supervise with greater confidence, Catherine founded special institutions for specific kinds of students, but even there the response from the public could be discouraging. When Ivan Betskoi and Prokofei Demidov established the School of Commerce to train the sons of merchants in commercial and entrepreneurial skills, they decided to limit the enrollment to one hundred students. But they had difficulty filling all of the places because virtually no merchants brought their sons to the school.[4]

Catherine also tried to reach parts of the literate public through the creation of educational societies. In 1765 she chartered the Free Economic Society for the Encouragement of Agriculture and Husbandry in Russia. To spread useful ideas and information among landowners, the Free Economic Society published a journal, *Trudy,* that contained a few speculative articles on social and economic questions and a much greater number of technical pieces on agronomy and mechanics.[5] Once again, however, the results were disappointing. By 1774 the Free Economic Society could count scarcely one hundred members, most of whom were aristocratic courtiers or scholars at the Academy of Sciences.[6] Few landowners in the provinces ever read *Trudy* or tried to profit from its advice.[7]

Another society, the Association of Those Who Are Dedicated to the Translation of Foreign Books into Russian, received a grant of fifty thousand rubles and a great deal of encouragement from the empress to make foreign books available to Russians who could not read them in the original. Between 1768 and 1783 the organization translated 112 foreign works selected for their practical value to society.[8] Its efforts were eventually supplemented by several official and semiofficial publications bearing such titles as *Sobranie luchshikh sochinenii (Collection of the Best Writings), Moskovskaia vedemost' (Moscow News),* and *Ekonomicheskii Magazin (Economic Journal).* Over the years Russia's presses turned out an average of 166 secular titles a year, but even though they printed only a few hundred or at best a few thousand copies of each title, they still managed to sell only a small percentage of their output.[9]

Catherine's desire to acquaint educated Russians with the utilitarian aspects of the Enlightenment also underlay her interest in Diderot's *Encyclopédie*. Amid the furor over deism, anticlericalism, and hostility to tradition that led the French government to suppress the first edition of the *Encyclopédie*, Catherine never lost sight of the fact that its editors had conceived it as a "rural glossary" and had devoted most of its pages to articles on agronomy, science, and technology. Moreover, the most controversial aspects of the *Encyclopédie* had little relevence to eighteenth-century Russia and attracted equally little notice. Catherine gave the publication the warmest possible reception and even invited the editors to transfer their operations to St. Petersburg or Riga. Newspapers in St. Petersburg and Moscow advertised the arrival of each new volume, and partial translations into Russian began appearing in 1767.[10] Instead of translating each volume in turn, however, the Russian editors brought together in one volume many articles on a single topic that had been scattered through several volumes of the original. At Catherine's instigation, M. M. Kheraskov began publication of such translations in 1767 with three volumes containing a total of twenty-seven articles on scientific subjects. Subsequent installments devoted to agriculture, commerce, economics, medicine, and the like appeared yearly, with occasional interruptions, until 1804. The earlier volumes were printed in editions of twelve hundred, but as unsold copies of volume after volume piled up in warehouses, that figure was reduced to six hundred and then to three hundred.[11] The Russian government could make the *Encyclopédie* available to its subjects, but it could not make them read it or profit from it.

Catherine's most extraordinary effort to disseminate useful, progressive ideas among her subjects involved the Legislative Commission that she convened in 1767 for the purpose of drafting a new code of laws. In her *Instruction* to that commission Catherine made an ambitious and imaginative attempt to acquaint her subjects with the ideas that had influenced her own thinking. By presenting those ideas to the public with all the fanfare she could manage, the empress hoped to broaden their influence and thus facilitate the improvement of Russia. She saw to it that seven editions of her *Instruction* were published in Russia between 1767 and 1776. Copies of those editions were still being sold for fifty to seventy kopecks in the 1780s, when an eighth edition appeared, to be followed in the 1790s by a ninth edition.[12] The *Instruction* was also read aloud, first in its entirety and then in parts, to the deputies who came to the commission from all over the empire. Owing to the election procedures established by the government, the majority of those deputies presumably enjoyed some measure of esteem among the noblemen, merchants, Cossacks, or other local constituency they represented, and the government sought to enhance their prestige with titles and special insignia. The empress may well have cherished the hope that many of the deputies would be converted by their experiences and would go back into the provinces as missionaries for enlightenment and progress. But the former deputies returned home only to be reabsorbed into provincial life, and the public remained equally uninspired by Catherine's *Instruction.* In 1784 the deputy director of the Academy of Sciences opposed publication of the eighth edition on the grounds that so many copies of the previous editions were still unsold.[13]

Catherine's government gained little leverage from its efforts to disseminate enlightened ideas among the public. Yet such efforts had to be made. They did help to spread progressive thinking among the elite, among the individuals whose opinions mattered most, and they were an essential component of any long-range program to develop Russia. But enlightenment from above had the same defects and limitations as reform from above: Its impact diminished rapidly as it moved downward and outward into Russian society. It had some effect upon the elite in the capitals, but it did nothing to enable that elite to move Russia forward. In spite of Catherine's efforts to inspire reform, she and her statesmen faced the daunting task of trying to enforce it.

Catherine's first program to promote the development of the Russian Empire avoided some of the difficulties of trying to transform provincial Russia by settling thousands of foreign immigrants in the fertile but largely uninhabited steppes of the southeast and the south. Impressed by the examples of Prussia and Austria and by the writings of Justi and Sonnenfels, Catherine saw immigration and the colonization of empty spaces as a relatively quick and seemingly simple means of increasing the population and the productive capacity of her empire. Without requiring extensive, controversial reforms or placing an excessive burden on the state administration, immigration promised to further the government's aims by helping to fill the underpopulated and unproductive regions of the empire with foreigners whose customs and techniques of production might inspire Russians to improve their own.

To administer the recruitment and settlement of foreigners in Russia, Catherine created the Chancellery for the Guardianship of Foreigners (Kantseliariia opekunstva inostrannykh) and appointed her favorite, Gregory Orlov, to be its president. In three decrees dated July 22, 1763, the empress defined the responsibilities of the chancellery and specified the terms and privileges it could offer to foreign immigrants.[14] Under those provisions the chancellery succeeded in bringing more than thirty thousand foreign settlers into Russia between 1763 and 1775.[15] Although Catherine's original manifesto of December 14, 1762, had invited foreigners to settle wherever they wished within the boundaries of her empire, in practice the chancellery focused its efforts on establishing colonies along the lower Volga. Concentrating the foreign settlements in one geographically limited area did not eliminate administrative problems, but it helped to make them manageable.

A separate effort to settle the western reaches of the steppe with Russians, Ukrainians, and immigrants from southeastern Europe was entrusted to A. P. Mel'gunov, an ally of Nikita Panin. By dividing the responsibility for colonizing the steppe, Catherine tried to accommodate the conflicting aims of the Panin and Orlov factions within her government. Orlov advocated a policy oriented toward the steppe and the Black Sea and an alliance with Austria against the Turks, whereas Panin sought peace in the south and a policy oriented toward the Baltic. By making Orlov president of the Chancellery for the Guardianship of Foreigners, Catherine allowed her favorite to pursue his interest in the steppe, but by excluding the chancellery from the sensitive region of the steppe north of the Crimea, she kept him from imperiling Panin's policies by provoking the Tatars and the Turks. That arrangement lasted until the mid-1770s, when Catherine's policy changed and the colonizing activities begun by Orlov and Mel'gunov were superseded by the vastly more ambitious program of colonization directed by Gregory Potemkin.

A second program to promote the development of the Russian Empire involved the use of foreign and commercial policy to stimulate production and trade. Such a program suited the capabilities of the Russian government in the 1760s because neither foreign policy nor commercial policy required an extensive bureaucracy in order to be effective. Both policies could be implemented in St. Petersburg, yet their effects would be felt throughout much of the empire.

Apart from Catherine herself, the principal authors of that program were N. I. Panin and G. N. Teplov. By October 1763, after more than a year of competition against Bestuzhev-Riumin and the Orlov brothers, Panin had emerged as the dominant figure in the new regime. As the leader of an extensive network of officials connected by bonds of kinship and patronage, Panin had allies and clients in posts throughout the government and used them to control or at least to influence virtually all of its affairs.[16] Teplov, who had gained considerable experience in commercial and economic matters as a protégé of P. I. Shuvalov, allied himself with Panin in 1762 and became an important link between Panin and the empress. Catherine trusted Teplov and employed him as her agent in a number of important and politically sensitive roles. In addition to working as Catherine's private secretary, Teplov directed the abolition of the Ukrainian Hetmanate, acted as secretary to the Commission on the Liberty of the Nobility, and served as one of the five original members of the Commission on Commerce.

In two very similar memoranda drafted at Catherine's request for the consideration of the Commission on Commerce, Panin and Teplov outlined a commercial and economic program for the new regime. Assigning the greatest importance to Russia's role as an exporter of raw materials and agricultural commodities, the two statesmen made the expansion of that role the critical element in their program to increase Russia's commerce, its domestic production, and its population. To achieve those goals, they called upon the government to eliminate the harmful burdens and restrictions that it currently imposed on economic activity and to adopt a rational, consistent policy for nurturing economic activity with favorable tariffs, commercial treaties, and other forms of indirect assistance. In the latter category Panin emphasized improved transportation, and Teplov called for measures to train and encourage Russia's merchants.[17]

Although Panin's assignments forced him to devote most of his attention to foreign affairs, he believed that foreign policy was linked with economic and commercial policy by a common need for peace—not just a temporary respite from war, but a stable, durable peace. Having opposed the Orlov-Bestuzhev proposal for an alliance with Austria that would have facilitated Russian expansion toward the Black Sea, Panin continued to insist that Russia was already too large and too thinly populated; it should strive to consolidate previous gains and develop its abundant but underutilized resources. On several occasions in 1762 Panin told the French minister Breteuil that, more than anything else, Russia needed a long period of peace in which to improve its administration and develop its economy.[18]

Panin's desire to keep Russia at peace and to develop the lands it already possessed caused him to assign relatively low priority to the southern steppes and the Black Sea region and to concentrate on Russia's western frontier and its Baltic trade route. His grand scheme of foreign relations called for the conclusion of a "northern accord," a defensive alliance through which Russia, Prussia, Denmark, and Great Britain could control the weaker governments of Poland and Sweden and frustrate the revanchist aims of France, Spain, and Austria. When Britain and Prussia rejected Panin's proposal for such a comprehensive alliance, he set out to secure its essential components through a series of bilateral agreements. As Catherine's de facto foreign minister, Panin's first major act was the conclusion of a formal military alliance between Russia and Prussia. With Frederick and Catherine cooperating to install and maintain Stanislaus Poniatowski on the Polish throne and to support the antimonarchical party in Sweden, Panin could forsee a long period of peace with Russia's western neighbors along a frontier stretching from the Arctic Circle to the lower reaches of the Dnepr River.

In 1765 Panin concluded a defensive alliance with Denmark. Reversing the policy of Peter III, who had been preparing for war against Denmark for the sake of his native Holstein, Panin and Catherine agreed to end Russia's involvement with Holstein in return for Danish support for their policies regarding Britain and Sweden. But Panin, who had served as Russia's ambassador to both Denmark and Sweden, was also eager to secure Danish good will concerning the Danish Sound, through which most of Russia's foreign commerce had to pass on its way to western Europe. Danish dues and regulations had interfered with the growth of that commerce, and Panin hoped to remove those obstacles through diplomacy. The alliance of 1765 subsequently became the basis for Russia's pleas to Denmark for more favorable treatment of its goods, ships, and merchants.[19]

The final piece of Panin's system fell into place in 1776 with the conclusion of a new commercial treaty between Russia and Great Britain. In his negotiations with the British, Panin pursued his dual objectives of guaranteeing the peace of northern Europe and enhancing Russia's position in international trade. By using the lure of a commercial treaty, to which the British government attached the greatest importance, Panin tried to bring Britain's policies toward Prussia and Sweden into line with those of Russia. He achieved only part of that goal, but he enjoyed somewhat more success in revising the previous Anglo-Russian trade agreement to Russia's advantage. The treaty of 1776 revoked Britain's privilege of trading directly with Persia through Russia and forced British merchants to deal with Russian middlemen; it placed British merchants in Russia under the jurisdiction of Russian courts; it required them to pay larger commercial fees; and, over British objections, it reserved Russia's right to "make such specific arrangements as she finds advantageous for the encouragement and development of her own navigation."[20] By 1766 Panin's diplomacy had enhanced the security and accessibility of Russia's major avenue of commerce all the way from St. Petersburg to the English Channel and the Atlantic.

The Baltic trade offered Catherine's government an expeditious means of stimulating the national economy. The docks of Riga, Narva, and St. Petersburg handled more than 95 percent of Russia's foreign maritime trade,[21] thus presenting the autocracy with a geographically limited area in which to administer policies that could stimulate development throughout the provinces. That was especially true of St. Petersburg. Although Riga's exports exceeded those of St. Petersburg in the 1760s, the patterns and volume of Riga's trade were too well established to be improved by the government's intervention. As a part of Livonia, a province ceded to Russia by Sweden in 1721, Riga was also governed by special laws, treaties, and customs that restricted the government's ability to interfere with its commerce. Moreover, many of the goods that were exported from Riga originated in the Polish-Lithuanian Commonwealth rather than the Russian Empire. Narva's less advantageous location and its more limited access to the interior offered little potential for rapid commercial growth. With the development of St. Petersburg, Narva's share of Russia's maritime trade had been diminishing throughout the century and would continue to decline in the future.[22] The trade of St. Petersburg, on the other hand, had grown rapidly during the preceding half-century and possessed significant potential for future expansion. In 1714 only 16 merchant ships had sailed from the newly created harbor. By 1725 their number exceeded 100, and by 1759 it had risen to 723.[23] In trade with countries west of the

Danish Sound St. Petersburg continued to trail Riga by a significant margin in the 1760s, but the gap contracted with each successive decade until it disappeared altogether in the 1790s.[24] With its exports and its own consumption St. Petersburg generated a demand for Russian goods and commodities that reached far into the interior of the empire. Just how far can be seen from Table 5, which shows the embarkation points for all of the 5,997 boats and barges arriving in St. Petersburg from the provinces in the year 1770. Catherine's claim that St. Petersburg had "given more circulation to money and commerce in forty years than Moscow had done in the five hundred years it has existed" may have been a factual exaggeration, but it was an accurate reflection of the government's perceptions.[25]

Although Russian trade statistics of the eighteenth century are notoriously unreliable, their evidence, supported by British, Dutch, and French records, indicates that Russia maintained a favorable balance of trade in all but a few years of the eighteenth century. Russia imported woolen cloth, tropical and colonial products such as sugar, coffee, and spices, and various luxury items. It exported timber, tar, pitch, hemp, tallow, hides, furs, horsehair, flax, linen, pig iron, and natural and processed goods. More than half the ships carrying cargo to and from St. Petersburg in any given year came from Britain, and nearly all of the others came from the Netherlands, the Hanseatic cities, and France, in that order.[26] At Riga the Dutch were the principal carriers, with the British and Germans accounting for most of what remained.[27] In their memoranda on commerce both Panin and Teplov expressed concern that Russian ships carried only a negligible amount of Russia's seaborne trade and pointed to the development of Russia's own carrying trade as an obvious commercial opportunity.[28]

The greatest possibilities for increasing Russia's role in international trade lay, as Panin and Teplov had noted, in the increased export of raw materials and agricultural commodities. The rapid growth of British manufacturing suggested a rising demand for Russia's flax, linen, and iron, and the expansion of the royal navy and the merchant marine held the same implications for Russia's timber, hemp, pitch, and tar. France's search for an alternate source of tobacco also opened the possibility of developing a new cash crop in the Ukraine. The greatest prospect of all for increasing Russia's exports lay in supplying grain to western Europe, where the burgeoning population was outstripping the increase in agricultural production. In western Europe the widening differential between the production and consumption of food would give rise to the studies and experiments of Arthur Young and Jethro Tull, the great enthusiasm for *agronomie* in the elegant salons of Paris, and the pessimistic forecasts of Thomas Malthus. For Russia, on the other hand, it raised the prospect of greater demand and higher prices for exported grain.

The settlement and cultivation of the black earth region in southern Russia and the Ukraine had created a surplus of grain in those areas. In the 1750s the abolition of internal tariffs encouraged the shipment of surplus

TABLE 5. EMBARKATION POINTS OF
BOATS AND BARGES ARRIVING IN
ST. PETERSBURG IN 1777

Point of Origin	Number
Ladoga Canal	245
River Sias	194
Tikhvin Posad	158
Rivers Vir and Pasha	47
Ladoga-Sosninskaia region	879
Rivers Tigoda, Pchovzha, and Oskui	11
River Vishera	18
Novgorod	117
Ilmen region	221
River Shelon	146
Staraia Russa	186
Ostashkov, Kholm, Velikie Luki	431
River Pola	186
River Msta	428
Torzhok region	279
Tver	166
Rzhev Volodimir	121
Gzhatsk	464
Sosninskii Warff	116
Kashin region	103
Rybnaia Sloboda	823
Kama River	92
River Ufa	107
River Chusovaia	146
Elsewhere	314
TOTAL	5,997

Source: M. D. Chulkov, Istoricheskoe opisanie
rossiiskoi kommertsii, 7 vols. (St. Petersburg, 1781–
1788), IV, 638.

grain from the south to grain-deficient areas in northern Russia, but the export of Russian grain through the Baltic ports was forbidden until March 1762, when the government of Peter III repealed that prohibition. Despite its fear of shortages and soaring prices in St. Petersburg and other areas of northern Russia, Catherine's government decided to encourage the export of Russian grain from St. Petersburg and other ports on the Baltic.[29] In 1766 the Commission on Commerce wrote that decision into the new legislation on tariffs, which permitted the unrestricted export of all agricultural commodities and nonessential products at a duty of only 5 percent.[30] In response to arguments that higher grain prices would create hardships for Russian consumers and unbalance the government's budget by raising the costs of military procurements, those who favored the unhampered export of grain countered that higher prices for grain would stimulate production and create wealth from which the state and all classes of its subjects would eventually benefit.[31]

To increase exports of grain, Catherine's government merely had to step aside and allow experienced producers and middlemen to respond to an expanded market. On the other hand, any attempt to enhance the opportunities created by the international market, was likely to exceed the government's capabilities if it required Russians to do something they were not already doing. Teplov's attempt to supply the French market with Ukrainian tobacco is a case in point. Sensing France's desire not to purchase tobacco from the colonies of its British opponent if an alternative were available, Teplov revived P. I. Shuvalov's scheme to develop such an alternative in Russia. In England or France the initiative and direction for such an undertaking would almost certainly have come from growers or merchants; in Prussia it would probably have come from the agencies of provincial administration. In Russia it had to come from the imperial government in St. Petersburg. An imperial decree of 1763 offered Ukrainian growers free seeds and cash subsidies for the cultivation of tobacco, and in 1765, Teplov, who directed the entire venture, even published a book on how to plant and cultivate that crop. Russian exports of tobacco finally began in 1773. They rose impressively in the mid-1770s but then declined precipitously after Teplov's death in 1779.[32] Teplov's personal involvement accounted for the transient success of that exceptional undertaking. As a general rule, however, the imperial government could not assign one of its chief ministers to projects of that sort, nor could it direct the growing and marketing of more widely dispersed crops.

With an effective bureaucracy in place, Frederick II could ignore the arguments advanced by contemporary theorists in favor of freer trade. Without such a bureaucracy, Catherine found them persuasive. From a practical point of view the easiest and quickest way for her government to stimulate the Russian economy was to eliminate some of the restraints its predecessors had imposed on economic activity and allow foreign and domestic demand for Russian goods to encourage increased production through the operation of a freer market. The tariff of 1776 incorporated the principle of freer trade with respect to imports as well as exports. It eliminated import duties on all essential products and commodities not produced within the empire and reduced the duty on those that would compete with Russian products to a moderate 30 percent. In defense of the latter provision the Commission on Commerce argued that a duty of 30 percent should suffice "for the encouragement of our factories" but that if it failed, then "there is no advantage in holding on to such factories."[33]

Catherine, Panin, and Teplov shared a common conviction that monopolies of the kind that Empress Elizabeth had handed out so freely damaged the national economy for the personal benefit of a few individuals. The new government acted swiftly, therefore, to eliminate all private monopolies and several state monopolies.[34] More slowly, it also moved to free manufacturing from the mercantilist restraints imposed by its predecessors. With the avowed aim of increasing industrial production, a decree of July 31, 1762, eliminated the need to obtain a special license in order to establish a sugar refinery or a mill for the manufacture of printed fabric.[35] In October of that year a decree calling for a greater dispersal of manufacturing stated that "anyone of whatever rank who wishes to erect or expand a factory for the purposes enumerated in this decree, outside Moscow but in other towns and uezds, may do so."[36] A decree promulgated in 1767 proclaimed that "no trade or handicraft by which people may legally produce their sustenance shall be restricted and all of the so-called unlicensed mills that have been confiscated shall be restored to their owners."[37] For the stated purpose of "multiplying all kinds of handicrafts," a decree of October 30, 1769, declared that "anyone who wishes to operate a weaving machine or even several such machines in his home will not be prevented or hindered in any way or have anything done to him because of it."[38] Extending the principle of unfettered production, a decree of March 17, 1775, abolished the fees that manufacturers had to pay to the treasury and proclaimed that "the freedom to carry on handicrafts of all kinds would not be hindered in any way or subjected to approval or denial."[39] Having thus lost its reason for existence, the Manufacturing College withered away and was eventually abolished.

The government's desire to liberate the economy from unnecessary constraints faltered when it came into conflict with the privileges of the various social orders into which Russian society was divided. Personal and corporate privileges had the same economic consequences, but in other respects they represented different problems. For centuries the autocracy had assigned economic privileges to the different orders of society along with the taxes and/or services it demanded from them. Unlike personal monopolies, therefore, such privileges were seen not as raids on the treasury but as essential aspects of the social order. Most Russians agreed that society should be organized into classes or orders and that each class should have a particular set of privileges and duties, but there the consensus ended. The task of defining the orders of society and specifying their privileges and duties remained the most controversial legal problem facing the Russian government in the second half of the eighteenth century. The legislative commissions of 1754–1763 and 1767–1774 devoted most of their attention to those issues and brought the conflicts out into the open as each class tried to improve its position at the expense of the others. As M. M. Shcherbatov, an outspoken champion of the nobles' interests, wrote of Catherine's commission: "Several of the Cossacks and peasants sought in their proposals to take away the very air that the nobles and merchants breathed; the merchants sought to extend their rights at the expense of the noble landowners; and even the nobles, though they were moderate . . . , tried to usurp each other's rights."[40]

Similar conflicts arose within the government. In the 1750s P. I. Shuvalov and R. L. Vorontsov clashed over the allotment of privileges and duties to the nobility. When the necessity of confirming or repealing Peter III's decree freeing the nobles from compulsory service to the state pressed Catherine into taking some kind of action on the issue, she succeeded in putting off a decision she did not want to make at that time. She appointed a committee of dignitaries to investigate the matter and formulate proposals, but she failed to carry out its recommendations.[41] While the question about the nobles' privileges remained unresolved, the five members of the Commission on Commerce divided over the privileges of the merchants. Opposing the exclusive rights of merchants to engage in many kinds of commerce, Teplov and I. M. Minikh proposed that those activities be opened to peasants for the purpose of increasing the total amount of economic activity within the empire. Significantly, they also pointed out the impossibility of defending the merchants' prerogatives in practice: Peasants were engaging in trade in violation of current laws, and the state possessed insufficient means to prevent them.[42] In rebuttal commission members Murav'ev, Ia. P. Shakhovskoi, and Timofei von Klingshtedt maintained that economic expansion was less important than the principle of social ordering, which required merchants to trade and peasants to farm. Like the merchants themselves, those three statesmen insisted that peasants could and should be excluded from commerce through the rigorous enforcement of explicit laws that would prevent the different orders of society from encroaching upon one another's prerogatives.[43] Pulled in opposite directions by its desire to reaffirm the hierarchical ordering of society and its desire to remove many of the legal obstacles to economic growth, Catherine's government would wrestle with the issues of socio-economic organization for more than twenty years.

Ever conscious of the importance and sensitivity of social and economic issues, Catherine wanted them resolved in a knowledgeable, orderly manner after due consideration had been given to all points of view, to all extenuating circumstances, and to all possible consequences. To carry on the work of legal reform and revision, Catherine reformed the Senate in December 1763 and summoned a new legislative commission to convene in January 1767. For reasons known only to herself, she then selected an obscure nobleman of military background, A. A. Viazemskii, to direct both of those agencies. Viazemskii's appointment as procurator-general of the Senate dismayed Panin and his allies, who had hoped to win control of the Senate for themselves. A man of limited imagination but great diligence, Viazemskii had no program of his own to advance, but he was a master of administrative routine. Since Viazemskii was also an outsider to the established cliques and factions in the capital, his appointment enabled

Catherine to retain control of the state administration and the process of legal reform.[44]

The Senate served as the focus of Catherine's initial campaign to enhance the capabilities of the imperial administration. As with most of her other efforts, that campaign began at the top, with the empress herself, and emanated outward from her person and outward from the capital with rapidly diminishing effect. The new empress took her *métier de roi* very seriously and worked harder at her duties than any autocrat since Peter I. In contrast to her recent predecessors, Catherine led an orderly, regular life and devoted much of her time to purposeful work.[45] To expand her capacity for business, she instituted the practice of hiring private secretaries to help her, selecting men of ability and involving them in the workings of government. Of the sixteen state secretaries she appointed between 1762 and 1796, nine eventually became senators, and a few, like Teplov and Alexander Bezborodko, became statesmen of major significance.[46] Catherine also reformed the Senate, the institution directly below the monarch, and expanded its authority as the central organ of control and supervison over the bureaucracy. During the first eighteen months of her reign she divided the Senate into departments, appointed new personnel, provided additional clerks and secretaries, revised procedures, and appointed a new procurator-general with greater authority than any of his predecessors.[47] With Viazemskii in charge, Catherine left the daily routine of government in the hands of the Senate and relied on it to demand from other agencies the same degree of competence that she required of it.[48] Her "Instruction to the Governors" of April 21, 1764, and a modest but necessary overhaul of the civil service completed the first stage of administrative reform by bringing the heads of provincial administration into line with the new system of supervision and by restoring the administrative apparatus of the state to minimally acceptable levels of performance.[49]

Viazemskii and the Senate also supervised the collection and processing of detailed information about the empire, a task that was intimately related to administration and lawmaking. The writings of Montesquieu, Bielfeld, Justi, and the physiocrats all taught that laws should never be imposed arbitrarily or transferred from one society to another without adjustment. To be effective, laws must conform to objective reality: They had to reflect the peculiarities of climate, geography, resources, and other conditions within a particular country as well as the general laws of nature. By the 1760s the general acceptance of such notions had made the unreconstructed Cartesianism of a man like Senator Ia. P. Shakhovskoi seem old-fashioned and unsophisticated. As a member of the Commission on Commerce, Shakhovskoi stood alone in asserting that the government should simply decide in principle what was best for the country and then enforce its decisions with consistency and vigor.[50] More typical of attitudes with the government was the position taken by Von Klingshtedt, Shakhovskoi's colleague on the commission, who argued that the central government could not generalize about the economic condition of the empire or the state of affairs in the provinces because it did not know enough about those subjects.[51] Expressing much the same attitude, their colleague Teplov demanded extensive information about Russia's merchants before he was willing to propose measures for promoting commerce.[52]

As one who appreciated the value of extensive, detailed information, Catherine began her rule under a severe handicap. Because Russia was so vast and because the collection and use of information about internal conditions was less advanced there than in most European countries, the Russian government in 1762 knew comparatively little about the lands and peoples it attempted to govern. During her first weeks in power Catherine was appalled by the government's lack of basic information about the empire and even about itself. She discovered that the Senate had no map of Russia, even though one could be purchased from the Academy of Sciences on the opposite bank of the Neva, that the Senate kept no complete, up-to-date roster of towns, even though they formed the basis of local and provincial administration, and that neither the Senate nor anyone else knew the total annual revenue of the imperial government.[53]

Because that kind of ignorance accounted for a large part of the government's incompetence, Catherine attacked it in her initial assault on administrative disorder. Her decree of July 5, 1762, dealing with governmental operations and administrative procedures, ordered officials and administrative agencies to submit prompt and regular reports on their affairs to the Senate.[54] Thereafter provincial governors and voevodas and the colleges, *prikazy, kantseliarii, ekspeditsii,* and *kontory* of the central administration concentrated a considerable portion of their time and effort on supplying the Senate with reports, and the Senate devoted by far the greatest portion of its time and effort to reading those reports, extracting information from them, and, if necessary, responding to points they raised. During the first week of December 1765, for example, the First Department of the Senate, meeting in formal session, heard reports from the governors of Siberia, Kiev, Orenburg, Arkhangel, and Novgorod, the voevodas of Mozhaisk, Mongozhaisk, Ruza, and Sol Kamskii, the Fifth Department of the Senate, the Moscow offices of the Senate, the Kammer College, the kantseliarii of Moscow Guberniia, Arkhangel Guberniia, Pereslavl Provintsiia, Iaroslav Provintsiia, and Valuev Uezd, the Main Magistracy, the Velikie Luki Border Commission, the Borovichi Rapids Office, the Naporetskaia Wharf, and the Bel'skaia Wharf.[55] Whenever it felt the need, the Senate could also demand specific information from agencies and officials. Thus, when an imperial decree of October 11, 1764, ordered the Senate to compile a list of all the towns within the empire for the purpose of reorganizing local and provincial administration, the Senate began by ordering the provincial governors to supply it with a list of all the towns within their guberniias, together with descriptions of all towns and their own recommendations for additions to and deletions from the list. Then, on the basis of the governors' responses, the Senate compiled and revised its own list of towns and reorganized the units of local and provincial administration.[56] Within a few years of Catherine's accession, the Senate was receiving or at least had access to great quantities of information and bureaucratic data collected by the various agencies of the imperial government.

In 1763 the Senate called Catherine's attention to the need for a new revision of the tax registers on which the government based its calculations of population, revenue, military recruitment, and other essential matters. In 1720, in order to provide a documentary basis for the assessment of the poll tax, Peter I had ordered the registration of all males who did not belong to one of the privileged orders of society. In the years 1741–1743 the government conducted the so-called Second Revision for the purpose of updating the rosters by adding the names of males born since 1720 and dropping the names of those who had died. At that time Empress Elizabeth established fifteen years as the proper interval between revisions, but she failed to authorize the Third Revision until November 1761. Amid the many disorders of the months that followed, nothing further had been done to set the process in motion.

Stressing the need for accurate, up-to-date information on which to base its decisions, the Senate asked the empress to authorize the appointment of special *revizory* (inspectors), the use of troops, and an appropriation of 800,000 rubles for the revision. Catherine ordered the Senate to proceed with the revision but denied its requests for money and personnel. Extending her policy on the collection of taxes to the compilation of new tax registers, Catherine insisted that the revision be conducted by the regular officials of the civil administration and its auxiliaries rather than by the army or by officials appointed especially for that purpose. She made every peasant village and every urban posad responsible for counting its own members and reporting the data to the local authorities. After making certain that every village and posad had complied, state officials needed only to compile the figures supplied to them and then send the information up the administrative chain of command for further compilation at higher levels.[57] At the top of the administrative ladder the Revision College collected the data from all over the empire and made it available to Viazemskii and the Senate, who used it to predict the consequences of decrees on taxation and recruitment, to reorganize local and provincial administration, to recognize elementary demografic shifts, to anticipate revenues, and to manage the salt and alcohol monopolies.[58] Conducted as Catherine had ordered, the Third Revision was completed, more or less, in just two years.[59] It was followed at fifteen-year intervals by the Fourth Revision and the Fifth Revision, each of which proved more thorough and more sophisticated in collecting and compiling data on population.[60]

Viazemskii also directed most of Catherine's efforts to collect and compile information about the physical characteristics of the Russian Empire. The progenitor of those efforts and thus the geographical counterpart of the First Revision was another decree of 1720, in which Peter I had ordered "those who study geodesy and geography at the Maritime Academy in St. Petersburg" to provide the government with maps of the provincial towns and their surrounding districts.[61] When the emperor examined the first of those maps in 1723, he issued a supplementary decree directing the *geodisti* to define the borders of each uezd, to identify the roads, canals, forests, hills, swamps, wastelands, and mills, and to compile an alphabetical index of all settlements.[62] Under the direction of the Academy of Sciences, I. I. Kirillov made use of those individual maps to produce the general, schematic map of the Russian Empire that he completed in 1734. At that time Kirillov proposed that a more precise map be prepared on the basis of trigonometric measurement and calculation, but the Senate ordered him to meet its more urgent need for a general, schematic atlas of the empire's many parts and regions. In 1754, after two decades of labor, the Academy of Sciences published Kirillov's *Atlas Rossiiskii*, which contained one general map of the empire and nineteen maps of specific areas.[63] By 1760, however, the Senate was calling for intensified efforts to collect geographical information and prepare a new, more detailed atlas, explaining that such knowledge "is not only useful to the entire people but is highly necessary for all the offices of government."[64]

Catherine's most ambitious attempt to amass information about the physical nature and condition of her empire occurred in conjunction with the General Survey authorized in 1766. Although the primary purpose of the survey was to verify and register landholdings, Catherine assigned it the additional task of producing maps and inventories of every territorial unit within the empire.[65] To carry out the survey, Catherine for once agreed to the creation of a special agency separate from the provincial administration and its auxiliaries. Composed of Viazemskii and three senators, the Mezhevaia Ekspeditsiia (Survey Office) was nothing more than a committee of the First Department of the Senate, but it supervised and directed the survey teams sent into the provinces to conduct the actual survey. The survey began in Moscow Guberniia in the summer of 1776, by which time the Mezhevaia Ekspeditsiia had managed to round up 101 surveyors from the army and various academies, who proceeded guberniia by guberniia through the empire.[66] The undertaking consisted of two stages, the fieldwork of measuring the land and collecting the data, which normally required two to five years per guberniia, and the paper work of compiling maps, statistical tables, and economic observations, which required another three to five years in most guberniias and as many as eight to ten in some others.[67] Both stages had been completed in nine guberniias by 1781 and in twenty-three out of fifty guberniias by 1800.[68]

The General Survey provided the imperial government with geographical information of unprecedented detail and abundance. Instead of schematic, impressionistic drawings, the local and provincial offices of the survey produced geometric projections drawn to a precise scale, with symbols used to indicate the exact locations of villages, factories, mills, roads, forests, hills, bridges, fords, and wharves.[69] In 1782 the survey office of Kaluga published an atlas containing a map of that guberniia on a scale of four versts per diuim (2.652 miles to the inch) and a map of each uezd on a scale of two versts per diuim (1.326 miles to the inch).[70] After seeing it, the Senate ordered similar atlases prepared for all guberniias of the empire.[71] The findings of the General Survey also enabled other agencies of the imperial government to prepare specialized maps such as the forest atlas produced by the Admiralty College in 1782 and the maps of inland waterways compiled by the Department of Water Communications in 1801.

The surveyors also collected economic data that they later standardized and quantified to produce statistical tables and economic observations (*primechaniia*). Because the methods used were far less precise than the surveying and cartographic techniques, the information contained in the compilations was less accurate and reliable than the maps produced by the survey, but it did provide officials with some notion, however imprecise, of the conditions to be found in various regions.[72]

Following the examples of the Academy of Sciences, the Army Cadet Corps, and the Free Economic Society, the Senate also collected economic data by distributing questionnaires (*ankety*) to individuals who either had or could obtain the information it wanted. According to the Soviet historian N. L. Rubinshtein, more than twenty official and unofficial questionnaires on topography, economic geography, and related subjects were distributed to government agencies, individuals, and private organizations between 1760 and 1795.[73] Unlike the Academy of Sciences, the Army Cadet Corps, and the Free Economic Society, the Senate had no interest in publishing the responses to its inquiries. In 1777, however, it ordered the governors to cast their replies to its new questionnaire in the form of a topographical description.[74] The descriptions arrived in St. Petersburg one by one over the next fifteen years until the project neared completion in the 1790s. Containing detailed inventories and statistical tables, the topographical descriptions provided the Senate with impressive amounts of data about the individual guberniias, but the standardization attempted in 1777 had been lost along the way as the Senate tried to refine and improve its original list of questions. The different categories and criteria used by different governors in collecting and compiling their information made it virtually impossible to compare one guberniia with another or to combine them into a statistical description of the empire.[75]

The Academy of Sciences supplemented the Senate's efforts to collect economic and geographical information about the empire by sending its members on scientific expeditions to interior and frontier regions. Among these kinds of expeditions, the best known are those of Academicians P. S. Pallas, J. A. Guldenstadt, and S. G. Gmelin, whose accounts of their travels and observations were published during the 1770s and 1780s, but the Academy also conducted smaller inquiries of a more limited scope and character. During the 1760s, for example, the investigations of several members of the Academy around Lake Ilmen in search of coal and other mineral deposits resulted in unpublished maps, charts, and topographical descriptions.[76]

The Legislative Commission convened in 1767 provided the government with a wealth of information about the views and perceptions of Catherine's subjects, as well as information about the groups and regions from which the deputies came.[77] There again it was Viazemskii who directed the collection and compilation of that information. Although Marshal Bibikov presided over the sessions of the Great Assembly, where all of the deputies met to hear speeches, discuss issues, and vote on various questions, Viazemskii supervised the administrative staff (*apparat*) of the commission and the fourteen committees or "partial commissions" charged with drafting the separate chapters of the projected code of laws. The apparat of the Legislative Commission predated the convocation of the deputies, and it continued to function until the end of Catherine's reign.[78] It read all of the instructions (*nakazy*) that the deputies had brought to the commission from their constituencies; it prepared extracts from the nakazy and the speeches given in the Great Assembly and organized them by topic; and it provided research and documentation for the fourteen committees.[79] The committees worked from 1768 or 1769 until 1771 or 1772, drafting projects of comprehensive laws on specified subjects. All of the committees had accomplished a significant portion of that work by the time they were disbanded, and several of them had completed their assignments.[80] As they disbanded, the committees turned over their drafts, notes, and research materials to Viazemskii and the apparat for use by the Senate and the empress in drafting new legislation.

In the 1760s Catherine's government did what it could to promote the development of the Russian Empire in the absence of an effective provincial bureaucracy by working around its administrative difficulties, by putting the central government into better working order, and by informing itself about conditions throughout the empire. For the time being, it made few efforts to reach into the provinces to confront those conditions directly, but its outlook and actions suggested that such efforts would have to be made in the not too distant future. In their memoranda on economic development Panin and Teplov had called attention to the need for an infrastructure of roads, canals, schools, and credit facilities that would require the imperial government to initiate and supervise improvements throughout the provinces. The government's administrative reforms and its efforts to inform itself about conditions in the provinces suggested that it intended to follow those recommendations. In the 1760s Catherine's government attempted few improvements of that sort, but they were on its agenda and would be taken up once adequate preparations had been made.[81]

As part of that preparation, Catherine appointed Jakob Sievers to the governorship of Novgorod and encouraged him to explore means of developing the provinces from that vantage point. Despite his lack of experience in civil administration and provincial affairs, Catherine selected Sievers to spearhead the development of the provinces, just as she had chosen Viazemskii, who also lacked appropriate experience, to head the central administration. Catherine appointed Sievers to the post in Novgorod on the day before she issued her "Instruction to the Governors," and it soon became apparent that those two steps were related. Before Sievers assumed his duties, the empress met with him more than twenty times to discuss the role he would play in her plans to improve conditions in the provinces, and she granted him the special privilege of corresponding with her about his affairs.[82] In a secret instruction sent to him a few months later Catherine told Sievers, "You must concern yourself with everything that leads to the welfare, enlightenment, and enrichment of your people," and she invited him to propose reforms based on his observations and experience.[83]

Sievers carried out Catherine's instructions with extraordinary zeal. He submitted lengthy reports on the conditions he encountered in Novgorod and showered the Senate and the empress with proposals for improving his guberniia and all of provincial Russia. At first Sievers's efforts led to few results, but in the early 1770s, when provincial reform and development moved to the top of Catherine's agenda, he became one of the most important officials in her government. His activities and his role within Catherine's government will be examined at length in the chapters that follow.

During Catherine's first five years in power she set in motion four distinct but interrelated programs to promote the development of the Russian Empire: the colonization of the southern steppes, directed first by Orlov and Mel'gunov and later by Potemkin; the program of peace, increased exports, and freer trade formulated by Panin and Teplov; the orderly reform of government and law entrusted to the Senate and the Legislative Commission under the supervision of Viazemskii; and the activist efforts to confront Russia's problems at the local and provincial levels, carried on by Sievers. Originally, those problems may have appeared to be complementary. Teplov, for example, worked simultaneously on behalf of all four and saw no inconsistency in advocating increased trade through the Black Sea while supporting Panin's plans to increase Russia's Baltic trade. More often, however, those programs represented alternatives that would compete for Catherine's support and for the limited resources at her disposal. In addition, personal hostilities and political rivalries among the statesmen identified with each program intensified and complicated their differences over policy. The conflict between Panin and Orlov and then between Panin and Potemkin was personal as well as professional, and Viazemskii regularly sided with Panin's opponents in order to restrain the dominance of the Panin faction and preserve his own freedom of action.[84] Sievers's attempts to combat provincial problems on his own or by going directly to the empress would bring him into conflict with Viazemskii and the Senate over their respective responsibility for government actions. Otherwise, Sievers tried to steer clear of disputes that did not involve his own undertakings and remained on good terms with both the Panin and the Orlov factions, but in the 1770s he would join Panin and his allies in their opposition to Potemkin.

Rivalries and conflicts between statesmen and factions constituted a permanent, integral feature of Catherine's regime. They preserved her independence from men who sought to dominate her in the way that previous empresses had been dominated by their favorites and statesmen, and they provided her with ready alternatives to policies that had outlived their usefulness. By retaining her freedom to choose between competing statesmen and strategic alternatives, Catherine remained the ultimate authority on all questions of policy, and her preference for one over another held far-reaching implications for all issues of foreign and domestic policy, including the development of provincial Russia.

III

The New Governor

UNTIL HE WAS NAMED GOVERNOR of Novgorod at the age of thirty-three, Jakob Sievers had acquired no experience in civil administration and virtually no exposure to provincial Russia. Although he was as well prepared as most of Russia's provincial governors, his appointment was more the result of favoritism and political patronage than a reflection of his professional or personal abilities. In retrospect his appointment may have marked the beginning of a new era in the autocracy's treatment of the provinces, but at the time it marked the culmination of Karl Sievers's efforts over twenty years to move his nephew from the margins of the Baltic German squirearchy into the ruling elite of the Russian Empire.

Jakob Sievers was born in 1731 in Estland. His father, Joachim Sievers, managed one of Baron Tisenhausen's estates, and his uncle Karl became one of the baron's personal attendants and accompanied him to St. Petersburg. There Karl ingratiated himself with Elizabeth Petrovna and entered her personal service. When Elizabeth seized the Russian throne in 1741, Karl Sievers began an extraordinarily fortunate and successful career at the imperial court. Elizabeth sent him to welcome her nephew, the future Peter III, to Russia and then dispatched him to the duchy of Anhalt-Zerbst to interview the future Catherine II and appraise her suitability as a bride for the heir to the Russian throne. He established such a close relationship with the young couple that when he subsequently married Elizabeth's best friend and confidante, a German widow by the name of Kruse, Peter and Catherine participated in the ceremony as his surrogate parents.[1] Through his contacts at court and in the government Karl Sievers eventually acquired several estates in the vicinity of St. Petersburg, copper and iron works in the Urals, and a paper mill at Krasnosel'sk, for which he obtained the monopoly on supplying paper to all the government offices in St. Petersburg.[2]

Karl Sievers had been quick to share his success with other members of his family. He arranged for his brother to acquire an estate in Livonia from the Rumiantsevs on which Joachim could settle into the traditional life of a country squire. Karl visited Joachim in 1744 on his return from the peace conference at Abo and brought his thirteen-year-old nephew Jakob back with him to St. Petersburg to begin a career in the imperial service. Through Karl's connections, Jakob was accepted as a *iunker* in the College of Foreign Affairs, a much sought after posting that served as a kind of training ground for future statesmen.[3] In 1747 Karl arranged his nephew's transfer to the diplomatic corps, in which Jakob served briefly in Copenhagen under J. A. Korff and then for eight years in London under P. G. Chernyshev. After the diplomatic revolution of 1756 Karl managed to have Jakob transferred to the army with the rank of major and a posting as division quartermaster to P. I. Shuvalov. Jakob had risen to the rank of brigadier by 1761, when, sick and wounded, he took an extended leave from the army to recover his health in Italy. In April 1764 Jakob Sievers was a retired major-general living with his parents in Livonia and collecting a pension of three hundred rubles a year when he received word that the empress had appointed him governor of Novgorod.

As Catherine's oldest acquaintance in Russia and chief marshal of her court, Karl Sievers had actively sought the post in Novgorod for his nephew. Karl's standing with the empress and her preference for appointing experienced military officers to provincial governorships resulted in the choice of Jakob from a field of twenty-five nominees.[4] Yet neither circumstance entirely explains why Catherine selected the retired soldier and diplomat to be her close collaborator in the development of provincial Russia. She may have spotted special qualities in Sievers at their preliminary meetings during her visit to Livonia in May 1764, or she may simply have decided to work closely with whomever she named to the governorship of Novgorod because of that guberniia's proximity to the imperial capitals. In any case, she could hardly have found a better man for the job. As a leader in the effort to enlighten provincial Russia, Sievers would provide another example of Catherine's uncanny ability to discover and make brilliant use of otherwise unrecognized talents in men like Viazemskii, Potemkin, Bezborodko, and many others.

Although Sievers brought little practical experience to his new assignment, his personality and ideology were well suited to the intimidating task of promoting progress in provincial Russia. Sievers's most outstanding qualities were a religiously motivated sense of duty and a religiously inspired zeal to perform good works irrespective of the outcome or of material advantage to himself. Those qualities were unusual in Russia, but they were hardly unique in the wider context of eighteenth-century Europe. Although the religious currents within the Enlightenment have received less attention from historians than the materialism of the French and Scottish philosophes, in one country after another they were instrumental in prompting their adherents to undertake humanitarian efforts that "reasonable" men thought foolish. There was much evidence to support the philosophes' contention that the established churches of Europe were responsible for repression, exploitation, intolerance, and obscurantism, but there were equally impressive examples of Quakers, Methodists, Catholics, Calvinists, and Lutherans taking practical steps to combat slavery, ignorance, poverty, and human misery.[5]

In Sievers's case, the desire to make this world a better place sprang from the teachings of Lutheran pietism, one of the major sources of reform and modernization in eighteenth-century Germany.[6] Expanding upon the Lutheran doctrine of justification by faith, pietism emphasized the personal salvation of the individual as a free gift from God. An individual who accepted God's grace should then serve God on earth through the performance of good works undertaken in a spirit of gratitude. At the same time, pietism accepted the social and political status quo without question and regarded service to the state and ruler as a form of service to society and thus to God himself.

Sievers absorbed those teachings as a child and took them to heart. His father emphasized dutiful behavior in all aspects of life and insisted that everything be done properly (*in Ordnung*), even getting up and going to bed. In a letter to his brother Peter in April 1785 Sievers recalled: "'Tue Recht!' was the motto of our Old Man [*Greises*], which he was concerned to impress upon me with my earliest comprehension of things."[7] When the younger Sievers left Livonia to enter service in St. Petersburg, his father advised him at their parting, "Whatever you do, do it gladly."[8] Joachim had Jakob tutored by a Lutheran pastor, and the young man took his vows of confirmation in the Lutheran church in St. Petersburg in 1744. He attended services every Sunday in St. Petersburg and later wrote his father from London that he continued to do so there, although sometimes he went to an English rather than a German church. While Jakob was in London, his father admonished him to "be god-fearing and so disposed as were the ancient Romans. Believe in God and do the duty that you have to do. Also practice all the virtues and manners that a cavalier should know, as you are my son."[9] In a similar vein Karl Sievers advised his nephew, "Be diligent in Christianity and perform your duties to the best of your

46

abilities,"[10] and his letters to Jakob contained repeated exhortations on the subjects of religion and professional duty. Unlike some young men who received similar advice, Sievers absorbed it into his personal ethos. In his later correspondence Jakob wrote less about God than had his father and uncle, but he returned again and again to the themes of duty owed to his ruler and service owed to humanity. In October 1790, in one of the clearest expressions of his service ethic, Sievers wrote to his son-in-law, General Gunsel: "To do Good. Oh, my friend, what voluptuousness. I never ceased to practice that heavenly virtue until my strength failed me."[11] As the chief administrator of northwestern Russia, Sievers would practice that virtue to the detriment of his health, his marriage, and his personal fortune.

Sievers's reading in European literature had widened his intellectual horizons, but only in ways compatible with his original outlook. Thus, in his evaluations of French literature he later wrote that Rousseau's *La nouvelle Héloise* was "an excellently written novel that has corrupted many young hearts." He felt a fundamental aversion to Rousseau and believed that the philosopher lacked the talent to write anything "useful." Sievers admired Voltaire for his wit and clarity, but his favorite French author was Fénelon. During Sievers's residence in London his uncle had sent him a copy of *Télémaque*, in which Fénelon portrayed the ideal monarch as a ruler whose sole ambition is to promote the well-being of his people. Although written by a French Catholic bishop, *Télémaque* embodied a Christian vision of government and society that a German pietist could enthusiastically support. In a letter to his oldest daughter, written in 1790, Sievers recalled his lifelong enthusiasm for *Télémaque*: "This is a book for every age. I will soon read it again with my young one—for the tenth time in my life, I believe—four times at least in London."[12] In English literature Sievers read and enjoyed Wollaston, Bollingbroke, Middleton's *Life of Cicero* (which he read at least twice), and Shakespeare. In German he loved the poetry of Haller and Klopstock and praised the writings of Frederick II, whose *Anti-Machiavelli* he recommended as a classic book for the education of young princes.[13]

Sievers's travels in Europe had developed his mind without changing it in any fundamental way. While in London, he had received a letter from his father expressing surprise that the Herrnhuter sect, which had been expelled from several Continental lands, including Livonia, could be tolerated in England. But Jakob had come to understand that such toleration and the pluralism it fostered posed no threat to the government or the society of England. After his return to Russia and Livonia he continued to read English newspapers and keep abreast of English politics.[14] In a letter to Catherine written in 1780, Sievers characterized England as "that country which is without doubt the most enlightened country in Europe at present."[15] With growing sophistication, the younger Sievers had learned English and French, attended the Anglican church, and read Voltaire, but he found the government and society of all Roman Catholic countries alien and inimical. His father encouraged him to visit Paris for the experience, but he also advised him not to remain in France longer than six weeks because that country was "full of lies and hypocrisy."[16] Jakob followed his father's advice and managed to remain unimpressed by France. Later, in his correspondence with Catherine, he would even use the word "Normandy" as a synonym for inefficiency and corruption.[17] In Italy Sievers enjoyed the climate, the beautiful women, the art, and the artifacts of ancient Rome, but when it came to laws and institutions, his admiration was confined to the lands of northern Europe, from Livonia through Germany and Scandanavia to England. Although England remained the country he admired most, his hero and the only ruler since Trajan to evoke his unequivocal adulation was Frederick II of Prussia.

If one were to categorize Sievers's *Weltanschauung* the way his older contemporary Linnaeus categorized flora and fauna, it could be termed progressive, humanitarian conservatism. As a conservative, Sievers supported the fundamental elements of the social and political status quo without question. He assumed that monarchy, inequality, privilege, and the pre-eminence of hereditary landowners were essential components of civilization, and he would be profoundly disturbed when the French Revolution set out to abolish them. Sievers served monarchs as his duty and accepted titles, lands, and serfs as his due. But the nature of Sievers's conservatism was modified by his belief in humanitarianism and progress.

If monarchy and the hierarchy of classes gave society its essential structure, Sievers was convinced that moral sentiments held society together. Within the necessary hierarchy, Sievers believed, classes and individuals were connected to each other by bonds of duty, responsibility, philanthropy, and fellow feeling. Superiors should treat their inferiors with kindness, justice, and concern for their welfare; consequently, Sievers opposed torture, religious persecution, and the cruelty that some landlords inflicted upon their peasants. Good monarchs and good landlords could expect their people to respond with gratitude and love such as children feel toward their parents;[18] oppression or neglect could destroy the feelings that made society workable. For the sake of civilization, Sievers agreed that peasants who ran away or rebelled or killed their masters must be punished, but he was always prepared to believe that the original fault lay with the lords. He attributed much of the Pugachev revolt and the peasant uprisings in Bohemia to the serfowners' abuse of their rightful authority.[19] Similarly, he assumed that the French government was to blame for the deplorable events that occurred in 1789 and 1790: "The weakness of the king, the contemptuousness to which the queen has grown accustomed, and the empty-headedness of the ministers, will keep the lawlessness going for a long time to come."[20]

A more general application of Sievers's humanitarianism was his belief that every person in every station of life should strive to the best of his ability to serve society and promote the public welfare. Thus he condemned Russian nobles who avoided service to the state or who sought to pervert it to their private uses, but his sharpest words were reserved for the Polish nobles whom he encountered in 1793 as Catherine's envoy to the diet of Grodno. In their words and behavior he found "no love for the public good, no zeal to cooperate for its benefit—to put behind them the evils that have been practiced to exhaustion and replace them with a new order—everything is selfishness and self-interest."[21]

Sievers's belief in humanitarianism and service to the public welfare merged into his belief in progress. Although the first mainly concerned the moral content of an action and the latter the practical effect of an action on the future of society, Sievers assumed that the two went hand in hand —that humanitarian actions contributed to progress and that progress itself was humanitarian. In his own mind he was convinced that most forms of human misery were the products of vice and ignorance and that they could be eliminated through virtue and enlightenment. Far from believing that "whatever is, is right" or that "this is the best of all possible worlds," Sievers saw most elements of the status quo as ripe for improvement. He upheld and defended those elements of the status quo that reason and natural law had shown to be essential, but he had no great respect for those that appeared to be accidental products of history. In his letters and reports Sievers ignored history prior to the eighteenth century, except for an occasional use of the ancient Greeks and Romans as moral examples. In Novgorod he would be surrounded by the architectural monuments of Russia's greatest medieval city, but he showed not the slightest intellectual or emotional interest in any of them. In Sievers's outlook society was shaped by natural law and the presence or absence of enlightened moral sentiments, not by history, which was only a record or list of examples. Thus, some aspects of society should be supported because they had to be present in any civilized society; others should be promoted because they ought to be present in an enlightened society. But no aspect of society had any claim on Sievers simply because it was present. Indeed, as the products of a less enlightened age, most of the accidental elements of society could probably be altered and improved for the sake of the public welfare.

Such were the attitudes that Jakob Sievers carried into the provinces of northwestern Russia in 1764. They accorded in many respects with the aims and assumptions of the empress and other members of her government, and they made Sievers an excellent choice to test the waters of provincial development. The empress and the new governor agreed in principle that conditions in Novgorod Guberniia should be improved to promote the prosperity, productivity, and happiness of that region—and, by extension, of the empire as a whole—but exactly what that meant in practice would depend not only on the attitudes Sievers brought to Novgorod Guberniia but also on the circumstances he would find there and on the role he would play in the imperial government.

Peter the Great had incorporated the office of governor into the Russian state administration during the first decades of the eighteenth century. Of Swedish origin, it entered the Russian Empire with the occupation of Ingria (Ingermanland) in the first year of the Great Northern War. Peter placed A. D. Menshikov in charge of the occupied territory, and in 1702 he began referring to him as its *gubernator*.[22] In 1708 Peter divided Russia into eight governorships modeled on the one he had created for Menshikov, and by 1710 he had worked out a system of guberniia administration with the office of governor at its head.[23]

Almost from its inception the post of governor was shaped by two conflicting desires on the part of the imperial government. On the one hand, Peter saw an advantage in making a single individual responsible for the administration of a large territorial unit and wanted him to exercise leadership and control. On the other hand, Peter feared the concentration of power in the hands of any individual other than himself and wanted to limit the governor's ability to abuse that power. Aware of the Swedish, Livonian, and Russian precedents for his actions, Peter first attempted to counterbalance the governor's power. In 1713 he ordered the nobles in each guberniia to elect representatives to a *landratskaia kollegiia* (council), whose members were to make decisions jointly with the governor and countersign his orders. Peter's decree stipulated that "the governor is not to be their ruler but their president . . . and is not to do any business without them."[24] The effort failed, however, because Russian noblemen could not or would not play the role Peter had assigned them. Peter then subordinated a number of provincial agencies to the Senate and the central administrative colleges instead of to the governor.[25] The governor's authority was broadened significantly under Peter II and Anna, but under Elizabeth it was again diminished in favor of the colleges and the Senate.[26] At the time of Sievers's appointment a governor held the fourth rank in the Table of Ranks and received a salary of 1,875 rubles a year, but his duties were vague and his powers limited.[27]

Catherine's "Instruction to the Governors" helped to clarify the governor's responsibilities, but it did little to enhance his authority. The instruction identified the governor as the responsible official of the guberniia and ordered him to obey no one but the monarch and the Senate. It named him commander of the garrison, head of the guberniia chancellery, and guardian (*opekun*) of all state agencies in the guberniia that were not subordinate to the chancellery. In an emergency the governor could take command of army units within his guberniia, even though the regular army commander might outrank him, and only he could receive secret instructions from the Senate and the first three colleges. The governor was to see to it that all state business was conducted properly, to prosecute corrupt officials, to ensure order and tranquillity, to take measures to suppress all forms of lawlessness, to traverse the guberniia once every three years, observing, correcting, and informing the Senate of all that he had seen and done, and to carry out orders from the Senate and the monarch.[28]

The governor's role in provincial affairs would continue to be limited by his need to obtain agreement and authorization from the Senate and/or other agencies of the central administration. Although the governor was responsible for seeing that the guberniia chancellery conducted its business properly and could issue orders to chancellery officials, he could not discipline those officials or force them to comply with his orders. Article three of Catherine's instruction stipulated that all disputes between a governor and a guberniia chancellery were to be referred to the Senate for resolution. Furthermore, many state institutions lay outside the jurisdiction of the guberniia chancellery and reported directly to agencies of the central administration. As examples, the instruction cited the border commissions, the police, and the coach and messenger service along the highways; a longer list might also have included the courts, the monastaries and churches, the former ecclesiastical estates, the armed forces, and the major commercial waterways. By making the governor the guardian of such institutions, article nine of Catherine's instruction allowed the governor to involve himself in their affairs, but it did not place them under his authority. For anything other than routine cooperation from those agencies, the governor would have to make his case with the appropriate supervisory agency in the capital. The governor also exercised little authority over other levels of the provincial administration. The Senate would continue to appoint and dismiss the uezd and provintsiia voevodas; if they refused to cooperate with the governor, he could only turn to the Senate for assistance. Article five did allow the governor to remove officials at all levels of provincial administration for alleged corruption, but their fate was to be determined by the Justice College. Although article two ordered the governor to keep an eye on everything, it then required him to inform the Senate or one of the colleges whenever he found something amiss. Article fifteen authorized the governor to recommend the repair of roads and bridges, and article eight invited him to express his opinions and to point out the advantages or disadvantages of anything that related to his guberniia, but those phrases hardly embodied grants of authority. The only provision that relieved the governor of his otherwise total dependence on the Senate came in article eight, which stated that if a governor had addressed the Senate on an important issue that required a prompt decision and had not received one, he could then present his case to the empress herself.[29]

Catherine encouraged Sievers to enlarge upon the role outlined in her general "Instruction to the Governors." At a series of meetings in June 1764 the empress and the new governor went through that instruction point by point and discussed the ways in which he would implement its provisions. At that time Catherine also invited Sievers to correspond with her about his guberniia and his activities as governor. Sievers later recalled that Catherine also mentioned the terms of a special, supplementary instruction but that she did not give it to him at that time.[30] When he received such an instruction several months later, Sievers regarded it as a confirmation of his special relationship with the empress.

Longer and more detailed than the "Instruction to the Governors," Catherine's "secret" instruction to Governor Sievers set forth a broad range of activities that the new governor was to undertake for the purpose of promoting the development of his guberniia. Several of its twenty-four paragraphs dealt with the need to learn everything possible about local conditions. The governor was to collect and organize data on geography, topography, and demography and observe the morals and customs of his people. He was to know about the soils, the crops, and the methods of cultivation. He was to know the number of merchants and the kinds of business in which they engaged. He should even know the kinds and quantities of fish that could be pulled from the local lakes and rivers.[31]

With that knowledge the governor was to act as a tutor to the people of his guberniia and as an adviser to the central authorities. Having informed himself about agriculture, he was to praise good landlords and educate bad ones with advice "so that everyone can see that the governor knows about his affairs." He was to foster agricultural productivity by recommending better tools and more advantageous crops and to promote conservation of the forests by teaching the peasants to make fences with thorn bushes instead of wood. In the towns he was to help the magistracies create a more "policed order" by advising them on town planning, sanitation, and related matters. However, the instruction also enjoined the governor "not to upset anyone with strong commands" and ordered him not to divulge its content or even its existence to his chancellery.[32]

Anything beyond the giving of advice would require authorization from the central authorities. In some cases that authorization had already been granted, and the governor was simply urged to enforce with greater vigor the existing laws on fire prevention, official corruption, and the return of fugitive serfs. Where new measures were required, the instruction merely invited the governor to make proposals to the empress and the Senate. In that regard it specifically mentioned the draining of swamps, the improvement of roads, and the joining of streams, but near the end the invitation broadened and placed such matters at the discretion and initiative of the governor. Having impressed upon the new governor her ideas for the improvement of his guberniia, Catherine concluded: "The empress expects suggestions for relieving the obviously miserable condition of Novgorod and the decline of its commerce and industry; and if the governor should come up with something that is not mentioned in this instruction, he should draft a proposal and send it to the Senate or to the empress herself."[33]

In his first eight years as governor Sievers spent most of his time and effort informing himself and the central government about his guberniia and proposing measures to promote its development. His first major memorandum, signed on December 9, 1764, set the tone for much of his future correspondence with the empress. Based on six months of experience and investigation, the thirty-four-page document dealt with a wide range of subjects grouped under five headings: Means of Restoring and Improving the Town of Novgorod; Highways, Water Communications, Cataracts; Finances, Saltworks, Chancelleries, Schismatics, the College of Economy; A New Law Code, Police; Estates, Forests, Wood, Peat, Coal, the Rural Economy, and a Society of Economy or Agriculture. On virtually all of those subjects, however, his proposals consisted either of requests for authorization to take some action or of suggestions for action by the empress or the Senate. Except for auditing the accounts of the chancellery, there was little he could do on his own.[34]

One aspect of Sievers's efforts to provide useful information about his guberniia is exemplified by his yearly reports on the number of births, deaths, and marriages. In her secret instruction Catherine had proposed that the parish churches record the number of births, illegitimate births, foundlings, deaths, and deaths due to violence and drunkenness "so that we may follow in this manner measures taken in the future to improve the people's morals."[35] Looking into the matter, Sievers found that the churches in his guberniia were already recording the number of births, deaths, and marriages and forwarding their information to the ecclesiastical authorities.[36] In 1765 Sievers began compiling that data and sending it to the Senate in the form of a table showing the number of births, deaths, and marriages in each provintsiia.[37] Like Catherine, he was particularly interested in the number of deaths and in determining the causes of any fluctuations he noticed in that figure. In 1768, for example, he informed the empress that the number of deaths had increased by 12 percent in the preceding year and blamed the bad harvest and the high price of grain.[38] In 1767 Sievers began submitting a second table of figures showing the specific ages at which males died, and in future years he would divide the first year of life into smaller units—first quarters and then individual months—in order to obtain more precise information about infant mortality.[39] In 1772 he expanded his efforts once again by trying to determine the causes of all the deaths that had occurred during the previous year.[40] The Senate welcomed Sievers's initiative in compiling such information and ordered other governors to prepare similar tables.[41]

Sievers spent much of his time traveling through his guberniia to observe local conditions, which he then described to the empress and the Senate. In the spring of 1765 he voyaged from Novgorod to St. Petersburg by boat and gave the Senate a report on the waterways based on his own observations.[42] He spent the summer of 1766 traveling some two thousand miles through the northern part of his guberniia, and at the instruction of the Senate he spent the following summer journeying a comparable distance through the southern part. He kept a diary of his travels and reported to the empress and the Senate on the roads, waterways, towns, soils, and anything else that seemed important.[43]

The Senate also sent Sievers to investigate specific problems. In 1765, for example, when the voevoda of Olonets reported a serious famine among the state peasants in the Kargopol region, the Senate ordered Sievers to investigate the matter on its behalf. Sievers's report confirmed the voevoda's assessment of the situation. He proposed that the government sell grain to the peasants on credit and that it excuse them from paying taxes for the next two years. Convinced by two separate, concurring reports, the Senate incorporated Sievers's proposals into a decree that the empress signed just nine weeks after the receipt of the voevoda's report.[44]

The costs of Sievers's journeys and the other expenses of his office helped persuade him to marry his cousin Elizabeth. Having retired as chief marshal of the court in the spring of 1767, Karl Sievers wanted to arrange a marriage between his high-spirited daughter and his hard-working nephew in order to keep her dowery in the family. Jakob visited his relatives at their estate near Narva in June 1767 and acceded to his uncle's wishes. Just before his wedding the following year Sievers wrote Catherine that he hoped his marriage would salvage his perilous finances.[45] After the wedding he continued to show far more interest in his job than in his wife, and his travels kept them apart for long periods of time.[46] For her part, Elizabeth Sievers was as devoted to pleasure and amusements as her husband was to work, and she hated life in the provinces. In the first years of their marriage she complained bitterly about his long absences and told him frankly that his zeal was ridiculous.[47] Eventually they worked out an arrangement whereby she remained in St. Petersburg to advance his interests at court and to keep him informed of what transpired there. For a number of years her efforts contributed to his standing with the empress, but the explosive breakup of their marriage in 1778 severely strained the personal relationship between Catherine and Sievers.

Sievers found that his job as a provincial governor consisted mostly of processing various kinds of documents and drafting reports. In May 1768 he complained to Catherine: "It is already the fourth year of my governorship, and I have never yet had the satisfaction at the end of my working day of saying to myself, 'Look, your work is completely finished.' On the contrary, the more time passes, the more the papers in front of me multiply."[48] In his memorandum of December 9, 1764, Sievers mentioned that he had asked the Senate for more clerks for his chancellery. Now, in May 1768, he was appealing to the empress for permission to hire a secretary and several clerks for his chancellery, adding: "It is useless to approach the Senate again, having already written them many times about this."[49]

By the late 1760s Sievers was becoming increasingly frustrated with his role in the imperial government. Under the administrative system used by Catherine and Viazemskii, officials in St. Petersburg received reports from governors and other officials in the provinces, checked their statements against information from other sources, weighed their proposals against other considerations, and then made decisions that the governors had to accept. In an emergency Sievers could prevail. In 1765, for example, he informed Catherine of a serious famine in the area around Velikie Luki and proposed emergency measures to aid the people of that region. The empress responded that other information indicated a simple shortage rather than a severe famine. She told Sievers to investigate further and to be on guard against local noblemen who might try to use the shortage to start a run on the state granaries. After checking, Sievers borrowed from the state granaries to feed the peasants of the College of Economy—and informed the empress a year later of what he had done.[50]

Under normal circumstances, however, a governor could do little without prior authorization from the Senate, and Sievers found that restriction increasingly intolerable. After the Senate had denied a number of his requests, he began to complain to the empress about being overruled on matters in which he believed his own knowledge and experience should have been decisive: "The Senate will always believe that it sees better with its telescope than I with my eyes."[51] Sometimes, as with his requests for clerks, the Senate simply gave no answer, but in many others it took the matter under consideration and proceeded to investigate and deliberate for years. Such a situation created a genuine dilemma for Sievers, who sincerely believed that rules and formal procedures provided essential safeguards against tyranny, favoritism, and other abuses of power but who was nonetheless impatient for progress and reform. In some instances—as when the Senate took seven years to consider fully his proposal to create four new towns in his guberniia—Sievers could not contain his frustration with a system that obstructed what he saw as obvious solutions to the problems of provincial Russia. Having presented his case several times in great detail, he responded sarcastically to the Senate's request for additional information and took his case to the empress. He asked her repeatedly to intervene on his behalf with the Senate and even urged her at one point to create the towns "with a stroke of your pen."[52] When the Senate ignored his repeated suggestions for improvements to the waterways, Sievers asked Catherine to take the provincial agencies in charge of those waterways from the Senate and place them under his authority.[53] He then castigated the Senate's management of the waterways in his letters to the empress and prosecuted the Senate's principal agent in charge of those waterways for embezzlement.

Sievers's tactics earned him the lasting enmity of Procurator-General Viazemskii and some other members of the central administration. In 1772, however, his hard work began to pay off. The final dismissal of the committees of the Legislative Commission in 1771 and 1772 marked the end of the preparatory period of study and deliberation that Catherine had felt necessary before launching major reforms, and the crises of the early 1770s had intensified the need for action. In 1772 the empress began to overrule the Senate and grant many of Sievers's requests. For several years thereafter Sievers became her principal adviser on provincial affairs and played a major role in her government's program to reform and develop provincial Russia.

IV

Novgorod Guberniia in the 1760s

HEN HE ACCEPTED THE GOVERNORSHIP of Novgorod Guberniia, Sievers assumed responsibility for administering a vast and underpopulated territory that extended from the Polish border to the shores of the White Sea. Encompassing almost all of the territory that was later divided into the four guberniias of Pskov, Novgorod, Tver, and Olonets, Novgorod Guberniiia in 1764 measured approximately eight hundred miles along its southwest to northeast axis and some four hundred miles along its shorter axis running from the southeast to the northwest between the upper Volga and the port of St. Petersburg.[1] With an estimated area of 200,000 square miles, Novgorod Guberniia in 1764 was as large as the kingdom of France.

Tax records and revision data provide a basis for estimating population. In April 1765 Sievers supplied the Senate with figures showing that Novgorod Guberniia contained 815,751 males who paid the polltax and another 30,674 males who were registered as merchants.[2] If one allows for the downward bias of tax rolls, for a normal, slight predominance of females over males, and for the absence from the tax registers of nobles, clerics, and officials, Sievers's figures would suggest a total population of about 1,800,000. Such a figure is not too far out of line with the estimates of the Soviet demographer V. M. Kabuzan, who used data from the Third

NOVGOROD GUBERNIIA IN THE 1760S

Revision of 1762 to determine what the male populations of the later guberniias of Pskov, Novgorod, Tver, and Olonets would have been in that year. Kabuzan's calculations for an area very nearly congruent with the Novgorod Guberniia of 1764 yield a total of 957,124 males of all classes, which would imply a total population of approximately 2,000,000.[3]

Taken together, these estimates of area and population indicate that the population density of Novgorod Guberniia was only nine to ten persons per square mile. In some respects, however, that figure is misleading, because the guberniia's rather arbitrary boundaries made it seem even more rustic and remote than it actually was. Most of the population was concentrated in the southwestern half of the guberniia, leaving the vast reaches of the northeast almost uninhabited. The uezds of Tikhivin and Beloozero, for example, contained fewer than one inhabitant per square mile.[4] Although Novgorod Guberniia included no major urban area, it lay between Moscow and St. Petersburg, the two largest centers of population in the empire. The proximity of both cities and the lines of trade and communication that passed between them exerted a significant influence on some areas of the guberniia.

Its location between the interior guberniias of Moscow and Smolensk to the south and the maritime ports to the north constituted the dominant feature in the economic geography of Novgorod Guberniia. The guberniia straddled a low continental divide that separates the headwaters of the Dnepr and Volga river systems from those of the Western Dvina, the Velikaia, the Volkhov, the Sias, the Svir, and others that flow toward the Baltic. No where else in the world do so many river systems arise in such close proximity at such low elevations. Short portages and canals across the divide connected virtually the whole interior of European Russia with the northern sea routes to Europe. Nearly all of the boats and barges that arrived in Narva or St. Petersburg in any given year either originated in Novgorod Guberniia or passed through it on their way from the interior, and so did many of the river craft arriving in Riga, Reval, and Arkhangel. With only slight exaggeration, Sievers could write Catherine in 1768 that the whole foreign trade of the empire passed through his jurisdiction.[5]

The most important trade route in Novgorod Guberniia, and one of the most important in all of Russia, was the so-called Vyshnii Volochek System of rivers and canals that formed a continuous waterway from Tver on the upper Volga River to St. Petersburg on the Gulf of Finland. Without it, St. Petersburg could not have become a metropolis or have exerted much influence on the national economy. The Vyshnii Volochek System and possible alternatives to it had been an important subject of discussion between Sievers and Catherine before his departure for Novgorod, and it became a major item of concern to him throughout his service as governor.

Of the 633 miles of waterway that composed the Vyshnii Volochek System, approximately 525 miles lay within Novgorod Guberniia and formed its economic and geographical axis. The system began at Tver,

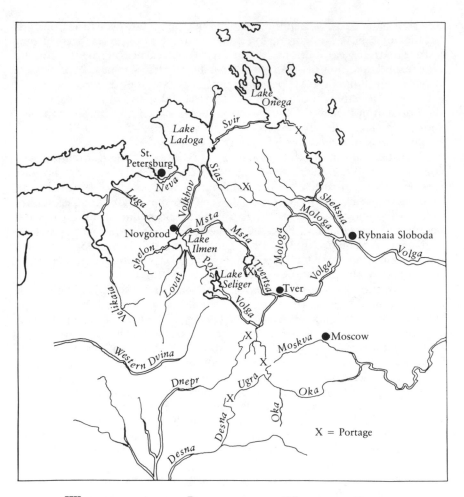

WATERWAYS AND PORTAGES IN WESTERN RUSSIA

where boats left the upper Volga and entered its tributary, the Tvertsa, to
begin the journey over the continental divide. Boats arriving from downstream carried grain, vodka, pig iron, salts, and other commodities produced along the Volga and its tributaries to the south and east as far away
as the Urals. Those arriving from upstream carried flax, linen, oats,
manufactured articles, and increasing quantities of rye and hemp loaded in
Rzhev, Zubtsov, and Gzhatsk after portage from the Dnepr River system.
Every boat or barge destined for St. Petersburg had to stop in Tver to hire
the ten horses, four teamsters, one pilot, and two assistants needed to as-

cend the Tvertsa.[6] Those arriving late in the year, usually from the more distant points of origin, had to spend the winter in Tver because the Tvertsa normally froze in November and thawed in late March or early April. One great caravan of more than a thousand boats normally began the ascent of the Tvertsa in April, to be followed by another in mid-summer, and a third in the autumn. The shallowness of the Tvertsa, which often fell below the two feet required by a fully loaded boat or barge, caused great difficulty for the summer and autumn caravans and sometimes prevented the latter from reaching St. Petersburg before winter.

After an ascent of 118 miles in twenty-five to thirty days, the caravans reached the continental divide at Vyshnii Volochek, an important *iam* (station) on the Moscow–St. Petersburg highway at an elevation 213 feet higher than Tver. Through the center of the settlement and across the continental divide lay the Tvertskoi Canal, some eight thousand feet in length, joining the Tvertsa with the Tsna, whose waters emptied eventually into the Gulf of Finland. Very shallow and less than eight miles in length, the Tsna was dammed, interrupted by a short canal, and augmented by water from other streams nearby. The canals, sluices, and reservoirs that made it possible to cross the continental divide without portage had been created for Peter the Great by a private concessionaire named Michael Serdiukov. Until 1764 Serdiukov's descendants continued to collect a fee from every boat and barge passing Vyshnii Volochek and to operate saw mills, grist mills, distilleries, and farms within the concession. Then, in response to merchants' complaints about deteriorating conditions, the Senate took over the management of the concession and put a Colonel Pisarev in charge. Between 1765 and 1773 an average of 2,400–3,000 boats and barges carrying 160,000–250,000 metric tons of cargo passed through the locks at Vyshnii Volochek each year.[7]

At Vyshnii Volochek the captains hired new pilots for the descent through the Msta River. Connected with the Tsna through Lake Mstino, the Msta ran and tumbled 260 miles down the northern slopes of the Valdai Hills into Lake Ilmen. Of the three sets of rapids that made the Msta especially treacherous, the worst were at Borovichi, where the river fell 367 feet in twenty miles and the boats had to pass through ten stretches of white water in eleven miles.[8] The Borovichi Rapids Office, under General Murav'ev, struggled to improve conditions there by removing the worst obstacles and installing wooden guard rails and tow lines. The owners of damaged or grounded boats had little choice but to hire local labor at exorbitant prices, and they occasionally accused the local residents of arranging accidents on purpose.[9] Low water in the Msta sometimes halted caravans entirely and forced them to lay over.

Upon arriving at Lake Ilmen, boats and barges had to brave its dangerous waters and sudden storms before arriving safely at Novgorod. So many boats were lost in the process that the nakaz of the merchants of Novgorod to the Legislative Commission proposed that the Msta be joined directly to the Volkhov by a canal that would bypass the lake.[10] After regrouping in Novgorod, the caravans descended the Volkhov in three to six days. The Volkhov also contained several cataracts, but they were less serious than those of the Msta. At Novaia Ladoga, at the mouth of the Volkhov, the caravans left Novgorod Guberniia to enter St. Petersburg Guberniia and the Ladoga Canal, which joined the Volkhov to the Neva. The entire trip from Tver to St. Petersburg normally required fifty-seven to sixty-nine days, depending on the weather, the water levels, and unforeseen mishaps.[11]

Some goods crossed the divide between major river systems on wagons or sleds. A portage between the Somina and Tikhvinka rivers at Tikhvin and another between the Kovzha and the Vytegra to the north connected tributaries of the Volga with streams leading to St. Petersburg. Other portages in the southwestern corner of the guberniia enabled cargoes to pass between the Dnepr and the Western Dvina.

The commercial traffic that passed along its waterways contributed heavily to the economy of Novgorod Guberniia. Among the most obvious and most important byproducts were the hiring of local labor and the purchase of lodging, food, repairs, and other goods and services. Each summer the waterways employed thousands of pilots, teamsters, constructon workers, and government workers of many sorts. According to one specialist, most of the wage labor in the city of Tver was connected directly with the waterways.[12] The same was no doubt true for most of the settlements clustered along the main route from Tver to Novaia Ladoga and even for those at some distance.[13] Using the data from the Topographical Description of 1783, one historian has estimated that the average peasant family in what was essentially Tver Provintsiia could raise only 37 percent of its annual cash needs from the sale of agricultural products and had to earn the remainder from other occupations, of which seasonal work on the waterways was the most common.[14] A pilot earned as much in a summer as a master craftsman made in a year, and a teamster made as much as a blacksmith and more than a shoemaker.[15]

Commercial traffic to and from various parts of Novgorod Guberniia played an even greater role in the local economy than did the transit trade. According to the General Survey, Novgorod Guberniia contained a total of 1,276 navigable rivers and 1,020 lakes,[16] most of which led eventually into one of the major systems. The ready availability of transportation enabled the local inhabitants to obtain grain, alcohol, salt, and other needed commodities from other regions of the guberniia or from guberniias to the south and southeast. Like many areas in northern Russia, Novgorod Guberniia was both a buyer and a seller of grain, depending on the harvest and the season, and commercial traffic along the waterways helped to regulate the supply and the price. Thus, when two bad harvests in a row led to a severe shortage of grain in the uezds of Velikie Luki, Opochka, Pustorzhev, Toropets, and Ostrov during the early months of 1771, Sievers could inform the empress that a good harvest in the neighboring uezds of Smolensk Guberniia would alleviate the difficulty by making grain available at reasonable prices.[17]

The waterways also provided producers in Novgorod Guberniia with easy access to markets on the coast. Figures for the year 1777 show that approximately 60 percent of the 5,997 boats and all of the 5,425 timber rafts arriving in St. Petersburg from the interior had taken on their cargoes in Novgorod Guberniia (see Table 5).[18] The Velikaia and Western Dvina rivers provided the western and southwestern regions of the guberniia with comparable access to Narva and Riga.

The exploitation of mineral resources played a relatively small role in the economy of northwestern Russia. Salt was mined in several locations; the most important deposit was to be found south of Lake Ilmen near the town of Staraia Russa. Limestone from the Valdai Hills and the Olonets region and clay from the area around Novgorod supplied materials for the construction of St. Petersburg. Although traces of coal were discovered on the Msta near Borovichi in the 1760s, no coal was actually mined there until much later. Low-grade deposits of sulphur pyrite and iron ore were found throughout much of guberniia, but production occurred only on a small scale. The smelting and working of iron, though actually declining in the once important centers of Novgorod and Tikhvin, was increasing in the uezds of Beloozero and Ustiuzhna.[19] Except for salt, the mineral deposits in Novgorod Guberniia employed relatively few people and contributed only marginally to the overall economy.

Forests and forest products, on the other hand, figured prominently in both the geography and the economy of Novgorod Guberniia. The data from the Economic Observations and the Fifth Revision, as compiled by the Soviet specialist N. L. Rubinshtein, indicate that forests covered more than two-thirds of the land area of the guberniia.[20] The eastern and northeastern provintsiias of Olonets and Beloozero were the most heavily forested and Tver the least, but even in Tver Provintsiia forests covered 63.8 percent of the land, or twice the amount devoted to agriculture. Only in the extreme south along the upper Volga did the forest range decrease to as little as 50 percent of the total area.[21] Local forests provided the inhabitants of Novgorod Guberniia with most of their building material and virtually all of their fuel. They also supplied the raw materials for the tools and implements of daily life as well as for the handcrafted goods sold for cash. The nakaz of the nobles of Tikhvin, for example, informed the Legislative Commission that the peasants of their region earned the major part of their income by fashioning wood into yokes, barrels, tubs, and other products, selling them, and using the money to buy grain and to pay their taxes and *obrok* (money dues).[22] Tar, timber, and pitch ranked high among the leading exports of the guberniia and were especially important along the Velikaia River in the west and throughout Olonets Provintsiia to the north. Along the waterways of the entire guberniia, the forests provided timber for the boats and barges that carried goods to market. Those boats that reached St. Petersburg were in turn broken up to supply the city with firewood.

Despite the seeming abundance of forests, the guberniia's inhabitants and the government worried about deforestation. Significant deforestation had already occurred in other parts of the empire. According to the nakaz of the nobles of Tula, for example, the glass and metal industries had caused once great forests to vanish, and the Demidov iron works alone were consuming 400,000 logs a year.[23] Novgorod sustained no industrial enterprises comparable to those of Tula; nevertheless, its nobles expressed anxieties about the rate at which the forests were declining and asked the government for measures to limit wood consumption.[24] In fact, the imperial government had been trying since 1723 to manage Russia's forests more intelligently, but Sievers and Catherine agreed with the nobles that more conservation measures should be undertaken.[25]

In contrast to the prevalence of handicrafts, large-scale manufacturing was almost unknown in Novgorod Guberniia in 1764. The only significant exceptions were the saltworks at Staraia Russa, where production revived in the 1760s, and the state distillery in Ustiuzhna. Otherwise, the two small factories that opened in Tver in 1761 ranked among the largest industrial employers in the guberniia. One was a rope walk that employed twelve hired workers and one serf; the other, a leather goods factory, maintained eight hired workers and one serf.[26] According to E. G. Istomina, a typical manufactory in Novgorod Guberniia in the 1760s consisted of a master craftsman and three to five hired laborers.[27]

All these forms of economic employment, plus fishing and seasonal labor in St. Petersburg, provided a necessary complement to agriculture. Although agriculture alone could not support the population, most of the inhabitants spent some portion of their time raising crops and animals. As important as it was in economic terms, agriculture held an even greater significance in the culture and tradition of the Great Russian people, who regarded the cultivation of the earth as man's natural employment. It enabled him to live and work in harmony with nature, God, and the community. That assumption and the minimal, if inadequate, security that agriculture provided made peasants reluctant to abandon it completely. The landowners and the government were equally unhappy to see peasants leaving the fields for other occupations. To a considerable extent they shared the peasants' belief in the propriety of agricultural and village life, but their desire to keep the peasants on the land was also connected with a crude notion of economic development that associated an expanding population with a larger agricultural work force and thus with increased production.

In spite of their ideological commitment to agriculture, both the landlords and the peasants of Novgorod Guberniia understood that in reality it was a relatively unrewarding occupation. Lying between the fifty-sixth and the sixty-third parallels of latitude, Novgorod Guberniia enjoyed only a short growing season under normal conditions. It was subject to sudden, unseasonable frosts at the beginning and the end, and the short summers were often cool and wet. The various types of podzol soils that predominated throughout the guberniia contained too much acid and too few of the minerals that most crops need in order to thrive, and in the midst of so much water the soils in many areas were waterlogged or marshy. The southern rim of the guberniia offered the best growing conditions for most food crops, but even in Tver Provintsiia, between the border of Moscow Guberniia and the southern slopes of the Valdai Hills, less than half the land was used for crops. In the areas around Rzhev, Zubtsov, and Staritsa between 40 and 50 percent of the land was under cultivation; in Tver Provintsiia as a whole, only 30 percent of the land was farmed. In the northern half of the guberniia cropland accounted for less than 10 percent of the total acreage.[28] Despite the economic and demographic pressures on both the peasants and the landlords, vast acreages remained uncultivated. The accessibility of the St. Petersburg market and that city's demand for foodstuffs encouraged some noblemen to cultivate a demesne under the barshchina regime of serfdom, but barshchina predominated only in the food-growing areas around Valdai and Borovichi—and then just barely. Outside of the flax-growing regions of the west, the great majority of serfowners turned the land over to the peasants for an obrok of two to three rubles a year.[29]

The principal food crops included in the three-field rotations were rye, wheat, oats, barley, peas, lentils, and buckwheat.[30] The Topographical Description recorded that crops of rye, oats, and peas normally yielded four times the seed throughout the guberniia and five or six times the seed in Valdai and Krestets.[31] But those figures are hardly compatible with S. I. Volkov's evidence that yields of rye on court estates near Moscow averaged scarcely twice the seed over a ten-year period from 1750 to 1759.[32] Had grain been yielding four times the seed in Novgorod Guberniia, we can assume that more land would have been under cultivation, that obrok payments would have been higher, that more landlords would have converted their estates to barshchina, and that fewer peasants would have left agriculture for other kinds of employment.[33] More credible is the report of the Free Economic Society. On the basis of questionnaires returned by landowners, it determined that the grain harvest in Tver Provintsiia, which embraced much of the best cropland in the guberniia, normally returned only twice the amount that had been sown.[34] In the more northerly uezds of Kirillov and Ustiuzhna, Istomina found that the harvest produced only enough grain to last from four to six months before the peasants had to begin purchasing additional supplies.[35] With unseasonal frosts and with cool, wet summers so common, the frequency of crop failures may have been even more discouraging to agriculture than consistently low yields. A Senate study of crop failures in 1767 concluded that such calamities were most common in the guberniias of Arkhangel, Novgorod, Smolensk, and Moscow.[36]

In addition to field crops, Novgorod Guberniia also produced fruit, meat, milk, and vegetables. Orchards were common on the northern slopes of the Valdai Hills and in the region around Novgorod. Valdai, Bezhetsk, and some other regions of the Valdai Hills boasted some excellent pastures, and the amount of land devoted to grazing in those areas was three to four times the guberniia average of 2 percent of the total land area. As a general rule, the peasants ate meat only on feast days, but in the more remote areas of the north and east hunting provided an important component of the diet.[37] Growing vegetables for one's own table was a nearly universal practice even in the towns.

Except for trees, the only commercially important plants that grew consistently well in Novgorod Guberniia were flax and hemp. Flax was a major crop in the western region that included Pskov and Velikie Luki, where it was raised as a cash crop for export through the Livonian harbor of Riga. Hemp, a garden rather than a field crop, was grown in increasing quantities throughout the guberniia, but more toward the south and west. It did not thrive there to the same degree that it did farther south, but proximity to the Baltic ports and the rising demand for Russian hemp in western Europe made it economically significant. Between 1761 and 1795 hemp exports from Russian harbors more than doubled, from less than 25,000 metric tons to more than 55,000 metric tons. St. Petersburg's share of those exports rose very rapidly between 1761 and 1785, but then they declined even more rapidly thereafter.[38]

Kabuzan's data on the social composition of the four guberniias (Pskov, Tver, Novgorod, and Olonets) into which Novgorod was divided after 1775 are presented in Table 6. They indicate that more than 95 percent of the inhabitants of northwestern Russia in 1762 were classified as peasants. More than half of the guberniia's total population (56.6 percent) was enserfed to the nobles; another quarter (24.2 percent) had been enserfed to the church but had become "economic peasants" after the secularization of ecclesiastical estates. Crown and votchina (appanage) peasants made up about 5.7 percent of the population, and state peasants accounted for another 8.6 percent. State peasants were concentrated in the northern region that would later become the guberniia of Olonets. There they constituted 80 percent of the male population, while peasants enserfed to noblemen accounted for only 4.6 percent. At the other extreme stood the western region that would later become the guberniia of Pskov, where three-quarters of the population (74.5 percent) was enserfed to pomeshchiks (noble landowners). In the central regions that subsequently became the guberniias of Novgorod and Tver, privately owned serfs accounted for 52.6 percent and 60.9 percent of the total population, respec-

TABLE 6. MALE POPULATION OF NOVGOROD, TVER, PSKOV, AND OLONETS GUBERNIIAS IN 1762 BY FISCAL-ADMINISTRATIVE CATEGORY

Guberniia	Crown and votchina peasants		Ecclesiastical or economic peasants		State peasants		Nobles' peasants		Townsmen		Non-Taxed		Total
	no.	%	no.	%	no.	%	no.	%	no.	%	no.	%	
Novgorod	18,458	7.80	81,089	34.29	899	0.38	124,488	52.63	5,944	2.51	5,635	2.38	236,473
Tver	20,996	5.57	102,562	27.24	2,159	0.57	229,541	60.97	18,157	4.82	3,034	0.81	376,449
Pskov	15,165	6.14	39,138	15.85	1,678	0.67	183,893	74.49	6,201	2.51	798	0.32	246,873
Olonets	—	—	9,340	9.60	77,701	79.83	4,478	4.60	5,734	5.89	76	0.08	97,329
TOTAL	54,610	5.70	232,139	24.25	82,437	8.61	542,400	56.66	36,036	3.76	9,543	0.99	957,127

Source: V. M. Kabuzan, *Izmeneniia v razmeshchenii naseleniia Rossii v XVIII—pervoi polovine XIX v* (Moscow, 1971), pp. 83–86. Of course, the individual guberniias of Novgorod, Tver, Pskov, and Olonets did not come into existence until after 1776. Kabuzan has reconstructed their population at the time of the Third Revision for purposes of comparison with later data. The territory of those four guberniias was almost but not exactly co-extensive with the territory of Novgorod Guberniia in 1762. The territorial reorganization that followed the reform of 1776 will be explained in Chapter V.

tively. Economic peasants were especially numerous in both of those territories, amounting to 34.3 percent of the population of Novgorod and 27.2 percent of the population of Tver. In the uezds of Novgorod, Tver, Kirillov, and Staraia Russa, economic peasants accounted for more than half the population and for slightly less than half in the uezd of Krestets.[39]

Large estates were less common in Novgorod Guberniia than in any other region of the empire, and the ratio of serfs to pomeshchiks was correspondingly low. In December 1764 Sievers informed the empress: "There is no provintsiia and no guberniia where the nobility is more numerous and more impoverished than that of Novgorod."[40] A Soviet study of serf ownership in the 1720s lends credence to the governor's impression. N. M. Serpukov found that fewer than 5 percent of the nobles in Novgorod owned more than one hundred revision souls, and more than 65 percent of the nobles possessed fewer than twenty. The comparable figures for the empire as a whole are 8.7 percent and 59.5 percent, respectively. Serpukov also found that small holdings of land and serfs were more prevalent in the region around Tver than anywhere else in the empire.[41]

Since the number of revision serfs owned by an eighteenth-century Russian nobleman or his parents usually provides a reliable index of his wealth, income, and education,[42] we can reasonably infer that the nobles of Novgorod Guberniia had neither the capital nor the knowledge to provide economic leadership for the development of agriculture. The prevalence of obrok would appear to substantiate that inference. Thus we can dispose of any notion of latifundia run by westernized landlords attempting to introduce modern agricultural techniques. Generally speaking, the possessional serfs of Novgorod Guberniia were on their own when it came to surviving and meeting their obligations, and they responded in terms of their own culture to necessity and opportunity, not to ideas of modernization and development that had no way of reaching them.

The former ecclesiastical serfs were in much the same position. Before secularization most of them had belonged to one of the great central monasteries (the Holy Trinity–St. Sergius, for example, or the Joseph of Volokolamsk), to the local episcopal domain, or, less commonly, to a local monastery. Ecclesiastical estates were generally much larger than those of the local pomeshchiks, and one might therefore expect that they could be exploited and developed more effectively.[43] The available evidence suggests, however, that the church was so backward in its management that its estates deteriorated instead of improving.[44] Under those circumstances, the transfer of management from the church to the College of Economy amounted to placing a bankrupt enterprise in receivership. The state pacified the peasants, but it was not prepared to manage their affairs. In December 1764 Sievers complained that the one administrator and two assistants sent to Novgorod by the College of Economy could not begin to meet their responsibilities to the twenty thousand revision serfs under their authority. As a result, "the peasants govern themselves in republican fashion, and that government is usually stormy and incompatible with the welfare of each individual."[45] From the standpoint of the imperial government, the decentralization of decision making among the peasants complicated and intensified the already serious problems inherent in their demographic decentralization and doubled the government's difficulty in making positive changes in what it regarded as their backward and unenlightened way of life.[46]

In the early 1760s Novgorod Guberniia contained several genuine towns and a number of partially urbanized settlements. Unfortunately, the legal-administrative categories in use at that time make it virtually impossible for us to determine how many settlements and how many people could be characterized as urban on the basis of economic, sociological, or demographic criteria. Although the term *gorod* is commonly translated by the English word "town," it was used to designate a settlement that had no landlord or owner, contained a voevoda and a garrison, and served as a center of public administration. In 1764 twenty-two settlements in Novgorod Guberniia were officially recognized as goroda, but some of them were visibly less urban than others that were not goroda. Sievers noted that Ostrov, for example, was more like a village than a town: it contained 150 dwellings; its male population numbered approximately 240; its fortifications lay in ruins; and the government offices were located in a straw hut. In Sievers's opinion the neighboring gorod, Opochka, represented only a slight improvement over Ostrov.[47] In contrast Ostashkov, a *sloboda* (suburb) managed by the College of Economy, had a population of 2,249 males in 1753 and by 1764 supported 111 merchants, including 38 first guild merchants who boasted a total capital of 37,700 rubles.[48] Sievers believed that it would make a "fine town,"[49] as, in his opinion, would Vyshnii Volochek, the settlement on the continental divide where the Moscow–St. Petersburg highway crossed the waterway linking the Volga with the Neva. In 1764 Vyshnii Vokochek had a population in excess of 1,000, but it belonged to the Iamskaia Kantseliariia, and its inhabitants were entered in the government's records as iamshchiks.[50]

The English word "townsman" is even less commensurate with Russian terminology of the 1760s. The imperial government classed and counted people according to their legal registration in one of several groups, each of which owed different obligations to the state. The term *posadskii chelovek*, which is often translated into English as "townsman" (pl. *posadskie liudi*), applied only to the members of an urban commune (*posad*) who received specified privileges within the settlement in return for bearing a communal burden (*tiaglo*) of taxes and services that they apportioned among themselves. Membership in a posad was restricted to the three merchant guilds, to the *meshchane* (who were too poor to qualify as merchants), and to some trading peasants who had obtained permission from the posad and their own masters. The term *posadskie liudi* did not include the noblemen, priests, government officials, and retired soldiers who might live in a gorod.[51] For example, merchants constituted only 41.6 percent of the population of the town of Novgorod in 1764.[52] Conversely, the inhabitants of Ostashkov, Tikhvin, Pogoreno Gorodishche, and other settlements that were not goroda had been allowed to organize posady and to be counted as posadskie liudi and merchants.[53]

In the 1760s the merchants of Novgorod Guberniia numbered 26,600 and constituted 14.2 percent of all the merchants in the empire. In this category Novgorod Guberniia ranked second only to Moscow Guberniia's 39,900 merchants (21.7 percent).[54] Once again, however, the legal-administrative terminology conveys only a vague representation of the socio-economic reality. An unknown and probably indeterminable number of merchants in the third guild, whose membership included the great majority of all merchants, were not merchants in any economic or sociological sense but artisans, laborers, or even farmers. On the other hand, some individuals registered in the peasantry and other classes engaged in trade and commerce in violation of the laws restricting those activities to merchants.[55] In 1768 Sievers wrote that most of the merchants in his guberniia carried on their business "without any order, seldom with written documents, without books, and almost without numbers."[56]

The society and economy of Novgorod Guberniia could not be fitted neatly into the various legal-administrative categories that the state had devised to record and govern them. In many respects they also defy categorization by such modern terms as "urban" and "non-urban." Many of the guberniia's inhabitants lived in small settlements and combined agriculture, hunting, fishing, and beekeeping with handicraft production for the market and seasonal wage labor on the waterways or in the capitals or a local town. The Topographical Description of 1783, for example, counted inhabitants in the city of Tver as 15,095 but labeled only 11,252 of them as permanent residents.[57] The precise number of the guberniia's urban population thus appears to be as much a semantic and methodological problem as a historical one. But whatever small number may have lived as real townsmen in a socio-economic sense, a much larger proportion were affected by the pull of St. Petersburg, by the growth of towns and other settlements within the guberniia, and by the increasing importance of economic pursuits outside of agriculture. It also appears that many individuals adjusted to those changes while retaining their roots in the peasantry.

The largest, fastest growing, and most incontrovertibly urban settlement in Novgorod Guberniia was the city of Tver (officially a gorod). In 1764 the Third Revision recorded the male population as 6,428, a substantial increase over the 3,903 recorded by the Second Revision of 1749.[58] According to the records of the Commission on Commerce, 2,800 of those townsmen were registered as merchants: 87 in the first guild, 140 in the second, and 2,578 in the third.[59] Among the first guild merchants were 49 with a combined capital of 91,700 rubles who traded at the port.

Twenty-three of them dealt in grain.[60] Most of the third guild merchants worked at one of the many trades and crafts practiced in the city, but some were simple laborers, as were most of the meshchane.[61] With the exception of the clergy, the garrison, and some of the state officials, nearly everyone in the city derived his income directly or indirectly from the trade along the Volga and Tvertsa rivers. In addition, we should note that in 1765, 11 members of the first merchant guild, 22 members of the second merchant guild, and 102 members of the third merchant guild were performing services without compensation for the treasury and other agencies of the imperial government.[62]

An Orthodox seminary founded in 1727 helped to promote intellectual interests and enlightened attitudes among some of the inhabitants of Tver. From 1759 to 1761 the rector of the seminary was the monk who ultimately became St. Tikhon Zadonskii. Influenced by Johann Arndt's *Wahres Christentum*, Tikhon incorporated principles of pietism into his own belief. In his lectures at the seminary and subsequently in his published works on theology, Tikhon argued that faith should be nurtured with learning and expressed in concern for the welfare of one's fellow man.[63] After Tikhon's departure from Tver, V. I. Vereshchagin, who taught rhetoric at the seminary, and D. I. Karmanov, a townsman who had recently graduate from the seminary, became the nucleus of a group of clerics and laymen devoted to intellectual discussion and the propagation of learning. After becoming a monk in 1767, Vereshchagin left Tver for a few years, but returned in 1775 as Bishop Arsenii. Karmanov became Tver's first public notary, a local historian, and a leader in civic affairs. In addition to studying theology, philosophy, and history, the group around Vereshchagin and Karmanov wrote and argued against the Old Belief, which has many adherents in some of the towns west of Tver. Its members also worked to broaden the curriculum of the seminary, to make Russian rather than Latin the language of instruction, and to spread learning and education among the laity.[64] Their leadership and the favorable response of the local inhabitants made Tver unusual among the provincial towns of Novgorod Guberniia. Both Sievers and Catherine were impressed by the progressive attitudes and civic spirit exhibited by the townsmen of Tver and by the noblemen of the surrounding countryside.

The physical appearance of Tver underwent a drastic alteration in the 1760s. Until then, Tver, like every other town in the provinces, had retained the characteristic look of old Russia, untouched by the example of St. Petersburg. Divided into four sections by the Volga, Tvertsa, and T'ma rivers, the city had grown over several centuries into a jumble of houses, churches, shops, and gardens connected by footpaths and narrow, winding streets. The typical dwelling, possibly combined with a place of business, sat in the middle of its own plot of land, its *dvor*, and was surrounded by sheds, workshops, pens, refuse heaps, and fences that separated it from its neighbors. When they left the isolation of their dvory, the townsmen socialized not in the streets but in and around the local markets, the parish churches, and the taverns. The seventeenth-century cathedral inside the kremlin provided a center of social intercourse for the city as a whole. The administrative offices of the imperial government stood nearby inside the kremlin wall, and just outside the wall a large open square served as the center of commercial activity. Permanent stalls and shops lined two sides of the square, and on Tuesdays, Thursdays, and Saturdays the square itself became the city's central market. Except for the major churches, the kremlin wall, a few government buildings, and the masonry house belonging to the wealthy grain merchant F. I. Volkov, the entire city was built of wood, and, like all Russian cities, it suffered periodic conflagrations. In May 1763 a fire broke out in the bishop's residence, swept through the kremlin and the center of the city, and burned the entire gorodskaia section to the ground. The reconstruction of Tver, which marked a turning point in the autocracy's efforts to modernize provincial Russia, was already underway when Sievers arrived there in the spring of 1765, and the new governor gave it his full and enthusiastic support. On the basis of its location, size, wealth, commerce, communications, transportation, civic spirit, and administrative importance, Sievers believed that Tver offered the greatest potential for development of all the settlements in his guberniia.

Historical tradition and administrative convenience rather than urban vitality accounted for the location of the guberniia capital in the ancient city of Novgorod. Since the dawn of Russian history, large areas of northern Russia had been governed from Novgorod, and the city's direct line of communication with the imperial capital maintained its tenure as a seat of administration in the eighteenth century. As one of Russia's major metropolitan sees, Novgorod also retained its importance as a center of ecclesiastical administration. But as an urban or commercial center, eighteenth-century Novgorod hardly measured up to its former significance. Resembling Tver before the fire of 1763, the settlement stood in ironic and depressing contrast to the imposing kremlin with its magnificent eleventh-century cathedral. In 1764 Novgorod contained fifty-eight stone and masonry churches but only two masonry houses. With 4,050 male inhabitants, Novgorod was only the seventh largest town in the guberniia.[65] Some small manufacturing enterprises operated there, but none employed more than five workers. The city's economy depended almost entirely on the transit trade, the church, and the state administration.

Sievers's first memorandum on the condition of his guberniia (December 1764) contained a section entitled "Means of Restoring and Improving the Town of Novgorod." His proposals included providing interest-free loans to anyone who would establish a tannery or a cloth factory, subsidizing the construction of brick and stone houses, erecting new public buildings, planting gardens and orchards, opening schools for the sons of nobles and merchants, and improving the seminary.[66] However, in a communication written in September 1765 the governor suggested that the main highway between St. Petersburg and Moscow be routed away from Novgorod in order to make it straighter and shorter. Recognizing the obvious implications of his proposal, Sievers also recommended that the guberniia capital be moved to a more appropriate location and that the town of Novgorod be reduced to the status of a provintsiia capital.[67]

Pskov, the other ancient metropolis of northwestern Russia, had suffered an even greater decline than Novgorod. By the 1760s its male population had shrunk to only 450, and its economy was weak. Because it was located in an area whose economy prospered from the cultivation and export of flax, Sievers saw a possibility for Pskov to become a center of the flax trade and of linen manufacture, but he noted that the local merchants had failed to take advantage of those opportunities in the past and showed little initiative for the future. In Pskov, as in Novgorod, the contrast between the city's past and present left Sievers completely unmoved.

In addition to Tver, Sievers found several flourishing towns whose potential for development aroused his enthusiasm. In the western end of the guberniia the most impressive town was Toropets, a settlement with some four thousand male inhabitants. Located in the provintsiia of Velikie Luki at the head of navigation on the Toropa River, it served as a major collection point for flax grown in the surrounding region. Toropets also exported leather goods and metal wares produced by its own craftsmen. Sievers called Toropets "the wealthiest town in the guberniia" and ranked its subsequent physical development "second only to that of Tver."[68] The neighboring town of Velikie Luki resembled Toropets in most respects, but it was smaller and less impressive. The other settlements in the western end of the guberniia were towns in name only and, except for the presence of administrative offices, were indistinguishable from villages.[69]

None of the towns in the northeastern region of the guberniia moved Sievers to optimism. Although a 1764 report of the Main Magistracy indicated that more merchants lived in Olonets than in any other settlement in the guberniia, Sievers had nothing to say about the town's prospects. That was in keeping with his attitude toward the entire northeastern region, which he considered an unwanted burden that should be transferred to another jurisdiction. For that reason he took no interest in the town of Ustiuzhna, even though it was the site of an important distillery. Finding the town of Kargopol in ruins after a major fire, Sievers concluded that the inhabitants were far too poor to carry out the kind of extensive reconstruction planned for Tver and other prosperous towns, and he took far less interest in its recovery. Of Beloozero, Sievers noted only that its economy was weak and that its merchants had only five thousand rubles of capital.[70]

In the central regions of his guberniia Sievers found several towns with good prospects for development. In the far south Rzhev claimed slightly more than four thousand male inhabitants and enjoyed a location near the head of navigation on the Volga in one of the most productive agricultural regions of the guberniia. Sixty-three first guild merchants resided in Rzhev, compared with eighty-nine in Tver, but, according to a report of the Commission on Commerce, they possessed 299,800 rubles of capital while their counterparts in Tver had only 91,700.[71] Clearly, Rzhev was a substantial town, but like Toropets it had only limited prospects for dynamic growth or for more than local significance.

Zubtsov, situated several miles down the Volga from Rzhev, was only half the size of its neighbor, but it dominated the juncture where the small Vazuza River entered the Volga. With increasing quantities of Ukrainian grain and hemp floating down the Gzhat into the Vazuza, Sievers believed that Zubtsov's importance was bound to increase in consequence. He thought that government assistance could help to make Zubtsov a flourishing town, but he found its inhabitants "apathetic."[72]

Those circumstances were reversed at Torzhok, a town with only fifteen hundred male inhabitants on the Tvertsa between Tver and Vyshnii Volochek. Its location conferred no special advantages, but the morale and progressive attitude of its citizens greatly impressed Sievers. For that reason he later referred to Tver and Torzhok as his favorite towns.[73]

Two other towns in the central region whose potential for development attracted Sievers's attention were Staraia Russa and Novaia Ladoga. The former lay to the south of Lake Ilmen, some nine miles below the mouths of the Polist, Lovat, and Pola rivers, amid excellent beds of salt. Staraia Russa had a population of 4,188 males in 1761, and Sievers believed that the revival of the saltworks and the increased volume of trade that would result from improvements to the waterways were certain to increase its size and importance.[74] Novaia Ladoga had less than half the population of Staraia Russa, but its location at the mouth of the Ladoga Canal made it a necessary stopping place for virtually all of the waterborne traffic to St. Petersburg. At Novaia Ladoga, moreover, the waterway crossed the main highways from the capital to Arkhangel and Siberia.

Two towns of the central region, Porkhov and Staritsa, appeared as unimpressive as some of those to the east and west, but Sievers also found several settlements that exhibited the potential to become substantial towns with the cooperation and assistance of the imperial government. He was especially interested in four settlements—Ostashkov, Vyshnii Volochek, Valdai, and Borovichi—located in the Valdai Hills in the very center of the guberniia, where there were no official towns at all in 1764.

As points of concentration and dissemination, where the centralized state and the national economy made contact with the countryside, provincial towns possessed an importance greater than their size and number might suggest. Linked to each other and to the imperial capital by roads and waterways, provincial towns were essential features of the networks of transportation, communication, and administration that tied Russia together.[75]

In Novgorod Guberniia towns and other settlements tended to cluster around the navigable waterways that were such a prominent characteristic of the landscape, but the same climate and topography that made water transport relatively easy made overland travel that much more difficult. There were few good roads anywhere in eighteenth-century Europe; Russia's distances and Novgorod's marshy terrain magnified the problems of transportation and communication overland. The main lines of overland communication between major cities and towns in mid-eighteenth-century Russia were highways known as "tracts." In contrast to other roads, tracts were relatively wide and straight, improved with some sort of paving, and served by a professional coach and messenger service. The empire as a whole maintained thirteen tracts, three of which originated in St. Petersburg and crossed the entire width of Novgorod Guberniia. The most important of the three and probably the most important road in the empire was the tract between St. Petersburg and Moscow, laid out at the command of Peter the Great in the first two decades of the eighteenth century. It followed approximately the same course as the Vyshnii Volochek System of waterways and passed through Novgorod, Krestets, Valdai, Vyshnii Volochek, Torzhok, and Tver. The roadbed consisted of tree trunks laid side by side at right angles to the thoroughfare and of piles driven into the marshes and low-lying soft spots. Covered with a layer of gravel, sand, or dirt, such a roadbed was supposed to provide a firm and relatively smooth surface for the passage of vehicles, but the rotting of the wooden base, the erosion of the surface, and the gradual subsidence of long stretches into the soft, marshy soil kept it in a permanent state of disrepair. Still, the improvements made since the time of Peter the Great, including the construction of bridges over the rivers and larger streams, had reduced the travel time over its 825 kilometers from five weeks to two.[76] A similar tract led westward from St. Petersburg to Pskov, and a third diverged from the St. Petersburg tract at Novgorod and proceeded south through Staraia Russa, Kholm, Toropets, and Velikie Luki to Smolensk. In addition, a section of the Moscow-Arkhangel tract traversed the northeastern corner of Novgorod Guberniia and passed through the town of Beloozero.

On all tracts a hereditary class of coachmen and messengers known as iamshchiks provided postal service and supplied fresh horses and drivers to travelers. The stations (*iamy*) were often located in monastaries to help protect them from brigands and horse thieves, and the iamshchiks lived in nearby villages surrounded by the fields and meadows from which they fed themselves and their horses.[77] Thirteen iams manned by 12,907 iamshchiks lined the tract between St. Petersburg and Moscow; five iams with 2,870 iamshchiks served the short tract between St. Petersburg and Pskov.[78] Travelers in various parts of the empire reported that under good conditions they could proceed along a tract at an average speed of five kilometers an hour.[79]

Important secondary roads also linked the major settlements, but they had no iam service and no roadbed. Such a road was simply a cleared expanse some two hundred to five hundred feet wide on which people were forbidden to erect structures or plant crops. At Novaia Ladoga a major secondary road from St. Petersburg to the east divided into a northern branch that led through Kargopol to Arkhangel and an eastern branch that led through Ustiuzhna to Siberia. In 1766 the northern branch became a tract: Forty-four iamy were established along its 1,160 kilometers, and four komissars and eighteen soldiers were charged with policing it.[80] A side road connected that route with Olonets, which was otherwise inaccessible by road from the central regions of the guberniia. From Novgorod one important secondary road led southward through Staraia Russa, Ostashkov, Rzhev, and Zubtsov to the Ukraine, and another led west and then south through Pskov, Ostrov, Velikie Luki, and Toropets. The guberniia's other roads and trails were primarily of local significance.[81]

An exchange of letters between Sievers and Catherine's secretariat on the subject of roads illustrates the imperial government's ignorance of and lack of control over provincial Russia at the start of Catherine's reign. In response to a request from the secretariat for information about the roads in his guberniia, Sievers wrote: "In my chancellery I cannot find any information on the subject of roads, especially those which connect one town with another. I shall have to send out officers immediately."[82]

At the time Sievers assumed his duties Novgorod Guberniia was divided for administrative purposes into five provintsiias and somewhere between eighteen and twenty-one uezds.[83] According to the government's staffing charts, that distribution would mean that Sievers had between 367 and 412 civil servants (depending on the number of uezds) with which to administer the entire guberniia.[84] In fact, he may have had even fewer, for he complained that the recent abolition of compulsory service for nobles and the nobles' reluctance to serve in the provincial bureaucracy made it difficult if not impossible to staff all of the administrative positions he was authorized to fill.[85] To supplement the small number of salaried officials, the state relied upon military garrisons, upon special ekspeditsii sent into the guberniia to perform specific tasks (such as the clearing of the Borovichi rapids or the rebuilding of Tver), and upon the uncompensated services performed by private individuals and groups as part of their obligations to the state. In 1766, for example, 289 merchants of Novgorod Guberniia were performing such service at various levels of administration.[86] Under such circumstances the state had little control over the quality of administrative service. Thus, when the police in the city of Novgorod were indicted for corruption, Sievers attributed their malfeasance to the absence of salaries, efficient organization, and clear subordination to a superior authority.[87] Outside the towns the only police were peasant *sotskie*, who communicated with the government through their parish priests because they themselves could not read or write. To remedy that situation, Sievers proposed that starshinas (officers) be elected or appointed from among the local nobles to "establish . . . some order." He suggested that their duties include "the building and repair of churches, the publication of decrees, the supervision of the roads, and the maintenance of peace and tranquillity."[88] For the time being, however, the government had no means of checking the banditry, lawlessness, and violence that prevailed in rural areas.[89] When the government felt the need to acquaint the common people with a new law or to announce something to them, it had the document read in churches after the liturgy.[90]

No matter how many officials the state might appoint to assist him, Sievers found the guberniia and its subdivisions too extensive to be governed in any but the most superficial manner. Novgorod Guberniia in 1764 retained the organization given it in 1727, and it embodied the outlook of the imperial government at that time. When viewed from the capital and seen in terms of its relationships with that city, Novgorod Guberniia looked like a reasonable unit of administration. Encompassing the provincial hinterland of the capital and all the lines of trade and communication that connected St. Petersburg with the interior, it formed a broad arc around St. Petersburg Guberniia, which in turn formed a smaller, almost concentric arc around the capital city. From the standpoint of the imperial government, it may have made sense to include all of that sparsely populated territory in one jurisdiction. After considering it from within, however, Sievers concluded that the guberniia had no internal raison d'être and must be treated as three separate regions, each of which extended across the width of the guberniia from the interior toward the sea.

The western end of Novgorod Guberniia, consisting of the provintsiias of Pskov and Velikie Luki, was the smallest of the three regions. Its trade routes tied it to Narva, Reval, and Riga rather than to St. Petersburg, and the cultivation and export of flax made agriculture more profitable there than in the other regions. As a result, the great majority of the region's landlords demanded barshchina rather than obrok from their serfs. The other dominant feature of the western region was the long boundary that separated it from Estland and Livonia to the west and Poland to the southwest and south. Smugglers and bandits took advantage of those frontiers, and serfs dissatisfied with their lot in Russia could easily escape into Poland. In their nakazy to the Legislative Commission, the nobles of the western region complained that the practically open frontiers, especially the one with Poland, imposed a serious hardship on landowners, and in a 1768 memorandum to the Legislative Commission the guberniia chancellery of Novgorod assigned the highest priority to strengthening the empire's border with Poland and Livonia and preventing the escape of runaway serfs.[91] The absence of any effective, cooperative authority on the other side made the Polish border an especially troublesome problem for Sievers, who once complained to the empress that he should not be expected to close 612 versts of frontier with four hundred old soldiers, two hundred dragoons, and pickets organized from among the local peasantry.[92] In 1770 and 1771 he proposed that the treaties to end the Turkish War should also give the western region of his guberniia a more natural and more manageable frontier. "If the Duna formed my border," he suggested, "the provintsiias of Pskov and Velikie Luki would be worth twice as much. Think of that, Your Majesty, when it comes to making peace."[93] Even better, in his opinion, would be the separation of the western region from the other territories under his jurisdiction, which in fact occurred temporarily in 1772. In his final memorandum, written as he was leaving office in 1781, Sievers urged the empress to detach the western region permanently.[94]

Sievers also longed to rid himself of the largely subarctic region at the opposite end of his guberniia, which comprised the uezds of Olonets and Kargopol. Separated from the rest of the guberniia by Lake Ladoga and vast expanses of empty forests, that region contained a high percentage of state peasants and a sizable Finnic population but few pomeshchiks. In 1765 it was reorganized as Olonets Provintsiia, but Sievers was not satisfied for long. In 1770 he referred to it as a "monster," and in 1771 he complained that he had not been able to attend to a serious emergency there because his presence was required on the Polish border almost eight hundred miles away. From then until the time he left office ten years later, Sievers continued to request that the northeastern region be transferred to another jurisdiction.[95]

The central region of Novgorod Guberniia, which included the provintsiias of Tver, Novgorod, and, with less certainty, Beloozero, contained all of the routes of trade and communication between the upper Volga and the capital. These in turn, together with their branches and feeders, tied the region together. Thus, in the mid-1760s, when the Senate considered transferring the southern uezds of Rzhev and Zubtsov from Tver Provintsiia to the Viazma Provintsiia of Smolensk Guberniia, the nobles and merchants of the affected areas petitioned the Senate and offered four reasons for their opposition to the scheme: they had no traditional or commercial ties with either Viazma or Smolensk; Viazma was more distant from both Rzhev and Zubtsov than was Tver; they had direct water transportation to Tver but not to Viazma; and all of their goods and products passed "down that one waterway . . . through Tver and Novgorod to the port of St. Petersburg."[96] The Vyshnii Volochek System of waterways and the St. Petersburg–Moscow tract, which formed the central axis of the entire guberniia, was also the axis of the central region, connecting not only the two imperial capitals but also the guberniia's capital with its largest city, Tver. For those reasons, Sievers devoted far more attention to the central region than he did to the others and took a much greater interest in its development. In his final memorandum to the empress Sievers termed the components of the central region "inseparable" and argued that they were enough for any one man to govern.[97]

In 1764, however, Sievers set out not only to govern the whole of his vast territory but also to improve it. In detailing a similar (although hypo-thetical) situation, the historian Fernand Braudel came very close to de-scribing the challenge that confronted Sievers in 1764—so close, in fact, that his words are worth repeating here. Asking what a modern economist could have done to accelerate the growth of the French economy in the time of Philip the Fair, Braudel pointed out the obstacles that would stand in his way:

> [H]e would see too many changes result in immobility or quasi-mobility, however violent they may have been in the short term. He would never have a manageable economy in front of him, nor really hold a whole people in his net, binding them to the decisions of leaders or specialists. Practically everything would elude him because political obedience is one thing and economic obedience another. But, more than anything else, his efforts would come up against insurmountable obstacles, the hazards of the harvest, the slowness or lack of transport, incomprehensible and contradictory demographic movements, hostile attitudes, lack of reliable statistics, and the chronic deficiency of power sources.[98]

Similar obstacles, notwithstanding, Sievers remained convinced that the state could improve the condition of provincial Russia, and he show-ered the empress and the Senate with proposals to that end. Most of those proposals dealt with very specific objectives, but they implied two general lines of approach: direct action to provide the provinces with an infra-structure of urban centers, transportation, education, health care, and eco-nomic enterprises, and fundamental legislation to create a more rational and progressive order. Sievers was more than willing to devote himself to efforts of the first kind, even at the expense of his health, his marriage, and, for a while, his personal fortune; but at the same time, he pressed for the improvement of the legal-administrative system as a prerequisite for the success of those efforts. In his detailed memorandum of December 9, 1764, the new governor implored his sovereign: "I throw myself at the feet of Your Imperial Majesty to beg that she press on with the new code that is being drafted." Deeming it "a necessity," he argued that the lack of a cogent and progressive code of laws "hurts everything," and he contrasted the salutary effect of Frederick II's code upon Prussia with the confusion and corruption of Normandy.[99] Sievers assured Catherine that the news of the opening of the Legislative Commission "has been a celebration for our good subjects in this province, not all of whom are Normans even though there is a good number of such," and he foretold of laws "more gentle, more conforming to humanity in the more enlightened century of Your Imperial Majesty."[100] In October 1768 Sievers wrote to Catherine about "that object so precious of Your Majesty, the code, which carries all my hopes," and reminded her of the great importance that he attached to the work of the Legislative Commission.[101] After the commission's dismissal, Sievers continued to press for legal reform and to plead with Catherine to provide him with statutes that would facilitate his efforts to transform northwestern Russia.

Convinced of the need for legal reform, Sievers was more than an interested observer of the legislative process. As the governor of Novgorod Guberniia, he was to play an important role in shaping and implementing the legislation that would reorganize and reform provincial Russia.

V

The Reorganization
of Provincial Russia

IN ORDER TO APPLY WESTERN MODELS and rationalistic theories of development to provincial Russia, Catherine and her officials first had to replicate the administrative and social framework that rulers and theorists in other European countries took for granted. Obliged by their assumptions to create rational units that could be comprehended and managed from above, Russia's lawmakers sought to organize a new provincial order based on six components: smaller, more effective areas of administration staffed by a larger, more competent bureaucracy; planned provincial towns inhabited by an enterprising middle class; and consolidated landholdings owned as private property by the members of a provincial gentry. Because the Russian Empire of 1762 lacked all of those components to one degree or another, the first problem facing Catherine's government was not how to use those elements more effectively but how to create them from the materials at hand. To a considerable extent, that basic difference in Catherine's situation accounts for some of the more obvious differences between her reforms and those of enlightened monarchs in other European lands.[1]

The reorganization of provincial Russia extended over two decades, and in some cases its specific objectives did not come clearly into focus for many years. The process began in the 1760s with the gathering of information, the launching of the General Survey, and the taking of the first, cautious steps toward reform; it turned a crucial corner in the mid-1770s with the promulgation of the Fundamental Law for the Administration of the Provinces; and it ended in the mid-1780s with the enactment of comprehensive laws and charters. Catherine presided over these activities, directing them and making major decisions, but Sievers, the Senate, the Legislative Commission, and other government agencies carried on much of the effort and made major contributions of their own. All six components of the new provincial order developed more or less together, but their place and purpose in Catherine's reorganization of provincial Russia will be seen more clearly if each is examined separately while its connections to the others are borne in mind.

Administrative Units

Except for recent additions such as the Ukraine and the Baltic provinces, the administrative units of the Russian Empire lacked the indigenous institutions, local estates, distinctive laws, and particularistic traditions of the *pays* of France or the *Lande* of the Hapsburg Empire. The oldest and most basic of those units, the uezd, was simply an area administered from a specific town by the agents of the autocracy. Established in the distant past, uezds had been grouped and regrouped to form larger units of administration, but they had not otherwise been altered in any significant way since the sixteenth century.[2] The uezds in existence when Catherine II came to power in 1762 were almost without exception the same physical units that Ivan IV had known two centuries earlier, and any purpose or principle they may once have embodied had been completely lost or forgotten.

Catherine's first attempt to reorganize the administrative units of the empire evolved quite naturally from her campaign to eliminate the appalling disorder she discovered in the operations of the imperial government during her first months in power. Her later recollection that the Senate at that time had no roster of towns and no certain knowledge of their number is verified by documents from the Senate's own archives. In a decree of December 15, 1763, Catherine put the number of uezd or town chancelleries at 165,[3] a figure based on information provided by the Shtats-Kontora, the personnel office of the imperial government. Subsequent complaints that other chancelleries existed but were not being funded led her to order the Senate to investigate the matter. The Senate collected information from the Shtats-Kontora, the governors, and the specially appointed Commission on Towns (Komissiia o gorodakh), but it could not immediately determine whether there were 165, 166, 167, or 169 towns in the Great Russian guberniias.[4]

In response to such confusion, the empress instructed the Senate to review and revise the existing distribution of towns and uezds. Her decree of October 11, 1764, enunciated the principles on which that revision was to be based and set forth seven explicit procedures that the Senate and the governors were to follow in carrying it out. First, the governors were to collect from the provintsiia chancelleries and forward to the Senate information on all the uezds in their guberniias. If an uezd contained fewer than ten thousand revision souls, it was to be disestablished, and the governor was to propose its merger with one or more existing uezds. If an uezd contained more than thirty thousand revision souls, the governor could propose the creation of new uezds on that territory. In either case, distance as well as population should be taken into account. Second, governors should try to reorganize the units of administration to the advantage of the local residents and see to it that they were governed from the town closest to them. Third, governors were to propose the creation of komissariats for individuals who for one reason or another resided too far from the nearest town. Fourth, governors were to provide written justification for all of the changes they proposed. Fifth, the governors were not to propose shifting a town from one provintsiia to another. Sixth, governors were to comment on the situation of each agency of local administration. And finally, the Senate was to review the governors' submissions and use them to prepare a new roster of towns and uezds.[5]

On April 29, 1765, six months to the day after receiving a copy of that decree from the Senate's courier, Sievers submitted his response. In a twenty-eight-page memorandum the governor proposed thirty-four transfers of territory and population affecting all but four of the existing uezds of his guberniia. Taken together, his recommendations would produce six major results. First, Novgorod Uezd, one of the most populous in the empire, would be divided among seven uezds so that its population would decline from 253,136 revision souls to a more manageable 61,682. Second, Olonets Uezd and a part of the former Novgorod Uezd would form a new provintsiia, with its center in Olonets. Third, the uezd chancelleries of Pustorzhev and Zubtsov would be abolished and the uezds divided among their neighbors. Fourth, five newly created uezds would be centered on the settlements of Novaia Ladoga (with a secondary center in Tikhvin), Porkhov, Ostashkov, Valdai, and Vyshnii Volochek. Fifth, three komissariats would be created, two in Olonets Uezd and one in Kargopol, where the low density of population meant that some areas were too far from the seat of administration. Finally, population would be equalized among uezds so that none would contain fewer than 26,000 revision souls and only three would contain more than 40,960.[6] In scope and number, Sievers's proposed changes far exceeded those submitted by other governors.[7]

Aware that his proposals most likely reached well beyond the limited reorganization envisioned by the Senate and perhaps by the empress, Sievers defended them as beneficial to both the state and its subjects. To the Senate he gave specific justifications for each change and the general observation, buttressed by a reference to the complaints of his predecessors, that smaller units would bring government closer to the people.[8] Two days before he dispatched his proposals to the Senate, Sievers made the same argument at greater length to the empress, using his privilege of direct communication with the sovereign to circumvent the Senate and increase his own influence on the reorganization of local administration. "I have tried," he wrote of his proposals, "to carry out Your Majesty's intention, so full of humanity and so salutary for your innumerable people, which is to locate every town in the center of its uezd and the people at a distance convenient to receive justice and to render unto Caesar that which is due to Caesar." Smaller, more numerous units of administration, he went on, would improve supervision and the collection of information, bring subjects closer to the hand of their "benefactress," and induce the far-flung populace to enter into civilized society.[9]

The Senate referred the governors' submissions to the Commission on Towns, which was to draft the proposal on local administration that the Senate would submit to the empress. Composed of Senator D. V. Volkov, Shtats-Komissar S. Ashitov, and a third, unidentified member, that commission labored from 1765 to 1767 to reorganize the units of local administration. It began by having maps prepared to represent the changes proposed by the governors. Then it worked its way through each proposal, accepting, rejecting, or modifying the specific points. By 1766 it began sending preliminary proposals for the reorganization of individual guberniias to the Senate.[10] In the case of Novgorod, the commission accepted most of Sievers's suggestions, with some modification, and advised that additional komissariats be established in the uezds of Toropets and Kargopol, "pending evaluation by the governor."[11] When the Senate referred the commission's recommendations to Sievers, he accepted them and asked in addition that the proposed komissariat of Vytegra be raised to the status of an uezd and that an entirely new uezd be created around Borovichi.[12] After a year of negotiation among the governors, the commission, and the Senate, the Senate submitted its own recommendations to the empress on January 19, 1768.

In its proposal on the reorganization of local administration, the Senate called for a reduction in the total number of administrators and a corresponding reduction in state expenditures for that purpose. It recommended the abolition of forty-four uezd chancelleries and the creation of twelve new ones, for a net reduction of thirty-two, to be made up in part by the creation of twenty-seven new komissariats. Since komissariats cost less than uezd chancelleries and garrisons, the reorganization advocated by the Senate would reduce the costs of local administration by 24,747 rubles per year (see Table 1). However, the Senate's recommendations for Novgorod Guberniia led in the opposite direction. In response to Sievers's proposals, the Senate consented to the creation of one new provintsiia (Olonets), three new uezd chancelleries (Valdai, Ostashkov, and Vyshnii Volochek), and four new komissariats (two in Olonets Uezd and one each in Kargopol and Toropets). Even with the proposed elimination of one uezd chancellery (Pustorzhev), those recommendations entailed an increase of 9,717.54 rubles in administrative expenses.[13] The reorganization initiated in 1764 was implemented in the early 1770s, but it was quickly subsumed in the more sweeping reform enacted in November 1775.

Three months after the Senate completed its consideration administrative reorganization, another agency began a broader and more far-reaching study of that subject. In three "assignments" (*uroky*) dated April 29, May 20, and May 29, 1768, Catherine charged the Partial Commission on the Order of the Realm, a committee of the Legislative Commission, with the task of examining virtually every aspect of Russia's internal administration and proposing improvements. Points eight, ten, and eleven of her first assignment specifically included within that charge the division of the empire into guberniias, provintsiias, and uezds, and her second assignment established guidelines to follow in determining the size and configuration of those units. Allowing that Siberia, the capital regions, and the frontier and maritime provinces would constitute exceptions, the empress stated that in principle guberniias should be of moderate size, that ideally their borders should be equidistant from their capitals, and that wherever possible the boundaries of all administrative units should coincide with rivers, lakes, mountains, and other natural features of the terrain.[14]

The Partial Commission held 248 working sessions between April 1768 and October 1771.[15] Its journal shows that its earliest meetings were devoted to studying the agencies of administration but that even as that work progressed, the commission's members began to collect the information and materials they would need to reorganize the units of administration. These included excerpts from Catherine's *Instruction* and from the nakazy and speeches presented to the Legislative Commission, Catherine's three assignments to the Partial Commission, the instructions she had given the Senate regarding the reorganization of local administration, data on population from the Third Revision, a map of the empire obtained from the State War College, and a report from the Iamskaia Kantseliariia showing distances between towns. With those materials the commission turned its attention to reorganizing the units of administration. On October 16, 1768, it reached its first major decision: The future guberniia of Moscow should consist for the most part of the present provintsiia of Moscow, with boundaries approximately ninety versts from the city limits.[16]

An additional source of information and opinion for the Partial Commission was the memorandum on Novgorod Guberniia that Sievers had submitted to the Senate on April 29, 1765. The Senate sent a copy of that memorandum to the Directing Commission, which in turn distributed copies to several other commissions. The journal of the Partial Commission on the Order of the Realm records that on December 26, 1768, the members "looked over the submission on population and the proposals concerning Pskov and Velikie Luki provintsiias and discussed them." At its next two sessions, on December 29 and January 2, the members read and discussed Sievers's memorandum for a total of four hours and forty-five minutes and devoted most of the two sessions that followed to reading and discussing the Senate's responses to it.[17]

The Partial Commission had difficulties obtaining and working with some of the materials it needed. The Directing Commission, for example, was initially reluctant to provide it with data from the Third Revision because that information was regarded as a state secret (*gosudarstvennaia taina*).[18] The Senate's register of guberniias, provintsiias, and uezds, which was still undergoing revision, did not become available until March 23, 1769, by which time the Partial Commission had already spent five to six months working on its own reorganization of those units.[19] Noticing that the Senate's register showed few uezds with a population greater than thirty thousand revision souls, the Partial Commission asked if some decree had set that figure as the maximum number allowable. Unable to identify Catherine's decree of October 11, 1764, the Directing Commission replied that no such instruction could be found.[20] On several occasions the Partial Commission also found that the information it received was either incomplete or unreliable. For example, commission members decided on October 16, 1768, that a definitive reorganization of Novgorod Guberniia depended on their obtaining a more accurate reckoning of the number of souls inhabiting the territory north of the Svir River between Lakes Ladoga and Onega.[21] The most serious problem of all was the lack of accurate maps. The Partial Commission quickly observed that in some cases the boundaries of guberniias were not even indicated on the map supplied by the State War College and that in other cases they were shown incorrectly.[22] Similar problems turned up in the maps of individual guberniias. On August 10, 1769, when the members of the Partial Commission tried to complete the reorganization of central Russia, they could not find the towns of Medyn and Novosil anywhere, while the single town of Volkov appeared in two different locations.[23]

In spite of such problems the Partial Commission on the Order of the Realm completed much of its assignment by October 6, 1771, the date of the last session recorded in its journal. In August 1769 the members finished the territorial reorganization on which they had been working for the past twelve months and noted with satisfaction that, according to their plan, all uezds would contain between 25,000 and 40,000 revision souls, provintsiias would contain 70,000–120,000, and guberniias 450,000–600,000.[24] On September 10, 1769, according to the commission's journal, the members "looked over the register of the newly proposed guberniias, provintsiias, and uezds with the number of souls in each" and thereafter turned their attention to other matters.[25] By October they had drafted their reply to Catherine's first two assignments, but unspecified differences of opinion created such delays that by September 29, 1771, the response to the first instruction was still being revised.[26] Whether the responses were finished or not, the drafts and other materials collected and generated by the Partial Commission remained in the archives of the Legislative Commission and were available for the empress and other agencies of government to use in reforming provincial administration.

Between 1771 and 1775 the imperial government increased the number of guberniias, provintsiias, and uezds by extending them into new areas and by dividing units already in existence. In 1773 part of the Belorussian territory acquired in the first partition of Poland entered the empire as the guberniia of Mogilev; the remainder was combined with most of Pskov Provintsiia to form the new guberniia of Pskov.[27] Guberniias were also authorized for the newly acquired territories of Novorossiia and Azov. The new guberniias of Tver, Iaroslav, Tula, Vladimir, Kursk, and Penza, on the other hand, were to be carved out of the old guberniias of Novgorod, Moscow, and Kazan, bringing the total number of guberniia's for the entire empire to twenty-five.[28]

By 1775, however, the Pugachev rebellion had convinced Catherine that the weakness of Russia's provincial administration posed a serious threat to the security of the empire, and from that conviction came a rapid and comprehensive reorganization. In less than nine months Catherine composed a 215-page statute of provincial reform: the Fundamental Law for the Administration of the Provinces of the Russian Empire (Uchrezhdeniia dlia upravleniia gubernii vserossiiskoi imperii) enacted on November 7, 1775. In this endeavor she had to rely on the materials prepared by the Senate and the Legislative Commission and on the advice and recommendations of experienced officials. Her closest and most influential collaborator in that effort was Governor Sievers, who had spent more than a decade struggling against the shortcomings of Russia's provincial administration and proposing measures to correct them. Catherine consulted Sievers personally about the reform, read his many memoranda, asked his advice on troublesome issues, rewarded and honored him for his contributions to the reform, and made it clear that he would be the first to introduce the new provincial order.[29]

Two provisions of the Fundamental Law led directly to the most extensive redistribution of administrative units ever undertaken by the tsarist regime. The elimination of the provintsiia as a unit and the stipulation that henceforth all guberniias should contain between 300,000 and 400,000 revision souls and all uezds between 20,000 and 30,000 led to the redrawing of most administrative boundaries and to the creation of new guberniias and uezds throughout the empire.[30] That process began in January 1776, when Sievers established the new guberniia of Tver. By 1781 the area that in 1775 had been partitioned into twenty-five guberniias and some 200 uezds comprised forty-one guberniias and 374 uezds, and by 1796 the extension of the reform into new areas had raised those totals to fifty guberniias and 493 uezds.[31] The area under Sievers's jurisdiction was increased by the addition of two densely populated uezds (Kaliazin and Kashira) in the Volga Valley below Tver and was reduced by the removal of a larger but less populous region in the eastern part of the former provintsiia of Beloozero. With those exceptions, the territory that had been organized as one guberniia with five provintsiias and twenty uezds in 1764 would become four guberniias with thirty-five uezds by 1781.

Despite subsequent adjustments and reshufflings, the administrative units created between 1776 and 1796 lasted until the end of the tsartist regime and constituted one of the most enduring legacies of Catherine's reign. They also presaged the creation of similar units in Hungary in 1785, in France in 1781, and, to a lesser degree, in the Northwest Territories of the American Republic in 1781—all of which embodied a similar element of rationalization and abstract uniformity. More immediately, the reform of November 6, 1775, provided Catherine's government with a systematic framework within which it could apply cameralistic principles to the sprawling expanses of the Russian Empire. In addition to facilitating financial operations, recordkeeping, and the integration of frontier provinces into the empire, that structure became the foundation of Catherine's subsequent efforts to improve the condition of the provinces.

Administrative Agencies

Expansion and rationalization of the provincial bureaucracy accompanied the reorganization of administrative units. In both cases Catherine's initial concern was to replace the confusion and disarray that prevailed at the time of her accession with an intelligible and manageable system of governmental operations. In addition to reorganizing the Senate and other agencies of the central administration, Catherine's decree of December 15, 1763, set the number of salaried civil officials at 16,500, thus bringing on to the state's payroll an undetermined number of government agents who had previously been allowed or expected to support themselves with state funds. Besides making minor adjustments to the Table of Ranks, which determined rank and salary within the state service, the decree also raised the salaries of many underpaid officials and designated more of them as eligible for pensions.[32] Catherine's Instructions to the Governors of April 21, 1764, began the practice of defining the duties and responsibilities of provincial officials, and her demand that they report regularly to their superiors increased their accountability. With bureaucratic controls came discipline, as the government began to prosecute or remove officials for acts of corruption that had been the normal practice under previous regimes.[33] By 1767 such measures had shaped up the provincial bureaucracy to the point where it could replace the army in the collection of the poll tax and the revision of the tax registers.[34]

In her assignments to the Partial Commission on the Order of the Realm, the empress revealed her intention to push beyond mere *rétablissement* to a full-scale reorganization of public administration. Her first assignment asked the members of the commission to make a thorough study of all aspects of the state administration and, after considering the nakazy and the speeches of the deputies on that subject, to determine the defects and deficiencies of the existing administration.[35] In her third assignment Catherine asked the Partial Commission to prepare a detailed plan for the reorganization of the state administration, specifying whether some agencies should be abolished or merged with others, whether new agencies should be created, and what their number, personnel, duties, purposes, locations, and interrelationships should be.[36]

On May 12, 1768, the Partial Commission made two decisions: It sent Andrei Shuvalov to the Directing Commission with a request for rosters (*shtaty*) of all existing agencies of central and provincial administration, and it divided the nakazy among the five members for reading and for excerpting relevant materials.[37] The commission's journal refers to excerpts being read aloud at some sessions, but it gives no indication of the thoroughness with which members examined the nakazy. Certainly they would have found no lack of comment on the faults and flaws of Russia's public administration, especially in the provinces. The nobles' nakazy, for instance, devoted more attention to that subject than to any other. Raising one complaint after another about the inadequacy and incompetence of the courts and the administrative agencies, the nobles portrayed an empire whose chaos and lawlessness bore not the slightest resemblance to the government's ideal of a well-ordered state.[38] By September 17, 1769, the members of the Partial Commission finished their study of the nakazy and began a similar examination of relevant excerpts from the record of speeches given in the Great Assembly.[39]

The journal of the Partial Commission on the Order of the Realm describes in detail only one substantive proposal for reforming the agencies of administration. On September 28, 1769, its members agreed, after much discussion, that several organs of the central government should be eliminated. They recommended that all of the functions of the Manufacturing College be reassigned to the Commerce College, that some duties of the Estates College and the College of Economy be performed by an agency of the guberniia administration, that the tasks of the Revision College be shared by an agency of the uezd administration and a department of the Senate, and that the responsibilities of the Main Magistracy be divided among the town magistracies, the guberniia magistracies, and the Senate.[40] Those proposals were included in the Partial Commission's response to Catherine's third instruction and thus were sent to Viazemskii and the Directing Commission when the Partial Commission disbanded in October 1771. The recommendations implicit in the commission's report—that some of the operations of the central government should be decentralized in the provinces, that the functions of the guberniia administration should be expanded, and that at least some of the guberniia agencies should report directly to the Senate-subsequently appeared in the reform of 1775, but the available evidence does not permit us to say whether Catherine borrowed directly from the Partial Commission in this instance or whether such notions were already current among the ruling circles in St. Petersburg.

Other elements of the 1775 reform appeared in an earlier state in the May 1773 legislation that established civil administrations in the territories acquired in the first partition of Poland. Combining those territories with part of the former provintsiia of Pskov to form the new guberniias of Pskov and Mogilev, the imperial government used the occasion to introduce several important innovations into the structure of its provincial administration. One was the appointment of a single governor-general with authority over both guberniias, even though each would have its own governor and its own administration. Second, the number of salaried employees was dramatically increased at the guberniia level of administration. Whereas the law of December 15, 1763, had authorized the hiring of 47 employees, including clerks, at a cost of 9,346 rubles per year for each guberniia, the law of May 8, 1773, authorized 247 positions for Pskov and an equal number for Mogilev, at a cost of 40,076.25 rubles per guberniia. The staff of each new provintsiia, on the other hand, was to have only 20 employees at a cost of 3,296 rubles rather than the 25 at a cost of 3,926 rubles prescribed by the law of 1763. A third innovation was the absence of any chief executive at the uezd level of administration in the two new guberniias. Functions performed by a voevoda in existing uezds of Pskov Guberniia were to be divided in the reorganized uezds of Pskov and Mogilev among class courts elected by the local inhabitants and komissars appointed by the state to serve as the agents of officials at the higher levels of administration. The election of courts and judges by the local inhabitants constituted a fourth innovation of major significance enacted in the law of 1773.[41] Several provisions of that law were still in the process of being implemented when they were superseded by the broader and more comprehensive reform of 1775.

The Fundamental Law of November 7, 1775, coordinated and elaborated various recommendations for and experiments in administrative reform that had gained acceptance over the past decade, and it carried them to their logical conclusion. In the preamble Catherine summarized the many faults her government had discovered in the administration of the provinces and then stated the purposes and principles of her reform. In effect, she tied the Fundamental Law and the structures it created to the ideology of what has come to be known as "enlightened absolutism":

> To eliminate all these and many other hindrances too numerous to
> mention and above all to establish a better order and an unrestricted
> delivery of justice, we have now thought it appropriate to issue a statute
> for the administration of the guberniias and to furnish each of them, as
> component parts of the Russian Empire with an administration to
> provide for and assist the better and more exact execution of the very
> beneficial legislation to be issued in the future.
>
> This, Our decree, as everyone can perceive, separates the courts from
> the guberniia administration, prescribes the duties and rules for each
> agency, and makes it possible for them to carry out instructions.[42]

As the representative of the crown, the governor-general (*namestnik*)
assumed responsibility for the proper functioning of guberniia administration and for the general well-being of his guberniias. Without making the
responsibility a formal provision of the Fundamental Law, Catherine followed the precedent set in 1773 and assigned two or more guberniias to
each governor-general.[43] In each guberniia five separate departments divided most of the operations of government. The Guberniia Administration (*pravlenie*), composed of the governor and two councilors, supervised
the police and handle all of the government business not specifically entrusted to one of the other departments. The board of public welfare (*Prikaz Obshchestvennago Prizreniia*), with the governor as its president and
two members from each of the three elected courts, established and managed the public and charitable institutions described in another section of
the law. Each of the three remaining departments bore the designation
palata (chamber), a direct translation of the German word *kammer*. The
financial chamber (*Palata Finantsov*), composed of the vice-governor, the
guberniia treasurer, the director of economy, a councilor, and two assess-
ors, supervised the collection and handling of all state revenue, thus assuming some of the functions of the Revision College and the College of
Economy. The chamber of criminal affairs and the chamber of civil affairs,
each with a president and two councilors, assumed the functions of the
Justice and Estates Colleges and supervised the courts. The superior land
court, the guberniia magistracy, and the superior rasprava—each composed of an appointed president and elected members—formed the courts
of appeals for the nobles, the burghers, and the state peasants and *odnod-
vortsy* (where appropriate) of each guberniia. An equity court (*Sovestnyi
Sud*) consisting of an appointed judge and two members elected by each of
the aforementioned classes was to deal with matters not covered by the letter of the law. A procurator, a surveyor, an architect, and an engineer
(*mekhanik*) completed the list of officials who would staff the administrations of the new guberniias.[44]

Incorporating another precedent set in 1773, the Fundamental Law left the administration of each uezd without a chief executive. Instead, it subordinated the officials and agencies at the uezd level to those at the guberniia level. Under the direction of the guberniia administration, police functions were assigned to an appointed police chief or a commandant in the towns and to an ispravnik or captain elected by the nobles in the countryside. The nobles, burghers, and state peasants (where applicable) also elected their own courts, which were subordinate to the courts of appeals at the guberniia level and through them to the chambers of criminal and civil affairs. The nobles and the free peasants also chose two deputies apiece to assist the ispravnik in maintaining law and order. A treasurer, a surveyor, a doctor, and a pharmacist with two assistants and two apprentices completed the roster of uezd officials.[45]

For each guberniia the Fundamental Law authorized the employment of ninty-three officials, and for each uezd, thirty-seven.[46] Unlike the figures associated with the laws of 1763 and 1773, those totals do not include clerks and laborers. Combined with the introduction of smaller and more numerous units of administration, the staffing provisions of the Fundamental Law produced a dramatic increase in provincial officials both in absolute numbers and in relation to area and population. In northwestern Russia, for example, the territory that had been Novgorod Guberniia in 1764 differed only slightly from the territory that would be reorganized as the guberniias of Novgorod, Tver, Pskov, and Olonets in the 1780s, but those four guberniias and their thirty-five uezds would be administered by 1,668 officials rather than the 243 officials of comparable responsibility who had served there in 1764.[47]

The results of Catherine's administrative reforms cannot be calculated with the same precision for the empire as a whole because the total area covered by the uniform system of administration was greater in 1781 than it had been in 1763. But even when one allows that the figures for the 1780s include regions such as Kiev, Novorossiia, and Belorossiia that were not covered in the figures for 1763, the increase is enormous. By 1781, 16,662 officials other than clerks and laborers were administering the forty-one guberniias and 374 uezds organized in accordance with the Fundamental Law, as opposed to only 2,555 officials of comparable authority employed in accordance with the staffing rosters of 1763.[48] In 1763 the Senate estimated the cost of administering the territories covered by the staffing rosters at 540,235 rubles; even when allowance is made for the expansion of the territory to be administered, that figure is dwarfed by the 5,618,857 rubles that the imperial government would be spending on provincial administration by 1785.[49]

Emperor Paul considered such outlays excessive and significantly reduced both the number of administrative units and the number of officials per unit, but Alexander restored Catherine's system, and he and Nicholas expanded it anew. Nevertheless, the Russian Empire of the mid-nineteenth century has justly been described as a country suffering from "undergovernment" and "underinstitutionalization" in comparison with other European states.[50] That condition was due in part to the rapid growth of bureaucracy in Continental European states in the first half of the nineteenth century and in part to Russia's late start in the development of its provincial administration. If Russia at the end of the reign of Nicholas I was underadministered, then Russia at the end of the reign of Elizabeth Petrovna had scarcely been administered at all, and Catherine's efforts to provide the provinces with a civil administration constituted a major step from the one condition to the other.

Throughout Catherine's reign, quantitative expansion of the provincial bureaucracy took precedence over qualitative improvement. By separating powers within the guberniia chancelleries, Catherine sought to limit abuses of authority; by sending *revizory* (inspectors) into the provinces and prosecuting flagrant examples of graft and embezzlement, she hoped to curtail corruption.[51] But legal restraints did nothing to improve the initiative or the competence of provincial officials. With so many posts to fill, the imperial government simply could not be very selective in making appointments and tended to accept whomever it could get. By 1796 the provincial nobles were supplying the state with 4,053 officials through election; the burghers, 3,851; and the peasants, 2,704.[52] The remainder had to be found among local landowners, retired military officers, and the small number of noblemen who chose to make a career in the provincial civil service. The total number, irrespective of qualifications, was never adequate.[53] At various times Catherine, Viazemskii, Sievers, and other senior officials fretted over the caliber of provincial officials and expressed the hope that qualified individuals could be found to fill all of the elective and appointive positions. Significantly, they continued to think in terms of *finding* qualified provincial officials and not of training and educating them, as the Prussian government did.

Catherine's failure to follow the Prussian model in that instance was not so much a matter of choice as it was a matter of expediency and priorities. She saw the advantages of the Prussian system and copied it when she could. In the 1760s she had Senator N. I. Nepliuev review the service records of her officials and recommend personnel actions ranging from dismissal to promotion.[54] She looked upon her personal secretaries and the *protokolisty* (secretaries) of the Senate as administrative apprentices to be trained for higher offices, and she sent groups of young men, such as the famous one that included Alexander Radishchev, to prepare abroad for a career in government. But Russia's backwardness, its lack of schools and universities, its widespread illiteracy, and its confining social structure meant that such efforts were limited to the higher offices in the central administration. Improvement in the lower ranks and the provinces would depend on Russia's future development in general and on the establishment of a system of schools in particular. Catherine managed to establish a system of civil administration in the provinces, but it remained for her successors, especially Alexander I and Nicholas I, to begin to improve its quality and competence. Not until the end of the nineteenth century would Russia's provincial administration attain the capability that Prussia's had demonstrated in the second half of the eighteenth century.

Towns

As intermediaries between St. Petersburg and its provincial hinterland, Russia's towns were to play a leading role in Catherine's program of provincial development. All towns (*goroda*) were imperial territory: They had no other individual or institutional overlord, and each served as the seat of administration for its uezd, provintsiia, or guberniia, just as St. Petersburg did for the empire as a whole. The autocracy governed Russia from its towns, and it was in the towns that its officials came directly into contact with its subjects. Catherine's policy was to expand the role of provincial towns as outposts of administration and to transform them into centers of civilization as well. She planned to stimulate the development of the provinces by injecting them with elements of a more advanced and more progressive way of life modeled on the example of St. Petersburg. Catherine had no doubt that St. Petersburg had changed Russia for the better,[55] but its effect on the country was limited so long as it remained a unique experiment. To extend its influence into the provinces, Catherine sought to implant its characteristics in the towns of provincial Russia.

She began by taking control over the spatial organization and physical appearance of Russia's towns. Finding them irrational, congested, dirty, and highly combustible, she attributed their condition to the ignorance of their inhabitants and the lack of purposeful direction from above. To her mind, the spontaneous, undirected growth of towns presented a striking example of irrational disorder worth citing in her *Instruction:*

> [I]t has occurred similarly with the number of houses forming a city, for which a land plan has not been made before it was begun. In such a city, when it begins to be built, everybody occupies the place which has pleased him best, not taking the slightest notice of the correctness or the size of the place occupied by him; and so a heap of buildings is formed, which whole centuries of effort and diligent attention can barely bring into correct order.[56]

When she learned that a fire had destroyed the center of Tver in May 1763, Catherine commissioned General V. V. Fermor and the architects A. V. Kvasov, P. R. Nikitin, and M. F. Kozakov to plan the rebuilding of Tver in the style of St. Petersburg.[57] Having seized an opportunity to bring one provincial town into "better order," she then commanded that similar plans be prepared for all the towns in the empire in anticipation of the time when they would have to be rebuilt.[58] She extended that directive in the early 1770s to several new towns established in Novgorod Guberniia and then to the hundreds of towns created after 1775.

Catherine assigned responsibility for planning provincial towns to the Commission on the Masonry Construction of St. Petersburg and Moscow, which she had appointed in December 1762 to supervise construction in the two capitals. The commission's prominent members—Princess E. R. Dashkova, the future director of the Academy of Sciences; Count S. G. Chernyshev, the president of the War College; and Count I. I. Betskoi, the director of the Commission on Construction and future president of the Academy of fine Arts—entrusted the preparation of town plans to a staff of professional architects headed by A. V. Kvasov.[59] The architects would compose the plans, the governors would countersign them, and then the commission would review them before granting or withholding its approval. However, no plan could be implemented until it had received the personal confirmation of the empress. Local inhabitants were to play no role in planning their own towns, but they could petition the authorities to make changes.[60]

Under Kvasov and his successor, I. E. Starov, the employees of the Commission on Masonry Construction drafted thirty-nine town plans between 1763 and 1774. By 1796 that figure had risen to more than four hundred.[61] The pace of implementation also increased after the reform of 1775. In many of the smaller towns and in the centers of the more important guberniia capitals reconstruction began soon after the confirmation of the plan. Structures that did not conform were simply demolished. Elsewhere the state waited until some disaster or the passage of time made rebuilding necessary, but by the second decade of the nineteenth century virtually all the towns in Russia had been reorganized in accordance with approved plans.

The plans themselves reflected the inspiration of eighteenth-century rationalism and the example of St. Petersburg. They began by treating each urban complex as a unified whole, or, if it was divided naturally by rivers, as two or more unitary "sides." That view dictated the elimination of walls, street plans, and legal jurisdictions that had previously shaped urban areas as conglomerations of separate settlements, quarters, and neighborhoods. Walls were pulled down; surrounding communes (*posady*), settlements (*iamy*), and villages (*sela*) were incorporated into the gorod; and broad, straight streets were laid out in radial and grid patterns that covered the entire town or side and recalled the Admiralty District or the Vasilevskii Island of St. Petersburg. Wherever feasible, historic kremlins and cathedrals were preserved intact and used as the focal point of the plans. The central axis was made to fall along the principal thoroughfare, which was often the continuation of an interurban highway. At the focal point that thoroughfare would open into a large square containing the government offices and other public buildings. Farther on, it might be interrupted by a second square, which would serve as the center of commercial activity.[62]

The government's plans divided towns into three concentric zones and prescribed the kinds of structures that could be erected in each one. The first zone, in the very center of the town, was reserved for expensive, impressive buildings of brick and stone—churches, government offices, public buildings, and the homes of officials, wealthy merchants, and resident noblemen. Private dwellings in the first zone were to be two stories in height and flush with the street and with each other to form a continuous facade. In some cases the plans for smaller, poorer towns omitted the first zone for practical reasons and included the center in the second zone. That zone was to be filled with smaller residences and neighborhood shops built of wood on stone foundations. To limit the spread of fire among those more flammable structures, they were to be spaced farther apart than buildings in the first zone, so that settlement in the second zone would be less dense and less compact. The third zone included all the land between the second zone and the town limits and was normally larger than the other zones combined.[63] Structures there could be built entirely of wood, provided they were flush with the street and were spaced sufficiently far apart to retard the spread of fire. In accordance with the instructions given the surveyors in 1766, the town limits were to be situated two versts from the center on all sides.[64]

Considerations of cleanliness, hygiene, and sanitation also entered into the creation and implementation of urban plans, which regularly included features such as water pipes, fountains, and drainage ditches. The stables of the coach and postal service were to be located at the very edge of the town, and cemeteries well beyond it, "away from any habitation."[65] Efforts were also made to locate factories in the outskirts and suburbs of towns and to move tanneries, slaughterhouses, and other sources of filth and pollution downstream.[66]

The imperial government assumed a large part of the cost of rebuilding towns to conform to the new plans. Its military engineers and soldiers laid out the streets, and its Commission on Construction erected the governmental and public buildings that were to form the nucleus of each town. It also subsidized the construction of private shops and dwellings. In the first zone of construction the imperial government would lend money free of interest to the builder of a two-story stone or masonry edifice and would excuse him from paying any taxes on it for five years.[67] Preference was given to wealthy merchants, but after one year any lot in the first zone that had not been sold to a merchant could be sold to a nobleman on the same terms. If the purchaser of a building lot in the first zone failed to erect a suitable structure within five years, the property would revert to the state.[68] In the other two zones the state normally subsidized construction by freeing the inhabitants from some of their obligations to the state. For example, when Tikhvin was reconstructed in 1770, its inhabitants were exempted from the poll tax for six years and from compulsory state service for three.[69] In many towns, especially the larger and more important ones, the state also constructed markets (*gostinye dvory*) of brick or stone and sold or rented the shops and stalls to local merchants and tradesmen.

As another measure to bring the towns of Russia into line with Catherine's notion of proper order, the Statute on Police (*Ustav Blagochiniia*) of April 8, 1782, constituted a logical sequel to her directives on planning. The statute divided towns into sections (*chasti*), subdivided them further into blocks (*kvartali*), and assigned police agents to each unit. Each block was to have its own policeman (*nadziratel'*) and deputy policeman. Each section was to have a section chief (*chastnyi pristav*), a fire chief (*branmeistr*), a police sergeant, and a garrison of thirty-four soldiers. And each town was to have a commandant or *gorodichnii* (police chief) in command of the entire force, a director of civil affairs, and a director of criminal affairs. In addition, the residents of each block and section would be organized into fire brigades and night watches.[70]

Application of those provisions to the towns of northwestern Russia entailed some confusion over the size of the intended units and the amounts of money that would be spent. In August 1782, after Sievers had been replaced as governor-general by Ia. A. Bruce, Governor T. I. Tutolmin of Tver Guberniia informed the empress that he was prepared to establish police agencies that would prevent crime and disorder "through the dependence of every condition of urban dweller on the police."[71] Later that month Bruce submitted a staffing roster for the urban police of Tver Guberniia. Either created or authorized by Tutolmin, it called for the division of all twelve towns into blocks containing between eighty and one hundred houses, with the number of blocks and sections dependent on the size of the individual town. The plan would have cost the state 48,950 rubles a year.[72] Instead, the state created a staffing roster for the urban police of Tver Guberniia that provided for sections only in the guberniia capital and divided the other eleven towns into only two blocks apiece, irrespective of their size, at a total cost of 19,400 rubles per year, including outlays for firefighting equipment.[73] At the same time, the state allocated 27,200 rubles per year for police in the ten towns of Novgorod, of which 9,440 went unspent because a number of positions were not filled.[74]

Catherine intended the urban police to be the guardians of physical and moral order in the towns. In addition to preventing crimes against life and property, they were to control prostitution, drunkenness, loitering, vagrancy, littering, and other forms of misconduct. They were responsible for preventing the spread of contagious diseases, for enforcing building codes, for maintaining sanitary conditions, and for removing or reducing fire hazards. Furthermore, the police were to look after the appearance of the towns and ensure that the streets were paved, swept, and lighted.[75] In keeping with that broad assignment of responsibility, the Statute on Police placed the fire department, the town architect, the local physician, and the local pharmacist under the authority of the commandant or gorodnichii and included them in the table of organization of the urban police. Together with the town plans and the building codes, the police were to make Russia's urban centers a part of the civilized world—a world that Catherine and some of her contemporaries referred to in a characteristic phrase as *le monde policé*.[76]

Catherine's measures to control the externals of urban life served several purposes. The most obvious and prosaic was that of making the towns less unhealthy and less flammable. Beyond their manifest concern with the health and safety of urban dwellers, however, those measures embodied a desire to mold people and activities to suit the policies of the state. Combining an eighteenth-century view of human nature with a traditional practice of the Russian autocracy, they sought to change human character by shaping environment and prescribing outward behavior in the hope that external conformity would lead to internal conversion. Peter the Great had employed similar, albeit more direct and more tyrannical, methods to westernize the government and the nobility, and Ivan Betskoi was striving to create "a new race of people" in the schools he founded. Without expecting miracles, Catherine believed that a proper urban environment would inevitably promote the enlightenment of Russia's townsmen. A third purpose of those measures was largely symbolic. To a public more familiar with icons than with books, Catherine's towns proclaimed the presence of the imperial government in the midst of the provinces and surrounded that presence with the kind of order that Catherine considered an essential prerequisite for the prosperity, productivity, and happiness of her subjects.

By expanding the functions of local government, the Fundamental Law also enhanced the civilizing mission of provincial towns. The new courts, for example, allowed many of Catherine's subjects to resolve civil and criminal cases more quickly and conveniently in the nearest town rather than with an agency or an official far removed from the local scene.[77] The appointment of a professional surveyor, a physician, and a pharmacist to every uezd town enabled provincial Russians to find in the nearest town important services that had been almost entirely absent from the provinces before the implementation of the Fundamental Law. That statute also called for the creation and maintenance of socially useful institutions in the capital of every guberniia, including a school, a hospital, an orphanage, a home for the aged, an insane asylum, a lazar house, a workhouse, and a jail. The imperial government gave the responsibility for establishing and managing those institutions to the board of public welfare in each guberniia, together with a one-time grant of 15,000 rubles. A board could then raise funds for support of the institutions in two ways: by accepting charitable contributions from the public, and by lending its capital at interest to local landowners. As institutions of credit for the local landowners, the boards would be extending yet another element of modern civilization into the provinces through the provincial towns.[78]

The implementation of the Fundamental Law required the establishment of hundreds of new towns to serve as centers of uezds, and their creation helped to disseminate urban influences throughout the provinces. Critics of Catherine's reforms have tended to mock the new towns created after 1775 for being either legal fictions or artificial implantations with no economic base.[79] That certainly was true of some of them: Where the uezds delineated in accordance with the Fundamental Law contained no appropriate settlements, administrative centers were located in small agricultural villages, which thereby acquired the status of towns. Yet such compromises were by no means typical. Most of the new towns created during Catherine's reign were provincial settlements with a minimum of several hundred inhabitants that had previously belonged to some government agency, such as the College of Economy, or, in rare instances, to a pomeshchik. Strictly speaking, the only difference between such settlements and others already recognized as towns was the presence of an office of the provincial administration, and even that was no infallible indication of a settlement's size or importance. In the 1760s Sievers had pointed out that some towns such as Beloozero "were poor and resembled villages," whereas settlements such as Tikhvin, Valdai, Vyshnii Volochek, and Ostashkov were towns in everything but name.[80] After 1775 the imperial government erased that discrepancy by locating administrative offices in such settlements and recognizing them as towns in law. Had the government been interested in nothing more than strengthening internal security and tightening its administrative grip on the provinces, it needed to do nothing more. Instead, it was the additional effort to increase the urban character of such settlements through planning, reconstruction, and the availability of some public services that bespoke the government's desire to spread its conception of civilization and progress into the provinces.

Townsmen

As it strove to transform the physical character of Russia's towns, Catherine's government also sought to organize a class of townsmen or burghers comparable to the urban classes of central and western Europe. Although the empress and her statesmen accepted the social and political dominance of the nobility as natural and proper beyond question, they also believed, on the basis of western models and theories, that the formation and development of a third estate or bourgeoisie would contribute significantly to the wealth, vitality, and welfare of the Russian Empire.[81]

As of 1762, Russian law made no provision for a class defined in terms of urban residence or participation in trade and commerce. For centuries the subjects of the Russian monarch had been defined and classified on the basis of their individual or, more commonly, their collective obligations to the state. The classification of some men as *posadskie liudi* conveyed an urban and commercial connotation, and indeed, state documents sometimes employed the term "merchants" with legal imprecision as a synonym for *posadskie liudi*. However, as we have seen in the example of Novgorod Guberniia, the status of *posadskii chelovek* did not necessarily denote residence in a gorod or involvement in trade and commerce. It identified only the registered members of a posad—a communal tax-paying unit located either in a gorod or in some other kind of settlement, whose members shared a communal burden of taxes and service and received in return exclusive economic privileges of which the most important was a monopoly on urban retail trade. The members of a posad commonly resented the other residents of their settlements for being exempt from their obligations and hated other traders for illegally usurping their economic privileges.[82]

The first direct challenge to the existing laws on townsmen and merchants came from Jakob Sievers in April 1765. In his response to Catherine's decree on the reorganization of local administration, Sievers proposed that the administrative seats of the new uezds he wanted to establish be recognized as towns and that all of their inhabitants be registered as merchants.[83] Those propoasls were the first step in Sievers's plan to form a middle class or third estate by merging many of the groups in Russian society who were neither nobles nor agricultural workers, by freeing them from unnecessary impositions, and by encouraging them to develop the spirit and outlook of a genuine bourgeoisie. In his very first memorandum to the empress, written on December 9, 1764, Sievers had urged the imperial government to equate the taxes and service obligations of all the iamshchiks and trading peasants who actually lived and/or worked in urban settlements with those of the posadskie liudi.[84] Seven years later Sievers gave full expression to his thoughts on the development of a Russian bourgeoisie:

> In spite of the encouragement of commerce and the abolition of monopolies, the spirit of the burghers is little improved. It seems that the domination of the poll tax, which carries with it the humiliating idea of servitude, is one of the great obstacles to industry, to enterprise, to acquisitive desires, to the security of property—in a word to the praiseworthy ambition of each individual to improve his lot and that of his posterity. The same is true of corporal punishment.

Noting also that the "nobleman regards the burgher as the serf of the crown and treats him no better than the serf of a gentlemen," Sievers believed that the state should act to elevate the status of townsmen:

Without losing revenues in money or emoluments, the state could immediately inspire other sentiments in the burghers, who should form the third estate [*tiers état*] of this vast empire if they were delivered from the humiliating domination of the poll tax. They would unwittingly acquire the consciousness befitting a class of subjects *whose estate should be free* [underlined in original] and from whom the state should expect great advantage for commerce, the liberal arts and crafts which are the raison d'être of the third estate, but which fall because of this great abuse into the hands of the serfs to the crown or of the nobles. A law which would bring to life the word *liberty* [underlined in original] that powerful awakener of the soul, would bring about a visible and happy revolution in the morals and morale of the townsmen.

More concretely, Sievers then listed thirteen practical steps that the government should take to foster the development of a third estate: replace the poll tax with a tax on capital; use the money raised from the townsmen's taxes to improve the towns; change the laws requiring merchants to collect the salt and alcohol excises; allow easier immigration into towns and easier admittance to the status of townsman; compile a new roster of townsmen with each revision; reduce the capital requirements for entrance into the merchant guilds, especially in poorer areas; exempt townsmen who could read and write from corporal punishment; encourage literacy by other means; renew and enforce the laws excluding peasants from urban commerce; open a school in each town to be supported by the population; implement a law on bank notes and bills of exchange that had already been drafted; order the governors to protect arts and crafts; and set a fixed sum for which a serf could buy his freedom and enter the bourgeoisie.[85] Clearly, Sievers believed that liberty for the townsmen must be combined with state tutelage, which could be reduced as it succeeded in enlightening them so that they could be given increased amounts of liberty. The state, in other words, had the responsibility to bring up its subjects the way parents might bring up their children.[86]

Sievers eventually saw most of his ideas on the formation of a third estate enacted into law—but only after years of discussion, consideration, and bureaucratic infighting that sorely tried his patience. In 1765, for example, the Senate was unwilling to accord town status to new administrative centers and to register their residents as merchants at the behest of one provincial governor. It agreed, on the basis of existing legislation, that any resident of those settlements who possessed the requisite three hundred rubles of capital should be allowed to register as a merchant and join a posad, but it wanted the others to retain their status as iamshchiks and economic peasants. The Senate consented to recognize Valdai and the adjoining Zimmorodskii Iam as a single town, but it wanted to keep Borovichi and Ostashkov as *slobody* of the College of Economy and Vyshnii

Volochek as a iam.[87] By doing so, however, the Senate itself was proposing a break with the established rule, which identified all administrative seats as goroda. Catherine intervened in May 1770 with an order that all four settlements be recognized as towns "on the same basis as other Russian towns."[88] Unwilling to concede any more than necessary, the Senate then proposed that all of the inhabitants of the new towns who failed to qualify as merchants under existing legislation should be expelled from those settlements and relocated elsewhere.[89] That proposal led to two more years of conflict, with the Senate, the Iamskaia Kantseliariia, and the College of Economy supporting it and Sievers opposing it on the grounds that it would destroy the economic viability of the settlements in question.[90]

For seven years Catherine ignored all appeals that she decide the issue of urban citizenship that Sievers had raised in 1765. The only solid clue to her own thinking on that subject appears in her manifesto on the elections to the Legislative Commission, which assigned the urban franchise to "all the inhabitants of towns" instead of limiting it to the members of the merchant guilds or posady.[91] That provision was so unprecedented, however, that the Senate had to nullify the election of several deputies chosen exclusively by posadskie liudi or by merchants before its meaning became sufficiently clear.[92]

On the subject of urban citizenship, Catherine's *Instruction* to the Legislative Commission was less consistent than the manifesto of the previous year. She employed at least three different terms to designate the inhabitants of towns: *gorodskie zhiteli, liudi srednego roda,* and *meshchane.* The first included all the residents of a town; the other two were vaguely more exclusive. In Chapter Fifteen she implied a broad tripartite division of Russian society into husbandmen, burghers, and nobles, but then she defined burghers (*meshchane*) as those who inhabit towns and are employed in arts, sciences, trades, and commerce. In Chapter Sixteen she began by talking about burghers (*meshchane*), then switched to "people of the middle sort" (*liudi srednego roda*), for whom she repeated the definition previously given for burghers but then broadened it to include the graduates of schools and seminaries and the children of officials. In Chapter Seventeen she returned to the word *meshchane* and defined it anew as those who are interested in the welfare of the town, who possess a house and property therein, and who pay certain taxes. She specifically excluded others from sharing in their advantages.[93] Although the statements in Chapters Fifteen and Sixteen seemed to support the formation of a middle class or third estate along the lines proposed by Sievers and other reformers, those in Chapter Seventeen suggested support for the continued existence of a narrow, exclusive class similar to the *posadskie liudi.*

Having addressed most of the possibilities in her *Instruction,* Catherine turned the issue of urban citizenship over to the Legislative Commission and assigned it, with continuing ambiguity, to two partial commissions, the Partial Commission on the Towns and the Partial Commission on the Middle Sort of People. Like the Partial Commission on the Order of the Realm, those commissions studied existing Russian law, Catherine's *Instruction*, relevant excerpts from the nakazy and speeches presented to the full commission, and foreign laws, especially those of Prussia and its Baltic neighbors. By 1771 both partial commissions had produced draft articles for the new law code that included new definitions of urban citizenship. The Partial Commission on Towns, which counted three townsmen among its five members, sought to change the basis of urban citizenship from membership in a posad to ownership of a house or other immovable property and also to transfer the existing privileges and duties of posadskie liudi to property owners.[94]

The Partial Commission on the Middle Sort of People, dominated by Prince Michael Shcherbatov, wanted to identify urban citizenship with membership in a broad, conglomerate middle class based on occupation. It defined the members of the middle class as individuals who lived in towns, who were neither nobles nor agricultural workers, and who were employed in the arts, sciences, trades, and crafts. Among those specifically identified were wholesale and retail merchants, shopkeepers, peddlars, artisans, workmen, wage earners, the regular clergy, physicians, pharmacists, graduates of secondary and higher schools, foreigners, free peasants, and the children of officials. The partial commission's draft proposed conferring certain civil rights upon all townsmen covered by its definition and transferring the privileges and duties of the posadskie liudi to specific subcategories within the urban population.[95] Despite their differences, both partial commissions wanted to salvage the traditional role that the posad had played in the legal administrative system of the Russian Empire while transforming the posad itself into a more rational unit with a different legal basis that would include other groups of urban residents.

Some agencies of the imperial government opposed broader definitions of urban citizenship because they feared a loss of authority over the groups slated for admission to the ranks of townsmen. The Orthodox church, for example, objected to the inclusion of the regular clergy on the grounds that the hierarchy's control over priests and deacons would be diminished. Metropolitan Gavriil of St. Petersburg, the deputy of the Holy Synod to the Legislative Commission and a member of the Directing Commission, denounced the article drafted by the Partial Commission on the Middle Sort of People for recommending in effect that members of the regular clergy be given a legal right to join the army, engage in commerce, or change their occupation like other townsmen. As an alternative to including some clergy in the urban middle class, Gavriil proposed that the entire clergy be organized as a separate, privileged order.[96] The Academy of Sciences raised similar objections regarding the proposed inclusion of its members in the urban middle class and countered that they too should be given a special, privileged status of their own.[97] Despite some minor differences among the four positions, the Holy Synod and the Academy of Sciences were in substantial agreement with the Iamskaia Kantseliariia and the College of Economy, which opposed Sievers's plan to register iam-shchiks and economic peasants as townsmen.

With the discussion exhausted, the decisions began. On April 2, 1772, the empress finally resolved the longstanding dispute between Sievers and the Senate over the new towns of Novgorod Guberniia. She ordered the Senate to allow all the inhabitants of Valdai, Borovichi, Ostashkov, and Vyshnii Volochek to register as merchants.[98] After 1775 that precedent was extended to hundreds of other new towns; decrees implementing the Fundamental Law in individual guberniias normally included the stipulation that "all new towns are to be established on the same basis as the towns of Novgorod."[99] In 1785 the Charter to the Towns applied the Novgorod ruling to all Russian towns, old as well as new, when it defined townsmen (gorodskie obyvateli, meshchane, liudi srednego roda) as "all those who are long-time residents in a town or who have been born there or have settled there or who own houses or buildings therein."[100]

By defining urban citizenship in terms of residence, Catherine's government eventually eliminated almost all of the traditional divisions between groups of urban residents, but it replaced them with new distinctions based primarily on wealth. A decree of March 17, 1775, clarified the earlier ruling of April 2, 1772, by ending the confusion between urban citizenship and registration as a merchant that had complicated the dispute between Sievers and the Senate. It upheld the Senate's position that a man must have a minimum of five hundred rubles of capital to qualify as a merchant and ordered that all townsmen who failed to meet that requirement be expelled from the merchant class. They were to retain their status as townsmen, however, and be enrolled in the meshchanstvo, a classification of urban citizens distinct from and inferior to the merchants (kupechestvo).[101] Two months later the government divided the merchants into three guilds according to the amount of capital they possessed: in the first guild were those with more than ten thousand rubles; in the second, those with one thousand to ten thousand rubles; in the third, those with five hundred to one thousand rubles. Movement between guilds and between the kupechestvo and the meshchanstvo was to occur automatically as a townsman's wealth increased or diminished.[102] The Charter to the Towns of 1785 raised the capital requirements for entry into each of the guilds but otherwise confirmed the provisions of the 1775 reform.

The merchant class that emerged from the reforms of 1775 constituted a small, privileged elite among the townsmen, a bourgeoisie amid the citoyens. In all of Russia only 24,470 individuals qualified as merchants under the new law, while 194,160 others were enrolled in the meshchanstvo.[103] In the city of Tver, where the figures were 356 and 2,874, respectively,[104] the merchant Mikhail Tiulpin recalled in his memoirs that friction quickly arose between the two groups, and Sievers's successor,

Iakov Bruce, observed in a letter to Catherine that in Novgorod "the merchants and the meshchanstvo, now divided, hate each other."[105]

In the 1770s and 1780s preferential treatment for the wealthier townsmen became an important element of the government's urban policies. In addition to separating the kupechestvo from the meshchanstvo, the decree of March 17, 1775, removed the stigma of the poll tax in exchange for a levy of 1 percent per year on each merchant's capital. The Charter of 1785 confirmed that distinction and freed all merchants from compulsory state service and allowed them to purchase an exemption from military conscription. It also granted to members of the first and second merchant guilds immunity from corporal punishment and permitted them to use certain status symbols such as coaches and carriages.[106] Although they shared in all of the civil and property rights enjoyed by all townsmen, the members of the meshchanstvo were denied the special privileges granted to the merchant guilds. As townsmen they could not be deprived of their status, their lives, or their property without due process of law,[107] but they remained subject to the poll tax, compulsory service, military conscription, and corporal punishment—liabilities common to all the lower orders of Russian society.

The government's preference for wealthy townsmen was also revealed in its rules on immigration and residence. Afraid of what Catherine termed "an excessive accumulation of workingmen" in the towns, the Senate in 1780 restricted new enrollments in the meshchanstvo on the grounds that expansion "does the towns no good, considering the poverty of the newly enrolled."[108] Two years later the Senate closed the remaining loopholes and prohibited enrollment in the meshchanstvo because it "does not in the least correspond to the interests of the treasury and increases the number of poor in the towns."[109] Enrollment in the merchant guilds, on the other hand, remained open to state and economic peasants who met the capital qualification, provided they paid both the poll tax and the levy on capital until the next revision. Even a serf could enroll as a merchant on those terms if he could present a letter of permission (*uvol'nitel'noe pis'mo*) from his master.[110] With much the same attitude, the zoning regulations within towns welcomed the wealthy to the center and invited them to build their houses beside the government buildings and the homes of state officials. Those same regulations implicitly restricted the meshchanstvo to the outlying districts, farther from the government and closer to the peasantry.

As one who wanted to form an urban middle class in Russia, Sievers had mixed but generally favorable views on the post-1775 reorganization of the urban population. He was especially enthusiastic about Catherine's efforts to upgrade the status of the merchants. When the government excused the merchants from the poll tax, Sievers praised the empress: "No monarch has ever accorded so many benefits or boons as Your Majesty has just conferred with her edict of March 17."[111] That members of the meshchanstvo failed to share in the privileges of the merchants did not concern him greatly, so long as they were free to acquire them by enriching themselves. He thought it quite proper that the state should provide potential members of the bourgeoisie with incentives and opportunity and leave the rest to them, but he considered the capital requirements to be much too high, especially for the smaller towns and poorer regions of the empire.[112]

What upset Sievers most was the legal barrier that kept enterprising serfs from enrolling themselves as merchants without the permission of their masters. In his memorandum on towns written in the early 1770s he had favored setting a fixed price at which a serf could purchase his freedom and become a townsman irrespective of his master's wishes.[113] In July 1775 he asked Catherine to expand her legislation of March and May by allowing peasants who were already engaged in commerce to purchase freedom for themselves and their families for 500 rubles and to register as merchants.[114] And in 1780, responding to a draft of the Charter to the Towns that Catherine had sent him, Sievers wrote:

> The right of everyone to enroll himself as a townsman or merchant as soon as he possesses or produces the required capital concerns humanity and the natural rights of man, of the industrious man who has the means to improve his condition but to which an abuse of the laws places insurmountable obstacles. The ancient laws permitted this, but the laws of the Senate have added an inhibiting clause requiring the *permission of the master* [underlined in original], which reduces that privilege to a *sachal*, subject to avarice and ambition.[115]

At the time he wrote those words Sievers and his friend A. P. Mel'gunov, the governor of Iaroslavl, were trying to prove that the "ancient laws" had in fact given serfs the right to purchase their freedom at a price set by the state. The two governors produced a ruling to that effect by the old Kholopii Prikaz, but the Senate disputed the import of the ruling, and Catherine agreed with the Senate.[116] In that instance as in others Sievers found that the absolute authority of the serfowners placed definite limits on the opportunities and incentives with which he and his allies hoped to promote the development of the provinces.

Sievers also failed in his efforts to protect the economic activities of townsmen from peasant competition. If they were to be excluded from the merchant guilds, Sievers wanted peasant traders banned from the towns as well. His proposals represented a minor contribution to a major controversy. Russia's merchants wanted to restrict the right to engage in trade and commerce in order to protect their profits, but many noblemen wanted to extend that right to all peasants as a means of increasing their own revenues. The state's interest was less certain. The commercial activities of peasants would retard the growth of towns and the formation of an urban bourgeoisie, as Sievers argued, but they would promote the growth of the national economy as a whole. In the end the government's determination was consistent with its earlier decisions to eliminate specific monopolies. The Charter to the Towns allowed peasants to engage in handicrafts and to sell their products in the towns.[117] It also suggested that noblemen might enroll in the merchant guilds and participate in urban commerce, but the government soon decided that such an innovation was carrying consistency too far, and in 1790 it ruled that such activities were inconsistent with the status, honor, and duty of a nobleman.[118]

As it replaced the legal category of *posadskii chelovek* with that of townsman, the government also substituted new forms of corporate organization for the posad. The manifesto of December 14, 1766, initiated both processes when it called upon the inhabitants of towns to convene and elect a head (*Glava* or *Golova*) to a two-year term to preside over the elections to the Legislative Commission and over any assemblies of urban residents "that the state may find it necessary to convoke."[119] Later the Fundamental Law called for regular elections of heads for three-year terms and made them members ex officio of the orphans courts in the towns and of the boards of public welfare. It also specified that all elected town officials and courts were to be chosen by an "urban society" (*Gradskoe Obshchestvo*), a term that received little definition or elaboration at that time but included by implication both the merchants and the meshchanstvo.[120]

The Charter to the Towns set forth a complicated scheme of corporate organization within the towns. It divided citizens into six categories: actual citizens who owned property in the town; guild merchants; artisans; merchants from other towns and foreign countries; honorary citizens; and posad people, an old term used in a somewhat new sense to include laborers of various kinds. Each group was to have its own organization to hold meetings, conduct common business, and elect representatives to town agencies. The existing merchant guilds and artisan associations, for example, were to function within the new structure. Each of the six groups was to choose delegates to the town council (*Gradskaia Duma*), whose size and composition were to depend on the size and complexity of the town in question. The town council in turn would select one representative from each of its six constituent groups to sit on a six-member council (*Shestiglasnaia Duma*); since the former met only once every three years, its responsibilities devolved upon the six-member council. Besides the agencies and officials based on the new division of urban society, the Charter to the Towns created others elected by the triennial assembly of the urban society. Participation in the assembly was restricted to males over the age of twenty-five with an annual income in excess of fifty rubles and would be effectively controlled by the wealthy merchants. That body selected the head or mayor, the members of the various urban courts, the judges, the elders, and the town's representatives on the police board.[121]

The pattern of corporate functions described in the Charter to the Towns is confused, ambiguous, and inconsistent in many of its specific details but reasonably clear in its general outlines.[122] As a corporation, the town became a person in the eyes of the law and could act on its own behalf. The urban corporation and its constituent class organizations could contribute to the welfare of the town by encouraging order and purposeful activity from the townsmen and by settling disputes among them. In virtually every instance, however, towns were to function as auxiliaries or adjuncts to the bureaucracy and the police, which retained control and supervision over them. The Fundamental Law and the Statute on Police circumscribed the Charter to the Towns and defined the context of authority and tutelage within which the townsmen might exercise their liberty. Although Catherine's government wanted to share some of the responsibility for the development of Russia with a bourgeoisie and a middle class, it believed that those groups were still at an early stage of development. They could begin to assume some responsibility for their own affairs, but they needed the guidance of a parental state to mold them into mature citizens.

Catherine's government sought to raise Russia's townsmen to responsible maturity by surrounding them with a proper environment and teaching them how to behave. Town planning, urban reform, social institutions, credit facilities, improved means of transportation, schools, and the urban police were all supposed to contribute to that effort. In addition, the state lectured townsmen on morals and good conduct. In a section of the Statue on Police entitled "The Mirror of Good Order" ("Zertsalo Blagochiniia"), Catherine sought to acquaint her urban subjects with rules of civilized behavior and good citizenship.[123] She also wrote, commissioned, or published moralizing books and prescribed their use in schools. The most extensive and inclusive work of that kind, *On the Duties of Man and Citizen*, published in 1783 and introduced into the schools in 1786, set forth a complete moral and civic catechism for Catherine's subjects to learn and follow.[124] Like its German and Austrian counterparts, whose publications it imitated, Catherine's government wanted to enlighten its people, for that too was an essential component of progress.

Estates

Outside the towns the basic unit of rational organization was to be the estate (*pomestie*), a clearly delineated piece of land controlled by a single noble owner. By bringing order to such estates, Catherine's government sought to establish a basis for improving conditions in the countryside and for ending the unmanageable confusion that prevailed there at the time of her accession.

The nobles' nakazy of 1767 portray disputes over land ownership as an extremely serious and nearly universal problem.[125] A century of transfers and subdivisions carried out in the absence of clear and accessible records had made it virtually impossible to determine who owned what.

When a landowner died, his properties or claims thereto were normally divided in such a way that each heir received a piece of land in each field of each village and a proportionate share in the yields of woods and meadows. That principle caused confusion enough, but when parts of the legacy were sold separately or passed to the next generation, informal understandings among close relatives turned into quarrels among neighbors.[126] Rather than wait twenty years or more for the courts to settle their disputes, landowners often used their peasants as private armies to assert control over what they claimed. In his first major memorandum as governor of Novgorod Guberniia, Sievers informed the empress that violence arisng from conflicting claims of ownership was an everyday occurrence in the countryside and that only an official survey of landholdings could end it.[127]

No general survey or registration of landholdings had taken place in Russia since 1686, and even that one had been based on informal agreements that bore little relationship to official records.[128] Since then, Empresses Anna and Elizabeth had authorized new surveys, but little had come of their efforts. In her decree of May 13, 1754, Elizabeth gave three reasons for ordering a new general survey: to verify with legal documents the possession of lands and serfs, to secure state lands from illegal encroachment, and to eliminate the common ownership of villages and fields by consolidating holdings.[129] In pursuit of those aims the state attempted to use the records of the Pomestnyi Prikaz and the Votchina College to determine legal ownership, but those documents proved so unreliable that the chief effect of the survey was to intensify existing disputes and create new ones. With the government's attention distracted by the Seven Years War, Elizabeth's survey came to a halt after determining the boundaries of some fifty estates in the uezd of Moscow.[130]

Catherine's survey succeeded where others had failed because it concentrated on measuring and recording at the expense of litigation. In August 1765 her Commission on the State Survey (Komissiia o gosudarstvennom mezhevaniia) submitted a report that attributed the failure of Elizabeth's survey to three principal causes: the intense opposition to the expulsion of people from lands claimed by the state; the inexperience of government officers and surveyors; and the enormous number of disputes demanding resolution.[131] In her own legislation on the survey Catherine sought to remove, or at least reduce, those obstacles. Her manifesto of May 25, 1766, subsumed other considerations to the speedy resolution of disputes. More important, the state sacrificed its own interest in recovering lands that it may once have owned. Instead of challenging the present ownership and boundaries of such lands on the basis of old records, it agreed to accept and record de facto possession. Intruders who had settled on lands that clearly belonged to the state would be allowed to purchase the property in question.[132] To reduce the number of disputes to which the state was not a party, Catherine prompted the claimants to settle with-

out litigation by requiring parties to produce documentary proof of ownership in court, which few landowners could do, and by claiming 10 percent
of all disputed properties for the state. Under such pressure the landowners
reached private settlements in ten cases out of eleven.[133] In many instances their agreements produced consolidated blocks of territory whose
boundaries needed only to be secured with markings, maps, and survey records. In others they produced accords on how to divide an area among
the various owners and claimants, and the surveyors were empowered to
effect an equitable division. Multiple ownership of estates and divisions of
single villages were avoided in every possible instance.[134]

As the General Survey proceeded from one guberniia to another, it
provided a precise and reliable reference for determining ownership and
resolving disputes. The introduction of the Fundamental Law increased the
value of the survey by creating the administrative and judicial machinery
needed to apply its findings on a continuing basis. The statute assigned a
surveyor to the administrative staff of every guberniia and uezd and created the uezd courts, the superior land courts, and the chambers of civil
affairs to resolve property disputes among noblemen. Those agencies assumed the functions of the central Estates College and replaced the judicial
system that the nobles had castigated in their nakazy of 1767. They were
intended to make the resolution of property disputes simpler, easier, and
quicker, and by most accounts they succeeded.[135]

The final step in the creation of rational, manageable estates came in
1785, when the Charter to the Nobility secured the pomeshchiks' rights to
control the property they owned. Abandoning her predecessors' attempts
to regulate the economy and manage the disposition of resources through
the Estates College, the Mining College, the Manufacturing College, the
Admiralty, and other agencies of the central government, Catherine removed virtually all legal restrictions on landowners' use of their movable
and immovable property. The charter accorded them the right to establish
mills, mines, factories, and dams on their estates and to sell on the open
market anything grown, processed, or manufactured within their boundaries. The only serious limitation on a landowner's control over his property was the provision governing its passage from one generation to the
next. The charter's requirement that property be divided according to a legal formula rather than in keeping with the wishes of a deceased owner
was aimed at protecting noble families from their individual members. The
same principle applied to cases in which a nobleman was to be deprived of
his property as punishment for a crime: The charter required that the
property be divided among his legal heirs instead of being confiscated by
the state.[136]

The property rights granted to the Russian nobility in 1785 reflect the
peculiar mixture of influences and considerations affecting the government
of Catherine II. Although the Charter to the Nobility echoed the enthusiasm for liberty and property and the opposition to mercantilism and eco-

nomic regulation that had spread across Europe from England and France in the course of the eighteenth century, it did so within a context of absolutism, social hierarchy, and serfdom that distorted the significance of those principles. Catherine and her associates could be fairly open-minded about modifying certain details in order to make Russian society more rational, more manageable, and more productive, but they took the context itself for granted. Seen from that point of view, the entire Charter to the Nobility and its companion Charter to the Towns represented efforts to emulate Prussia and other German states in rationalizing the traditional class structure by providing a legal definition of the membership, organization, and privileges of the separate corporate estates within society.[137] In spite of Catherine's opposition to *individual monopolies* that restricted economic growth, her charter recognized the ownership of estates and serfs as an exclusive *corporate privilege* of the nobility.

Although the charter as a whole reflected the influence of German models, the property rights it assigned to the nobility did not. The Prussian *Standestaat* was also a *Poliseistaat* in which the government's presumption to control the use and development of natural resources and to manage the economy in the national interest set narrower limits on the nobles' control of their estates. Catherine's decision to accept the pomeshchiks' control over forests, mineral deposits, water, and other resources may have coincided with ideas emanating from England and France and with the desires expressed by the nobles in their nakazy to the Legislative Commission almost twenty years before, but it was also consistent with the structure and capabilities of the Russian state. Despite Catherine's expansion of the provincial bureaucracy, the imperial government could not hope to match Prussia's success in managing and developing the resources of rural areas as it could hope to emulate that success in managing and developing the towns. Rural Russia lay beyond the control of the imperial administration. Unable to govern and develop rural areas and unwilling to leave them confused and primitive, Catherine's government had no practical alternative other than to rely on the nobility. The creation of consolidated, clearly defined estates under the authority of single owners with full power to make economic decisions and undertake improvements in the hope of increasing their own revenues presented Catherine with a plausible, if uncertain, means of enhancing the productivity, prosperity, and happiness of rural Russia. The qualifications of Russia's provincial nobles to act as responsible landlords left much to be desired, but the state had some hope at least of enlightening the nobles. It had no hope of performing or even supervising the tasks it left to them.

Although the Charter to the Nobility said nothing explicit about serfs, their status as movable property was understood. On that issue Catherine either ignored or perverted the position of the French physiocrats and agronomes, whose teachings on private property were otherwise in complete accord with her charter. Physiocrats and agronomes argued that individual cultivators should be free to make their own decisions about the use of their property, but they denied that the possession of serfs or other so-called feudal rights constituted a valid form of property.[138] The charter made no real change in the status of Russia's serfs, but its very silence marked a significant shift in Catherine's stand on the peasant question.

In the 1760s several statesmen proposed that the state should mitigate the worse abuses of serfdom by bringing the relations between serfs and their masters within the purview of Russian law. Nikita Panin, the most influential figure in the government at that time, sympathized with notions of that sort, and his brother Peter produced a report that deemed the lack of restraint on serfowners' authority as the principal cause of peasant desertions from the western guberniias to Poland.[139] Sievers came to the same conclusion. He advised Catherine that the unmitigated power of the serfowners was "without a doubt the primary cause of the thousands of fugitives who go to populate Poland and Lithuania."[140] A few years later he blamed the "insupportable yoke" of serfdom for the jacqueries associated with the Pugachev rebellion and predicted, as did some other critics of serfdom, that it would someday cause the fall of the Russian state.[141] In addition to his and Mel'gunov's campaign to have the state set a price at which any serf could purchase his freedom, Sievers wanted the state to limit both the amount of labor that masters could require of their serfs and the punishments that they might impose without a formal hearing.[142] He also suggested that Catherine borrow from his native Livonia a law that allowed serfs to select their own mates. Such a law, he argued, would encourage masters to treat their serfs humanely because no one would want to marry the serf of a bad master.[143]

Sievers offered those suggestions in the belief that Catherine was planning to move against the evils of serfdom. In January 1766 he implored her on behalf of the serfs: "The unfortunates are men—often more so than their masters. It is the cause of Humanity, my Gracious Sovereign, and it is your cause. Assuring the property of the subject will be the most beautiful and durable monument of the reign of Catherine, the friend and partisan of humanity."[144] Almost four decades later Sievers maintained that one of Catherine's motives in summoning the Legislative Commission had been to bring the serfs under the protection of the law.[145]

In the 1760s Catherine too had hoped that the impending reorganization of society might include some improvements in the status and condition of the serfs. In a secret memorandum to the procurator-general, in the famous essay contest that she sponsored through the Free Economic Society, in several articles of her *Instruction*, and possibly in the injection of certain arguments into the debates of the Legislative Commission, Catherine raised the questions of limiting the serfowner's absolute control over the person of the serf and of allowing serfs to own private property.[146] Like the physiocrats and agronomes in France, she tried to persuade the nobles that it was in their own interest to yield some of their rights over the peasants. For example, the winning essay in the competition of the Free Economic Society was judged to be that of Beardé de l'Abayé, a French agronome who argued that the ownership of a small piece of property would make serfs more industrious, more contented, and more dependent on their masters.[147] But the serfowners would not be persuaded. The discussions of the Legislative Commission indicated that the serfowners would not endorse the kinds of reform Catherine contemplated, and the fear engendered by the *pugachevshchina* only a few years later made it certain that they never would. Catherine thus abandoned her efforts to bring the serfs under the protection of the law.

In seeking a personal political motive for Catherine's démarche on serfdom, historians have ignored the institutional aspects of the issue. Opposition to limits on the serfowners' authority came not from the influential nobles and politicians of the capital, whom Catherine might have reason to fear, but from the provincial nobles who played no role in court politics or in the overthrow and elevation of monarchs. The provincial nobles did, however, hold a crucial place in the affairs and order of rural Russia; without their cooperation the government in St. Petersburg had no acceptable means of enforcing any laws it might enact for the benefit of the serfs. The fate of Paul's decree limiting labor services to three days per week is a case in point. A state that lacked the means to govern the serfs without the pomeshchik also lacked the means to govern the serfs against him.

The Nobility

Between 1762 and 1785 Catherine's government reorganized the Russian nobility by enrolling the noble landowners of every guberniia in corporate associations and assigning them collective functions and obligations. Incorporation enabled the government to resolve the problems created by Peter III's Manifesto on the Liberty of the Nobility by treating the dvorianstvo as a landed gentry with whom the state could share some of its responsibilities for the government of provincial Russia.[148]

Until 1762 the compulsory service instituted by Peter I had shaped the nobleman's identity and defined his role in society. It removed noblemen from the isolation of their estates and brought them together in schools and regiments to be trained and socialized. State service determined membership in the nobility as well as status and precedence within it.

With his manifesto of February 18, 1762, Peter III ended the defining function of compulsory service without replacing it. At the time he announced his intention to abolish compulsory service, the emperor added some remarks about putting the Russian dvorianstvo on the same legal footing as the Livonian nobility, but in the four remaining months of his reign he took no further steps in that direction.[149] After seizing the throne, Catherine charged the Commission on the Freedom of the Nobility with the task of finding solutions to the problems raised by her husband's manifesto. However, when that commission recommended that the manifesto be confirmed and that it be supplemented with civil liberties and economic privileges, the empress tabled its report and left the matter unresolved. As a result, the many nobles who left imperial service after 1762 found themselves at odds with their new situation. As the nakaz from the nobles of Pskov to the Legislative Commission put it: "The Russian nobility has only the freedom not to serve, and that alone, but having neither the resources nor the power for anything else, they live on their estates with a few poor possessions and many dependents; and even if someone wants to work at something useful to the Fatherland, his capability and his inclination are constrained to perish for want of means on the one hand and for want of permission on the other."[150]

Catherine's refusal to adopt the proposals of the Commission on the Freedom of the Nobility reflected her concern that the privileges of the nobility should not be defined in isolation from the interests of the merchants, the peasants, or the state. On the last point she was not persuaded by the commission's confident assertions, echoing those of the manifesto, that during the past fifty years Russian nobles had been so thoroughly enlightened and had so internalized the civic, patriotic lessons of Peter I that further compulsion was unnecessary. She suspected that more than a few noblemen would sever all ties with the progressive state and sink back into the indolence, selfishness, and ignorance from which the service requirements of Peter the Great had forcibly removed them.

Catherine's first attempt to create new institutional ties between the state and the emancipated dvorianstvo came in connection with the elections to the Legislative Commission. In language very similar to that which applied to the gatherings of townsmen, Catherine ordered the nobles of every qualified uezd to convene and elect a marshal (*predvoditel'*) to oversee the elections to the Legislative Commission. The marshal would retain his title for two years and preside over any future gathering of the nobles "that the state may find it necessary to convoke."[151] The manifesto gave the townsmen a new form of organization and a new kind of official, but it gave the provincial nobles their first organization and their first class official of any kind since the time of Peter I. These innovations also opened for the imperial government a new means of communicating with the nobles and of using them for its purposes. During the crisis of the early 1770s, for example, the government at various times ordered the marshals of the nobility to assist the state administration in collecting military conscripts, preventing the spread of epidemics, and halting the transportation and sale of contraband.[152]

Sievers saw the corporate organization of the nobility as a potential instrument of order and progress. Following the elections to the Legislative Commission, he informed Catherine that more than five hundred noblemen had attended the meetings in the five districts (*piatiny*) of Novogord Uezd and that in drafting their nakazy they had addressed themselves to many of the same issues that concerned him.[153] When the nobles of Novgorod again gathered to elect a marshal in January 1769, Sievers sought and won their agreement to contribute ten kopecks for every revision soul in their possession to a fund for the repair of the road from Novgorod to Moscow.[154] In the autumn of that same year, while many noblemen were present in the town for other reasons, Sievers called them together in order, in his words, "to make them several propositions concerning the establishment of a better internal order in the immense uezd of Novgorod." He reported to Catherine that the nobles had agreed unanimously to three resolutions: to divide the uezd into komissariats of five parishes each, to elect noblemen to serve as komissars, and to contribute one kopeck per revision soul to pay the salaries of the komissars; to elect a supervisor for the construction of the road to Smolensk and to contribute five kopecks per revision soul to hire labor for the repair work, rather than depend on peasant corvée; and to contribute five kopecks per revision soul to pay for a land survey in order to put an end to the lawsuits and violence arising from property disputes.[155] Those proposals reflected Sievers's strong conviction that provincial estate owners should contribute their time, money, and effort to the improvement of their local areas both as an act of public service and as an act of enlightened self-interest. In his first major memorandum as governor of Novgorod Guberniia Sievers had suggested that the local landowners be made to pay for a much needed survey "because they will receive the benefits of it." At the same time, he had complained of the difficulty of staffing minor positions in the provincial administration because the nobles could no longer be compelled to serve.[156] In the corporate institutions of the nobility Sievers believed that he had found a solution to both of those problems, a solution that was demonstrably successful in his native Livonia and one that, moreover, was consistent with the interests of both the provincial nobles and the imperial government.

Ideal though that solution may have seemed to a provincial administrator like Sievers, it faced powerful opponents in the capital. One member of the Commission on the Freedom of the Nobility explicitly advocated the involvement of the provincial nobles in local affairs on a corporate basis, and another is known to have favored such an arrangement. But the omission of any such proposal from the report that the commission submitted to the empress suggests that a majority of those high-ranking statesman were opposed to the idea.[157] Nikita Panin, a member of that commission, omitted any corporate role for the nobility from his own proposals for developing the provincial economy.[158] The same omission is also apparent in the nakaz from the nobles of Moscow Uezd, a document supposedly composed by Panin.[159] Prince Viazemskii, frequently pitted against Panin on other issues, also opposed the involvement of provincial nobles in public affairs. As the chief bureaucrat of the central administration, Viazem-skii considered public affairs the preserve of the bureaucracy, and he was determined that the provinces would be administered from the center through the bureaucratic chain of command.[160] Until 1775 Catherine took a position between those of Viazemskii and Sievers and drew a distinction between the election of class courts, analogous to those of the townsmen, and the election of officials with executive responsibilities. Her statute of 1773 on the new guberniias of Pskov and Mogilev directed the resident nobility to elect land courts, but one year later her decree ordering the creation of four komissariats in St. Petersburg Guberniia specified that the komissars were to be appointed.[161] The same distinction carried over into the first and second drafts of the Fundamental Law, which originally prescribed the election of the members of the uezd court and the appointment of the judge of that court, as well as the appointment of uezd officials with duties similar to those of the komissars described in her decree of the previous year. In the second draft, however, the phrase "are to be appointed by the governor" was crossed out and replaced by the phrase "are to be elected every three years by the nobility."[162]

On the recommendation of her principal adviser, Sievers, Catherine turned to the provincial nobles to supply some of the additional manpower required by the Fundamental Law. At the end of her reign, when implementation of the reform had led to the formation of fifty guberniias and 493 uezds, the nobles were responsible for filling 4,053 posts by electing their peers. The great majority served as judges and as members of the class courts, but 493 served as ispravniks, the chiefs of the rural police charged with enforcing the laws and maintaining order in the countryside. They were assisted by 986 deputies chosen by the nobles and another 986 chosen by the state peasants.[163] The importance of nobles to the reform of 1775 can be judged from the comment of Governor-General R. I. Vorontsov on the creation of Vladimir Guberniia in 1779: "I did not watch over the regular outline of an uezd so much as I strove to see that in every uezd there would be a sufficient number of noblemen to perform public service."[164] Similarly, after Catherine observed that the uezd of Pskov was too extensive, Sievers replied that a new uezd might be organized around the settlement of Pechersk, but he was worried that it would contain too few noblemen.[165]

Although he praised the Fundamental Law for putting to good use noblemen "who have been loafing since 1762 and who have all but lost interest in the public good and in their duty to their country,"[166] Sievers envisioned a much larger and more comprehensive corporate role for the nobles than that law provided. As the first governor-general to implement the reform, he took the lead in enhancing the importance of the nobles' assemblies. He identified the establishment of each new guberniia with election meetings of the nobility and spent a few thousand rubles on ceremonies and amusements.[167] On his own authority he had the nobles elect a marshal for the entire guberniia who was thereafter to preside at the meetings, and he imposed a property qualification for voting and for seeking office in order to interest the more substantial landowners in the elections.[168] Resuming his efforts to broaden the scope of the assemblies' activities, Sievers in December 1777 asked the nobles' assembly of Olonets to support a school for young noblemen. When they agreed unanimously to contribute five kopecks per revision soul to a school fund to be managed by the guberniia marshal, Sievers proudly informed the empress: "Behold, Most Gracious Soverign, the monument that I dedicate to Your Majesty— I dare to congratulate myself upon it—to have elevated the souls of your subjects."[169] He then presented similar proposals to the other assemblies and received the same response.

Catherine treated Sievers as an authority on all matters related to provincial reform and nobles' assemblies. She allowed him to set the precedents that the other governors-general were to follow in implementing the Fundamental Law, and she sought his advice on amendments to that statute. In April 1777, for example, she asked him if it might not be better to deny elected servitors a temporary rank in the Table of Ranks and to allow governors-general to dismiss elected officials at their discretion. Sievers replied that both proposals had some merit, but he succeeded in convincing her that the first would tend to discourage worthy candidates and that the second would "degrade and humiliate the nobility."[170] Before the second round of elections Sievers asked the empress to confirm each of the innovations he had introduced during the past three years. Catherine responded affirmatively and promulgated a decree, dated November 25, 1778, that made them official throughout the empire. She formally recognized the assemblies as corporate institutions with officers and a treasury and some degree of autonomy from state officials. That decree also helped to pave the way for the Charter to the Nobility to resolve many of the issues raised by the manifesto of Peter III.[171]

Although it adopted most of Sievers's views on the nobles' assemblies, Catherine's government refused to grant them all of the authority he believed they should have. Commenting on a draft of what was to become the Charter to the Nobility, Sievers proposed that the assemblies be empowered to fine individuals who failed to attend their meetings and suggested maximum penalties of fifty rubles for the first absence, two hundred for the second, and five hundred for the third. Even more drastic was his proposal that the assemblies be empowered to levy assessments for the support of projects such as improvements to the roads. Unlike the voluntary contributions voted in the past, Sievers wanted future assessments to be binding on all serfowners, including noblemen who failed to attend the assemblies and the state as the owner of crown peasants.[172] The government incorporated some of Sievers's other suggestions into the charter, but it balked at the notion of assemblies assessing fines and taxes.

The Charter to the Nobility recognized the nobles' association (*dvo-*

rianskoe sobranie) of each guberniia as a corporate institution possessed of rights, duties, and liability before the law. Each association was to be run by its own elected officers: a marshall, his deputies, a secretary, and a treasurer. It was to maintain its own headquarters, preserve its own archives and records, operate its own printing press, record information about its members, collect and disperse revenue, care for noble widows and orphans, petition the state, direct corporate activities that would promote the interests of its members, and elect officials in accordance with the Fundamental Law. Within that structure the nobles of each uezd formed a separate chapter or branch that elected its own uezd marshal and officials of the uezd administration.[173]

As in the case of townsmen, the corporate concerns of the nobles were intermingled with those of the state. The nobles chose the ispravniks and their deputies, but the governor-general selected the guberniia marshal from two candidates nominated by the nobles. The marshals were essentially class officials, but they served on the boards of public welfare and performed various services for the state. Although the state paid them no salary, it did accord them a service rank in the Table of Ranks. The associations could petition the state, but they could also be fined for presenting an illegal proposal, and even the class organs and class activities of the nobles were subject to state supervision.[174] The associations were created to serve as auxiliaries of the bureaucracy, not as its competitors, and their limited autonomy represented a practical division of labor rather than a legal separation of powers.

Just as it reorganized the nobility on a different legal basis, the charter created a new relationship among noble status, estate ownership, and state service. By equating membership in a nobles' association with ownership of an estate in a particular guberniia, the charter identified nobles as landowners. Landless nobles could exercise all of the personal liberties granted to the nobility, but they were excluded from all corporate functions and privileges and thus became a kind of technical or artificial nobility with an anomolous status like that of personal nobles or even *raznochintsy*. The issue of state service was resolved in a somewhat similar fashion: all noblemen were granted the personal liberty to serve or not to serve, but only those estate owners who had entered the service and won a commission could attend the assemblies, vote, or run for elective office. Landowners who had not attained commissioned rank in the service were to be enrolled in the associations, but they would be denied the privilege of active participation in corporate activities.[175] By substituting a social sanction for a legal sanction, the charter managed to combine liberty for the individual nobleman with the needs and interests of the state.

The new rules prescribed for registering nobility also resolved some longstanding problems. The charter ordered the guberniia marshals and their deputies to examine the credentials of everyone claiming membership in the associations. If they accepted someone's claim, the marshals and deputies were to enter his name in the book of nobility of that guberniia and record specific information about him, his family, and his estate.[176] By having the associations assume the responsibilities of the Heraldry Office, the state simultaneously relieved itself of a burden, enhanced the significance of the nobles' corporate institutions, provided better service to the nobles, and, in all probability, improved the collection of information and records.

Catherine's charter completed the transformation of the dvorianstvo from a service nobility supported by the possession of estates to a landed nobility that was expected to serve. In the 1760s Catherine had feared that nobles freed from compulsory service might sink back into the stupidity and indolence from which Peter I had forcibly removed them. In the associations she found a means of tying the nobles to each other and to the state. Instead of trying to communicate with many thousands of noblemen scattered over the vastness of Russia, the imperial government could now deal with a maximum of fifty associations with headquarters in the guberniia capitals. The associations involved the provincial landowners in civilizing activities, and by encouraging them to contribute to the welfare of their country, their localities, and their class, the associations would assist the state in bringing the benefits of order and civilization to the provinces.

By concentrating on the bureaucracy, the burghers, and the nobles, and by giving the nobles more authority over the countryside than it gave the burghers over the towns, Catherine's reorganization of provincial Russia exemplified the social and political biases of her government. Moreover, in both of those regards it also matched the reforming capabilities of the Russian state in the last quarter of the eighteenth century. The limited power of the imperial government in the provinces was exercised in the towns and from the towns, and even that weak presence represented a significant increase in governing and reforming capabilities. In the first two decades of the eighteenth century Peter the Great reformed the central government, the capital, and the court—all of which lay directly under his personal supervision and control. But his efforts to extend those reforms had accomplished very little because the provinces lay beyond his administrative grasp. By the last quarter of the eighteenth century the state had acquired the capability of bringing a program of modernization *to* the provinces, but still it could not project reform very deeply *into* the provinces. Catherine could only begin to do at the intermediate levels of government and society what Peter I had done at the uppermost levels. The lower levels of government and society continued to function outside the administrative control of the national government and would remain unreachable for decades (some would say centuries) to come.

VI

The Development of Northwestern Russia, 1764–1796

IN AN OVERREACTION to the German chauvinism of Blum's biography of Sievers, the Russian nationalist historian D. I. Ilovaiskii once belittled the governor-general as "an official who believed in the possibility of creating national prosperity through a rearrangement of administrative details, symmetrical borders, and straight roads."[1] Yet in his own account of Sievers's career Ilovaiskii provides an abundance of material that belies that statement. Certainly Sievers believed that rational units and systems fostered progress and that irrational ones impeded it, but within that framework he was essentially a voluntarist who assumed that progress began with the initiatives of groups and individuals. His reports reveal a man compelled by his own nature to try to improve virtually everything that came to his attention. Most of his contributions to Catherine's reforms started as specific initiatives to ameliorate conditions within the territories he governed. His successors, Count Ia. A. Bruce (1782–1784) and N. P. Arkharov (1784–1797), developed fewer projects of their own to promote progress in northwestern Russia, but they assumed responsibility for those begun by Sievers and for those required by the reforms of the 1780s.

The reports of the three governors-general of northwestern Russia to the central government contain important, if incomplete, information about the various attempts to promote the development of provincial Russia. Together with information from other sources, they enable us to see how conditions in the provinces changed—or failed to change—in response to the state's initiatives. However, in using them to appraise the character and success of the government's policies, we must be aware of two considerations that helped to define the content and style of those reports. The first is geographical. Sievers had little to say about the guberniias of Pskov and Olonets except to request that they be removed from his charge, and indeed, his successors were freed of them. Consequently, if we want to compare the conditions that Sievers reported in 1764 with those reported in the 1770s, 1780s, and 1790s, we must confine our inquiry in most instances to the parts of the old guberniia of Novgorod that became the guberniias of Novgorod and Tver after 1775.

The second consideration involves the role that the governors-general played in the imperial government and the nature of the information they reported. Although they were willing or, in Sievers's case, eager to advise the Empress and the Senate on broad issues of policy, governors-general were provincial administrators, not lawmakers, and they normally reported the details of specific concerns. The financial practices of the Russian government also forced them to request special appropriations for all but the most routine operations of government and to explain and justify each request in detail. Rather than discussing "urban development," therefore, the governors-general simply reported on the growth of towns they had recently visited or proposed the reconstruction of one that had just been destroyed by fire. Information of that kind also served the needs of the central government, which had few means of perceiving provincial development in abstract, quantified terms. It could count the number of towns or the number of taxpayers or the number of schools, but it had no sophisticated means of assessing urbanization, industrialization, average personal income, or other measures of development employed in the twentieth century. For the most part, Catherine's government had to form its impressions and conclusions from examples.

Many of the improvements that concerned the governors-general of Novgorod and Tver can be fitted into one of five categories: transportation and communication, towns, public institutions, industry and commerce, natural resources and agriculture. Such categories are neither comprehensive nor discrete. Public institutions, for example, existed only in towns, and improvements to transportation constituted an important form of assistance to commerce. But by using these categories as convenient devices for organizing the myriad concerns of state officials into a few comprehensible topics, we can obtain a clearer picture of the government's efforts to promote the development of northwestern Russia.

Transportation and Communication

When he resigned his office in 1781, Sievers advised Catherine that the affairs of Novgorod and Tver guberniias were so intertwined with those of the Vyshnii Volochek System of inland waterways that responsibility for all three should always be assigned to a single governor-general.[2] Having acquired such an assignment for himself, Sievers observed that the Vyshnii Volochek System demanded as much attention as an additional guberniia, and on at least one occasion an opponent, Senator M. A. Dedenev, referred to Sievers sarcastically as "the governor of locks and barges."[3] Governor-General Arkharov shared Sievers's opinion, and in 1797, when Paul brought Sievers out of retirement and gave him authority over all inland waterways, Arkharov resigned in protest.[4]

Sievers saw immediately the vital importance of the Vyshnii Volochek System to both the local and the national economy, but his original assignment as governor of Novgorod Guberniia included no formal responsibility for its operation. The Vyshnii Volochek Office, the Borovichi Rapids Office, and the Volkhov Office, located at the three major bottlenecks along the route, collected tolls, kept the system in repair, and made minor improvements as time and money allowed. The three offices reported directly to the Senate, which followed the collection of tolls with some interest but referred all questions of hydroengineering to Senator Dedenev, who considered himself an expert on the subject.

Despite his lack of formal responsibility, Sievers could not ignore a matter that he considered so important. In his first major memorandum to the Empress the new governor offered four suggestions for improving the Vyshnii Volochek System:

> 1) have General Murav'ev investigate the mischief that the peasants are doing at Borovichi; 2) have General Murav'ev or someone else examine the locks at Vyshnii Volochek next summer in my presence. They are in a bad state, and it is through them that St. Petersburg lives; 3) have an officer examine the Volkhov cataracts next summer and find ways to clean them; 4) look into General Kutuzov's plan to connect the source of the Volga at Lake Seliger with the Pola, which flows into Ilmen. This seems very practical. It will improve abundance in the capital and attach to it provinces that nature has put at a distance."[5]

The first three suggestions intruded into the affairs of all three Senate offices along the Vyshnii Volochek System, and the fourth envisioned the opening of an alternate route from the Volga to St. Petersburg. Sievers's remarks about the inland waterways earned him the lasting enmity of Senator Dedenev, but they also alerted Catherine to problems along the waterways that might jeopardize the provisioning of St. Petersburg and the growth of Russia's exports.

On March 24, 1765, the empress commissioned General A. N. Vil'boa (Villebois) and Senator Dedenev to examine the costs and feasibility of opening new water routes from the interior provinces to the capital. Vil'boa was to study the possibility of linking the Volga with Lake Ilmen via Lake Seliger and the Pola River to the southwest of the existing route. Dedenev was to investigate the practicality of linking the Volga with Lake Ladoga through the Sheksna, Kopia, Lida, Tikhvin, and Sias rivers to the northeast of the existing route.[6] Dedenev's report, submitted on January 16, 1767, accompanied by twenty-two maps, estimated the total cost of the northeastern link as 5,175,092 rubles.[7] Just when Vil'boa completed his report or what he proposed is not clear from the Senate's documents. The Senate forwarded its own recommendation endorsing Dedenev's plan on October 9, 1774, but neither project was funded during Catherine's reign.[8] That inaction left improvement of the difficult and barely adequate route through Vyshnii Volochek as the only means of increasing the volume of goods and commodities that could be shipped across the continental divide from the interior provinces to St. Petersburg.

By 1768 both Dedenev and Sievers had submitted detailed memoranda to the Senate proposing improvements to the Vyshnii Volochek System. Although their recommendations differed in certain respects, the two men agreed on the need to augment the flow of the Tvertsa and Msta rivers. In May of that year Sievers sent Catherine the first of his many complaints about the Senate's delay in authorizing improvements to the waterways. He pointed out that in the previous autumn two hundred barges laden with grain for St. Petersburg had been halted by low water in the Msta and forced to spend the winter near Borovichi. He also assured the empress that the improvements he was outlining would cost less than the 130,000 rubles required for Dedenev's "exorbitant project."[9]

By October 1768 Sievers felt sufficiently secure to request full authority over the waterways within his guberniia.[10] While he waited five years for Catherine's decision, the governor continued to remove rocks from the waterways and to undertake other improvements that did not require anyone else's approval. Whenever he did so, he promptly notified the empress of his accomplishment, and on one occasion he even sent her two large blocks of granite that had been removed from the Volkhov.[11] Although Sievers normally complained that war interfered with his projects, he also tried to turn it to his advantage whenever he could. In 1769 he pointed out that the Turkish War had increased the importance of water communications and the need for improvements to the Vyshnii Volochek System.[12] In the same vein he later informed the empress that low water had halted caravans of iron and timber destined for the Admiralty.[13]

In November 1773 Catherine appointed Sievers director of water communications in Novgorod Guberniia.[14] At Sievers's suggestion, the state repurchased the Serdiukov concession at Vyshnii Volochek in 1774 for 176,000 rubles,[15] and 1778 the Senate reorganized the Department of Water Communications under Sievers's authority and provided it with a staffing chart.[16] The next year Catherine ordered the Senate to give special attention to requests from the director of water communications.[17] Within that structure Sievers, Bruce, and Arkharov held managerial responsibility for water communications, but for major improvements requiring extraordinary expenditures they were still obliged to seek authorization from the Senate.

In a memorandum to his successor Sievers declared that his goal as director of water communications had been to make possible the uninterrupted passage from one end of the system to the other.[18] That meant eliminating the bottlenecks at Vyshnii Volochek, at Lake Ilmen, and at the rapids of the Msta and Volkhov. Above all, it meant providing enough water to operate the locks at the continental divide and to maintain an adequate draft in the Msta and Tvertsa rivers on the divide's slopes. Seasonal rains, deforestation, and the eutrophication of lakes and swamps sent too much water into the system in the spring and too little in the summer and fall.

Serdiukov had succeeded in creating a water link at Vyshnii Volochek by damming the Tsna River to create a reservoir with which to operate the locks of the canal. To provide more water, Sievers hired Johnan Gerhard, a German hydroengineer, to create a system of aqueducts through which the waters of several small rivers and four small lakes were eventually brought into the main reservoir on the Tsna. After it was used in the locks, water from the reservoir was released into the Tvertsa to augment its natural flow.[19] In the 1780s several tributaries of the Tvertsa were also dammed to retain the spring runoff and to release water into the river in coordination with the passage of the spring and autumn caravans. On the other side of the divide a lock was built at the spot where the Msta emerges from Lake Mstino, and six dams were constructed on the tributaries of the Msta. Those projects served to regulate the depth and current of the river and helped to ease the passage at its cataracts.

At Vyshnii Volochek itself, Colonel Pisarev had failed to maintain the works on which the whole system depended. Between 1774 and 1778 Gerhard repaired the rotting, leaking, wooden dams and locks while the Senate and the empress ignored Sievers's pleas to have them rebuilt in stone. In January 1783 Bruce renewed the request for funds to rebuild the works at Vyshnii Volochek in stone, pointing out that the project would cost far more than the 4,382 rubles in surplus tolls that the canal produced each year after salaries and other expenses had been met.[20] After a similar request from Arkharov, Catherine authorized the reconstruction in January 1785. She appropriated 35,000 rubles at that time and promised another 20,000 rubles per year for the next five years.[21] The project took longer and cost more than expected, but by the end of Catherine's reign the locks and dams had been rebuilt in stone.[22]

The state also improved the movement of traffic through the waterways by organizing vessels into caravans, scheduling their passage, and coordinating them with the release of water from the various reservoirs. In a last memorandum to his successor, Sievers urged that his goal of uninterrupted passage through the system could be achieved once the dams on the tributaries of the Tvertsa were in operation. Then, if the officials in Tver organized the traffic properly and posted schedules for commencing the journey, a caravan of three hundred to four hundred vessels would be able to proceed from Tver to Lake Ilmen without having to halt because of low water.[23]

Through such efforts Sievers and his successors increased the efficiency of the Vyshnii Volochek System. Boats passed through it more quickly, and there were greater numbers of them. In 1778 the grain caravan from Gzhatsk passed through the canal at Vyshnii Volochek two months earlier than in previous years, and in 1781 Sievers reported with pride that 500 barges carrying iron and other goods from Siberia had passed through Vyshnii Volochek in August instead of spending the winter in the Tvertsa as they had been forced to do in the past. The earlier passage not only saved money for the Siberian merchants; it also made workers, horses, and water available for the immediate use of the spring caravan carrying grain to St. Petersburg.[24] A total of 1,742 boats and barges passed through the locks at Vyshnii Volochek in 1769; by 1779 their number exceeded 2,000.[25] The total rose to 3,520 in 1786,[26] and from 1797 until the opening of the railroad in 1851 it fluctuated between 4,000 and 4,600 vessels per year.[27]

Improvements to the channel on the lower part of the system virtually eliminated the cataracts of the Volkhov as hazards to navigation. In 1781 Sievers reported that only five or six vessels had been damaged out of a total of some four thousand and that in those cases the owners had been careless. But he was annoyed that a salmon weir, operating in full compliance with the law, continued to impede traffic along the Volkhov, and he reminded Catherine of the need for a code of navigation.[28] Sievers also cleaned the channel of the Lovat, a river emptying into Lake Ilmen from the south.

Of all the problems that confronted Sievers when he became director of water communications in 1773, only that of Lake Ilmen remained in 1781 as he had found it. Because that lake held too much water in the spring and too little in the summer and fall, some caravans were swamped in sudden squalls while others became stuck in the mud. The obvious solution was to build a canal less than ten kilometers in length from a point near the mouth of the Msta to a point on the Volkhov through which the caravans could bypass the lake. Agreement on that plan had been reached by 1775, but once again Sievers and Dedenev advocated different routes, and the Senate failed to reach a decision. Later, as director of water communications under Paul, Sievers finally supervised the creation of a Msta-Volkhov canal. Opened in 1804, it was named the Sievers Canal in his honor.

The improvements to inland waterways during the reign of Catherine II ended decades of neglect under her predecessors, but they were dwarfed in turn by those initiated during the brief reign of her successor. In 1797

Paul gave Sievers responsibility for improving water transport throughout the empire, and the following year, at Sievers's suggestion, he created an imperial Department of Water Communications.[29] The fruits of Paul's collaboration with Sievers were the Sievers Canal, the Berezina Canal linking the Dnepr with the Western Dvina, and the Sias, Svir, and Mariiansk canals linking the Volga with the Neva by way of Lakes Beloe and Onega. They also formulated plans to link the Dnepr with the Niemen by way of the Priepet and to bypass the Dnepr rapids.[30] Paul took a close personal interest in Sievers's projects and supported them as strongly as Catherine had supported Potemkin's efforts to settle the Pontic Steppe. He personally ordered the Assignats Bank to provide Sievers with 250,000 rubles over seven years to build the Msta-Volkhov canal,[31] and in 1799, when the war against France prevented Paul from appropriating funds for what would become the Mariiansk Canal, Empress Maria Fedorovna came forward and put up her own money to finance the first year's work.[32] As Paul's director of water communications, Sievers received the kind of attention and support he had always wanted from Catherine and was happier and more effective in his work.

In eighteenth-century Russia, as in almost all the rest of Europe, good roads were out of the question. Given the harsh climate, unstable soils, and great distances, the government's problem was to maintain passable roads for the sake of communication and, as a secondary consideration, for commerce. As of 1764 Russia's roads were constructed by the Chancellery for the Construction of State Roads and maintained by corvée imposed on nearby villages. Sievers's first inspection convinced him that such measures were insufficient, and in his memorandum of December 9, 1764, he proposed a number of changes: the obligation to maintain roads should be imposed on all inhabitants of an uezd and not just on those who lived along the right of way; komissars should be appointed to supervise the fulfillment of that obligation; and the penalty for failure to perform corvée should be changed from corporal punishment to a fine, with the funds collected to be used to finance further improvements. In support of the third proposal Sievers argued that serfowners were not embarrassed if their peasants were whipped occasionally but would not want to see money taken from them.[33] At the time, the government ignored those proposals, but eventually the need for a better system of building and maintaining roads led it to some of the same conclusions.

In 1766 Catherine called upon the governors to describe the roads in their guberniias.[34] In that year she also included a chapter on roads in her instructions for the General Survey. The surveyors were to allow thirty sazhens (64 meters) for most rights of way—ten sazhens (21.3 meters) for the road itself and ten sazhens on each side for a border. The main highway from St. Petersburg to Moscow was to have borders fifty meters in width; minor roads were to be only six meters wide without borders.

Landlords in the immediate vicinity were to be responsible for seeing that their peasants kept the roadbed in repair and that they refrained from planting on the borders.[35] In 1775 the Fundamental Law charged the ispravnik and the lower land court of each uezd with seeing that the roads were maintained and that the landlords and the peasants met their obligations.[36] The Chancellery for the Construction of State Roads was abolished in 1780 and replaced within a few years by a separate commission on roads in each guberniia, headed by the vice-governor.[37] That decentralized arrangement endured until 1800, when Paul created the Expedition on the Roads of the Empire to supervise the construction of roads and bridges.[38]

Most of the official correspondence about the roads in Novgorod Guberniia deals with the highway between St. Petersburg and Moscow and reveals the difficulty involved in maintaining the most important artery of communication in the empire. With the outbreak of the First Turkish War, the Senate sought to facilitate the movement of troops and supplies along that route toward the south. It instructed the governors of St. Petersburg, Novgorod, Moscow, Belorossiia, and Kiev to notify the Chancellery for the Construction of State Roads of any major repairs that would be necessary and to estimate the amounts of time and money required. The chancellery would supply the necessary materials and dispatch officers to direct the corvée. After reading the Senate's plan, Sievers stated his objections to the empress in two letters: the plan was too military in its outlook and ignored the welfare of the provinces; the existing road was beyond repair and should be rebuilt along a route that could shorten it by 100 kilometers; the four officers and forty soldiers assigned to Novgorod by the chancellery could not supervise corvée along all 560 kilometers of highway, no matter what the Senate believed; the corvée should be converted into a monetary assessment of three to five rubles levied on all the landowners of the guberniia (except those of Olonets and Kargopol), not just on those who happened to live along the highway; and the funds collected should be used to hire willing laborers who would continue to work for as long as they were needed.[39]

The Senate summoned Sievers to Moscow to discuss his objections, and, under the pressure of war, the two parties resolved their disagreements. The Senate authorized Sievers to relocate the stretch of road between Novgorod and Tsarskoe Selo that he had described as virtually impassable, and the governor promised simply to repair the remainder. To finance the project, Sievers persuaded the assembled nobles of the guberniia to agree unanimously to contribute ten kopecks per soul for road work.[40] A compromise between the governor and the Senate subsequently converted that agreement into an assessment of three kopecks per soul to be imposed on all landowners in lieu of corvée. When additional funds were needed, the Senate, which had none to spare, allowed Sievers to use accumulated revenues from the river tolls at Borovichi.[41] By May 1771 Sievers could report that the work was progressing well and nearing completion.[42]

In 1780 the Senate reversed itself. Having prohibited new assessments voted by the nobles' assemblies after 1776, it extended that ruling to include the 1771 accord on the construction and repair of roads. Sievers, who had reached the point of exasperation in his dealings with the Senate, appealed to the empress. Protesting both the specifics of the Senate's ruling and the senators' alleged enmity toward him, he complained:

> It states in writing that the improvement must be carried on through corvée or voluntary contributions. Whom shall I ask to volunteer to make a contribution? As for corvée, I am convinced that Your Majesty's fairness and justice would never require several small uezds to construct the highways of the empire. Moreover, the corvée is always converted into cash contributions within the communes. I saw evidence of that last summer. To forestall intrigues and accusations against me, I must insist upon an explicit decree. The fairest thing of all would be for me to be able to say that the roads will be constructed at the expense of the imperial treasury as before the Turkish War; that burden has remained upon these two guberniias since the start of the war. Let Your Majesty's fairness decide.[43]

Within a month Sievers received Catherine's personal decree of November 19, 1780, which renewed, on the same basis as before, the assessment of three kopecks per soul for the maintenance of the highway between St. Petersburg and Moscow.[44]

In that same decree the empress called for a description of needed improvements to the highway and a detailed estimate of the costs.[45] In the wake of Sievers's resignation, Governor Protasov of Novgorod responded on November 11, 1781, with a proposal that 249 kilometers of the highway in Novgorod Guberniia be rebuilt, including 110 kilometers along which it would be necessary to sink piles into the soft ground. He estimated that the project would cost 105,425 rubles to complete, plus 26,689 rubles per year for maintenance.[46] When Bruce finally arrived to replace Sievers, he prepared a second response dealing with minimal repairs as opposed to complete reconstruction. Observing that "the road lying between the two capitals is in such bad condition that one can travel only with the greatest difficulty" and that "these problems will increase throughout the coming fall and spring," the new governor-general explained that the three-kopeck-per-soul assessment in Novgorod Guberniia brought in only 7,717 rubles per year with which to maintain 326 kilometers of highway containing many low spots and swampy places. At the same time, wood needed for repairs to the road was becoming scarce and more expensive. Bruce estimated that 13,000 rubles would be needed just to make the road passable for the next summer, and he pointed out that the Senate had twice refused to allow more than the 7,717 rubles to be collected from the landlords.[47]

Just before leaving office in 1784 Bruce requested 44,920 rubles to repair seventy-two bridges along the St. Petersburg–Moscow highway in Novgorod Guberniia.[48] The response was apparently favorable, for a year later Arkharov reported that the repair of wooden bridges along the highway was more than half finished, and he asked permission to use any unexpended funds for improvements to the roadbed.[49]

Finally, in 1786, after the creation of a commission on roads in each guberniia, the state authorized a complete reconstruction of the highway between St. Petersburg and Moscow. In order to pave most of the route with stone in place of increasingly expensive and less durable wood, it ordered the peasants who lived near the road to collect paving stones and deliver them to the construction sites. Instead of corvée, however, the state authorized the hiring of 1,369 laborers in Novgorod Guberniia alone. At the end of the first year Arkharov reported that the work had gone very well.[50] Looking to the future, however, he pointed out that construction would be more difficult and more costly in Novgorod Guberniia than in Tver because of the swampy soil. Nevertheless, more money was actually available in Tver than in Novgorod. He asked permission to combine both sums into one fund under his personal control.[51] The highway still presented difficulties to travelers in the 1790s, but it was in better condition than at any time since its creation. Unfortunately, we have no record of the amount of traffic over the road, since the state did not collect tolls on the road as it did on the waterways.

The only other road to receive more than passing mention in the reports of the governors and governors-general was the new highway from St. Petersburg to Nizhnii Novgorod, which was intended to connect with existing roads to Kazan and Tobolsk. As a replacement for the route through Moscow, the new highway would shorten the distance between St. Petersburg and Ekaterinburg by five hundred kilometers. On its way through nine guberniias it would traverse the most remote section of Novgorod Guberniia, where it would open a direct route from Ustiuzhna through Tikhvin to St. Petersburg. In 1778 Sievers reported that traffic on the new road was already significant, even though the work was far from finished.[52] The following year he noted that the inhabitants of the region were happy to build the road because it promised to double or triple the value of their produce.[53]

A related measure for the improvement of communications through provincial Russia was the expansion of a postal service along the highways. The initial impulse for that effort came from A. P. Rumiantsev, the governor of Malorossiia, who proposed the creation of an extensive postal service in his guberniia in 1764. In 1765 he was authorized to establish nine postal routes over 2,358 kilometers of road, to be served by seventy-two post offices, fifteen postmasters, 165 postmen, and three hundred horses.[54] Later that year the empress ordered the governors of Novgorod and Arkhangel to cooperate in the creation of a rapid postal service along the highways from Arkhangel to St. Petersburg.[55] Just one month later she instructed the governors of Novgorod, Moscow, and Nizhnii Novgorod to appoint postmasters to supervise the postal service between St. Petersburg, Moscow, and points east.[56]

In response to the first of those orders Sievers submitted a detailed outline in September 1766 for the organization and operation of a postal service between St. Petersburg and Arkhangel. In a covering letter to Teplov he bemoaned the isolation and ignorance of provincial Russia and praised Catherine's efforts to improve communications.[57] In May 1768 Sievers proposed that each iam between St. Petersburg and Moscow should have a post office where private letters could be dispatched and received as they were in the two capitals.[58] Four such offices were opened during the next ten years, and in the summer of 1778 the Senate sent Sievers eight thousand rubles to complete the system by establishing fifteen more.[59] In 1781 the Senate authorized postal service on the new highway to the east through Tikhvin and Ustiuzhna. At the same time, Sievers continued to seek a similar authorization for the highway between St. Petersburg and Smolensk, arguing that without postal service the highway through six guberniias lost much of its potential value.[60] The following year Governor Tutolmin of Tver made a similar request regarding the secondary route along the upper Volga, "for the use of merchants and for convenient communications among the guberniias of that region."[61]

All of the evidence on canals, roads, and postal service indicates that Catherine's government made a number of significant improvements. Yet it also shows that in almost every instance these improvements were undertaken as individual projects to be proposed, discussed, authorized, funded, and implemented case by case. In some of the central government's requests for information and proposals and in Sievers's appointment as director of water communications we see significant steps toward the systematization of progress in transportation and communication, but it is only with the accession of Paul that a favorable attitude was transformed into a strategy and that a series of ad hoc decisions was replaced by a genuine program.

Towns

In the Fundamental Law, the Statute on Police, the Charter to the Towns, and other general legislation Catherine expounded a comprehensive program for the development of provincial towns. Provincial administrators supervised the implementation of that program, and they also sought additional, specific improvements to certain towns. They discussed these actions in their correspondence with the central government, and from time to time they reported on the physical development of individual towns.

The city of Tver enjoyed a special relationship with the imperial government. Sievers and Catherine identified it as their favorite provincial town, and they treated it as something of a demonstration project for the development of all provincial towns. Sievers repeatedly declared that its burghers and the nobles of the surrounding countryside were more public-spirited than those he encountered elsewhere, and the natural advantages of its location increased with every improvement to the Vyshnii Volochek System.

When the great fire of May 1763 destroyed the center of Tver, Catherine fed the displaced inhabitants for an entire year at her own expense and appropriated 200,000 rubles for the planning and reconstruction of the gorodskaia district. Another fire in May 1773 led to the planning and reconstruction of the districts across the Volga and Tvertsa rivers. Such an effort was bound to arouse Sievers's enthusiasm, and as early as the summer of 1766 he began to submit his own suggestions for the improvement of Tver.

Contemporary accounts describe the physical transformation of the city as the reconstruction progressed. According to local writer Dmitrii Karmanov, the central district in 1775 contained a commercial market (*gostinyi dvor*) built of stone, numerous public buildings, and one thousand private dwellings arranged in lines along the streets. The latter figure included one hundred houses of brick, and more were under construction. In the other districts the rebuilding had only just begun. As a whole, the city contained nineteen churches built of stone and brick and only ten of wood. The main streets had been paved, and the four sections of the city had been connected by bridges floated on rafts and barges. Karmanov put the population of the city in 1775 at ten thousand.[62]

In 1781 Sievers reported: "There has been much construction in Tver in the past two years."[63] Not long after that, Governor Tutolmin informed the empress that Tver contained 178 houses of stone and 993 houses built of wood upon stone foundations.[64] The Topographical Description of 1784 catalogued 237 houses of stone or brick, 1,044 of wood on stone foundations, and 800 of wood, and it put the total permanent population of the city at 15,095.[65] In 1782 Governor-General Bruce, who had been very critical of conditions in Novgorod, described Tver as "a masterpiece of order, obedience, and exactitude."[66] The city made a similarly favorable impression upon the British traveler William Coxe, who visited it in the 1780s. Among other things, Coxe noted that the state had recently constructed a courthouse, a prison, schools, and residences for the bishop and governor and that it was offering loans to any private citizen who would build a brick house.[67] From all accounts, the transformation of Tver justified Catherine's opinion, expressed in a letter to Baron Friedrich Melchior Grimm: "After St. Petersburg, Tver is the most beautiful city in the empire."[68]

Tver had also become much safer. The wide, regular streets, the stone construction, and the presence of night watchmen, chimneysweeps, and a fire department, as required by the Statute on Police, had greatly reduced the threat of fire. By the 1790s major conflagrations—as common in the wooden towns of Russia as crop failure in the countryside—had become a thing of the past in Tver. The threat of major floods, which had been almost as frequent as major fires, had also been diminished by the dikes that Sievers had erected along the Tvertsa after the serious inundations of 1770, 1771, and 1772.[69]

The physical improvement of Tver and the simultaneous increase in its commerce and prosperity went hand in hand with the rising morale of the inhabitants, which expressed itself in the citizens' enthusiasm for Catherine and in their willingness to cooperate with and to contribute to the improvement of their city. In 1776, at the conclusion of the first elections held under the Fundamental Law, the nobles of Tver Guberniia voted to erect a statue of Catherine in the city and raised 13,283 rubles for that purpose.[70] Dmitrii Karmanov addressed a panegyric to Catherine in 1778 on behalf of the citizens of Tver, and in 1785, in response to the promulgation of the Charter to the Towns, the burghers raised 7,504 rubles to erect a triumphal arch in honor of Catherine, a monument that was subsequently destroyed at the command of her successor.[71]

Although Novgorod's importance as an administrative center surpassed that of Tver before 1776 and equaled it thereafter, its development as a town received much less attention from the government. Resigned to its continuation as the capital of the guberniia, Sievers proposed some modest embellishments to Novgorod in his memorandum of December 9, 1764, and in 1768 he asked the empress for money with which to build masonry houses and shops in the city.[72] Significant improvement did not begin until the confirmation of a plan for the reconstruction of Novgorod in June 1778, fifteen years after Catherine ordered the immediate preparation of plans for all the towns of Russia. The delay may reflect the absence of serious fires in Novgorod during that period, or it may be a measure of the government's lack of concern for the city. Although it was Sievers's only official residence until 1776, he wrote less about Novgorod than he did about several other settlements. In June 1780, however, he reported that there has been "much construction in the city," and he mentioned three hundred new houses, a school, and repairs to the cathedral.[73] Still, it was not until March 1, 1781, that Sievers asked for a subsidy for the reconstruction of Novgorod and Pskov.[74] That spring a fire destroyed twenty-four houses in Novgorod, and on May 20, 1781, the very day on which he tendered his resignation, Sievers asked for a subsidy of one thousand rubles to rebuild the burned-over quarter entirely of brick.[75] He had only recently submitted plans and estimates for the rebuilding of the governor's residence,[76] and it was only after he had retired to his estate in Livonia and was tying up the loose ends of his affairs that he sent to the Senate plans for dikes in Novgorod similar to those he had constructed in Tver.[77]

Soon after his arrival in 1782 Bruce sent Catherine a disparaging report on conditions in the city of Novgorod. He noted some signs of progress but found them few and insufficient. In words that addressed one of Catherine's personal concerns he concluded: "There are absolutely no communications here. Everyone lives in his own lair, and to go to one another means the farthest possible distance and mud up to your knees."[78] The following month he added, in direct contradiction to Sievers's comment of 1780, that there was little building going on in Novgorod.[79] According to the *Geographical Dictionary*, Novgorod in 1782 contained more than thirteen hundred houses, forty-two of which were built of brick.[80] Estimates of its population at that time range from 7,000 to 11,500.[81]

For the smaller uezd centers, the pattern that emerges from the reports of the governors-general resembles that of the guberniia capitals. In virtually every instance the settlements that excited Sievers's interest in the 1760s flourished under continuing attention from the government while the others experienced less development and received less attention. The law treated all provincial towns alike, but the state's officials understood that some had significant prospects for improvement that others would never match.

When a serious fire destroyed much of Torzhok in 1766, Catherine provided fifty thousand rubles in interest-free loans to help the inhabitants rebuild their homes and their businesses. Sievers supervised the implementation of the urban plan and reported that forty townsmen had agreed to build houses of brick or stone.[82] By the early 1780s Torzhok contained eighty-three houses of masonry construction and 1,792 dwellings of all kinds.[83] In both categories it ranked second to Tver. Had it not been situated so close to that city, Torzhok would almost certainly have become the capital of a guberniia.

Staraia Russa, the second city in Novgorod Guberniia after the reorganization of 1776, had been destroyed by fire in 1763. Catherine provided ten thousand rubles in interest-free loans for its reconstruction, and the reopening of the saltworks in 1764 strengthened the local economy.[84] Between 1761 and the mid-1780s its population (in round figures) increased from eight thousand to twelve thousand.[85] In 1780 Sievers reported that agreements had been signed for the building of twenty-four brick houses and 250 wooden houses on stone foundations. Forty stalls had been erected in the reconstructed market, and another eighty had been agreed upon.[86] By the 1780s Staraia Russa contained about 1,100 dwellings of all kinds.[87]

The development of Vyshnii Volochek, Ostashkov, Borovichi, and Valdai, the four settlements that Sievers had converted into towns after seven years of struggle, justified his expectations for them. Vyshnii Volochek grew from two thousand inhabitants in 1773, when it became a town, to three thousand in 1783 and to four thousand in 1795.[88] Undoubtedly, much of the increase was due to the expansion of traffic along the waterways and the St. Petersburg–Moscow highway. Catherine's decree of April 2, 1773, offered immunity from taxes for five years to anyone who would build a house of stone or brick in Vyshnii Volochek, and by 1782, 14 of its 804 dwellings were of brick.[89] The pace of masonry construction increased rapidly in the last two decades of the century, and by 1800 Vyshnii Volochek contained 303 houses of brick or stone.[90]

Tutolmin's report of 1782 on masonry construction in Tver Guberniia referred only to Tver, Torzhok, and Vyshnii Volochek. By 1783, however, Ostashkov contained 3 masonry houses and 159 dwellings of wood on stone foundations out of a total of 890; another 3 houses of masonry and 110 of wood on stone foundations were under construction.[91] A marketplace of masonry construction containing 102 stalls was opened in Ostashkov in 1788.[92] Between 1770 and 1783 the male population of Ostashkov increased from 1,846 to 3,078, but it ceased to grow thereafter and stood at only 3,024 in 1795.[93]

Borovichi in Novgorod Guberniia witnessed an increase in its male population from 773 to 2,574 between 1770 and 1783.[94] In that year Bruce recorded a favorable impression of Borovichi, noting that it enjoyed, in addition to its wharf and the work provided by the rapids of the Msta, a rather enterprising merchantry. He noted that 248 houses had been built in accordance with the urban plan and that 9 of them were brick.[95] Later in the decade Borovichi contained 16 houses of brick, 317 of wood on stone foundations, and 373 of wood.[96]

Sievers found the inhabitants of Valdai poorer than those of the other three settlements he had converted into towns. In 1783, however, Bruce reported that Valdai boasted 14 houses of brick and 226 of wood on stone foundations, totals that rivaled those of Vyshnii Volochek and surpassed those of Ostashkov and Borovichi.[97] In his *Journey from St. Petersburg to Moscow* Radishchev railed against Valdai as a notorious center of prostitution, an activity that may have accounted for the rapid increase in its wealth once it escaped the control of the church and the College of Economy. During his visit in 1783 Bruce concurred with the townsmen on the need to pave the large square in front of the major church and on a site for more brick houses with arcades and shops beneath.[98]

The town of Kargopol, located in Olonets Guberniia after the introduction of the Fundamental Law, provides a good example of a settlement that was too poor to be transformed into the state's conception of a real town. Sievers arrived there in July 1766 to organize the town's reconstruction after a disastrous fire. Showing the inhabitants the plan prepared by the state architects and confirmed by the empress, he asked them to choose building lots and sign agreements to erect the kinds of dwellings prescribed for those lots. The citizens, however, responded that they were too poor to build even stone foundations and that the retail merchants could not afford stone shops. Believing them, Sievers did not insist on strict adherence to the building code. In December 1771 he reported only that Kargopol had been completely rebuilt with straight streets.[99]

Rzhev, on the other hand, offers an interesting example of a very different kind. In the 1760s its merchants possessed more capital than those of Tver, and by 1783 it was the third largest town in its guberniia, after Tver and Torzhok. However, Tutolmin's report of 1782 on masonry construction indicates that no brick houses had been built there, and the reports of the governors-general are strangely silent about the development of a town 50 percent larger than Vyshnii Volochek, one whose merchants played a crucial role in the increasingly important trade between the Ukraine and St. Petersburg. We know that Old Believers founded Rzhev and that they remained especially numerous there and in the nearby town of Zubtsov. It may be that they were largely responsible for both the commercial vitality and the urban conservatism of those settlements. The state associated commercial enterprise with a westernized bourgeoisie and with towns that were modern in eighteenth-century terms, and because it believed that these characteristics were necessary complements, it presumed that the vitality of a town could be determined from its outward appearance, the way a patient's health could be determined from his temperature. However valid that assumption may have been for St. Petersburg or Torzhok, it obviously did not hold for Rzhev.

The twelve remaining towns of Tver and Novgorod guberniias—Staritsa, Kashin, Kaliazin, Bezhetsk, Krasnyi Kholm, and Vyshegonsk in Tver, and Tikhvin, Kirilov, Cherepovets, Krestets, Beloozero, and Ustiuzhna in Novgorod—engendered fewer expectations and received less attention from the state than the larger settlements. They were intended to serve as administrative centers and local markets, and most of them should be classed with Kargopol rather than Staraia Russa or Vyshnii Volochek. Tikhvin and Ustiuzhna were the most promising of the lot, but they were out of the way in the remote eastern end of Novgorod Guberniia. They would experience significant development in the nineteenth century as a result of increased traffic along the new highway through that region and the opening of new waterways between the Volga and the Neva. In the autumn of 1783, however, Bruce passed through Ustiuzhna, Cherepovets, Valdai, and Borovichi, and although he informed Catherine of encouraging improvements in the latter two towns, he had nothing at all to say about Ustiuzhna or Cherepovets. Sievers visited Beloozero in March 1776 and reported that its inhabitants "resemble those of Novgorod with respect to poverty and indolence. I found little change there since my first visit."[100]

Although Sievers tended to ignore the less promising of the newer settlements, he made an exception in 1778, when the inhabitants of Krestets agreed to build 22 houses of masonry construction and 260 of wood upon stone foundations. In a burst of enthusiasm Sievers wrote the empress: "This will seem unbelievable to Your Majesty. In three years the town will be a match for others without a kopeck of encouragement—just my good words and their good will."[101] In that instance, however, Sievers's enthusiasm was misplaced: Krestets failed to become a genuine town, and, like Kirilov, Cherpovets, and Krasnyi Kholm, it was disestablished in the 1790s.

Catherine liked to give the impression that her government had created hundreds of towns like Tver and Torzhok and Ostashkov. On the other hand, historians hostile to Catherine, having helped to perpetuate the myth of the "Potemkin village," have emphasized the failure of towns like Krestets and Krasnyi Kholm in order to demonstrate the disparity between Catherine's claims and her accomplishments.[102] The truth in this instance does not lie between the two extremes; it encompasses them both. Where the settlements converted into towns had some vitality of their own, the state's assistance and guidance produced undeniable improvement. That condition was met in many cases, but it was not and could not be found throughout provincial Russia.

Public Institutions

Among her efforts to bring civilization to the provinces of Russia Catherine included the establishment of public institutions intended to contribute to the welfare of society. Chapter Twenty-five of the Fundamental Law identified eight such institutions that were to be founded in all provinces of the empire: schools, orphanages, hospitals, poorhouses, lazar houses, insane asylums, workhouses, and jails. The Fundamental Law described those institutions in some detail and assigned responsibility for creating and operating them to the boards of public welfare in each guberniia. The experience of Novgorod and Tver guberniias illustrates the difficulties that the boards and other agencies encountered in fulfilling that directive.

The only schools to be found in Novgorod Guberniia before the introduction of the Fundamental Law were the Cadet Academy in Novaia Ladoga and the ecclesiastical seminaries in Novgorod, Tver, and Pskov. The latter offered some possibilities for the expansion of public education. The son of a poor townsman, Dmitrii Karmanov received an education at the seminary in Tver in the 1750s, but only because he made such a great impression on his teachers that they were willing to translate books into Russian for him to read. The new rector of the seminary, Makarii Petrovich, favored instruction in Russian, and he himself taught philosophy and theology in that language. Later, Karmanov and one of his teachers, Arsenii Vereshchagin, wrote a pamphlet, "The Plea of the Children of Merchants and Others," in which they argued the necessity of educating more young laymen at the seminaries by broadening the curriculum and by teaching in Russian.[103] But although Catherine transferred 17,268 rubles from the College of Economy to the seminary in Tver to replace the building destroyed in the great fire and appropriated 2,000 rubles to create a library for the seminary in Novgorod,[104] she made no concerted effort to convert them into institutions for the education of the broader public.

Seminaries could play an important role in the enlightenment of Russia, but they could not meet the nation's need for literate nobles and townsmen. The nobles themselves perceived the need for schools in the provinces. In their nakazy to the Legislative Commission the nobles of several uezds complained that their sons' inability to obtain decent educations limited their usefulness to the fatherland—a tactful way of saying that it confined them to the lowest ranks in the army and bureaucracy and virtually guaranteed that the sons of poor noblemen would remain poor. The solution, as they saw it, was for the state to open schools for young noblemen in the provinces and to support them financially.[105] In the case of townsmen, the call for schools and education came almost entirely from officials of the imperial government. In contrast to the urban nakazy of 1767, which expressed almost no interest in that subject, the members of Catherine's Commission on Commerce saw the education of young townsmen as an essential means of molding the bourgeoisie or third estate that they believed Russia needed.[106] In his memorandum of December 9, 1764, Sievers recommended that a gymnasium and a high school be opened in every major city for the children of nobles and burghers, with grammar schools in all the lesser towns. A few years later he insisted: "Schools in the towns are an absolute necessity."[107] Although they disagreed on particulars, the members of the Partial Commission on Schools also agreed in principle that Russia needed a national system of primary and secondary education.[108]

In July 1775, while Catherine was hard at work on the Fundamental Law, Sievers suggested that every governor be ordered to open primary schools in the towns of his guberniia. He assured her that he could do so in all twenty towns of Novgorod Guberniia for less than five thousand rubles.[109] Instead, article 384 of the Fundamental Law assigned to the boards of public welfare the responsibility for endeavoring (*starat'sia*) to establish primary schools in all towns and then, when that had been accomplished, in the more populous villages of the state peasants. Enrollment would be voluntary, and fees would be assessed on a sliding scale according to the parents' income, with the children of the poor admitted free. The pupils were to be taught reading, writing, arithmetic, drawing, and the Orthodox catechism.

The report of the board of public welfare of Tver Guberniia for the years 1776–1779 indicates that it ranked the creation of elementary schools as its highest priority and that it tackled the problem with a greater sense of urgency than the language of article 384 required. The board claimed to have opened elementary schools in all the towns of Tver Guberniia by the end of 1777, with the result that two hundred pupils were enrolled in Tver, sixty in Kaliazin, forty in Kashin, thirty in Bezhetsk, twenty-five in Vyshegonsk, thirty-five in Vyshnii Volochek, forty in Ostashkov, one hundred in Rzhev, thirty in Staritsa, thirty in Zubtsov, and two hundred in Torzhok. The report stated that the schools were open to children of merchants and meshchane and that the pupils studied reading, writing, drawing, world history, and the Orthodox catechism. Examinations were held at the end of June, and the better graduates could go on to the high school in Tver to study German, geography, and bookkeeping. The board would also arrange apprenticeships for the sons of meshchane.[110]

That article 384 of the Fundamental Law, plus the initiative of the board of public welfare, could lead to the creation of eleven schools for 790 pupils by 1779 engenders skepticism. So do the round numbers ending in 5's and 0's. On the other hand, historian Vladimir Kolosov used a different, unidentified source to determine that a school for the children of burghers was opened in Tver in 1776 and that similar schools appeared in all the other towns of Tver Guberniia in the following year. On June 3, 1779, Sievers informed Catherine: "Eight hundred burghers attend the new schools. Every town has one."[111]

An alternative to total acceptance or total rejection of the achievements claimed by the board of public welfare in Tver can be constructed from information provided by Governor-General Bruce about the board of public welfare in Novgorod. In the first of two reports written in August and October 1782 Bruce informed the empress that, to his surprise, the board of public welfare "has nothing but two rooms in the old governor's house where several people are being taught to read." In the second he explained: "A school for teaching Russian reading and writing exists in Novgorod and the other towns, but no special buildings have been constructed to house them."[112] Bruce's remarks suggest that the schools in Tver Guberniia were probably classes provided by one or two teachers and that the number of pupils was considerably smaller than Sievers and the board of public welfare had claimed. The latter inference is strengthened by a question that Sievers raised with the empress in March 1781 when asking for guidance on a number of problems: "Final question: what means should be employed to oblige the inhabitants of towns to build schools and to send their children to them. Your Majesty in her wisdom will find a compromise between compulsion and free will."[113] An achievement in popular education that was very modest and tenuous but nonetheless real would also correspond with the state's accomplishments in other aspects of provincial development.

The grammar schools opened immediately after the introduction of the Fundamental Law were absorbed into the national school system created in 1786. At that time Catherine's general injunction to the boards of public welfare was superseded by a direct order to the governors-general. In December of that year Arkharov replied: "I have received Your Imperial Majesty's order of August 12 regarding the preparation of everything necessary for the opening in Tver and Novgorod guberniias on the twenty-second of September of high schools in the guberniia capitals and of lower public schools in several of the towns."[114] That the central administration gave the governor-general only forty days to prepare for the opening of as many as forty schools in two guberniias suggests that the task involved a reorganization of schools already in existence rather than their creation *ab novo*. In that sense both the direct order to the governors-general and the educational statute of August 15, 1786, bespoke a more thorough and carefully prepared effort to provide the provinces with schools. So did the activities of Catherine's Commission for the Establishment of Public Schools, which had been at work for several years prior to 1786 training teachers, printing textbooks, and preparing a unified curriculum.[115] Even so, Arkharov's reference to "several of the towns" reveals the continuing problem of finding qualified teachers and willing pupils and weakens the contention of some historians that Catherine made a conscious (and presumably free) decision to limit the spread of education by failing to open schools in the villages and make attendance compulsory (as Joseph II had done in Austria).[116] The limited objectives of Catherine's educational statute reflect a realistic assessment of the state's capabilities rather than an ideological decision to exclude peasants. The schools were open to children of all classes, and approximately one-third of the pupils who enrolled were peasants.[117]

Sievers's role in creating schools for the sons of poor nobles was more overt and more dramatic than his involvement in the education of young townsmen. As he introduced the Fundamental Law into the guberniias assigned to him, Sievers took the lead in persuading the assembled landowners to contribute money for the support of a school for the young noblemen of their guberniia. In every instance he received a favorable response: the nobles agreed to assess themselves several kopecks per revision soul to build and operate such schools. As usual, Tver was to provide the prototype. In January 1779 the 434 nobles who attended Tver's assembly agreed unanimously to contribute ten kopecks per revision soul for the construction of a school and five kopecks per revision soul for its maintenance. With 122,547 revision souls in the guberniia, Sievers calculated that five kopecks for each one would enable the board of public welfare to provide two hundred young noblemen with free tuition, room, and board.[118] Informing Count A. R. Vorontsov of the nobles' decision, Sievers wrote: "I hope that in a few years I shall see at Tver an institute for 200 young noblemen supported by the nobility."[119] A few months later he described the nobles' school in Tver to Catherine as "the most evident proof of the effect that the new institutions have had on morals and morale."[120]

In his enthusiasm Sievers underestimated both the costs of operating the nobles' schools and the opposition that his schemes would arouse in St. Petersburg. Sievers's hopes for the schools were founded on the assumption that the assessments voted by the nobles' assemblies would be binding on all landowners in the guberniia in accordance with the precedent set in connection with the construction and repair of roads. The Senate, however, objected to granting the assemblies the power to levy what amounted to taxes. Catherine supported the Senate on the general principle but tempered the effect of her decision in the case of the nobles' school in Tver by offering a subsidy of ten thousand rubles a year and by allowing Sievers to use the money already contributed to erect a monument to her.[121] That, plus money contributed voluntarily by the nobles, would have to suffice. Consequently, when the school opened in makeshift quarters in July 1779, Sievers found that he could admit only 120 students rather than the 200 he had predicted.[122] In October 1780 Sievers told Catherine that her ruling against compulsory assessments threatened the very existence of the school.[123]

To make matters worse, the nobles' school in Tver and the prospect that more like it would be founded in other guberniias provoked the enmity of Ivan Betskoi, who saw Sievers's activities as a threat to his own ambitions to control schools and education throughout Russia. The dispute became entangled with Sievers's marital difficulties, and Betskoi used those problems to discredit the governor-general with the empress, who ignored Sievers's requests for additional subsidies to the school.[124] Sievers kept the school operating in spare rooms in the survey office and in the governor's palace by using the money designated for school building to supplement the insufficient contributions from the nobles.

In February 1781 he again asked the empress for 20,000 rubles for a building and a perpetual subsidy of 7,000–8,000 rubles per year. His request outlines the conditions undoubtedly faced by all governors-general: "Of all the subjects that require my attention, the most interesting of my concerns and the one for which I have the strongest feeling is the nobles' school in Tver."[125] He pointed out that the guberniia contained a total of 980 young noblemen, of whom 271 were below the age of seven and 174 were above the age of fourteen. Of the remaining 535, only 136 had parents who could afford to educate them at their own expense; 138 were currently enrolled in the school at Tver, and another 261 sought admittance. Those fortunate enough to be admitted studied Russian, French,

German, geography, mathematics, drawing, and dance. Knowing Catherine, Sievers added that their health and morals received as much attention as their minds.[126] Catherine's response was swift and negative. Less than two weeks after requesting the subsidy, Sievers wrote again to, acknowledge receipt of her decision. He thanked the empress for having agreed to some of his requests but regretted that they could not compensate him for the loss of the nobles' school in Tver, for which he would gladly have sacrificed the other favors she had granted him. In what he had promised would be his last plea on behalf of the school, Sievers reminded the empress that many of the pupils were in rags and that they had no hope of obtaining an education elsewhere. He pointed out that there were 980 young noblemen in Tver, 1,200 in Novgorod, and 800 in Pskov whose lives and talents should not be wasted for want of schooling.[127]

Denied a subsidy in spite of his pleas, Sievers supported the school with the money that the nobles had raised for a monumental statue of Catherine. His successor, Bruce, apparently unaware that Catherine had given Sievers permission to spend that money on the school, reported Sievers's last-ditch effort to save the school as though it were an improper use of public funds. He informed the empress that all of the money had been spent and that the teachers had not been paid for the last three months. Now faced with the prospect of closing the school and sending the pupils home, Bruce concluded: "I await your Imperial Highness's order."[128]

The school was not closed. Catherine provided money to keep it open for another year or two, after which it was reorganized under the nobles' association founded in accordance with the Charter to the Nobility. The details of its rescue and continued operation are unclear, but the Economic Observations of 1825 listed among the public buildings of Tver "a nobles' school founded on June 28, 1779."[129] A smaller school founded in Novgorod in 1780 also managed to survive, but the plan to open a similar school in Pskov failed for lack of money.[130]

A few foundling homes and orphanages were established in northwestern Russia before the introduction of the provincial reform of 1775. In Novgorod Sievers supported foundlings at his own expense during his first years as governor, but the results were discouraging. In 1769 he reported that nineteen of the twenty-one foundlings he had tried to save had died. The other two had been transferred at the age of three to the Vospitatel'nyi Dom in Moscow.[131] In the early 1770s Sievers worked with Betskoi, whom he described to the empress as "ce bon père des orpheiins," to establish a branch of the Vospitatel'nyi Dom in Novgorod.[132] The Vashkalov family provided for the establishment of another branch of the Vospitatel'nyi Dom in Olonets in 1772, and in the following year the town magistracy of Ostashkov established yet another in response to criticism from the Senate that abandoned children in that town were being left to die without care. In the town of Beloozero a merchant by the name of Karak'ev opened a branch of the Vospitatel'nyi Dom in his own house in 1775.[133]

The evidence from northwestern Russia indicates that the creation of orphanages after 1775 followed much the same pattern as the creation of primary schools. Article 385 of the Fundamental Law ordered the boards of public welfare to establish and maintain orphanages or foundling homes in all the towns with sufficient need for them and elsewhere to provide for the care of abandoned children in the homes of foster parents. In northwestern Russia the boards moved with surprising speed on this issue, but their efforts fell short of full compliance with the letter of the law. In a report on its activities from 1776 through 1779 the board of public welfare of Tver Guberniia claimed that it had opened poorhouses and orphanages in all the towns of that guberniia by the end of 1777.[134] That statement was subsequently clarified by Sievers's report of June 3, 1779, in which he informed the empress that every town in Tver Guberniiia contained a poorhouse that also accepted foundlings.[135] The one exception, according to Kolosov, was the city of Tver, which in 1777 supported a genuine orphanage in a separate building.[136] However, Bruce's report of October 1782 on the board of public welfare in Novgorod Guberniia observed that in the city of Novgorod abandoned children were still being placed in foster homes (otvedennye domy).[137] Later, after the board in Tver had taken time to revise the makeshift arrangements of the 1770s, the orphanage in Tver became the guberniia orphanage, and foundlings from the uezd towns were sent there when (and if) they reached the age of six. That arrangement paralleled the system of major and minor schools prescribed by the school statute of 1786.

With the promulgation of the school statute of 1786, Catherine also began to bring the educational practices of the orphanages into line with those of the public schools. Thus, when Governor-General A. P. Mel'gunov of Iaroslavl reported to Catherine in 1786 that some private citizens there had raised thirty thousand rubles to build and maintain an orphanage, she stipulated that the money be donated to the board of public welfare so that the donors' intentions would be carried out in a manner approved by the state. She also enjoined the governor-general and the board of public welfare to ensure that the children were educated "in accordance with the regulations of the Commission for the Establishment of Public Schools and the methods it has prescribed."[138]

The report of the board of public welfare, Sievers, and the historian Kolosov agree that poorhouses for both males and females were operating in all the towns of Tver Guberniia by 1779.[139] However, in his report on the board of public welfare in Novgorod Governor-General Bruce noted that no new poorhouse had been built in that city; consequently, men and women were still being sent to the old one.[140] Although we can not be certain, Bruce's information suggests that in at least some instances the board of public welfare in Tver may simply have taken over poor-houses that were already functioning, perhaps under the authority of the town magistracies.

The other public institutions authorized by Chapter Twenty-Five of the Fundamental Law received far less attention from the boards of public welfare in Tver and Novgorod guberniias. Tver had a hospital with forty beds by 1777, and Novgorod had a hospital by 1782, but none existed in the smaller towns.[141] In Novgorod some individuals were admitted to what was called a workhouse, but, according to Bruce, they were lodged without work in a tower of the kremlin awaiting the construction of a proper facility. Bruce also pointed out that no homes for the incurably ill, for patients with contagious diseases, or for the insane existed in the city of Novgorod or in any of the uezd towns.[142] None of those institutions had been established in Tver Guberniia as of 1779 or even 1825.

In his history of social welfare in Russia, published in 1818, A. Stog called Catherine the originator of a generalized, nationwide system of social welfare.[143] His claim is justified in the sense that Catherine created permanent agencies with authority and resources and charged them with combatting ignorance and misery in every guberniia of the empire. But those achievements should not be interpreted to mean that the state itself assumed responsibility for such efforts. The autocracy put up "seed money" with its one-time grant of fifteen thousand rubles and with special grants for the construction of schools; the governors-general provided supervision and occasional assistance; and the governors offered leadership as chairmen of the boards of public welfare. But the members of those boards were the marshals of the nobility, the heads of the urban corporations, and the judges of the guberniia class courts, and most of the funding was to come from the general public in the form of charitable contributions. Catherine's government directed, organized, and encouraged the development of socially useful institutions; unlike the government of Joseph II, however, it would not insist that they be made to function in the face of public indifference or hostility. Beyond the problems of finding qualified doctors and teachers, the boards of public welfare had to find patients and pupils and financial support in the local communities.

Popular support for the institutions entrusted to the boards of public welfare varied enormously from one locality to another. Sievers was distressed by the problem of inducing townsmen to take advantage of the classes offered in the smaller towns of Tver Guberniia. In the city of Tver, on the other hand, when the burghers set out in 1786 to raise a thousand rubles to support a public high school, they collected fifteen hundred rubles in contributions.[144] Formal medical care drew the same mixed reactions. In their nakazy of 1767, for example, the townsmen of Iurev Polskii and Epifan argued that there should be a professional doctor in every town, but the townsmen of Uglich objected to having to support a doctor because no one except noblemen ever consulted physicians.[145]

Such differences of attitude underlie Stog's data on the cumulative increase in the capital of the boards of public welfare. At the rate of 15,000 rubles per guberniia, the state's contribution to the boards of public welfare would have totaled 750,000 rubles by the end of Catherine's reign. According to Stog, however, their total capital as of 1803 amounted to 5,486,360 rubles in assignats, 786,820 rubles in silver, 31,630 rubles worth of German thaler, and 7,857 rubles worth of high-carat gold.[146] So impressive a total demonstrates that the 30,000 rubles donated to build an orphanage in Iaroslavl was far from an isolated example of private philanthropy. Yet a breakdown of the total would also show that philanthropic sentiments were not distributed uniformly throughout the empire. To cite only the most extreme example, by 1786 the capital of the board of public welfare of St. Petersburg had grown to 444,337 rubles while that of the board of public welfare in Olonets Guberniia remained at 15,000 rubles, the identical amount it had received from the state in 1777.[147]

Industry and Commerce

Catherine's government did not consider industrial output a significant index of national development. Although the empress and her advisers accepted the fact that large-scale industrial production was advantageous to some branches of the economy, such as metallurgy and glassmaking, they remained suspicious and even fearful of factories. Catherine thought it desirable that every town contain a factory or two of moderate size to provide employment for surplus labor and to create a market for primary producers, but she wanted to avoid the concentration of industry in any one location.[148] Having observed in her disparaging appraisal of Moscow that "one must not overlook the number of large factories which create an excessive accumulation of workingmen," she herself would not fail to note their connection with the outbreak of bubonic plague in that city or their contribution to the "plague riot" of 1771.[149] The government also knew that the metal workers of the Urals were one of the most continuously discontented and insurrectionary groups within the empire.

On another level the empress questioned the suitability of large-scale manufacturing to the Russian economy. She thought that in some cases it might be appropriate to new industries that produced primarily for the foreign market, but she feared that it would dislocate existing modes of production within the domestic market.[150] When considering the applications of foreigners who sought to open factories in Russia, the government frequently denied permission unless it was reasonably certain that the new enterprises would not compete with established producers. In at least one instance the College of Manufacturing stated openly its opinion that factories which required large numbers of workers throughout the year represented a threat to agriculture whereas small factories and handicraft production provided a desirable complement to agriculture.[151]

Although the Russian Empire as a whole experienced some significant industrial development during the reign of Catherine II, most of that growth occurred in the Urals or in the central industrial region in and around Moscow and extending southward to Tula. Northwestern Russia, on the other hand, contained few enterprises employing more than fifty workers. With regard to iron production, for example, S. G. Strumilin has demonstrated that the number of blast furnaces in Russia doubled between 1760 and 1800 and that the production of iron and pig iron rose 270 percent in those four decades, which suggests large facilities.[152] In the northwest, however, iron was still produced in limited quantities at small works located in the remote eastern end of Novgorod Guberniia, where the industry received virtually no attention from the governors and governors-general.

By the 1780s and 1790s northwestern Russia supported only a few large industrial enterprises. In 1761 Tver's largest employer had been a rope walk with thirteen workers; by the 1780s several enterprises of moderate size were established there, including a linen mill and a glassworks owned by the merchant Tatarinsov that employed fifty-five workers.[153] In Novgorod the state actively promoted large enterprises in order to provide employment and strengthen the faltering economy of that city. In his memorandum of December 9, 1764, Sievers asked Catherine for permission to offer an interest-free loan to anyone who would build a tannery in Novgorod.[154] The merchant Fedor Ulasov expressed interest in such a venture but subsequently withdrew from the discussion. Seeking another entrepreneur, Sievers concluded a successful agreement with Semen Ivanskii, who opened a large tannery in 1767. The tannery prospered, and by 1775, when he was elected Glava of the city, Ivanskii had become Novgorod's richest merchant.[155] More directly, at Catherine's instigation the Admiralty moved its sailcloth factory from Moscow to Novgorod, where it resumed operation on January 3, 1780.[156] A privately owned brickyard employing one hundred workers opened in Novgorod in 1785.[157]

The saltworks in Staraia Russa, established in the 1670s to supply the state salt monopoly, closed in 1753 after the original deposits ran out. Soon after Catherine's accession the Academy of Sciences sent Professor Lehmann to Staraia Russa to search for new deposits. His success led to the reopening of the works in 1764. In his memorandum of December 9, 1764, Sievers informed the empress that the saltworks at Staraia Russa, "which are so important to the treasury and to the neighboring provinces," could be greatly expanded if Lehmann made further discoveries during the next summer.[158] Lehmann located important new deposits of salt along the Shelon River, and by the early 1770s the saltworks' production reached 50,000 or 60,000 puds (1 pud = 36 pounds or 16.33 kilograms) per year.[159] By the 1780s the saltworks employed more than twenty salaried officials and more than one hundred wage laborers.[160]

The output of individual craftsmen and small-scale manufacturing, though virtually impossible to quantify, must certainly have increased more rapidly than that of industrial enterprises. In his study of the towns of northwestern Russia Iu. V. Klokman discovered a dramatic increase in the number of smithies, tanneries, rendering plants, and other enterprises employing fewer than ten workers.[161] In addition to Ivanskii's large tannery, seven smaller ones operated in the city of Novgorod in the 1780s.[162] In Tver the percentage of craftsmen (tsekhovnye and remeslennye) in the city's population rose from 31.7 in 1765 to 42.8 in 1785.[163] In the 1780s the town of Ostashkov was home to a total of 574 craftsmen, including 90 smiths and 100 bootmakers.[164] Given the increase in small-scale production in the towns, the elimination of monopolies and similar restraints on producers, the low productivity of agriculture, and the prevalence of obrok in the great majority of the uezds under Sievers's authority, one can logically infer a significant increase in peasant manufacturing and handicrafts, but reliable, quantitative data are lacking. The state could neither control nor count such scattered, unfocused activities, and both its awareness of them and its encouragement of them were necessarily indirect.

One gratifying index of economic development to which the Russian government paid considerable attention was the growth of merchant commerce, which could be monitored by the magistracies and merchant guilds. In Tver the number of families engaged in trade and commerce rose from 343 in 1765 to 533 by 1785, and the number of families "trading at the port" rose during that same period from 49 to 80.[165] The merchants of Novgorod were also growing in number and wealth. Following Catherine's reorganization of the merchantry in 1775, the magistracy of Novgorod registered 188 merchants with a total of 84,939 rubles of capital; by 1786 the city was home to 360 merchants with a combined capital of 237,576 rubles.[166] Most of the heightened commercial activity in the guberniias of Tver and Novgorod centered around commodities such as grain, hemp, lard, hides, and timber, in their natural or processed forms. The merchants of the northwest largely acted as middlemen between buyers in the northwestern provinces or in St. Petersburg and producers in other regions. In 1768, for example, Sievers informed the empress that the merchants of Rzhev had subscribed 200,000 rubles for the purchase of Ukrainian grain and hemp that they planned to sell in St. Petersburg.[167]

The greatest stimulus to the commerce of northwestern Russia and to the general economy of that region came from the pull of St. Petersburg. According to Heinrich Storch, Russia's foreign trade increased by more than 500 percent between 1760 and 1797.[168] During that same period the population of St. Petersburg rose from 90,000 to 300,000. The growth of exports and urban consumption created an enormous demand for the products of northwestern Russia and for products from other regions that had to be transported through northwestern Russia to the benefit of its laborers and merchants. Improvements to the canals and the roads reduced the physical obstacles between the producers of the interior and the wharves and markets of St. Petersburg while changes in the laws reduced the man-made barriers to trade.

The government also acted to stimulate economic activity by putting more money into circulation and by making credit available to businessmen. Before 1768 Sievers had argued that a shortage of gold and silver coins in the provinces constrained and discouraged commerce. He urged Catherine to issue bank notes and cited the beneficial effect of bank notes on the economies of Denmark, Sweden, and England.[169] In the summer of 1768, having requested and received permission to lend state funds to merchants as a means of expanding commerce and production, Sievers proposed that banks be established for that purpose.[170] In that same year the empress made favorable mention of banks and credit in article 329 of her *Instruction* to the Legislative Commission: "In many states banks are established with good success, which by their credit, having established new signs of value, have increased the circulation in those states." On December 29, 1768, the Assignats Bank opened in Moscow, and by the end of 1769 it had put 2,600,000 rubles worth of bank notes into circulation.[171] In 1772 Sievers mentioned in a report to the empress that assignats were being accepted in his guberniia at their face value.[172] The government's subsequent misuse of bank notes to finance its wars and debts through a form of inflation is well known, but the words of Catherine and Sievers indicate that their original purpose was to stimulate and facilitate commerce. In his autobiographical memoir to Alexander's minister of the interior Sievers proudly claimed credit for inspiring the creation of the Assignats Bank and the circulation of bank notes, but he hastened to emphasize that the latter had not lost any of their value at the time he left office.[173]

In 1778 the empress extended for another four years Sievers's authority to lend state funds to merchants, but the governor-general continued to press for banks in the provinces. Finally, in 1780 he received word that the state was preparing to open banks in several provincial towns, including Novgorod and Pskov. Sievers was pleased but characteristically unsatisfied. He wrote Viazemskii of his pleasure and assured him that a banking office in Novgorod would be extremely useful to the commerce along the waterways and to the many employees on the state payroll. Then he pointed out that, although the bank in Pskov would not be useless, it would be less beneficial there than in Tver, "where water communications and the highway require the exchange of an incredible amount of money." Finally, he proposed that a bank with 200,000 rubles in capital be opened in the capital of every guberniia and that as much as 25,000,000 rubles in assignats be lent to merchants and noblemen in order to stimulate the economy throughout the provinces.[174] Just two days later Sievers suggested to the empress that a bank would be very useful to the economy of Velikie Luki, an uezd town in Pskov Guberniia.[175] In banking, as in so many subjects, Catherine's government took important, pathbreaking strides in the direction that Sievers wanted to go, but it would not or could not move as fast or as far as he desired.

Natural Resources and Agriculture

In the territories administered by Sievers, Bruce, and Akharov the state did comparatively little to improve the cultivation and exploitation of the earth. In his memorandum of December 9, 1764, under the heading "On Lands, Woods, Peat, Coal, the Rural Economy, and a Society of Economy or Agriculture," Sievers discussed the need to conserve the forests, the possibility of mining coal, and the desirability of improving agriculture. Except for the saltworks at Staraia Russa, he and his successors confined their interest in primary extraction to those three objectives; they accorded them a relatively low priority; and they achieved little or no success.

Forests played a crucial role in the economy of northwestern Russia, providing commodities and products with a multitude of uses and even helping, as Sievers noted, to regulate the flow of water in the streams and canals. For that reason he and his successors repeatedly expressed concern over the rapid deforestation of the areas close to the towns and trade routes. In the memorandum of December 9, 1764, Sievers complained that the excessive consumption of wood by St. Petersburg was depleting the forests of Novgorod Guberniia.[176] Thirteen years later he informed the empress that the shortage of wood was growing more acute and that the price of wood had jumped 300–400 percent in the past ten years. Later that same year he pointed out that the rising cost of wood was creating serious problems for all trade requiring boats and barges and for the rebuilding of towns and villages in accordance with the plans prepared by the state.[177] Subsequently, both Bruce and Arkharov blamed the growing scarcity and rising price of wood for hindering their efforts to repair the highway between St. Petersburg and Moscow.

In 1764 Sievers called for the appointment of foresters to supervise the forests and regulate their use. Such methods, he argued, had achieved considerable success in Prussia, Holstein, and certain provinces of France.[178] However, once he became better acquainted with the Russian provinces and with the weakness of state supervision there, he abandoned that proposal. Peter the Great had created the post of senior forester at the Admiralty and had called for the appointment of local nobles to serve as foresters in each uezd, but neither measure had proven effective.[179] The nobles' nakazy of 1767 also complained about deforestation and the state's failure to deal successfully with that problem, but their preferred solution was to prohibit commoners and especially manufacturers from cutting timber and to commission local noblemen to see that such prohibitions were enforced. Only the nakazy of Ruza and Pskov mentioned the planting of trees and the management of forest resources, and only that of Ruza, an uezd in Moscow Guberniia, called for a state program of forest management.[180]

A decree dated September 22, 1782, removed the forests from the jurisdiction of the Admiralty and entrusted them to the control of individual landowners.[181] In effect, the decree simply brought the law into line with practice. The Charter to the Nobility confirmed that decision, and a decree of March 28, 1786, further distinguished state property from that of private individuals (*chastnye luidi*).[182] In 1785 Catherine issued a law regulating the use of forests by state peasants, and in 1798 Paul created the Forest Department of the Admiralty College to manage the forests on state lands.[183] Otherwise, management of the forests depended on the enlightened self-interest of the pomeshchiks.

In 1777 Sievers proposed that the government either limit or prohibit the export of timber from St. Petersburg and that it encourage boats and barges to make a return trip inland so that they could be used again.[184] The central government, of course, paid no attention to the first proposal. Despite similar pleas from other quarters to reinstate the prohibition on the export of grain, the policy of Catherine's government was not to restrict exports but to maximize them. Over and over again its communications with subordinates in the provinces emphasized its concern to supply St. Petersburg with all the food and wood it needed for its own consumption and for sale to all the foreigners who wished to buy. In the 1780s Senator A. R. Vorontsov, as president of the Commerce College, joined two other senators in proposing that even more logs be sent to St. Petersburg by floating them through the waterways instead of shipping them on barges. The suggestion was dropped only when Bruce, as director of water communications, protested that free-floating logs would damage boats, locks, and wharves along the waterways and so interfere with the supply of grain and other commodities to the capital.[185]

Sievers's other proposal—to facilitate two-way traffic through the Vyshnii Volochek System—won the approval of the Senate. A towpath (*bechevnik*) along the Volkhov made it possible for boats and barges to return from St. Petersburg to Novgorod and even Borovichi, and the state began to pay rewards of up to fifty rubles to captains who made such a journey.[186] Had the Senate consented to Sievers's proposal for a towpath on the Msta, boats and barges would have been able to return all the way to the Volga. The motive for such a scheme can be seen in the estimates of one historian that 300,000–500,000 trees were consumed each year in the construction of boats and barges and that the price of boats in Rybno (Rybinsk) on the Volga rose from 16–30 rubles apiece in 1764 to 120–350 rubles apiece in 1794.[187] In practice, however, it proved too difficult to haul loaded barges up the Volkhov and the Msta, and the return of empty barges was economically inefficient. In 1783 Bruce informed the empress that it now cost twice the price of a new barge to haul an old one upstream to Novgorod or Borovichi, and the cost of repairs to the towpath along the Volkhov would make it even more expensive.[188] At the end of the 1780s Arkharov repeated Bruce's argument, noting that it cost 200 rubles to return a barge to Novgorod, where it could be sold for only 80–100 rubles.[189] The contribution of round trips to the conservation of timber is also questionable. Used barges were normally sold in St. Petersburg for firewood, which would have had to have been replaced from some other source.

In his memorandum of December 9, 1764, Sievers recommended the use of peat and coal as a means of reducing the amount of wood consumed as fuel. Professor Lehmann, whose prestige had been greatly enhanced by his discovery of a new bed of salt near Staraia Russa, believed that coal might be found in the area around Lake Ilmen. Excited by that possibility, Sievers told the empress that such a discovery could rival the reserves of Scotland and Newcastle and could even create a new export trade for the empire.[190]

Lehmann returned to Novgorod Guberniia in the summer of 1765 to supervise the saltworks and to continue the search for coal. He found additional indications of coal in the vicinity but failed to discover a workable vein. When Lehmann refused to renew the search the following summer, the Mining College sent its own expedition to the banks of the Msta. In January 1767 the Free Economic Society offered a prize of one thousand rubles to the first person to locate good quality coal in Novgorod Guberniia, and later that year it commissioned J. J. Stählin of the Academy of Sciences to prepare an instruction on the extraction and working of coal.[191] In 1768 the search for coal in the Valdai Hills was taken up by Academicians Gmelin and Pallas. In November of that year Sievers informed the Free Economic Society that coal had definitely been discovered near the villages of Ust'e and Borovichi on lands belonging to the Borovichi Rapids Office, and six months later Ivan Kniazov, an agent sent to Borovichi by the Mining College, confirmed the report.[192]

Why the deposits of coal were not exploited until the nineteenth century remains something of a mystery. Right after Kniazov's confirmation of the discovery, the crises of the early 1770s—Poland, the Turkish War, the plague, the Pugachev rebellion—absorbed virtually all of the government's resources and attention. Moreover the Free Economic Society's offer of a prize to anyone who could extract and break coal suggests that a lack of skills and technology delayed the exploitation of coal in Novgorod Guberniia. Yet experts could have been brought from England or Germany, as they were for other projects. In the 1780s Arkharov reminded Catherine of the coal and described its characteristics to her. Meanwhile, the governor of Novgorod had developed plans for mining and breaking it, but the outbreak of war with Turkey and Sweden brought the project to a halt.[193] The real problem may have been the absence of markets and demand. The British residents of St. Petersburg burned coal that they imported from home, but to Russians fuel meant wood.

Of agriculture Sievers wrote in his memorandum of December 9, 1764: "The rural economy of the provinces is still far from the point of perfection to which it has been brought by the English, the Germans, and the Swedes."[194] Catherine responded in her secret instruction of February 1, 1765: "Agriculture, the primary source of public wealth, is a subject of the greatest importance. . . . See how they farm and look for means and methods that promise a better result."[195] Most of the land in Sievers's territories was controlled by noble landlords, but much of the remainder was administered by the College of Economy. An outsider unacquainted with conditions in the Russian provinces might have reasoned, logically enough, that the latter offered the better opportunity for improving agriculture, since the lines of authority were more direct and since the state would have more latitude in dealing with its own property. However, Sievers's reports make dismal reading for anyone who ever imagined that the state bureaucracy could deal directly and effectively with the peasants.

Considering the history of the lands administered by the College of Economy, it was to be expected that the new governor would criticize the conditions he discovered there, but the criticisms continued throughout Sievers's tenure in office. In December 1771 he apprised Catherine that the revenues coming to the state from those lands were diminishing year by year, and he called for a drastic reform of the administration of state territories.[196] In November 1779 he raised the issue again when he included a reorganization of the College of Economy among his most urgent needs. Asking pardon for his frankness, Sievers termed Catherine's latest attempt to deal with the problem "a mild palliative" and reminded her: "One and a half million of your subjects await a radical remedy through your dedication and your wisdom."[197] In March 1781, referring to "the ancient malversations" of the College of Economy, "whose very name has been a horror," Sievers reported that its operation had improved somewhat through the addition of more officers to its staff. He expressed hope that the new arrangement would be retained pending a comprehensive law or instruction on the administration of the "economic" lands. Pointing out that the director of the economy in Tver, in his opinion the best of the three with whom he had to work, was resigning in frustration, Sievers insisted that the need for such a law was more urgent than ever, even though he admitted that "this instruction will be the most difficult and the most painful."[198]

Far from improving the practice of agriculture on its lands, the College of Economy barely managed to govern them. It maintained a modicum of order and collected its revenue, more or less, but otherwise it left the peasants to their own devices. Although Sievers regarded the Russian form of serfdom as "inhuman," he recommended serfdom as practiced in his native Livonia as an improvement over state administration by the College of Economy. In 1765, for example, he advised that the estates administered by the College of Economy be rented to army officers who would agree to introduce a new agricultural regime modeled on the practices of Livonia, where, in Sievers's words, "they cultivate assiduously within the limits set by law."[199] Emperor Paul went so far as to believe that the lands and peasants of the state would be better off in the hands of Russian pomeshchiks and began giving them away to private lords until the damage to the state budget forced him to stop. Sievers's comments on the College of Economy suggest that Paul's basic premise may not have been as wrong as is commonly supposed.

In 1765, in response to Sievers's proposal of the previous year, Catherine authorized him to introduce agricultural reforms, based on a Livonian model, on the economic estate of Korostina, located on the southwestern shore of Lake Ilmen. At the same time, she and Gregory Orlov, a charter member of the Free Economic Society, assigned Pastor J. G. Eisen von Schwarzenberg to conduct a somewhat more radical experiment along the same lines on the crown estate of Ropsha, near St. Petersburg. In both experiments the proprietors would receive full control of the estate and were to encourage the introduction of new crops and new techniques; the peasants were to receive a greater degree of personal freedom, and their obligations to the proprietor were to be defined in a legally enforceable contract. Sievers later claimed that Catherine's support for his efforts at Korostina and her convocation of the Legislative Commission were both directed toward a reform of serfdom and the rural economy throughout Russia.[200]

At the Legislative Commission Baron Ungern-Sternberg, the delegate of the Landrat of Estland, presented to the Subcommission on the Orders of the State a proposal on peasant tenure that was similar in its general outlines to the experiments of Eisen and Sievers. The project on the nobility drafted by that subcommission and presented to the full commission contained several vague references to "free villages," which may also be linked to the experiments of Eisen and Sievers and through them to the Baltic provinces of the Russian Empire.[201] In the General Assembly of the Legislative Commission, however, the idea of free villages was denounced by several of the noble delegates and failed to win endorsement. Eisen's experiment at Ropsha lasted about eighteen months. Sievers's experiment at Korostina lasted several years, but, ultimately, it too ended in failure.

With 4,373 male serfs, the estate at Korostina produced 5,817.5 rubles of revenue in 1764. In that year its harvest amounted to 187 chetverts of rye, 62 chetverts of barley, 250 chetverts of oats, and 31 chetverts of peas (1 chetvert = 5.75 bushels).[202] After inspecting the estate, Sievers reported to the empress that conditions there were generally good but that the fields needed to be redivided among the peasants and that two additional parcels of land had to be purchased for pastures. Sievers hired a fellow Livonian by the name of Engelhardt to manage Korostina and advised him to hire an agronomist, a master mechanic for the mills, and a blacksmith. Sievers promised the empress that Engelhardt would begin to introduce the new agricultural regime just as soon as he could terminate the existing one.[203] In February 1767 the governor wrote the empress: "Guided solely by the well-being of the inhabitants, I shall try at Korostina to increase the growing of grain and to raise the return on seed to six. That will require a free hand and no deceptions from the chancery."[204]

What actually happened at Korostina is not clear because Sievers had surprisingly little to say about his experiment in the years that followed. In his memorandum to Alexander's minister of the interior, Sievers recalled that the venture had progressed slowly because he could not devote sufficient attention to it.[205] In 1768 Sievers hired a Captain Volkersahm to introduce Livonian methods of agriculture at Korostina, but it is not clear whether Volkersahm replaced Engelhardt or merely shared the responsibilities with him.[206] By 1775 Korostina had passed to the direction of Catherine's former secretary I. P. Eliagin, who was simultaneously conducting an experiment with a model industrial community at Iamburg near St. Petersburg. In that year Sievers admitted to the empress that the peasants of Korostina had rioted and that Eliagin had been forced to flee, leaving anarchy behind him. As to the cause of the disturbance, Sievers noted only that it had coincided with Pugachev's success at Kazan. He added that he had written ten letters to Eliagin about the project at Korostina but had never once received a reply.[207] Korostina was one—perhaps the first— of a series of experiments that would subsequently include the military colonies and the so-called Kiselev reforms. In each case the imperial government tried, according to its lights, to institute order, reform, and progress among the peasants, and in each case the peasants responded, according to their own lights, by rebelling.

In an unaddressed memorandum written within a year or two of assuming office, Sievers identified the unlimited power of the nobles over their serfs as a major obstacle to the improvement of agriculture and proposed that the number of days of compulsory labor per week be determined by law.[208] He did not attack serfdom per se, merely the absence of legal restraints on the pomeshchiks' authority, and he pointed to Germany and Livonia as places where the rights of the nobles to own estates and serfs had been made compatible with legal protection for the peasants for the benefit of all concerned.[209] In Sievers's mind the moral and economic arguments against arbitrary despotism were closely related, for he was convinced that every man, including a serf, needed some measure of legal security and economic opportunity to inspire his labor and release his productive energies.

Sievers's belief that restraints on the serfowners' power would encourage agricultural production reflected the assumptions of the European Enlightenment, and it pleases modern sensibilities. But its truth was not self-evident to Russia's pomeshchiks. When G. S. Korob'in and Ia. P. Kozel'skii made that same argument in the General Assembly of the Legislative Commission, provincial noblemen scoffed at their analysis of agricultural economics and charged that those would-be reformers knew little about the realities of life in the countryside.[210] Defending the nobles' unlimited power to impose demands, the opponents of reform insisted that the Russian peasant had to be coerced into productive labor and implied that if less were demanded, less would be produced.[211] Men like Sievers, Korob'in, and Kozel'skii assumed that Russian peasants would respond in a predictably rational manner to the incentives of liberty and property, and their opponents were equally certain that they would not. A personal but by no means conclusive piece of evidence on that score comes from Sievers's wife, who complained that Sievers treated his own peasants so well that his estates brought in little or no revenue.[212]

In his memorandum of December 9, 1764, Sievers wrote that Russia needed an agricultural society to promote the dissemination and discussion of information and progressive ideas among the landlords. Although Sievers later claimed credit for conceiving the idea for the Free Economic Society, founded in 1765, it in fact had several influential proponents. As a national institution with offices in St. Petersburg and a disproportionate number of courtiers, aristocrats, and academics on its membership rolls, the Free Economic Society exerted only very limited influence on the provincial landowners. Oddly enough, in view of his interest in using the nobles' assemblies for progressive purposes, Sievers made no effort to organize local societies for the improvement of agriculture. Throughout Russia the provincial nobles also ignored that possibility. Although eighty of the nobles' nakazy written in 1767 called for the assemblies to elect some sort of land court to settle disputes, only two, Kostroma and Dmitrov, proposed that the assemblies create committees or societies to promote the improvement of agriculture.[213]

Some noblemen—especially the kind of wealthy, well-educated aristocrats who joined the Free Economic Society—drew up lengthy and detailed instructions for their stewards to follow in the interest of increasing agricultural productivity. For the most part, however, the nobles sought to enlarge their income by adding to the area under cultivation and by intensifying the use of traditional techniques. According to N. L. Rubinshtein, the increased demand for grain, reflected in its rising price, led directly to a great expansion of the area under cultivation, especially in the central provinces. For the empire as a whole, he estimates that the expansion ranged from 60 to 100 percent during the last quarter of the eighteenth century.[214] Despite the low agricultural productivity in Sievers's territories, the proximity of the St. Petersburg market created similar pressures to expand the arable land by draining swamps and clearing forests. On a constant scale, such practices tended to lower productivity even as they raised production by bringing more and more marginal land under the plow.

Pressure to expand the arable prompted Sievers to protest the ban on planting crops within thirty sazhens (sixty-four meters) of a highway. In 1765, when the Senate complained that Sievers was not enforcing that prohibition in his territories, the governor replied that he had never heard of such a prohibition in any other country. While conceding that the regulation promoted the safety of travelers and helped to provide food for their horses as well as for cattle being driven to market, Sievers objected that it was nevertheless "foolish and cruel" to leave the land untilled. The peasants, he wrote, bewailed the loss of cropland, and on their behalf he asked the Senate to change the law.[215] In response, the Senate issued a special decree allowing crops to be planted along the highways in Novgorod Guberniia until 1770.[216]

The desire to increase agricultural output by refining existing practices rather than by adopting new ones was also responsible for the widespread inclination to keep as many peasants as possible on the land. In articles 269 and 270 of her *Instruction* to the Legislative Commission Catherine criticized the growing practice of collecting serf dues in cash (*obrok*) on the grounds that it encouraged peasants to leave the land in order to earn money. She urged the landowners to extract their dues in a way that would not separate the peasants from their villages so that "the population will increase and agriculture become flourishing." The nobles' instructions to the Legislative Commission and the speeches of their delegates in the General Assembly of that body reflected a similar assumption that the word "peasant" meant "farmer" and that any other occupation was either a temporary expedient or a dangerous aberration.[217] Although he tried to balance that view against his desire to increase the number of townsmen and artisans, Sievers also assumed that the level of agricultural production depended on the number of cultivators and that the abandonment of agriculture was directly responsible for high grain prices and famine. To keep more peasants on the land, he urged that the landlords take a part of their obrok in grain and that the state conscript vagabonds, fugitives, criminals, surplus priests, and household serfs into the army in preference to field hands.[218]

Sievers's one effort to make agriculture more productive through innovation involved the introduction of the potato. In 1765 he asked the Senate to procure a store of seed potatoes from England or Ireland.[219] In that same year the Senate issued its own instruction on potato cultivation.[220] In July of the following year Sievers reported from Olonets Uezd that he had had the satisfaction of seeing potatoes being grown there.[221] According to E. G. Istomina, Sievers's first experiments with the potato were surprisingly productive, and he became very active in promoting their use. In the 1770s potatoes were successfully introduced in the uezds of

Novgorod and Staraia Russa.[222] We do not know the extent of potato cultivation in northwestern Russia before the end of the eighteenth century, but the economic observations fail to mention it as a major crop in any locality. Judging by the difficulties that the state experienced in promoting potatoes in the nineteenth century, we can reasonably infer that Sievers's efforts yielded only minor results.

The experience of northwestern Russia exemplifies the successes and failures of Catherine's program of state-directed development. The state reached its greatest achievements when it matched and enhanced the inclinations of the people at whom its efforts were directed, such as the grain merchants or the residents of Tver, or when it worked toward a physical objective that was specific and limited, such as the saltworks at Staraia Russa or the locks at Vyshnii Volochek. It was less successful when it aimed to change the attitudes and habits of its subjects, such as the nobles or the peasants, or when its physical objective was broad and diffuse, as in the case of forest conservation or the improvement of agriculture. The state found that it could act to better the condition of provincial Russia, and it made more improvements than in any comparable span of time in the past. However, it also found that the development of provincial Russia could not be accomplished easily or quickly. The effort was usually frustrating, and success was likely to come in small increments at best.

Sievers was convinced that he could have accomplished more if his projects had been given a higher priority, but the government in St. Petersburg, though it continued to promote the prosperity, productivity, and happiness of provincial Russia, had other concerns and other priorities—including faster, more effective, and more rewarding ways of increasing the wealth and power of the Russian Empire.

VII

The Obstacles and Alternatives to Provincial Development

N MAY 20, 1781, SIEVERS SUBMITTED his resignation to Catherine with the explanation that his ruined health made it impossible for him to continue in her service.[1] In his seventeen years as the chief administrator of northwestern Russia Sievers had suffered through many brief but intense bouts of illness and had often complained about the perilous condition of his health. In the weeks preceding his resignation a severe fever had at times rendered him too weak even to sign his name.

Sievers's explanation for resigning, though certainly credible, was probably not complete. After each previous illness he had returned to work with redoubled vigor, determined to make up for lost time. Even now, when Catherine accepted his resignation as governor-general but asked him to continue as director of water communications pending the arrival of his successor, Sievers readily agreed. Until November 1782 he carried out those duties with his customary diligence and spent as much time as ever on the road making tours of inspection and supervising important operations on the spot. Ten years later, when Catherine asked Sievers to replace Betskoi as director of the Vospitatel'nyi Dom and its associated institutions, he again cited his poor health as his reason for declining,[2] but several months later he agreed without hesitation to serve as Catherine's special representative to the Diet of Grodno to oversee the second partition of Poland. He immediately plunged into an exhausting round of negotiations, balls, and receptions. In 1797, when Paul offered to appoint him director of water communications for the entire Russian Empire and Empress Maria Fedorovna asked him to serve as director of the Vospitatel'nyi Dom, Sievers accepted both positions. His health was always delicate, but Sievers's concern for it varied with the circumstances.

In most situations Sievers valued public service and the performance of his duties more than he valued his health, his marriage, or his private fortune. In 1772 his wife had felt obliged to give him some advice on that particular subject: "I know that much remains to be done, but you also know that ten more like you would be necessary, and still you would hardly get everything done; so do not torture yourself. Forget everything but the essentials."[3] As their debts and her frustration continued to mount, she complained in 1774 that in her husband's career there were "always waterfalls, always swamps, always locks, always business, never peace, never promotion, never money."[4] After taking over from Sievers in 1782, Bruce conveyed to Catherine his astonishment at all that his predecessor had managed to accomplish with so little help; he was not at all surprised that Sievers had ruined his health in the process.[5] Such comments suggest that if the post of governor-general harmed Sievers's health, it was because Sievers allowed it to do so, not because the work had to be that all-consuming. Bruce was no healthier than Sievers when he accepted the post that Sievers had resigned. At the time of his appointment he was vacationing in Italy and France on doctor's orders, and when the news of his appointment caught up with him in Paris, it found him too ill to return to Russia for well over a year. Still, with Pskov and Olonets guberniias removed from his charge, Bruce managed to cope with his new duties by following the course that Frau Sievers had recommended to her husband: Except in extraordinary circumstances, he limited himself to inspecting and supervising the work of the governors and subordinate officials. It was possible for a man in poor health to serve as governor-general. Sievers had done it, and Bruce would do it, but in May 1781 Sievers decided he had had enough.

For seventeen years Sievers's willingness to perform his duties in the face of illness and other difficulties had been founded on inspiration from a personal vision of his role as a reformer. He saw himself as the lieutenant of an enlightened sovereign and an intermediary between her aspirations for a better Russia and the good works to be performed among her subjects. That vision sustained Sievers through many delays and disappointments, but by 1781 it had faded, and so had his motive for service. Physically Sievers might have been capable of serving beyond 1781 as an ordinary governor-general; psychologically, however, he could not go on.

From the time of his initial appointment Sievers believed that he enjoyed a special relationship with the empress. The many hours she spent in conference with him, the secret instruction she prepared especially for him, the privilege she granted him of writing directly to her about his affairs, and the interest she took in his projects had all convinced Sievers that he and Catherine were partners in the promotion of progress. The tone and style of his letters and reports reflect Sievers's assumption that his projects were matters of the utmost importance to the empress and that she looked forward to every detail and observation he sent her. He hungered for her approval and encouragement and complained when she was not forthcoming with them. Catherine saw that hunger and used it to her advantage, but on occasion she found it tiresome. In February 1776, when Sievers's importance reached new heights with the introduction of the Fundamental Law in the new guberniia of Tver, he reproached her for not writing: "Not to receive a single syllable from the beneficent hand that moves me to act, . . . that guides me and sustains me! That would destroy a courage less determined than my own."[6] In that instance Catherine perceived that Sievers was practically begging for attention. She in turn chided him for complaining and reassured him of her favor:

> From your letters and the extracts from your journal I see that there is no need to keep you under my thumb, that you are already strong and great. But what of these disjointed phrases that I find in your letters and do not understand at all, for example: "I have no strength to go into details now"; "I confess I am almost exhausted"; "My cares are endless"; "My spirit is even more depressed than my body." What is the matter with you, and what do you lack, letters from me? Well, here is one, and now you know that I am very well pleased with you.[7]

Sievers thanked the empress for her encouragement and explained that his complaints referred to the difficulties of his tasks, his awareness of his frailty, and the sleepless nights that were destroying his nerves.[8] A few weeks later, after telling Catherine of his exasperation with the Senate, Sievers identified the wellsprings of his resolve: "I do not despair, for my cause is good, and it is under the protection of the beneficent heart of my mistress."[9] By April 1776, however, he was complaining once again about Catherine's inattention and her failure to write to him.[10]

Believing himself to be Catherine's special agent, Sievers expected her to support him and his projects when they encountered opposition from other agencies of the imperial government, especially Viazemskii and the Senate. Viazemskii saw Sievers and his zeal as threats to the order and regularity of the state; Sievers in turn regarded Viazemskii and his bureaucratic methods as obstacles to progress. Viazemskii could never forgive Sievers for trying to cut him and the Senate out of the chain of command between the empress and provincial officials, and Sievers would never forget that of the many proposals he had sent to St. Petersburg in the 1760s, the one to convert four settlements into towns had been held up by the Senate for seven years and the others for almost as long. In exasperation

Sievers had appealed to the empress on March 10, 1771: "To my great displeasure I am all too well aware that my proposals are left lying with the procurator-general."[11] Within days Sievers began to receive favorable actions on some of his proposals, and a year later Catherine finally ordered the Senate to do as Sievers had requested about the four settlements in his guberniia. Disregarding other possible reasons for the long delay, such as the deliberations of the Legislative Commission, whose committees had remained in session until October 1771, Sievers interpreted the resulting decree on the four new towns in Novgorod Guberniia as a decisive triumph for his progressive efforts over the obstructionist practices of Viazemskii. But even as he rejoiced in his victory, Sievers understood that it was likely to intensify the enmity that his powerful opponent felt toward him. On June 28, 1772, Sievers warned the empress that hostility between the Senate and himself "could harm the public."[12]

When the decree of April 2, 1772 on the four new towns, was followed by the one on May 3, 1773, which drastically revised the system of administration into the new guberniias of Mogilev and Pskov, and by the decree of November 22, 1773, which appointed him director of water communications in Novgorod Guberniia, Sievers was convinced that the empress had decided to back him to the hilt. In December 1773 he rejoiced to Catherine: "It is now a matter of having insights, formulating plans, and making calculations—and if difficulties arise in administration in the future, a stroke of Your Majesty's pen can eliminate them."[13]

In 1775, when Catherine turned her attention to administrative reform, Sievers saw an opportunity to convert his personal influence, then at an all-time high, into institutional authority. As one of Catherine's principal consultants on provincial reform and as the first governor-general appointed under the Fundamental Law, Sievers tried to invest the office with all the authority any governor-general would need to order and develop the provinces. Believing that Catherine would follow the provincial reform with a reform of the central administration, Sievers tried to persuade her to restrict the Senate's control over provincial affairs and believed—or was led to believe—that he had succeeded. Consequently, when he left Moscow for Tver in January 1776, Sievers nourished high hopes that the line of authority would soon pass directly from the absolute monarch in St. Petersburg to himself as governor-general of northwestern Russia.

Although Viazemskii had failed to exert much influence on the content of the Fundamental Law or to block its promulgation, he retained Catherine's confidence and continued to hold a number of powerful positions in the government from which he soon managed to reassert his control over provincial affairs. First and foremost—in Sievers's opinion at least—he succeeded in persuading Catherine to abandon a projected reform of the central administration, which threatened to curtail the powers of the Senate.[14] Then, as procurator-general, he made full use of his power to appoint the procurators of the new guberniias. He ordered them to act independently of the governors and governors-general and to report regularly and directly to himself. Sievers wasted no time in complaining to Catherine that the procurator-general had failed to send him copies of the laws he would need to consult as governor-general but had ordered the provincial procurator in Tver to spy on his activities, to watch for breaches of legality, and to report everything that occurred in the administration of the guberniia.[15] Informed of Sievers's accusations, Viazemskii let the governor-general know that the empress agreed with the procurator-general's interpretation of the role and responsibilities of the provincial procurators. Adding insult to injury, Viazemskii included copies of the relevent sections of the Fundamental Law with his letter and admonished Sievers to read and obey them.[16] Stung to the quick, Sievers wrote to Catherine:

> I confess that I did not foresee this turn in my affairs, that in the
> event of a doubt arising about my implementation [of the reform]
> Your Majesty would, without hearing me or demanding my explanation,
> place me under the discipline of the procurator-general, who can only
> gloat over setting me straight. In this matter I have not lost sight of Your
> Majesty's goal, which is better known to me than to the procurator-general.
> I repeat frankly: the procurator-general will destroy your work as
> he has destroyed so many of your wise and beautiful reforms.[17]

Viazemskii had succeeded in taking an important aspect of provincial administration away from the governors-general, and for the remainder of his term in that office Sievers regarded the provincial procurators as the agents of his archenemy.[18]

As president of the First Department of the Senate and of its Office of State Revenue (Ekspeditsiia o gosudarstvennykh dokhodakh), established by Catherine's decree of February 25, 1773, Viazemskii also assumed control over the treasury boards (*Kazennye Palaty*) of the new guberniias.[19] That control was enlarged in 1780, when he was named state treasurer with expanded authority over all the agencies of the government that dealt with revenue and finance.[20] Even Bruce, who was on good terms with Viazemskii personally, was moved to complain to Catherine: "The treasury boards cannot obey my orders, only those of Prince Viazemskii."[21] Controlling the financial affairs of the central administration enabled Viazemskii to see to it that all of Sievers's requests for money passed through his hands, and it was from his post as state treasurer that Viazemskii blocked Sievers's plans to finance some of his projects with compulsory assessments voted by the nobles' assemblies. After forcing Sievers to swallow "that bitter pill," as Sievers called it, Viazemskii immediately attacked the governor-general on another front by charging him with impropriety and illegality in the appointment of a substitute *rentmeistr* (collector of rents).

Unable to argue that his actions satisfied the letter of the law, Sievers could only defend himself to the empress by countering that his decision had been both expedient and responsible.[22]

The degree to which Sievers's efforts to enlighten and develop his territories depended on the cooperation of the Senate can be seen in his unsuccessful attempt to establish a printery in Tver. Following Catherine's decree of January 24, 1773, on the creation of printing offices in the provinces, Sievers had searched for a printer who would be willing to set up shop in Tver. By 1778 he had reached a tentative agreement with the St. Petersburg printer Shnor. In return for opening an establishment in Tver, Shnor wanted a loan of 1,500 rubles free of interest for five years, rent-free quarters, payment for government work at prescribed prices, the right to open a bookshop, and the right to print and sell Russian and foreign books, calendars, and a periodical to be published under the title *Tverskoi Vestnik*.[23] Sievers consented and notified the empress that he would make a representation to the Senate to obtain permission.[24] Although Sievers argued that Shnor's operation would benefit both the government and the public, the Senate denied his request for the interest-free loan and rent-free quarters on the grounds that no other free press had ever received such privileges.[25] Shnor would not agree to other terms, and Tver remained without a printing office until the nineteenth century.[26]

By 1780 Sievers had learned to his chagrin that the Fundamental Law was not the grant of plenipotentiary authority he had imagined it to be. In the summer of that year the vice-governor of Novgorod had cited the Fundamental Law as a justification for refusing to obey a direct order from Sievers. Sievers wanted to throw the man into jail for insubordination, but the Senate, as the chief interpreter of the law and the adjudicator of disputes within the bureaucracy, ruled that the law was clearly on the side of the vice-governor. In defeat Sievers demanded of the empress: "What has become of the powerful, bombastic Chapter Four on the duties of the governor-general, who basically wields less power than the governor previously did?"[27]

Sometime after Viazemskii's death in 1793, Sievers gave Catherine his full, explicit appraisal of his old opponent's role in subverting the provincial reform of 1775. In his opinion, the shortcomings and failures of that reform could be understood only by looking back to the early years of the reign:

> One must go way back to the fatal moment when Your Majesty allowed herself to be persuaded by Prince Viazemskii to set aside the Senate reform and to retain him in the important post of procurator-general in addition to the post of treasurer-general, with which she had endowed him. From that moment he was procurator-general only to use his tricks against the new constitution and, through a host of decrees which he weaseled out of Your Majesty and still others in which the Senate partici-

pated, to undermine it always to the detriment of its needs, for our Majesty knows and remembers that the high-placed people did not love the new constitution, which brought your distant subjects nearer to Your Blessed Person through the governor-general.[28]

Viazemskii was only one of the statesmen Sievers antagonized in the course of his career. His successful efforts to gain control over the waterways of northwestern Russia made an enemy of Senator M. A. Dedenev, and his less successful attempt to control the nobles' schools within his guberniias converted Ivan Betskoi from an ally into a foe. The origin of Sievers's quarrel with Vice-Chancellor Alexander Golitsyn is unknown, but in January 1776 Frau Sievers identified him and Viazemskii as her husband's "greatest enemies."[29]

At that very moment, Sievers was acquiring yet another powerful opponent in the person of Gregory Potemkin. As favorite, general-in-chief of the armies, vice-president of the War College, commander of the Cossack forces, and governor-general of Novorossiia, Azov, and Astrakhan by January 1776, Potemkin had acquired the kind of plenipotentiary authority in the southern steppes that Sievers hoped to wield in the northwest. In addition to envying the power and influence of his fellow governor-general, Sievers believed that Potemkin was misusing them.

For one thing, Sievers deplored Potemkin's ability to direct the monarch's attention away from the civilized, European parts of the Russian Empire toward the empty, exotic lands of the south and southeast. Sievers had never traveled farther south or farther east than Moscow, and he had no interest in the steppes of Asia. He had spent his entire life in places like Livonia, Sweden, Denmark, England, and Italy, and he always thought of progress and development in terms of lands with limited expanses and settled populations. Like many other critics in the imperial capitals, Sievers considered Potemkin's expensive projects to populate and develop his guberniias to be enormous wastes of resources, indistinguishable from the grandiose spectacles and extravagant entertainments with which he debauched the empress and the court.

Even worse in the eyes of Potemkin's many critics was the likelihood that his activities would involve Russia in another war with the Ottoman Empire. Opposition to war had appeared in Russia during the last years of the Seven Years War and then flared anew during the Russo-Turkish War of 1768–1774. In addition to condemning the inhumanity of war and the suffering that it inflicted on its immediate victims, that opposition also decried the damage done to the prosperity and happiness of the country. Concurring with Catherine's statement of 1762 that she would seek peace "because the tranquillity and prosperity of our throne demand this," a number of prominent Russian statesmen and intellectuals insisted that peace was an essential prerequisite for progress.[30]

For Sievers, that proposition was an elemental truth. In October 1768 he expressed to Catherine his distress over the prospect that the impending war with Turkey would soon absorb her attention to the exclusion of all else, even the codification of the laws.[31] One year later, after Russia's armed forces had achieved unexpected successes, Sievers congratulated the empress in these terms: "The war, that cruel primary concern has estranged Her from me and my affairs. What joy should I not feel for the victories of Her arms since they have given Your Majesty the leisure to glance anew at the details of my secondary concerns."[32] When the war dragged on in spite of those victories, Sievers's New Year's greeting to the empress contained a reminder: "In addition to wishing my Most Gracious Sovereign a happy new year, I wish for one thing more, namely a glorious peace in the course of that year. When that is attained, I will begin to live again and to think of new towns and provinces, of the survey, of the economy, of canals and highways."[33] Two years later, when peace seemed imminent, Sievers broke off a discussion of a new water link between the Volga and St. Petersburg to exclaim: "Oh, this peace! How impatiently I long for it!"[34] As for the war's effect on Novgorod Guberniia, Sievers subsequently reported that it had taken more than fifty thousand ablebodied recruits away from productive labor in the fields.[35] He also referred to it as the cause of the government's decision to place the burden of maintaining the roads upon the local pomeshchiks and their peasants. In 1787 Sievers had responded to rumours of war by writing to his brother: "As good citizens we want to pray that where war is concerned the evil councils of ministers who are always fishing in troubled waters will be rejected."[36] Writing to his son-in-law, the governor of Vyborg, at the close of the Russo-Swedish War in 1790, Sievers recalled his own situation in 1775 and his antipathy for war, royal extravagance, and "courtiers": "With this peace, I wish you happiness once again and with it credit with the beneficent monarch that you may heal the deep wounds that this war has inflicted in your guberniia. If she gave you one-tenth of what the peace celebrations cost in 1775, the compensation would be paid, but the courtiers will propose invitations to a fête."[37]

Sievers's views on southern expansion and war with the Ottoman Empire coincided with those of Nikita Panin, but during the First Turkish War Sievers refrained from joining Panin and his associates in attributing the continuation of that war to the personal, unpatriotic ambitions of the Orlovs. He counted Gregory and Alexis Orlov among his personal friends and considered them respectable, virtuous men. But when Potemkin replaced the Orlovs as the champion of an active, expansionist policy in the south, Sievers joined Panin and his supporters in characterizing Potemkin as an unscrupulous adventurer whose unprincipled actions would lead to a new and ruinous war. Sievers saw no virtue in Potemkin and no ability apart from the personal pleasure he gave the empress. In January 1776, when Sievers heard that Potemkin had lost even that attribute, he dared to raise the matter with Catherine and to advise her in a postscript on the future employment of favorites:

> What I now say to Your Majesty will serve as a new proof of my feelings for her blessed person, moreover, it is to You alone that I dare to speak. The rumors from Moscow, which increase continually, give the favorite's position to another fortunate mortal and assert that Count Potemkin conceals his indifference and lack of capacity with overwhelming riches, visiting his guberniias and returning to the monk's robes, because he retains little—they say in Moscow—except his blue ribbon. The city that he loves so much says this. The wish of your good citizens—and there are quite a number of them—is that the favorite's successor should have no area of responsibility other than the happy one of pleasing the Benefactress who deserves his love. This is also the wish of the man who engraved the name of Catherine at Marmora, Iaspis, and Granit.[38]

Catherine's reply ended the discussion: "Zeal dictated your postscript. I have burned it."[39] Euphoric over is recent triumphs, Sievers had overstepped the bounds of his influence. He had offended Catherine and added Potemkin to the list of his enemies.[40]

Faced with hostility from statesmen as powerful as Viazemskii and Potemkin, Sievers remained confident that his personal standing with the empress was secure. After October 1778, however, his assurance was seriously weakened by a series of shocks that followed the breakup of his marriage. After a few unhappy years together, Jakob and Elizabeth Sievers had gone their separate ways. They corresponded regularly but saw each other only when Jakob came to St. Petersburg on business. For a while that arrangement suited them both, but it could not survive their disagreements over money. Sievers's expenses as governor and then as governor-general of northwestern Russia regularly outran his salary.[41] In January 1776, for example, he spent 4,000 rubles of his own money on entertainments to celebrate the establishment of Tver Guberniia.[42] Later that year, when his accumulated debts amounted to 90,000 rubles, Sievers asked his wife to sell her jewels to save him from bankruptcy. She refused and insisted that he seek help from the empress, in whose service he had spent the money but from whom he had received nothing beyond his official salary. Jakob took her advice, and in December 1776 Catherine awarded him 70,000 rubles and an estate in Belorossiia containing 1,021 revision souls.[43] According to Sievers, Elizabeth reacted to the sudden change in their fortunes by purchasing a townhouse, a dacha, furniture, servants, and a coach and team. When he arrived in St. Petersburg in September 1778 and discovered that she had spent an additional 11,500 rubles during the course of that summer, Sievers insisted that Elizabeth quit St. Petersburg and return with him to Novgorod.[44] Unwilling to trade her paramour, Prince Putiatin, and the society she loved for her husband and the provinces she detested, Elizabeth demanded a divorce. For help and advice she turned to her close friend Madame de Ribas, a personal attendant of the empress and the adopted daughter of Ivan Betskoi.

As someone who stood close to both Jakob and Elizabeth Sievers, Catherine intervened in their dispute in the hope of achieving a quick, quiet, and amiable settlement. Three days after Sievers's solitary departure from St. Petersburg, Catherine wrote advising him to remain calm and to submit the issues of debts, property, and children to arbitration.[45] Nine days later she sent him a gift of 15,000 rubles to ease his distress over money.[46] To her great satisfaction, Jakob and Elizabeth accepted her advice and agreed to settle their differences out of court.

The great change in Sievers's personal relationship with the empress came when he rejected the arbiter's decision awarding all three daughters and most of the property to Elizabeth. Charging that a "base cabal" had led to the selection of his enemy Alexander Golitsyn as the final arbiter of his divorce settlement, Sievers maintained that Golitsyn had deliberately exceeded his authority and perverted the law in order to injure him. Instead of informal arbitration, Sievers now demanded a formal decision from a court of law before which he planned to expose publicly Elizabeth's adultery with Putiatin. Then, with the assistance of his brother-in-law, Sievers broke into Elizabeth's apartment by night and took away the children, whom he concealed on an estate belonging to his friend Count Z. G. Chernyshev. When Catherine rebuked him for those actions, Sievers wrote her a long letter explaining his position and justifying his conduct. Accepting no guilt and making no apology, he told her frankly: "Your Majesty has given heed only to my enemies. Ask what Prince Orlov, Count Orlov, Count Chernyshev, or Count Panin think of my dealings with my wife. I assure Your Majesty that the public, that hard, unforgiving public, is completely for me, with the exception of my open enemies, four in number, who are without the civil ties of human society."[47]

Catherine was genuinely offended by Sievers's behavior. She accused him of traducing her favor and his own good name. The most she would allow him was that his passions had overwhelmed his true nature and taken possession of his soul. She warned him not to commit any further acts of violence and ordered him to calm his passions away from the capital.[48] Ignoring his responses, she let the matter lie for several months, corresponding with him as little as possible and including neither reprimands nor encouragement. In August 1779 she finally granted many of his official requests and began once again to seek his advice and encourage his initiatives.

Incapable of letting matters lie, Sievers took Catherine's rebuke and her subsequent silence to heart. In December 1778 he sent her a plaintive report:

Today I travel from Novgorod to Tver. I consider it my duty to inform Your Majesty that all matters are in good order and that the people are satisfied. I do not find this a field for observation as I would formerly, when my domestic misfortunes—made public and important by the intrigues of my enemies—did not impose silence upon me. How many questions would I not have raised had not the failure to answer my previous ones led me to fear that Your Majesty has not changed her pernicious impression of me. I insist that my service should not suffer for that.[49]

Although Catherine's expressions of renewed favor in the late summer and autumn of 1779 offered him encouragement, her rebuke left a permanent scar on Sievers's morale. He interpreted any decision that went against him as additional evidence of her disfavor and attributed it to his domestic misfortunes and the intrigues of his enemies. His anguish reached a peak in March 1781, when he learned that Catherine would not grant a subsidy to the nobles' school in Tver. Although she had acceded to many of his other requests, he responded with a *cri de coeur*:

I prostrate myself at the feet of Your Imperial Majesty; I implore your assistance, your beneficence, your tenderness as the mother of your subjects. If my zeal for your glory carries me too far, then deign to excuse me in favor of my goal, but one should not say that my loss of credit with Your Imperial Majesty or my personal misfortunes, which are a shame to my detractors and my enemies, could affect the welfare of your subjects entrusted to my care as easily as they could influence my private fortune.[50]

At that moment Viazemskii and Potemkin combined to humiliate Sievers over an entirely different matter. Some months earlier Viazemskii, as state treasurer, had complained about the tax receipts from the three southwestern uezds of Velikie Luki, Toropets, and Kholm, where 500,000 rubles of arrears had been allowed to pile up. With his pride at stake, Sievers asked the commandants of the local garrisons for assistance, but when the first commandant agreed to assign only four soldiers to that duty, Sievers lost his patience and ordered thirty soldiers from the regiment stationed in Velikie Luki and sixty from the regiment in Toropets to assist the ispravniks and their deputies in collecting the arrears. At that, Potemkin, as president of the War College, complained to the empress that Sievers was exceeding his authority by presuming to command detachments of the army. When Catherine asked Sievers to explain his actions, he pleaded expediency, just as he had in other cases involving conflicts of jurisdiction, and promised that his methods would reduce the arrears to only 200,000 rubles by the end of the current year.[51] Catherine had no choice but to agree with Potemkin. The Fundamental Law allowed a governor-general to command units of the regular army only in an emergency, and one of the orignal aims of her adminstrative reforms had been to remove the army from the process of tax collection. Nevertheless, Sievers felt that he had been humiliated once again.[52]

Sievers's defeats at the hands of Viazemskii, Betskoi, and Potemkin coincided with the defeat of Nikita Panin and his allies over the Austrian alliance. In April 1781 Panin withdrew to his estate near Smolensk, leaving Potemkin, Viazemskii, Bezborodko, and A. R. Vorontsov in effective control of the government. Personally, Sievers was on good terms with Bezborodko and Vorontsov, but he could not look to them for support and protection as he had looked to Panin, the Orlovs, and the Chernyshevs. Convinced by recent events that he had lost most if not all of his own influence with the empress and confronted by a government controlled by his greatest enemies, Sievers saw the end of his career as the developer and enlightener of provincial Russia. According to Blum, he discussed his resignation with his brother during a visit of Livonia in the fall of 1780.[53] His fever in April 1781 finally triggered a decision that was virtually certain to have come within the year.

Despite their disagreements, Sievers and Catherine remained on good terms after his departure from office. In his letter of resignation he asked for a cash subsidy to straighten out his finances, and within one month he received a gracious and favorable reply. The former governor-general and the empress continued to exchange letters several times a year, and he met with her in St. Petersburg on at least two occasions between 1781 and 1793. Catherine sought his advice on several subjects, including the drafts of the Charter to the Nobles and the Charter to the Towns, and he volunteered his advice on the introduction of the Fundamental Law in Livonia and the conduct of Russia's war with Sweden. In 1792, with Viazemskii and Potemkin still in power, he refused her offer of a position in her government. One year later, when he accepted a different position, Viazemskii and Potemkin were dead.

Sievers's letters and reports present a consistent interpretation of the development of the provinces under Catherine II. He believed that much had been accomplished by her government, but not all that could have or should have been achieved if she had followed his recommendations and had supported his efforts more fully. For those mistakes he blamed not Catherine but "courtiers," "favorites," and "tricksters" within her government who put their own selfish interests above those of their country and their sovereign. Catherine's only failing, in Sievers's estimation, was that she allowed people like Viazemskii and Potemkin to deceive her. Beyond that, Sievers spoke no ill of Catherine, although his biographer, Blum, expanded Sievers's version of events into an indictment of Catherine and her entire regime. Though different in tone and emphasis, Sievers's assessment of Catherine's reign is generally consistent with those presented by such other contemporaries as Shcherbatov, Fonvizin, and Radishchev, and with them it has helped to support the negative view of Catherine and Potemkin that has prevailed among historians throughout most of the nineteenth and twentieth centuries. The essence of that view is that Catherine sacrificed internal development and internal reform to the pursuit of extravagance, vainglory, expansion, and war.

For all its sincerity, its consistency, and its appeal to like-minded people, Sievers's view of Catherine's government was distorted by his perspective and his preconceptions. Like Shcherbatov, Fonvizin, and Radishchev, Sievers was completely lacking in objectivity when it came to discussing policies that interfered with or prevailed over those that he himself supported. Sievers never considered the possibility that Catherine might be making pragmatic choices between reasonable alternatives; he saw her confronted by moral decisions between virtue and vice and believed that she had chosen wrongly.

From Catherine's viewpoint, however, there were good, practical, even moral reasons for denying Sievers some of the authority and money he demanded and for according his efforts a lower priority than he thought they deserved. Her support of Viazemskii in some of his disputes with Sievers, for instance, was thoroughly consistent with her belief in legal monarchy and a system of checks and balances within government. Following Montesquieu, Catherine believed that adherence to the law distinguished legal monarchy from tyranny by restraining the arbitrary and capricious use of power. Sievers agreed with the theory, but in practice he did not understand how it should apply to him. What Sievers either failed to see or would not admit was that he represented only one element of a much larger system and that Catherine had never intended to support him in everything he wanted to do. Red tape restrained the actions of good officials as well as bad ones, but it also tied the administration of the empire together and gave it the character of systematic rationality that Catherine and most of her contemporaries admired. Catherine also intended that the various officials and agencies of administration should check and balance each other and that they should depend on her to be the ultimate arbiter of the conflicts that would inevitably arise among them. Over the years Sievers emerged victorious from most of his conflicts with other officials, but he always regarded the process with repugnance. Then, when several small but personally humiliating decisions went against him, he found it intolerable. Sievers may have disagreed with many of the specific measures taken by Paul during his five years on the throne, but that monarch's style of government, with its direct lines of authority and its willingness to use and to delegate autocratic power, proved easier and more satisfying to work with.

An exchange of letters between Catherine and Sievers in October 1779 illustrates the differences in their attitudes toward decision making. Putting aside her displeasure with Sievers's over his divorce, Catherine granted some of his requests and began to correspond with him on her former terms. Assured at last that the provincial reform would produce the results she wanted, she asked Sievers what other measures should now be considered most urgent. "Everything is equally urgent," he replied, "a criminal code and court procedure, a law on commerce, the statute on the department of finances, that on the director of economy, the municipal law of towns, the chapter on the nobility, the settling of the old affairs of the two capitals, and finally I add, *avec un coeur serré*, an economic law, that of humanity."[54] Catherine replied that many of Sievers's wishes would be satisfied in the not too distant future: the "chapters" on the bureaucracy, the nobility, and the salt and alcohol monopolies were ready for enactment; the chapter on the municipal administration of St. Petersburg would be completed during the coming year; and the one dealing with Moscow would be ready soon thereafter. Beyond that, she was pleased to assure him that she had already collected all of the statistical information needed to prepare legislation on military conscription, the land police, taxation, schools, and the duties of the imperial treasurer. She had gathered her preliminary thoughts on those matters and would soon compose her considered opinions regarding the content of the new legislation. The Senate had made similar preparations and would turn its attention to those matters when it finished the new statute on court procedure.[55] Whereas Sievers felt that everything was urgent, Catherine believed that nothing was so urgent that it should not be handled properly in due time. Delay, within reason, was the price that Catherine was willing to pay for order and regularity in the affairs of state. Her own list of pending legislation, moreover, made no mention of an economic law that would regulate serfdom.

Under certain circumstances Catherine was occasionally willing to cut through red tape and eliminate procedural checks and balances. Indeed, she considered a ruler's ability to act in such a manner to be one of the desirable features of monarchy, but she also believed that such action should be exceptional in the sense of being justified by extraordinary circumstances. After the Pugachev revolt, for example, she assigned such a high priority to the composition and implementation of the Fundamental Law that she freed Sievers from some of the restraints that normally encumbered him and accorded him greater influence than he normally enjoyed. Sievers suffered considerable frustration when he discovered that the same high priority did not apply to all of his undertakings, and he attributed the difference to his personal loss of favor rather than to the lessened importance of his work. In his zeal for good works, the governor-general could not agree that the creation of a nobles' school in Tver in 1780 was less urgent and less important than the introduction of a new provincial order had been in 1775 and 1776 or that the results of his many efforts to develop his guberniias failed to justify their exemption from normal bureaucratic procedure.

If Sievers's projects had contained the promise of extraordinary benefit to the empire, Catherine might have accorded him the authority he desired, but the plain, unsympathetic truth was that they did not. As the record of achievements surveyed in the preceding chapters indicates, the government's efforts to promote progress and development in northwestern Russia yielded only modest results. They promised continuing, incremental improvement but no immediate or dramatic solution to the problem of underdevelopment. Even if the government had given Sievers everything he wanted, it is doubtful that the results would have been significantly different. The greatest obstacles to the development of Sievers's guberniias after all were not the policies and officials of Catherine's government but the soil, the climate, the society, and the attitudes found in those guberniias. Confronted by such deterrents to the realization of her ambitions, Catherine supported programs of provincial development as part of an ongoing, long-range commitment to progress. Except for the introduction of the Fundamental Law, she refused to regard them as the most urgent items on the government's agenda.

With that policy Catherine created the breach between herself and Sievers. The governor-general saw no conceivable alternative to his kind of programs, no matter how modest their results might be, other than the immoral acceptance of continued underdevelopment. Aware that the state could not work miracles, Sievers nevertheless expected it to realize the potential of its lands and peoples, however limited, not just in his territories, but throughout the settled regions of the empire. Instead, Catherine assigned her highest priority to Potemkin's projects for the settlement and exploitation of the steppe. She made Potemkin a virtual despot over southern Russia and financed his undertakings with sums of money that Sievers could scarcely imagine. Her reputation as an enlightened ruler never recovered from the criticisms leveled at her decision to give Russia's expansion into the steppe a higher priority than the reform and development of the settled regions of the empire, but in a choice between two different strategies for developing the Russian Empire, that decision had much to recommend it. While Sievers, Panin, her son Paul, most of the aristocracy, and a number of intellectuals and writers saw Potemkin's actions in the Pontic Steppe as an obstacle to the development of Russia, Catherine saw them as a brilliant alternative.

Geography gave the southern steppe two great advantages over the northern and central regions of European Russia. First, it was able to produce an abundance of grain and other agricultural commodities. As we saw in Chapter IV, agricultural yields in northern and central Russia were low and crop failures frequent. Consequently, the nobles in those regions had to think of themselves as buyers as well as sellers of grain, which explains why their nakazy to the Legislative Commission advocated measures to increase the supply of grain and to stabilize its price at moderately low levels. Only in nakazy from south of Kadom (Voronezh Guberniia) did the noble landowners identify their interests exclusively with the sale of surplus grain.[56] In the same year that those nakazy were being written, the Senate tracked the prices of various kinds of grain backward along the supply routes that led to St. Petersburg and found, not surprisingly, that prices declined steadily as one moved southward toward Gzhatsk, Alatyr, and Kazan.[57] Such evidence supports the conclusion that all of northern Russia and much of central Russia was a grain deficient region whose ability to maintain, never mind increase, its population depended on shipments of grain from the steppe lands of the Volga Valley and the Ukraine.

Catherine's government could do virtually nothing to change that situation. Neither its cooperation in the experiments of Eisen von Schwarzenberg and Sievers at Ropsha and Korostina nor its sponsorship of the Free Economic Society had done much to accelerate the adoption of improved agricultural methods, and in 1801 Heinrich Storch would be justified in writing of Russia: "There is certainly no country in Europe where agriculture is practiced so negligently."[58] Poor methods of cultivation may have aggravated, but certainly did not create, the basic causes of low agricultural productivity, which were podzol soils, swampy terrain, short growing seasons, rainy summers, and unpredictably early frosts. Northern Russia was simply not a good place to grow grain, and central Russia was not much better.

If it could not hope to increase the agricultural productivity of northern and central Russia, Catherine's government had to find other ways to pursue its goals of increasing the population and expanding exports. One alternative was to increase overall production at the cost of lowered productivity by increasing the number of peasant cultivators and the amount of land under cultivation. Although that solution was economically inefficient, the serfowners favored it, the peasants were constrained to adopt it, and the government shaped its policies to accommodate it. In Sievers's territories that policy led to the draining of swamps, the cutting of forests, and the planting of crops along the shoulders of the roads. A second alternative was to encourage the movement of agricultural commodities from surplus regions in the south to consumers and exporters in the north. The empress and the Senate counted on the northward movement of southern grain to stabilize prices in St. Petersburg in the wake of their decision to permit the export of grain from the Baltic ports,[59] and Sievers relied on it to relieve food shortages in his territories. The movement of southern grain to northern Russia was promoted not only by the effect of higher prices within a free market but also by the improvements to the Vyshnii Volochek System under Catherine and the construction of additional canals under Paul. The government's third alternative was to direct its efforts to increase population and exports toward those regions in which food was more abundant and agricultural productivity was higher—that is, toward the steppe.

The physical conditions that restricted agricultural productivity in northern and central Russia were almost totally absent from the steppe. Its chernozem soils were deep, fertile, and well drained. The growing season was significantly longer and less likely to be broken by unseasonable frosts or heavy rains. Only an occasional drought threatened to interrupt a succession of abundant harvests. As a result, the regions of the steppe that were already settled by 1775 supported a dense and flourishing population. In 1775, when the Turkish envoy to St. Petersburg passed through the Polish areas on the right bank of the Dnepr, he reported that the territory between Zhvantes and the Russian frontier was filled with prosperous villages so close together that it was possible to see from one to another.[60] By the second decade of the nineteenth century the English traveler Sir Robert Wilson could record that in the Ukraine he found "as great a population and as richly cultivated land as almost any province in England can produce," and he observed with some surprise that "I do not think we saw a barren acre for five hundred miles."[61] With much of the steppe open and uninhabited as of 1775, the effort to bring more land into production there promised greater rewards than it did farther north. Black land commonly yielded four times the seed, but newly cultivated black land often produced as much as twenty times the seed during the first few years.[62] The nobles' nakazy of 1767 complained that many peasants fled from their owners and ran away to the Ukraine. Had it not been for the restraints imposed by serfdom, the movement of hungry people toward promising sources of food would doubtlessly have been much greater.

Abundant harvests not only freed the steppe from the subsistence crisis that afflicted northern and central Russia, but they also provided a marketable surplus at a time when grain prices were raising in northern and central Russia and throughout most of Europe. Fernand Braudel cites one French report of 1771 that claimed that "piles of corn the size of houses, enough to feed all Europe, are again rotting in Podolia and Volhynia" and another report from 1784 that noted that superabundant harvests had caused grain to be sold "at such a low price in the Ukraine that many landowners have abandoned its cultivation."[63] A government that wanted very much to increase Russia's population and expand the volume of Russia's exports could accomplish both of those aims if it could eliminate the barriers that separated the grain surpluses of the Ukraine from their potential customers. Since the 1750s the Russian government had been clearing the way for that surplus to reach northern Russia and the Baltic ports, and we have seen that some of it was moved each year from the wharf at Gzhatsk to the markets of St. Petersburg. However, in order to reach St. Petersburg from the Ukraine, grain had to be pulled up the Dnepr and the Desna and then hauled overland to the Oka, where once again it had to be pulled against the current of that river and its tributaries, the Ugra and the Vora. From there it had to be hauled overland to the wharf at Gzhatsk, from which it could be moved down the Gzhat, the Vazuza, and the upper Volga to Tver, the starting point for the arduous and expensive journey through the rivers and canals of the Vyshnii Volochek System.

The second great advantage that geography conferred upon the southern steppe was its relatively easy access to the sea. Between south central Russia and the Black Sea cargoes could be floated *downstream* without any need for canals, teams of horses, boatmen, or portages other than to circumvent rapids, such as the cataracts of the Dnepr. In comparison to the quantities that reached St. Petersburg, the volume of Ukrainian grain that could be brought to ports on the Black Sea was potentially enormous.

Was Catherine aware of the economic potential of the southern steppe when she decided to pursue its rapid development and exploitation against the wishes of many of her statesmen and much of the nobility? Or was she led to that decision by her lust for conquest, glory, and the favors of Potemkin, as the opponents of that decision insisted? Catherine's personal responsibility for Russia's southern policy can be inferred from the circumstances of Potemkin's rise to power. During the First Turkish War the critics of the war attributed that policy to Gregory Orlov, and they were pleased when Orlov fell from favor in the spring and summer of 1772. Had their premise been correct, Orlov's fall should have led directly to the triumph of the Panin faction, the abandonment of most of Russia's demands upon Turkey, a quick conclusion to the Turkish War, and a full return to a Baltic orientation in foreign and commercial policy. Without Orlov, Catherine frustrated the expectations of Panin and his allies on her own for a brief period before swallowing her pride in March 1773 and restoring Orlov to his titles and offices but not to his other role as her lover.[64]

Meanwhile, Catherine had been carrying on a correspondence with Potemkin, who was fighting with the army in the south. In November 1770 she recommended the otherwise obscure and insignificant Potemkin to his commanding officer, General Rumiantsev, as a man "filled with the desire to distinguish himself" and one who "had been born with gifts that the Fatherland can use."[65] She summoned Potemkin to St. Petersburg in February or March 1774, and it was only when she was satisfied with his potential as a counterweight to Panin that she finally dispensed with the support of the Orlov faction. Although Catherine had conferred no important offices upon Vasilchikov, Orlov's successor as her lover, she rapidly appointed Potemkin to a multiplicity of important offices that gave him full administrative and military control over the Pontic Steppe. Catherine's desire to develop and exploit the southern steppe not only determined the specific use that she chose to make of Potemkin's extraordinary ability, but it also assured the continuity of Russian policy toward the steppe and the Black Sea from 1768 to her death in 1796, in spite of Orlov's dismissal and Potemkin's death in 1791.

Without attributing Catherine's southern policy to any one specific motive, it is possible to demonstrate her appreciation of the steppe's potential contribution to the development of the Russian Empire. Her first systematic effort to realize that potential began in July 1763 with her manifestoes creating the Chancellery of Guardianship to promote colonization. Between 1764 and 1768 that effort settled thousands of foreign immigrants in the eastern steppe along the Volga.[66] In 1764 A. P. Mel'gunov followed this model in drawing up a plan for the systematic settlement of Novorossiia, a sparsely inhabited region north of the Crimean Khanate. For the next ten years the Russian government promoted the immigration of tens of thousands of settlers, mainly Ukrainians and Great Russians, into that territory.[67] Those programs provoked relatively little controversy at the time because most statesmen could see that the gradual settlement of fertile but empty areas within the Russian Empire was an obvious means of increasing Russia's population. The controversy really began with the First Turkish War. In 1768, soon after the outbreak of war, the Academy of Sciences dispatched two scientific expeditions to investigate the natural resources and the economic potential of the steppe. One, headed by Academician P. S. Pallas and including the Swedish physician I. P. Falk and the young scholars I. I. Lepekhin and V. F. Zuev, explored the eastern steppe in the vicinity of the lower Volga, the Caspian Sea, and the southern Urals. The other, headed by Academician J. A. Guldenstadt and including the botanist S. G. Gmelin and the junior scholar K. I. Gablits, headed for the Pontic Steppe, the Kuban, and the Caucasus. After six years in the field, Guldenstadt's expedition returned to the capital on December 20, 1774.[68] Six days later, at a formal session of the Academy, Guldenstadt presented a paper on the subject of improving Russia's balance of trade by increasing its export of raw materials and finished goods from the Ukraine and the Pontic Steppe through the Black Sea. Four years later, with Joseph II of Austria in the audience, Guldenstadt presented to the Academy a paper on the favorable prospects for increased trade between Russia and Germany via the Danube.[69] At least three other expeditions from the Academy of Sciences explored the Pontic Steppe and the Crimea between 1781 and 1794.[70]

Although it is possible that Guldenstadt's reports were used simply to provide an economic justification for a policy based on other motives, there can be no doubt that Catherine understood the economic implications of her southern policy. Catherine's critics have made much of her ambitious schemes to create a kingdom of Dacia and to revive the Greek empire of Byzantium, but those projects represented the fanciful extremes of her aims rather than the heart of her policy. From 1770 until 1796 the essential, minimal, and unwavering goals of Catherine's southern policy were the establishment of Russian ports on the Black Sea, navigation rights on that sea, and unrestricted passage from that sea into the Aegean and the Mediterranean.

In order to realize the economic potential of the steppe, Catherine's government had to provide protection for the cultivators, craftsmen, and traders who would settle there. In ancient times the Pontic Steppe had been a source of grain for the cities of Greece and Asia Minor, but for centuries before the Treaty of Kuchuk-Kainardji the marauding horsemen who roamed the steppe had made settled life there so dangerous that vast areas remained uncultivated in spite of their obvious fertility.[71] The crushing of the Pugachev revolt eliminated much of the threat that the Yaik Cossacks and the Bashkirs had posed to settled agriculture in the eastern reaches of the steppe. Farther west, Potemkin moved swiftly to dissolve the Zaporozhian Sech and bring the Don Cossacks under firmer control. He then began to erect fortified lines of settlements behind which immigrants could settle in relative security. As one line became stabilized, another would be set up beyond it. Finally, in 1783 Russia subdued the last stronghold of the steppe's marauders when it annexed the Crimea. When the comte de Ségur conveyed to Catherine France's opposition to that annexation, the empress strongly defended her action: "If you had in Piedmont or Spain neighbors who every year took into captivity 20,000 of your subjects, and I took them under my protection, what would you say."[72]

The second threat to Russian settlements in the steppe was the military might of the Ottoman Empire. Although Russia had satisfied its basic demands for ports and rights of navigation and passage in the Treaty of Kuchuk-Kainardji, diplomatic pressures and internal disorders had kept Russia from defeating the Turks in detail, and there were many reasons to believe that the Turks would eventually attempt to regain what they had lost. Against that eventuality Catherine maneuvered toward an alliance with Austria while Potemkin worked to make Russia's gains irreversible by reorganizing the armies, constructing cities and fortresses, and filling the previously empty land with settlers. The details of those undertakings lie beyond the bounds of this book, but their pace and scope provide a relevant contrast to what has been said about projects in other parts of the empire.[73] Faced with the threat of a Turkish attack that could undo everything she had accomplished in the south, Catherine pushed the development of the Pontic Steppe with unwonted impatience and determination. She gave Potemkin whatever authority he needed and supported his projects with few questions asked. In contrast to the relatively slow and deliberate manner in which the Chancellery of Guardianship settled foreign immigrants along the Volga, Potemkin organized an all-out effort to settle as many people as he could in the Pontic Steppe in the shortest possible time.[74] To the dismay of many Russian and Ukrainian noblemen, Catherine and Potemkin even permitted fugitive serfs to remain as settlers in Potemkin's guberniias.[75]

In addition to Panin and Sievers, the list of statesmen and intellectuals who opposed all or part of Catherine's southern strategy included I. F. Bogdanovich, S. G. Domashnev, D. I. Fonvizin, N. I. Novikov, A. N. Radishchev, M. M. Shcherbatov, P. S. Sumarokov, A. R. and S. R. Vorontsov, and Paul, the heir to the throne. We do not know how many less important or less verbal individuals shared in that opposition, but there are indications that their number was large. Crises, hardships, and rebellions had accompanied the First Turkish War, and Paul was not the only person in Russia prepared to attribute budget deficits, the slowdown or cessation of reform, high levels of military recruitment, plague, famine, and the Pugachev revolt to the prolongation of that conflict.[76] In the spring of 1772 several noncommissioned officers of the Preobrazhenskii Guards persuaded somewhere between thirty and one hundred officers and enlisted men to join them in a conspiracy to replace Catherine with Paul.[77] The prolongation of the Turkish War also increased the tensions between Catherine and the nobles of Moscow. In 1766 the nobles had authorized Nikita Panin to draft their nakaz to the Legislative Commission and had chosen his brother Peter to serve as their deputy. A crowd of Moscovites had cheered Paul in 1768 as their only true sovereign.[78] The bubonic plague brought to Moscow from the war zone in the south killed more than fifty thousand inhabitants of that city in 1771 and 1772 and instigated the so-called plague riot, in which an angry mob of commoners temporarily seized control of the Kremlin. In July 1774 many nobles of the Moscow region fled in terror of the *pugachevshchina*,[79] and later that year Sievers advised Catherine not to travel to Moscow: "The plague has not destroyed all of the political poison that grows in that city."[80] When Sievers denounced Potemkin to Catherine in the postscript to his letter of January 22, 1776, he cited "rumors from Moscow" and public opinion in that city to support his own assessment.[81]

The motives of the various groups and individuals who opposed Catherine's southern policy included a moral condemnation of aggressive or expansionist wars, a disdain for favorites and "accidental people," a disregard of the south's potential, and instinctive displeasure at the shift of resources and attention from the regions they inhabited to a region in which they had little interest. In some respects their position was similar to that of the American Federalists who would denounce the Louisiana Purchase of 1803. Unlike the Federalists, however, the critics of Catherine's southern policy could make a persuasive argument that the expansion they opposed was harmful, not only to their personal welfare and interests but also to those of the nation. In 1787 the long-expected war with Turkey finally erupted and brought with it all of the dire consequences that Potemkin's opponents had predicted. In January 1790 Edmond Genet, the French chargé d'affaires, penned a description of conditions in war-torn Russia:

> The great landed proprietors are beginning to raise their voices in all seriousness, and it has been necessary to dispatch to Moscow Monsieur Sheshkovskii, the chief of the Secret Chancellery to repress several of them; the people groan in every province to see the best cultivators torn from the land, and lamenting families being robbed of their sole means of support; money has completely vanished from circulation, and it is evident that the government, under the guise of bank notes, is manufacturing

a veritable paper currency; the harvest has been bad, next year's is going to be even worse; no snow has fallen, and it is freezing only at intervals, and the grain is fermenting and rotting in the bosom of the earth; the revenues from the crown lands have fallen; trade is languishing; the rate of exchange is sinking steadily; finally everything proclaims that it is time to finish the war and repair the evils that it has occasioned. In so alarming a situation, if the Turks refuse to negotiate peace directly, if they put forward unjust demands, it will be necessary either for the empress, deprived of our support, to throw herself into the arms of England, or else be crushed beneath the ruins of her empire.[82]

The Second Turkish War ended in 1792, but Russia's financial condition, which was commonly mistaken for its economic condition, remained critical at the time of Catherine's death in 1796. In that year the Prussian diplomat von Tauenzien reported that the treasury was empty, that the pay of the army and the bureaucracy was in arrears, and that the government was sending large sums of money abroad to cover its foreign debts. In reporting Catherine's death, von Tauenzien observed that in thirty-four years of false glory and illusory grandeur the "immortal Catherine" had destroyed the happiness and well-being of her state.[83] His judgment conformed to the general wisdom.

Sievers and Paul were among the many Russians who shared von Tauenzien's assessment of Catherine's reign. Steeped in the lessons of Fénelon's *Télémaque*, they saw Catherine as a classic example of a ruler who had sacrificed the happiness and welfare of her subjects before the false gods of conquest and military glory. Once in power, Paul moved swiftly to put Russia back on the high road to prosperity by replacing his mother's policies with those of the opposition. Condemning the wars, the extravagance, and the corruption of the previous reign, he began his own by promising peace and demanding virtue and discipline. In a clear reversal of his mother's priorities, Paul neglected the development of the Pontic Steppe and the Black Sea trade while empowering Sievers to construct canals that would bring the agricultural surpluses of the Ukraine to northern Russia and the Baltic ports.[84]

In the somewhat longer run, however, Catherine's decision to assign the highest priority to the conquest and rapid development of the south proved more advantageous to Russia than the alternatives preferred by her critics. After 1796 the development of northern and central Russia remained as frustrating and as slow to yield rewards as it had in Catherine's time. Incremental improvement continued, but dramatic change would not begin to occur until after the emancipation of the peasants, the coming of the railroads, and the beginning of rapid industrialization. In the meantime, the south provided much of the economic and demographic growth that kept Russia from falling even farther behind the European powers than it actually did between 1796 and 1856.[85] Between the Fifth Revision in 1795 and the Ninth Revision in 1850, for example, the male population of the eight guberniias that comprised Novorossiia and the Lower Volga regions rose from 1,179,865 to 3,166,922 while the male population of the eleven guberniias that comprised the northern lake region and the central industrial region rose from 3,957,796 to 4,978,904.[86] Because the immigrants to the south were generally less set in their ways than were the settled populations of the north, Potemkin and his successors also found it easier to introduce viniculture, marino sheep, and other agricultural innovations, as opposed to Sievers's difficulties with the potato. The southern cultivators also had a more fertile land to work. Agricultural exports from the south did not begin to rise dramatically until the early nineteenth century; thereafter the Pontic Steppe became the granary of southern Europe.[87]

The annexation of a rich land larger in area than the United Kingdom of Great Britain and its rapid settlement by millions of people altered the balance of power in eastern Europe. By 1815 it had helped Russia to eclipse the Ottoman Empire, to outstrip Austria and Prussia, to defeat Napoleonic France, and to become, for a while, the arbiter of Europe.[88] The shift in the balance of power that resulted from Russia's conquest and settlement of the Pontic Steppe might have been even more significant and long lasting had not the French Revolution and the industrial revolution upset that balance in ways that Russia could not readily assimilate. Even so, the opening of the Pontic Steppe enabled Russia to remain a major power in spite of its slower modernization in the first half of the nineteenth century, and in the late nineteenth century the enormous exports of grain from the Pontic Steppe would pay much of the cost of Russia's industrialization. Those advantages remained long after the sacrifices required to obtain them had been forgotten.

Unlike her critics, Catherine never regarded internal development and expansion as diametric opposites. In company with rulers more admired by her critics she regarded them instead as two different means of achieving the same objective. Despite the priority she accorded the south, Catherine continued to finance the development of northern and central Russia after the departures of Sievers and Panin, and to a considerable extent it was her "guns *and* butter" budgets that produced the monetary inflation she bequeathed to her successors.

Although Joseph II of Austria is commonly regarded as a more thorough and more dedicated practitioner of enlightened absolutism than Catherine, he shared her conviction that the conquest of desirable territory was the swiftest and most practical means of enriching one's state. Frederick II of Prussia had reached that same conclusion as early as 1740. Still, many critics failed to see the connection between those monarchs' desire for conquest and their desire to increase the wealth of their states. The same French physiocrats who lauded the domestic reforms of Joseph II were confounded by his aggressive wars and his determination to conquer

Bavaria.[89] In Russia the same statesmen who admired the laws and reforms of Frederick II—Sievers, Panin, and Paul, to name a few—conveniently forgot that Frederick's most significant contribution to the rise of Prussia was the seizure of Silesia, a conquest gained at the cost of two long, bloody, and expensive wars. Panin and his allies made an equally selective and distorted use of history when they glorified the legend of Peter the Great to support their own orientation toward the Baltic and to provide a belittling contrast to the woman who had usurped the throne of his descendants.[90] To be sure, Peter had placed Russia's capital on the Baltic, but he had done so only through conquest and twenty-one years of war—and only after he had first tried and failed to establish a Russian presence on the Black Sea. In their efforts to increase the wealth and power of the states they ruled Catherine, Peter, Joseph, and Frederick all perceived that the development of the provinces was a necessary but inadequate means of achieving their objectives.

Abbreviations

AHR	*American Historical Review*
CASS	*Canadian American Slavic Studies*
CMRS	*Cahiers du monde russe et sovietique*
CSS	*Canadian Slavic Studies*
IZ	*Istoricheskie Zapiski*
JGO	*Jahrubücher für Geschichte Osteuropas*
LOII	Leningradskoe otdelenie instituta istorii akademii nauk SSSR
PSZ	*Polnoe Sobranie Zakonov Rossiiskoi Imperii s 1649 goda*
RA	*Russkii Arkhiv*
RBS	*Russkii Biograficheskii Slovar'*
RES	*Revue des études slaves*
RR	*Russian Review*
RV	*Russkii Vestnik*
SIRIO	*Sbornik Imperatorskago Russkago Istoricheskago Obshchestva*
SR	*Slavic Review*
TsGADA	Tsentral'nyi gosudarstvennyi arkhiv drevnikh aktov
TsGIA	Tsentral'nyi gosudarstvennyi istoricheskii arkhiv
TsGVIA	Tsentral'nyi gosudarstvennyi voenno-istoricheskii arkhiv
ZMNP	*Zhurnal Ministerstva Narodnago Prosveshcheniia*

Notes

Introduction

1. M. M. Shcherbatov, "Primernoe vremiaishchislitel'noe polozhenie vo skol'ko let pri blagopoluchneishikh obstoiatel'stvakh mogla Rossiia samo soboiu, bez samovlastiia Petra Velikago doiti do togo sostoianiia v kakom ona est' v rassuzhdenii prosveshcheniia prosveshcheniia i slavy," in *Sochineniia kniazia M. M. Shcherbatova*, II, 13–22. Despite Peter's despotic methods, Shcherbatov praised him for bringing enlightenment to Russia. So for that matter did Voltaire in his *History of Peter I.*

2. A succinct and explicit definition of the Enlightenment in those terms is to be found in the opening paragraph of Peter Gay, *The Enlightenment: An Interpretation* (p. 3): "The men of the Enlightenment united on a vastly ambitious program, a program of secularism, humanity, cosmopolitanism, and freedom, above all freedom, freedom in its many forms—freedom from arbitrary power, freedom of speech, freedom of trade, freedom to realize one's talents, freedom of aesthetic response, freedom, in a word, of moral man to make his own way in the world."

3. John G. Garrard, "The Emergence of Modern Russian Literature and Thought," p. 13. See also Marc Raeff, "The Enlightenment in Russia and Russian Thought in the Enlightenment," pp. 35–37.

4. Karl Blum's four-volume biography of Sievers, *Ein russischer Staatsmann. Des Grafen Jakob Johann Sievers Denkwürdigkeiten zur Geschichte Russlands*, is remarkable both for its extensive use of primary sources and its pro-German, anti-Russian bias.

5. A. Cherkas, "Sivers, Ia. E.," in *Russkii biograficheskii slovar'*, XVIII, 410.

6. Some significant and highly influential examples of this interpretation of Catherine II are to be found in V. O. Kliuchevskii, *Kurs russkoi istorii*, II and IV; P. N. Miliukov, *Ocherki po istorii russkoi kultury*, III; and A. A. Kizevetter, *Istoricheskii siluety. Liudi i sobytiia*, pp. 7–28. The same interpretation is also apparent in more specialized works, such as those of I. I. Ditiatin, *Ustroistvo i upravlenie gorodov Rossii*, I, and Kizevetter, *Posadskaia obshchina v Rossii XVIII st.*, on the towns and townsmen, or that of V. I. Semevskii, *Krest'iane v tsarstvovanie Ekateriny II*, on the peasants. These were not the only interpretations of Catherine II to come out of tsarist Russia, but for several reasons

they have exerted the strongest influence on Western scholars. For a brief summary of the historiographical tradition of Catherine's alleged hypocrisy, see David Griffiths, "Catherine II: The Republican Empress," p. 325n.

7. Shcherbatov, Fonvizin, Sumarokov, Vinskii, and Radishchev were among the memoirists and publicists of Catherine's time who severely criticized the empress and her policies. Alexander Herzen provided a crucial link between those contemporary critics of Catherine and the liberal and populist historians mentioned in the preceding note. By publishing Shcherbatov's *On the Corruption of Morals*, Radishchev's *Journey from St. Petersburg to Moscow,* and Catherine's own memoirs, Herzen sought to discredit Catherine in particular and the autocracy in general. See, for example, his preface to the edition of Shcherbatov's *On the Corruption of Morals* and Radishchev's *Journey* published in one volume by Herzen's Free Russian Press in London in 1858.

8. For a survey of works on the reign of Catherine II published in the years prior to 1971 both in the West and in the Soviet Union, see Marc Raeff, "Random Notes on the Reign of Catherine II in the Light of Recent Literature." The many individual examples of the new scholarship on Catherine and her reign are too numerous to list here, but many of them will be cited at appropriate places in the text. The first general account of Catherine's reign to include much of the new scholarship is Isabel de Madariaga's *Russia in the Age of Catherine the Great*, which appeared as this manuscript was being revised for publication.

9. Examples are Theodore von Laue, *Sergei Witte and the Industrialization of Russia,* Walter Pintner, *Russian Economic Policy under Nicholas I,* and George Yaney, *The Systematization of Russian Government.*

Chapter I. Ideas of Development

1. "Razskaz imperatritsy Ekateriny II o pervykh piati godakh eia tsarstvovaniia," *RA*, 1865, pp. 470–490.

2. This comment, written in 1769, appears in a collection of notes on law and government to which Catherine added throughout her reign. TsGADA, f. 10, d. 17, p. 5.

3. Rudolph Daniels, "V N. Tatishchev: A Rationalist Historian and Theorist of the Petrine Service Nobility," pp. 154–156; N. L. Rubinshtein, "Ulozhenaia komissiia 1754–1766 gg. i ee proekt novogo ulozheniia 'O sostoiannii poddannykh voobshche,'" pp. 217–219, 240–249; Marc Raeff, "The Domestic Policies of Peter III and His Overthrow," pp. 1294–1300.

4. Rubinshtein, "Ulozhenaia komissiia," pp. 230–246.

5. Quoted in David L. Ransel, *The Politics of Catherinian Russia: The Panin Party,* p. 147.

6. According to G. Parry, "Enlightened Government and Its Critics in Germany," p. 183, this meaning was "universally" understood.

7. M. Shpilevskii, "Politika narodonaseleniia v tsarstvovanie Ekateriny II," argues impressively that population policy constituted the centerpiece of Catherine's social and economic policies. The most explicit statement of such a policy by one of Catherine's contemporary rulers came from Joseph II, who declared: "I consider the supreme object towards which the political, fiscal, and even the

military administration should direct their activities is the population, that is to say the maintenance and increase of the number of subjects." Quoted in T.C.W. Blanning, *Joseph II and Enlightened Despotism*, p. 54.

8. Quoted in G. G. Pisarevskii, *Iz istorii inostrannoi kolonizatsii v Rossii v XVIII v.*, p. 7.

9. Citations from Catherine's *Instruction* will be given by chapter and article so that they can be traced in any edition. In some cases I will quote from the *Instruction* using my own translation. When I quote from another translation, I shall use, for the sake of convenience, the most recent English translation by Paul Dukes, *Russia under Catherine the Great*, II.

10. A small but illustrative example of the government's use of western European models is provided by its first steps toward reform of the treatment of the mentally ill. On August 8, 1762, only two months after seizing the throne, Catherine suggested the creation of insane asylums "on the example of other European countries in which special *dolgauzy* are established for this." Accordingly, the Senate instructed the College of Foreign Affairs to order its residents in England, Holland, France, and elsewhere to gather information on the treatment of the insane in those countries and to transmit it to the Senate for study. Senate *doklad* (report) entitled "On the Designation of One Monastary in Each Guberniia for the Insane and their Support by the College of Economy at the Rate of Four Kopecks per day," TsGADA, f. 248, d. 2833, pp. 1–2.

11. Marc Raeff, "Pugachev's Rebellion," p. 164. Since serf dues tended to claim most of a peasant's after-tax surplus, taxes levied on the serfs reduced the income of their masters.

12. Quoted in Ernst Wangermann, *The Austrian Achievement 1700–1800*, p. 90.

13. Walter L. Dorn, "The Prussian Bureaucracy in the Eighteenth Century," p. 404.

14. Ibid. In contrast to the sometimes exaggerated assessments of the Prussian bureaucracy and its achievements presented by nationalist historians, Hans Rosenberg, *Bureaucracy, Aristocracy, and Autocracy: The Prussian Experience 1660–1815*, and Hubert C. Johnson, *Frederick the Great and His Officials*, emphasize the monarch's difficulties with the bureaucracy and the shortcomings of the bureaucracy when measured against the monarch's wishes and the ideals of cameralism. If the accomplishments of the Prussian bureaucracy were modest enough in those terms, they were nevertheless impressive compared with those of the Austrian and Russian bureaucracies.

15. Honore G. V. Riquetti, Comte de Mirabeau, *Die preussische Monarchie*, I, 87.

16. Eduard Winter and his associates deserve much of the credit for identifying the specific connections between the intellectual life of Germany and that of Russia in the eighteenth century. It was largely on the basis of their work that Marc Raeff argued that the intellectual ties between Russia and Germany were far stronger than those between Russia and France in "Les Slaves, les Allemands, et les 'Lumières.'" Raeff's "The Enlightenment in Russia and Russian Thought in the Enlightenment," pp. 25–47, describes Russia's continued commitment to German rationalism and natural law theory throughout the eighteenth century. And his "The Well-Ordered Police State and the Development of Modernity in Seventeenth and Eighteenth Century Europe: An Attempt at a Comparative Approach" provides a seminal discussion of the formation and development of this ideology.

17. Friedhelm Kaiser, "Der europäische Anteil an der russischen Rechtstermino-logie der petrinischen Zeit," pp. 261–262.
18. William H. E. Johnson, *Russia's Educational Heritage*, p. 36; Raeff, "The Enlightenment in Russia," pp. 28–31.
19. Walter Gleason, "Political Ideals and Loyalties of Some Russian Writers of the Early 1760s," pp. 562–563; Emile Haumant, *La culture française en Russie 1700–1900*, pp. 90–91.
20. Raeff, "The Enlightenment in Russia," pp. 33–34; Eduard Winter, introduction to Winter, ed., *August Ludwig Schlözer und Russland*, p. 19; Allen McConnell, "The Autocrat and the Open Critic," p. 158; McConnell, *A Russian Philosophe: Alexander Radishchev 1749–1802*, p. 42; Richard Pipes, *Karamzin's Memoir on Ancient and Modern Russia*, p. 29; Haumant, *La culture française en Russie*, pp. 97–98. In 1799, when Paul recalled Russian students from foreign universities, there were 36 Russian students at Leipzig and 65 at Jena; Henri Masson, *Secret Memoirs of the Court of St. Petersburg*, p. 291. The largest group of Russian students ever to study in "France" consisted of 44 students enrolled at the Alsatian and non-Catholic University of Strasbourg in 1786 to study medicine and natural science; Haumant, *La culture française en Russie*, pp. 99–100.
21. Haumant, *La culture française en Russie*, pp. 43–49.
22. Two statements of this hypothesis are George Yaney, *The Systematization of Russian Government*, pp. 22–28, and Richard Pipes, *Russia under the Old Regime*, pp. 74–76.
23. S. M. Troitskii, "Finansovaia politika russkogo absoliutizma vo vtoroi polovine XVII–XVIII vv.," p. 306. On Peter's provincial reforms and their attendant problems, see M. M. Bogoslavskii, *Oblastnaia reforma Petra Velikago: provintsiia 1719–1727*. On the so-called counter-reforms that followed Peter's death, see Iu. V. Got'e, *Istoriia oblastnogo upravleniia v Rossii ot Petra Velikago do Ekateriny II*, I. Arcadius Kahan, "Continuity in Economic Activity and Policy during the Post-Petrine Period in Russia," emphasizes the continuity of the autocracy's policies on tariffs, subsidies, contracts, etc. and the continued growth of industry under private ownership, but he concedes that state spending on public projects and what he terms "social overhead" (schools, roads, churches) experienced a significant decline.
24. According to S. M. Troitskii, *Russkii absoliutizm i dvorianstvo*, p. 166, expenditures on the court increased from 4.4% of the state's total expenditures in 1725 0 10.9% in 1767. According to Walter M. Pintner, "Russia as a Great Power, 1709–1856: Reflections on the Problem of Relative Backwardness, with Special Reference to the Russian Army and Russian Society," pp. 8–10, The Russian army in the middle of the eighteenth century approximately equaled that of France in size and clearly exceeded those of Austria and Prussia.
25. Troitskii, *Russkii absoliutizm i dvorianstvo*, p. 176, estimates a total of 12,500 civil servants in 1755. Catherine's decree of December 15, 1763 (*PSZ* no. 11991, Table X), gives a figure of 16,504 civil servants. Since that decree provided for a significant increase in the number of civil servants, an approximate figure of 14,000 for 1762 may, if anything, be too high. Dorn, "Prussian Bureaucracy," p. 261, says that Frederick II employed 14,000 officials of all kinds but does not tie that figure to a specific year. A very different estimate is

given by Johnson in *Frederick the Great and His Officials* (p. 17): "It is still possible that no more than three thousand persons composed the entire Prussian civil service in 1750." In a footnote Johnson goes on to break down that figure into 1,000 executive-level officials and about 2,000 subalterns of various degrees. However, on pp. 58–59 Johnson indicates that the figure given earlier refers only to the "core bureaucracy" and not to local officials.

26. The figure on Austria is from R. J. White, *Europe in the Eighteenth Century*, p. 209. Troitskii, *Russikii absoliutizm i dvorianstvo*, p. 265, says that in 1767 the Russian government spent 5,660,000 rubles on internal administration out of a total state budget of 25,000,000. In 1763 both the absolute figure and the percentage would almost certainly have been lower.

27. Troitskii, *Russkii absoliutizm i dvorianstvo*, pp. 275–285.

28. *Kniga Shtatov* no. 11991 (Dec. 15, 1763) combines the data reproduced here in Tables 1–4 with similar data for the guberniia of St. Petersburg to yield a total of 3,958 provincial officials for the empire, not counting the Baltic provinces and the Ukraine.

29. Troitskii, *Russkii absoliutizm i dvorianstvo*, p. 255. In Catherine's own words, provincial officials at the time of her accession were expected to "kormitsia s del." *RA*, 1865, p. 471.

30. Blanning, *Joseph II*, pp. 26–27; Dorn, "Prussian Bureaucracy, pp. 416–417.

31. Catherine complained that provincial officials regularly ignored her decrees until they had been issued for the third time. *RA*, 1865, pp. 370–371. In 1764 J. J. Sievers, the new governor of Novgorod, reported that his predecessor had been able to act on only two or three of the hundreds of petitions that local residents submitted to him each year. D. I. Ilovaiskii, Iakov Sivers," p. 466.

32. In a letter to Catherine dated June 7, 1778, Sievers referred to "ce que vous me dites sur l'Angleterre, comment vous l'avez cru le meilleur gouvernement de l'Europe et vous le croyez le plus mauvais presentement." TsGADA, f. 5, d. 130, p. 3.

33. Marc Raeff, "The Empress and the Vinerian Professor: Catherine II's Projects of Government Reforms and Blackstone's Commentaries," pp. 18–19; Robert E. Jones, *The Emancipation of the Russian Nobility*, pp. 219–220.

34. Transmission from Vorontsov to Catherine, dated July 15, 1766. LOII, f. 36, d. 398, pp. 219–235.

35. Quoted in Janet Marcum, "Simeon R. Vorontsov: Minister to the Court of St. James," p. 236.

36. Lionel Rothkrug, *Opposition to Louis XIV: The Political and Social Origins of the French Enlightenment*, pp. 249–371.

37. Ransel, *Politics of Catherinian Russia*, pp. 73–84.

38. Gleason, *Moral Idealists*, pp. 94–98.

39. Troitskii, "Obsuzhdenie voprosa o krest'ianskoi torgovle v komissii o kommertsii v seredine 60x godov XVIII v.," pp. 227–232.

40. Robert Derathe, "Les philosophes et le despotisme," p. 73.

41. Heinz Holldack, "Der Physiocratismus und die Absolute Monarchie," pp. 533–535.

42. Ransel, *Politics of Catherinian Russia*, pp. 148–150.

43. Arthur Wilson, "Diderot in Russia 1773–1774," p. 197.

44. Ibid., p. 189; Ivan Luppol, "The Empress and the Philosophe," p. 62.

45. Wilson Augustine, "The Economic Attitudes and Opinions Expressed by the Russian Nobility in the Great Commission of 1767," pp. 182–184; Jones, *Emancipation of the Russian Nobility*, pp. 56–90.
46. Augustine, "Economic Attitudes and Opinions," p. 164; W. H. Parker, *An Historical Geography of Russia*, p. 58. Karamzin urged Alexander I to restore the practice of allowing peasants to purchase substitutes for recruitment on the grounds that it was a major incentive for the peasants to work hard and to save their money. Pipes, *Karamzin's Memoir*, p. 162.
47. The physiocratic concept of *produit net* is most clearly stated in Pierre Samuel Du Pont de Nemours, *De l'origine et progrès d'une science nouvelle*, p. 25, and in Z. B. Le Thrône, *De l'administration provincale*, I, 29.
48. Arcadius Kahan, "The Costs of Westernization in Russia: The Gentry and the Economy in the Eighteenth Century," pp. 48–50.
49. For Catherine's views on this question, see article 378 of her *Instruction* and her letter to Marie Therese Jeoffrin published in *SIRIO*, I, 283.
50. Troitskii, "Obsuzhdenie voprosa o krest'ianskoi torgovle," pp. 232–234.
51. François-Xavier Coquin, *La grande commission legislative, 1767–1768. Les cahiers de doléance urbaines (Province de Moscou)*, pp. 108–123.
52. F. V. Taranovskii, "Politicheskaia doktrina v nakaze imperatritsy Ekateriny II," pp. 44–86; K. N. Lodyzhenskii, *Istoriia russkago tamozhnago tarifa*, pp. 113–116; Raeff, "The Empress and the Vinerian Professor," p. 20.
53. Joseph Sonnenfels, *Grundsätze der Policey, Handlung und Finanz*, I, 6.
54. Justi aknowledged Montesquieu as one of his predecessors in the introduction to his *Gesammelte politische und finanz Schriften*, I.
55. Quoted in Albion Small, *The Cameralists, Pioneers of German Social Policy*, p. 486.
56. David Ogg, *Europe of the Ancient Régime 1715–1783* p. 41–44.
57. Quoted in Small, *The Cameralists*, p. 508.
58. Dukes, ed., *Russia under Catherine the Great*, II, 18. According to August Ludwig von Schlözer, *Allgemeines StaatsRecht*, p. 123, Catherine awarded Bielfeld the Russian Order of St. Anne.
59. *RBS* XXII, 601.
60. N. D. Chechulin, *Nakaz imperatritsy Ekateriny II dannyi komissii o sochinenii proekta novago ulozheniia*, introduction; Chechulin, "Predposlednee slovo ob istochnikakh 'Nakaza.'" See also Dukes, *Russia under Catherine the Great*, II, 12–22.

Chapter II. The New Regime

1. See V. S. Popov's account of his conversation with Catherine in which the empress emphasized the need to prepare legislation with care and circumspection. *RA*, 1891, p. 5.
2. In dealing with the peasant question, Catherine was always extremely fearful of arousing exaggerated hopes and fears. In a confidential memorandum to Procurator-General Viazemskii she emphasized the need for secrecy in dealing with the peasant question lest rumor lead to unforseen results. P. I. Bartenev, ed., *Os'mnadsatyi vek: istoricheskii sbornik*, III, 390. For similar reasons Viazemskii opposed the publication of the winning entry in the essay competition sponsored by the Free Economic Society and argued that the Russian people

mistook anything published for a decree. Ilovaiskii, "Graf Iakov Sivers," p. 277.

3. See Chapter VI.

4. P. M. Maikov, *Ivan Ivanovich Betskoi*, pp. 397–399.

5. For a more complete account of the society's activities in Catherine's time, see V. V. Oreshkin, *Vol'noe ekonomicheskoe obshchestvo v Rossii 1765–1917*, pp. 18–86; A. I. Khodnev, *Istoriia imperatorskago vol'nago ekonomicheskago obshchestva*, pp. 1–30; and Michael Confino, *Domaines et seigneurs en Russie vers la fin du XVIII siècle*.

6. K. V. Sivkov, "Voprosy sel'skogo khoziaistva v russkikh zhurnalakh poslednei tretei XVIII v.," p. 554.

7. Confino, *Domaines et seigneurs*, pp. 150–152; Augustine, "Economic Attitudes and Opinions," pp. 96–98; John H. Brown, "The Publication and Distribution of the *Trudy* of the Free Economic Society, 1765–1796," pp. 342–346.

8. P. H. Clendenning, "Eighteenth Century Russian Translations of Western Economic Works," p. 748.

9. Valentin Gitermann, *Geschichte Russlands*, II, 480.

10. Françoise de Labriolle, "Le prosveščenie russe et les lumières en France 1760–1789," pp. 75–92; P. N. Berkov, "Histoire de l'*Encyclopédie* dans la Russie du XVIII siècle," pp. 47–48.

11. Labriolle, "Le prosveščenie russe," p. 77; Berkov, "Histoire de l'*Encyclopédie* dans la Russie," pp. 51–57.

12. *Svodnyi katalog russkoi knigi XVIII veka, 1725–1800*, I, 333–334.

13. Griffiths, "Catherine II," p. 326.

14. *PSZ* nos. 11879, 11880, and 11881.

15. Roger Bartlett, *Human Capital: The Settlement of Foreigners in Russia 1762–1804*, p. 66.

16. Ransel, *Politics of Catherinian Russia*, pp. 102–117; John Le Donne, "Appointments to the Russian Senate 1762–1796," pp. 41–43.

17. Ransel, *Politics of Catherinian Russia*, pp. 147–148; N. N. Firsov, *Pravitel'stvo i obshchestvo v ikh otnosheniiakh k vneshnei torgovli Rossii v tsarstvovanie imperatritsy Ekateriny II*, pp. 52–56.

18. Ransel, *Politics of Catherinian Russia*, p. 145.

19. Walter Kirchner, *Commercial Relations between Russia and Europe 1400–1800*, pp. 181–191.

20. Knud Rahbek-Schmidt, "The Treaty of Commerce between Great Britain and Russia 1765: A Study on the Development of Count Panin's Northern System," p. 116.

21. Jake V. T. Knoppers, *Dutch Trade with Russia from the Time of Peter I to Alexander I: A Quantitative Study in Eighteenth Century Shipping*, I, 154, 177–178, 191.

22. Ibid., pp. 177–178.

23. S. V. Bernshtein-Kogan, *Vyshnevolotskii vodnyi put'*, p. 29.

24. Knoppers, *Dutch Trade with Russia*, I, 155.

25. *Memoirs of Catherine the Great*, p. 365.

26. Lodyzhenskii, *Istoriia russkago tamozhnago tarifa*, p. 142; Rahbek-Schmidt, "Treaty of Commerce," p. 117; Kirchner, *Commercial Relations*, pp. 164–169.

27. Knoppers, *Dutch Trade with Russia*, I, 193–196.
28. Ransel, *Politics of Catherinian Russia*, pp. 146–148.
29. *PSZ* no. 11489 (March 28, 1762). B. N. Mironov, "Eksport russkogo khleba vo vtoroi polovine XVIII—nachale XIX v.," pp. 174–176.
30. Lodyzhenskii, *Istoriia russkago tamozhnago tarifa*, pp. 113–116.
31. Mironov, "Eksport russkogo khleba," pp. 174–176.
32. Kirchner, *Commercial Relations*, p. 186.
33. Lodyzhenskii, *Istoriia russkago tamozhnago tarifa*, pp. 113–116.
34. Ibid., p. 198.
35. *PSZ* no. 11689.
36. *PSZ* no. 11761.
37. *PSZ* no. 12872.
38. *PSZ* no. 13374.
39. *PSZ* no. 14275.
40. Shcherbatov, *Sochineniia*, I, 366.
41. For details see Jones, *Emancipation of the Russian Nobility*, pp. 108–117.
42. Troitskii, "Obsuzhdenie voprosa o krest'ianskoi torgovle," pp. 227–232.
43. Ibid., pp. 232–239.
44. Ransel, *Politics of Catherinian Russia*, p. 162. According to P. I. Ivanov, *Opyt biografii general-prokurorov i ministrov iustitsii*, p. 45, contemporaries were shocked by the appointment to such an important post of a man whom P. A. Rumiantsev characterized as "an ordinary quartermaster."
45. Catherine's activities on a typical day are described in William Richardson, *Anecdotes of the Russian Empire*, as excerpted in Peter Putnam, ed., *Seven Britons in Imperial Russia 1698–1802*, p. 147.
46. John P. Le Donne, "Appointments to the Russian Senate 1762–1796," p. 37.
47. Jones, *Emancipation of the Russian Nobility*, pp. 174–176.
48. Ibid. See also Ivanov, *Opyt biografii general-prokurorov i ministrov iustitsii*, p. 39, and James Hassell, "Catherine II and Procurator-General Viazemskii," pp. 23–30.
49. *PSZ* no. 11989 (Dec. 15, 1763) and no. 12137 (April 21, 1764). On the results of this administrative rétablissement, see Kerry Morrison, "Catherine II's Legislative Commission: An Administrative Interpretation," pp. 472–473. On the relationship of these measures to each other and to the administrative theories of cameralism, see Dietrich Geyer, "Gesellschaft als staatliche Veranstaltung. Bemerkungen zur Sozialgeschichte der russischen Staatsverwaltung im 18 Jahrhundert," p. 30.
50. Wallace Daniel, "Russian Attitudes Toward Modernization: The Merchant-Nobility Conflict in the Legislative Commission, 1767–1774," pp. 69–70.
51. Ibid., p. 67.
52. Ibid., p. 77.
53. "Razskaz imperatritsy Ekateriny II o pervykh piati godakh eia tsarstvovania," *RA*, 1865, p. 471.
54. *PSZ* no. 11598.
55. TsGADA, f. 248 (Zhurnaly i protokoly pravitel'stvuiushchego senata), d. 3688, pp. 36–47.
56. Doklad Senata o preobrazovaniiakh gubernskikh i uezdnykh pristustvennykh mest. TsGADA, f. 370 (Dela otnosiashchiesia do obrazovaniia razlichnykh gosudarstvennykh uchrezhdenii), d. 33, pp. 1–40.

57. "Razskaz imperatritsy Ekateriny II o pervykh piati godakh eia tsarstvovaniia," *RA*, 1865, p. 475.
58. For example, toward the end of 1782 Governor T. I. Tutolmin of Tver sent the Senate a report on the distribution and sale of salt in his guberniia in which he used population statistics to calculate the quantity of salt that would be needed in each uezd during the coming year and to project the amount of revenue the state could expect from its sale. TsGADA, f. 16, d. 788, part 3, pp. 341–346 ob.
59. V. E. Den, *Naselenie Rossii po piatoi revisii*, I, 89.
60. *PSZ* nos. 15278 and 15296. See also Den, *Naselenie Rossii po piatoi revisii*, I, 99, and Karl German, *Statisticheskie izsledovaniia otnositel'no Rossiiskoi Imperii*, p. 11.
61. *PSZ* no. 3682 (Dec. 9, 1720) and its supplementary instruction *PSZ* no. 3695 (Dec. 22, 1720).
62. M. A. Tsvetkov, *Izmenenie lesistosti evropeiskoi Rossii s kontsa XVII stoletiia po 1914 g.*, p. 66.
63. L. N. Pushkarev, "Akademiia Nauk i russkaia kul'tura XVIII veka," p. 32; I. E. German, *Istoriia russkago mezhevaniia*, pp. 159–160.
64. *PSZ* no. 10029 (Jan. 30, 1760).
65. *PSZ* no. 12474 (May 25, 1766), part 5, point 1.
66. German, *Istoriia russkago mezhevaniia*, pp. 91, 204.
67. L. V. Milov, *Issledovanie ob "ekonomicheskikh primechaniiakh" k general'nomu mezhevaniiu*, pp. 38–43.
68. M. A. Tsvetkov, "Kartograficheskie materialy general'nogo mezhevaniia," p. 91.
69. According to Milov, *Issledovanie ob "ekonomicheskikh primechaniiakh" k general'nomu mezhevaniiu*, p. 52, the surveying of one uezd of Nizhegorod Guberniia in 1783 produced a general plan of the uezd, a topographical map, a survey book, a catalog, "economic observations," an alphabetical listing of estates and their owners, and several statistical tables. The survey's effect on Russian cartography can be seen in a comparison of two maps of Novgorod Guberniia in the collection of the Central State Military Historical Archive. The first, produced in 1765 to portray a reorganization of local administration, is little more than a schematic drawing showing approximate boundaries, major towns, and little else. A scale for measuring distances in versts is provided but cannot be used with accuracy. The second map was composed by the *mezhevaia kantselariia* of Novgorod Guberniia in May 1785 and bears the title "Geometric Map of the Novgorod Viceregency." Notes on the map explain that the survey of Novgorod was begun in 1778 and that the entire guberniia had been divided into 14,843 *dachy* comprising 8,639,292 *desiatini* of land (1 desiatina = 2.7 acres or 1.092 hectares). A key in the lower right-hand corner gives the symbols for features such as villages, fords, and mills, and a separate note states that the scale is fourteen versts to the English inch. The detail evident in most areas of the maps is missing from the northeastern corner because, according to another note, the survey had not been completed in that region. TsGVIA, f. VUA, d. 20875 and 20876.
70. Tsvetkov, "Kartograficheskie materialy general'nogo mezhevaniia," p. 91.
71. *PSZ* no. 15688 (March 15, 1782).
72. E. G. Istomina, "Novgorodskaia guberniia vo vtoroi polovine XVIII veka.

Opyt istoriko-geograficheskogo issledovaniia," gives examples of the details included in the economic observations, but she notes on p. 253 that the data are unreliable and points out that the economic observations and the topographical descriptions used different categories and different criteria, so that it is difficult to check one against the other. On the other hand, Milov, *Issledovanie ob "ekonomicheskikh primechaniiakh" k general'nomu mezhevaniiu,* p. 20, argues that the economic observations are reasonably reliable and that they can be used as a credible source for economic history. S. E. Semevskii used the economic observations as his major source on the economics of serfdom, but Milov, who uses the same source to revise Semevskii, argues that Semevskii based his conclusions on too few examples.

73. N. L. Rubinshtein, "Topograficheskie opisaniia namestnichestva i gubernii XVIII v.—pamiatniki geograficheskogo i ekonomicheskogo izucheniia Rossii," p. 45.

74. *PSZ* no. 14671.

75. Thus, for example, the topographical description of Vladimir Guberniia, completed in 1784, followed the 20 questions posed by the Senate in 1777, but the one completed in Novgorod Guberniia at approximately the the same time was based on a different set of 40 questions; G. A. Riazhskii, introduction to Riazhskii, ed., *Topograficheskoe opisanie vladimirskoi gubernii sostavlennoe v 1784 godu,* p. iv. See also Istomina, "Novgorodskaia guberniia vo vtoroi polovine XVIII veka," pp. 109–110. This work was the author's *kandidatskaia dissertatsiia* at Moscow State University and will be referred to in all future references as Istomina, dissertation, to distinguish it from the *referat*, or published summary, which bears the same title. The latter work will be cited as Istomina, referat.

76. Istomina, dissertation, p. 132.

77. Catherine later observed: "The Legislative Commission gave me light and testimony on the whole empire. . . . It brought together all the parts of the law and sorted out the materials and would have done more had not the Turkish War begun." "Razskaz imperatritsy Ekateriny II o pervykh piati godakh eia tsarstvovaniia," *RA,* 1865, p. 480.

78. This is apparent from the registers retained in TsGADA, f. 342 (Novoulozhennaia komissiia), d. 111 (Opredeleniia komissii), parts 1–27, which includes payments to the staff of the Legislative Commission and authorization for expenses related to the staff. The first entry is dated Jan. 3, 1767. The second entry, dated Jan. 20, 1767, authorizes the staff to proceed from St. Petersburg to Moscow. The last entry that I have noted is dated Sept. 15, 1796, and authorized the payment of salaries to the staff in the total amount of 8,754 rubles.

79. These materials are preserved in TsGADA, f. 342, dd. 149–219.

80. Morrison, "Catherine II's Legislative Commission," pp. 482–484. In addition to the four projects mentioned by Morrison, a project on the status of the church and the clergy entitled "Dukhovno-grazhdanskoi glavnoi glavnoi proekta novago ulozheniia" was completed by June 3, 1770, according to I. Pokrovskii, "Ekaterininskaia komissiia o sostavlenii proekta novago ulozheniia i tserkovnye voprosy v nei 1766–1771," pp. 311–313. I have also seen projects entitled "O razmnozhenii naroda," "O zemlevladenii," and "O pochtakh i gostinitsakh" in TsGADA, f. 342, d. 261.

81. Except in grave emergencies (and sometimes even then), Catherine was a firm

believer in the need to prepare legislation carefully and slowly. See her statement to V. S. Popov cited in n. 1 above. In her notes on law and government
Catherine laid out a detailed agenda for the Legislative Commission that began with an examination of current circumstances and proceeded step by step
to proposals for new legislation. At the end she wrote: "Perhaps one will say
that all of this is pedantic, but without a method is there any means to do anything properly? It is necessary that the novel begin not with the end but with
the beginning because the one comes last and the other first." TsGADA, f. 10,
d. 17, p. 14.
82. TsGADA, f. 16, d. 785, pp. 6–22. Sievers's recommendations will be discussed in the following chapters.
83. Quoted in Blum, *Ein russischer Staatsmann,* I, 181–182.
84. Le Donne, "Appointments to the Russian Senate," pp. 27–33.

Chapter III. The New Governor

1. Ilovaiskii, "Graf Iakov Sivers," pp. 451–452. On p. 458 Ilovaiskii notes that
   the family's origins was always a delicate subject for its members and that the
   nobles of Livonia agreed only in 1754 to enroll the Sievers family in the nobility. Earlier, on p. 448, Ilovaiskii quotes the sarcasm that A. V. Khrapovitskii,
   Catherine's secretary, wrote in his journal on March 3, 1788: "Reviewing
   the Cabinet Register provides an explanation of various court figures of Elizabeth's time, to wit: Razumovskii was a choir boy and Sievers was
   a lackey."
2. *Ocherki istorii Leningrada,* vol. I, *Period feodalisma 1703–1861,* pp. 76, 354.
   According to entries in the Senate's journal for August and September 1765,
   Karl Sievers owned a copper foundry in Orenburg, and he and a member of
   the Repnin family were one of five sets of claimants to several other copper
   and iron works in the Urals. TsGADA, f. 248, d. 3684, pp. 514–515, and d.
   3685, p. 92 ob. I am grateful to Professor Roger Bartlett for sharing this
   information with me.
3. According to Blum, *Ein russischer Staatsmann,* I, 15, Sievers was one of
   twelve young men accepted for such service by the College of Foreign Affairs;
   only two of them failed to reach the third highest rank in the Table of Ranks.
   On the excellent career prospects of a young man selected as a *iunker,* see
   Troitskii, *Russkii absoliutizm i dvorianstvo,* pp. 191–193.
4. Blum, *Ein russischer Staatsmann,* I, 151–152.
5. For example, when De La Salle and the Brothers of the Christian Doctrine set
   out to spread literacy and education among the common people of France, La
   Chalotais attacked their efforts in his *Essai d'education nationale.* Voltaire
   then wrote to La Chalotais: "I am grateful to you for dissuading peasants
   from studying. I who cultivate the ground, forward to you a request for laborers, not for clerks. Send me especially some *frères ignorantins* to work my
   ploughs." Quoted in W. J. Battersby, *De La Salle: A Pioneer of Modern Education,* pp. 716–719.
6. This is a neglected subject in English. Until quite recently, historians emphasized the secular and materialistic aspects of the Enlightenment in Britain and

France as the immediate ancestors of the French Revolution, secular liberalism, and scientific positivism. An important exception is Raeff's "The Well-Ordered Police State and the Development of Modernity in Seventeenth and Eighteenth Century Europe." Donald Treadgold, *The West in Russia and China: Russia 1472–1917*, pp. 109–113, discusses some of the influences of pietism on eighteenth century Russians. The most important work on pietism as a source of reform and social action is Karl Hinrichs, *Preussentum und Pietismus in Brandenburg Preussen als religios-soziale Reformbewegun.* On the role of pietism in transmitting German political and social concepts into Russia, see Eduard Winter, *Halle als Ausgangspunkt der deutschen Russlandkunde in 18 Jahrhundert,* and Raeff's "Les Slaves, les Allemands, et les 'Lumières.'"

7. Quoted in Blum, *Ein russischer Staatsmann,* II 467.
8. Ibid., I, 13.
9. Ibid., pp. 37, 63.
10. Ibid., p. 14.
11. Ibid., II, 522.
12. Ibid., pp. 523–524.
13. Ibid., I, 23, 28; Ilovaiskii, "Graf Iakov Sivers," pp. 454–455.
14. Blum, *Ein russischer Staatsmann,* II, 534–535. Much earlier, Blum quotes from a letter that Sievers wrote to Catherine in 1766 in which he referred specifically to an article on grain prices that he had recently read in the *St. James Evening Post.* Ibid., I, 237.
15. Sievers to Catherine, March 12, 1780. TsGADA, f. 5, d. 130, p. 11. In a letter to Catherine in French dated Jan. 11, 1779, Sievers referred to "Liberty and Property" (in English) as "mon but et ma divise." TsGADA, f. 16, d. 788, part 1, p. 3.
16. Blum, *Ein russischer Staatsmann,* I, 51–54; Ilovaiskii, "Graf Iakov Sivers," pp. 456–457.
17. He used the words "Normandy" and "Normans" in this sense several times. The first usage occurs in his first major memorandum from Novgorod, dated Dec. 9, 1764. TsGADA, f. 16, d. 785, p. 17.
18. Sievers's theory of moral sentiments is most clearly spelled out in his judgment on the educational experiments of Ivan Betskoi, who had sought to create a new breed of Russians out of children cut off from their parents. Sievers wrote to his daughter in 1791: "All those who are graduated from the educational institutions of that scatterbrain Betskoi are possessed of a certain coldness that is rooted in contempt for social relations—the disposition of a bastard, which their teacher was. He maintained that tearing them loose from the ties of family would make them subjects and children of the state; he did not consider that by robbing them of those first feelings which nature instills through the instinct of gratitude he was, in spite of everything, rendering them incapable of the most beautiful feelings." Quoted in Blum, *Ein russischer Staatsmann,* II, 274.
19. Ibid., pp. 99–95.
20. Ibid., p. 535. Those words were written in 1790 in a letter to his daughter.
21. Sievers to Count A. K. Razumovskii from Grodno, Nov. 3, 1793. TsGADA f. 11, d. 1312, p. 9.

22. S. A. Korf, "Ocherk istoricheskago razvitiia gubernatorskoi dolzhnosti v Rossii," p. 131.
23. *PSZ* no. 2218 (Dec. 18, 1708); Korf, "Ocherk istoricheskago razvitiia gubernatorskoi dolzhnosti v Rossii," pp. 130–131.
24. *PSZ* no. 2673 (April 24, 1713).
25. Korf, "Ocherk istoricheskago razvitiia gubernatorskoi dolzhnosti v Rossii," pp. 134–136.
26. Ibid., pp. 136–137.
27. The rank and salary of provincial governors is given in the *Kniga Shtatov* no. 11991 (Dec. 15, 1763). The uncertainty surrounding the duties and powers of the governors is discussed in the introduction to Catherine's "Instruction to the Governors" ("Nastavlenie gubernatoram"), *PSZ* no. 12137 (April 21, 1764).
28. *PSZ* no. 12137 (April 21, 1764).
29. Ibid. Jones, *Emancipation of the Russian Nobility*, pp. 176–177, fails to make a necessary distinction between a governor's responsibilities and his authority.
30. Blum, *Ein russischer Staatsmann*, I, 153–154, provides this information in the form of a quotation from Sievers's autobiographical memorandum to the minister of the interior, composed about 1805. In it Sievers stated that Catherine showed him the "secret" instruction during their meeting in St. Petersburg, which would have been in June 1764, but that she did not give him that instruction until six months later, which would have been around December 1764. However, on pp. 172–173 of the same volume Blum gives the date of the secret instruction as Feb. 1, 1765. He then says that it was heavily influenced by Sievers's memorandum of Dec. 9, 1764. Although Blum's citations can be trusted, his interpretations, which consistently glorify Sievers and denigrate Catherine, cannot. The question of who first influenced whom cannot be determined on the basis of the available evidence.
31. Ibid., pp. 1, 173–180.
32. Ibid., pp. 175–182.
33. Ibid., pp. 1, 177–182.
34. Sievers to Catherine, Dec. 9, 1764. TsGADA, f. 16, d. 785, pp. 6–22 ob. A German translation of the memorandum appears in Blum, *Ein russischer Staatsmann*, I, 159–171, but for some reason the sections are given in a sequence different from that of the copy in the archives. A Russian paraphrase with quotations appears in Ilovaiskii, "Graf Iakov Sivers," pp. 467–470.
35. Blum, *Ein russischer Staatsmann*, I, 173.
36. According to Karl German, *Statisticheskie izsledovaniia otnositel'no Rossiiskoi Imperii*, p. 193, the Dukhovnyi Reglament of 1722 ordered the parish clergy to record such information and send it to the hierarchy every three years. Mikhail Shpilevskii, "Politika narodonaseleniia v tsarstvovanie Ekateriny II," pp. 23–24, says that soon after Catherine's accession August Ludwig von Schlözer proposed the compilation of *metricheskie knigi* (books recording births and deaths) and that Catherine ordered that such books be compiled in the guberniia of St. Petersburg. *PSZ* no. 12761 (Feb. 27, 1764). On p. 25 Shpilevskii goes on to point out that Sievers was the first to present the Senate with a general *metricheskaia tabel'*.
37. TsGADA, f. 16, d. 785, pp. 51–52.

38. Sievers to Catherine, Oct. 10, 1768. Ibid., p. 86 ob.
39. Ibid., pp. 68 ob., 88 ob., 162 ob., 217 ob., 233.
40. Ibid., p. 233.
41. Shpilevskii, "Politika narodonaseleniia v tsarstvovaniia Ekateriny II," pp. 25–26. He notes that as late as 1794 Catherine was still trying to develop a nationwide system of recording and analyzing population data from the *metricheskie knigi*.
42. A copy of his report, dated April 27, 1765, is preserved in TsGADA, f. 16, d. 785, pp. 46–49.
43. In a letter dated Sept. 8, 1766, Sievers informed Catherine that he had just completed a journey of more than 3,000 versts through the northern part of his guberniia. Ibid., p. 58. According to the unidentified author of a summary of Sievers's travel accounts, his report on that trip was read before the First Department of the Senate in the presence of the empress on Jan. 19, 1767. *RA*, 1892, p. 169. Sievers's report on the second journey, bearing the date 1768, begins: "Following the new instructions given by the Senate, I examined the southern half of my guberniia last summer." TsGADA, f. 16, d. 785, d. 89. In addition to the summary of Sievers's accounts of his travels published in *RA*, D. I. Ilovaiskii gives a longer, more detailed account in his article "Novgorodskaia guberniia sto let tomu nazad."
44. M. T. Beliavskii, *Krest'ianskii vopros v Rossii nakanune vosstaniia E. I. Pugacheva*, pp. 185–186.
45. Ilovaiskii, "Graf Iakov Sivers," p. 504. In fact, Sievers remained deeply in debt from his service until Catherine rewarded him generously in 1776.
46. Ibid., pp. 510–511.
47. Blum, *Ein russischer Staatsmann*, I, 308–309.
48. Sievers to Catherine, May 24, 1768. TsGADA, f. 16. d. 785, pp. 68–68 ob.
49. Ibid.
50. Blum, *Ein russischer Staatsmann*, I, 207–208.
51. Quoted in ibid., p. 387.
52. Robert E. Jones, "Jacob Sievers, Enlightened Reform, and the Development of a 'Third Estate' in Russia."
53. Sievers to Catherine, Oct. 23, 1768. TsGADA, f. 16, d. 785, p. 75 ob.

Chapter IV. Novgorod Guberniia

1. As part of its effort to reorganize the administrative units of the Russian Empire, the Partial Commission on the Order of the Realm, a committee of the Legislative Commission, noted in the minutes of its meeting of Thursday, Jan. 29, 1769, that the best maps available showed Novgorod Guberniia measured 1,150 by 600 versts (one verst equals 0.6629 miles or 1.067 kilometers). TsGADA, f. 342 (Novoulozhennye Komissii), d. 123 (Dnevnye zapiski chastnoi komissii o portiatke [sic] gosudarstva v sile obshchago prava), book II, p. 7. All figures for guberniias prior to 1776 are inexact because no one knew their precise size or limits. At its session on Tuesday, Jan. 19, 1769, the same partial commission complained about that very fact and pointed out that the boundaries of many guberniias were not indicated on any maps and that the

existing boundaries on many maps were "highly inaccurate, such that on the general map of Russia the boundaries indicated for Moscow Guberniia include Galich Provintsiia, which belongs to Arkhangel Guberniia, whose provintsiias and uezds are not indicated at all." Ibid., p. 5.

2. *Donoshenie* (report) from Sievers to the Senate dated April 29, 1765. As part of the reorganization of administrative units being considered by the Senate, Sievers proposed a realignment of the uezds in his guberniia and supported his proposal with a table showing the populations of all uezds as they stood then and as they would be under the terms of his proposal. TsGADA, f. 248 (Dela Senata), d. 3588 (komissiia o gorodakh), pp. 351–352. The Senate used identical figures in its own *Rospisanie gorodam* (sic) of January 1766. Ibid., d. 3716 (Pervyi Departament za 1765–1766), pp. 196–222.

3. V. M. Kabuzan, *Izmeneniia v razmeshchenii naseleniia Rossii v XVIII— pervoi polovine XIXv.*, p. 83.

4. Istomina, dissertation, pp. 61–63.

5. Quoted in Blum, *Ein russischer Staatsmann*, I, 397.

6. Bernshtein-Kogan, *Vyshnevolotskii vodnyi put'*, p. 53.

7. Ibid., pp. 17–28.

8. William Coxe, *Travels into Poland, Russia, Sweden, and Denmark*, II, 283.

9. Istomina, dissertation, p. 355.

10. *SIRIO*, CVII, 444.

11. Bernshtein-Kogan, *Vyshnevolotskii vodnyi put'*, p. 50. A complete voyage from the town of Dmitrovsk in the Ukraine to St. Petersburg is described in the journal of the grain merchant I. A. Tolchenov, *Zhurnal ili zapiski i prikliuchenii I. A. Tolchenova*, pp. 38–39.

12. Kh. D. Sorina, "K voprosu o protsese sotsial'nogo rassloeniia goroda v sviazii s formirovaniem kapitalisticheskikh otnoshenii v Rossii v XVIII v. (g. Tver')," p. 283.

13. The merchant Tolchenov recalled that in 1772 Sievers met his caravan at Vyshnii Volochek. After advising the captains how much to pay the hired workers, Sievers told Tolchenov's group that they were to hire workers only on the float at Gorodko and to take only those who resided in the uezd of Vyshnii Volochek and no others. Tolchenov, *Zhurnal*, pp. 61–62.

14. V. I. Pokrovskii, *General'noe soobrazhenie po tverskoi gubernii izvlechennoe iz podrobnago topograficheskago i kameral'nago po gorodam i uezdam opisaniia*, p. xiv.

15. Ibid.

16. Istomina, referat, p. 14.

17. Sievers to Catherine, March 24, 1771. TsGADA, f. 16, d. 785, p. 223.

18. M. D. Chulkov, *Istoricheskoe opisanie rossiiskoi kommertsii pri vsekh ee portakh i granitsakh ot drevnikh vremen*, IV, part 5, p. 638.

19. Istomina, referat, p. 17.

20. N. L. Rubinshtein, *Sel'skoe khoziaistvo Rossii vo vtoroi polovine XVIII v.*, pp. 209–222.

21. Pokrovskii, *General'noe soobrazhenie po tverskoi gubernii*, p. v.

22. *SIRIO*, VIII, 442. On the role of handicrafts in the peasant economy, see I. A. Bulygin, *Polozhenie krest'ian i tovarnoe proizvodstvo v Rossii, vtoraia polovina XVIII veka.*

23. *SIRIO*, IV, 407–408.

24. Ibid., XIV, 257 (Vodskaia Piatina of Novgorod), 261 (Derevskaia Piatina of Novgorod), 278 (Ostrova), 286 (Rzhev), 347–348 (Shelonskaia Piatina of Novgorod), 354 (Bezhetskaia Piatina of Novgorod), 394–395 (Pskov).
25. Denise Eckaute, "La legislation des forêts au XVIII siècle," traces the history of the government's efforts to manage Russia's woodlands and conserve its timber. In their early correspondence Sievers and Catherine agreed that the governor should seek means of preserving the forests, but they offered few concrete proposals.
26. Sorina, "K voprosu o protsese sotsial'nogo rassloeniia," p. 293.
27. Istomina, referat, p. 17.
28. Pokrovskii, *General'noe soobrazhenie po tverskoi gubernii*, p.v; Istomina, dissertation, p. 265.
29. Istomina, dissertation, pp. 284–288.
30. Ibid., pp. 268–269.
31. Ibid., p. 270.
32. S. I. Volkov, *Krest'iane dvortsovykh vladenii podmoskov'ia v seredine XVIII veka*, pp. 135–141. Volkov found very few cases north of the city of Moscow in which harvests yielded even twice the seed. Ibid., pp. 221–226.
33. Milov, *Issledovanie ob "Ekonomicheskikh Primechaniiakh" k general'nomu mezhevaniiu*, pp. 308–309, argues persuasively that obrok payments and the use of barshchina varied directly with the profitability of agriculture.
34. Rubinshtein, *Sel'skoe khoziaistvo v Rossii*, p. 364.
35. Istomina, dissertation, pp. 274–275.
36. Rubinshtein, *Sel'skoe khoziaistvo v Rossii*, p. 364.
37. Pokrovskii, *General'noe soobrazhenie po tverskoi gubernii*, p. ix. In their nakaz to the Legislative Commission, the peasants of Kargopol asked permission to hunt birds and game throughout the year. Cited in Augustine, "Economic Attitudes and Opinions," p. 160.
38. Edger Melton, "The Peasant Economy and the World Market 1785–1860."
39. Istomina, dissertation, p. 282.
40. TsGADA, f. 16, d. 785, p. 8 ob.
41. N. M. Serpukov, "Ob izmenenii razmerov dushevladeniia pomeshchikov evropeiskoi Rossii v pervoi chetverti XVIII–pervoi polovine XIX v.," pp. 390–391.
42. Jones, *Emancipation of the Russian Nobility*, pp. 5–18, 56–62.
43. In the uzed of Tver, for example, 60 different monasteries owned a total of 39,836 revision souls. V. I. Pokrovskii, *Istoriko-statisticheskoe opisanie tverskoi gubernii*, II, 20.
44. N. I. Pavlenko, "Monastyrskoe khoziaistvo XVIII v. po votchinnym instruktsiiam," pp. 314–318; A. I. Petrova, "Antifeodal'naia bor'ba monastyrskikh krest'ian tverskogo kraia v pervoi polovine XVIII veka," p. 10.
45. Sievers to Catherine, December 1764. TsGADA, f. 16, d. 785, p. 16 ob.
46. Some idea of the geographic dispersion of the population can be seen in a piece of information provided by Istomina on p. 64 of her dissertation. She states that the territory organized as Novgorod Guberniia after 1776, which encompassed about 30 percent of the territory of the old guberniia, contained 10 goroda, 31 slobody, 266 pogosti and vystavki, 377 sela, 1,363 seletsii, and 7,721 drevna. Faced with the difficulty of trying to communicate even

the most essential information to people under those circumstances, Sievers wrote to Catherine in the summer of 1769 to propose that a local nobleman be designated to communicate government decrees to the people of each *pogost*. TsGADA, f. 785, pp. 149–149 ob.

47. Ilovaiskii, "Novgorodskaia guberniia," pp. 496–497.
48. Kh. D. Sorina, "Ocherk sotsial'no-ekonomicheskoi istorii goroda ostashkova v kontse XVIII–pervoi chetverti XIX v.," pp. 6–7.
49. Blum, *Ein russischer Staatsmann*, I, 252.
50. Kh. D. Sorina, "Ocherk sotsial'no-ekonomicheskoi istorii g. Vyshnego-Volochka vo vtoroi polovine XVIII veka i nachala XIX veka," p. 123.
51. Jones, "Jacob Sievers," pp. 426–427.
52. Istomina, dissertation, p. 382. Istomina cites a report of the Commission on Commerce as the source of her data.
53. A report of the Main Magistracy to the Commission on Commerce in 1764 counted 268 merchants in Pogoreno Gorodishche, 529 in Kholm, 587 in Ostashkov, 876 in Tikhvin, and 544 in eight smaller settlements. None of those places was a gorod at that time. TsGADA, f. 291 (Glavnyi Magistrat), op. 3, d. 13066, pp. 12–16.
54. Istomina, dissertation, p. 319. The author cites no source, but her figure accords well with that of the Main Magistracy cited in the previous note (which counted 26,223 merchants in Novgorod Guberniia) and with the figures contained in two Senate documents drafted in 1766 in conjunction with a reorganization of local administration. One counted 28,375 merchants in Novgorod Guberniia and the other 30,674. TsGADA, f. 248, d. 3716, pp. 53 ob., 196–206.
55. In 1765 the merchants of the city of Novgorod petitioned the Senate via the Commission on Commerce to enforce the laws against nonmerchants engaging in commerce. They claimed that the commercial activities of peasants and iamshchiks were a threat to their own solvency. TsGADA, f. 397 (Komissiia o komertsii), d. 455/32, p. 18.
56. Sievers to Catherine, October 1768. TsGADA, f. 16, d. 785, p. 150.
57. Pokrovskii, *General'noe soobrazhenie po tverskoi gubernii*, p. ii. The figures for Kholm and Bezhetsk, both of which became towns after 1775, show differences of comparable magnitude between the total and the permanent populations, whereas those for Rzhev and Ostashkov show only minor differences.
58. Sorina, "K voprosu o protsese sotsial'nogo rassloeniia," p. 287.
59. TsGADA, f. 397, d. 445/55, pp. 1–3. In a report to the Senate written in 1764, the Main Magistracy put the number of merchants in Tver at 2,608. TsGADA, f. 291, op. 3, d. 13066, p. 12.
60. Report of the Commission on Commerce to the Senate, Dec. 2, 1764. TsGADA, f. 397, d. 445/55, pp. 1–3.
61. Ibid., pp. 5–11.
62. Ibid., p. 9.
63. According to the anonymous entry in *RBS*, XX, pp. 585–589, Tikhon's six-volume work on theology, published in 1785 amd 1803, was based on the lectures he had given at the seminary in Tver. Its title, *Ob istinnom khristianstve*, is a Russian translation of Arendt's *Wahres Christentum*. On

Tikhon's theology of service to humanity, see Georges Florovskii, *Puti russkago bogosloviia*, pp. 124–126.

64. Vladimir Kolosov, *Istoriia tverskoi dukhovnoi seminarii*. Also see the same author's introduction to D. I. Karmanov, *Sobranie sochinenii otnosiashchikhsia k istorii tverskago kraia.*

65. Donoshenie of the Main Magistracy to the Senate, 1764. TsGADA, f. 291, op. 3, d. 13066, pp. 12 ob.–15 ob.

66. Sievers to Catherine, Dec. 9, 1764. TsGADA, f. 16, d. 785, pp. 6–22 ob.

67. Ilovaiskii, "Novgorodskaia guberniia," p. 499.

68. Ibid.

69. See Sievers's comments on Opochka and Ostrov in ibid., pp. 496–497.

70. Sievers to Catherine, undated. TsGADA, f. 16, d. 785, p. 134.

71. Sorina, "Ocherk sotsial'no-ekonomicheskoi istorii," p. 7. The Old Belief was very strong among the merchants of Rzhev, who made most of their money selling Ukrainian grain and hemp in St. Petersburg.

72. Ilovaiskii, "Novgorodskaia guberniia," p. 499. The Old Belief was also strong in Zubtsov, which may be one of the reasons why Sievers found its inhabitants uninterested in what he considered progress.

73. Ibid., pp. 409–491. See also Ilovaiskii, "Graf Iakov Sivers," p. 524, and Blum, *Ein russischer Staatsmann*, I, 387.

74. Istomina, dissertation, p. 394; Blum, *Ein russischer Staatsmann*, I, 249.

75. Gilbert Rozman, *Urban Networks in Russia 1750–1800 and Premodern Periodization*, presents an ambitious, elaborate, and controversial theory that the growth of a network of towns of various sizes and functions proceeds apace with the modernization and development of a society and that therefore the former can be used to measure and evaluate the latter.

76. Bershtein-Kogan, *Vyshnevolotskii vodnyi put'*, p. 21; Parker, *Historical Geography of Russia*, p. 191.

77. Doklad of General-Porutchik Larion Aftsina of the Iamskaia Kantseliariia to Empress Catherine II, undated but obviously written between 1764 and 1766. TsGADA, f. 16, d. 264 (Ob ustroistve pocht i mnenie po etomu predmetu Iakova Siversa), pp. 8–8 ob.

78. Report of the Iamskaia Kantseliariia to Catherine II on the distribution of horses and iamshchiks along the tracts, written in response to Catherine's decree of May 2, 1763. TsGADA, f. 16, d. 264, pp. 12–16 ob.

79. Fernand Braudel, *Capitalism and Material Life*, p. 310, states that in 1766 Jacob Fries, a Swiss doctor serving in the Russian army, traveled the 890 kilometers from Omsk to Tomsk in 178 hours, averaging 5 kilometers an hour. In September 1775 the Turkish ambassador on his way to St. Petersburg reported: "From Kiev to Moscow posts were set up on the side of the road. . . . On each post there was written in Russian letters and numbers indicating how many posts it was to Kiev. They call the distance between every two posts a vers [verst]. They calculate that one travels at the rate of five versts an hour." Norman Itzkowitz and Max E. Mote, comps., *Mubadele: An Ottoman-Russian Exchange of Ambassadors*, p. 86. One verst equals 1.067 kilometers.

80. Report of the Iamskaia Kantseliariia, undated but written in late 1765 or in 1766. TsGADA, f. 16, d. 264, pp. 28–29. The distance between iamy ranged between 15 and 37 versts.

81. For additional detail on the relationship of the towns of Novgorod Guberniia to roads and waterways, see Bernd Knabe, *Die Struktur der russischen Posadgemeinden and der Katalog der Beschwerder und Forderungen der Kaufmannschaft (1762–1767)*, pp. 78–86.

82. Sievers to "Monsieur" (probably G. N. Teplov), Nov. 1, 1765. GsGADA, f. 16, d. 264, pp. 28–29.

83. As we shall see in Chapter V, the government was originally uncertain about the number of uezds in Novgorod Guberniia. According to a donoshenie of the Shtats-Kontora to the Senate dated July 5, 1764, Novgorod Guberniia contained the following administrative units: Novgorod Provintsiia, with the uezds of Olonets, Porkhov, Novaia Ladoga, and Staraia Russa; Tver Provintsiia, with the uezds of Staritsa, Torzhok, Rzhev, and Zubtsov; Beloozero Provintsiia, with the uezds of Ustiuzhna and Kargopol; Pskov Provintsiia, with the uezds of Pustorzhev, Gdov, Opochka, Ostrov, and Izborsk; and Velikie Luki Provintsiia, with the uezd of Toropets. TsGADA, f. 248, d. 3588 (Komissiia o gorodakh), pp. 3–7 ob. However, a second list bearing neither date nor attribution but entitled "Register of Towns in Which There Are Appointed Voevodas" omits Izborsk from the list of towns or uezds of Pskov Provintsiia (ibid., pp. 8–14), which suggests that Izborsk was an uezd de jure but not de facto. Complicating matters further is the fact that the Shtats-Kontora put the population of Porkhov and Novaia Ladoga uezds at 560 and 670, respectively, and that Sievers and the Commission on Towns recommended the creation of uezds around Porkhov and Novaia Ladoga, which suggests that each may have had an administrative staff whose jurisdiction did not extend beyond the borders of the town. The capital of each provintsiia was also the administrative center of an uezd, but the staffs of the provintsiia administrations apparently governed those uezds as part of their duties. Thus Novgorod Guberniia contained somewhere between 18 and 21 uezds but only 13 to 16 staffs of uezd officials plus the 5 staffs of provintsiia officials.

84. Using the figures presented in Tables 2, 3, and 4, the calculation is 13 uezds x 15 officials + 5 provintsiias x 25 officials + 1 guberniia x 47 officials = 367 officials, or 16 uezds x 15 officials + 5 provintsiias x 35 officials + 1 guberniia x 47 officials = 412 officials.

85. Sievers to Catherine, Dec. 9, 1764. TsGADA, f. 16, d. 785, pp. 14–15.

86. The totals for 1767 and 1768 were 246 and 264, respectively. Report of the Main Magistracy in response to the Senate's decree of May 24, 1769, requesting such information. TsGADA, f. 291, d. 15127, pp. 11–12.

87. Istomina, dissertation, p. 182.

88. Quoted in ibid., p. 103.

89. Brigandage is cited as a major problem in nakazy from the nobles of Vodskaia Piatina of Novgorod, Opochka, Beloozero, Tver, Obonezhskaia Piatina of Novgorod, Shelonskaia Piatina of Novgorod, Bezhetskaia Piatina of Novgorod, Pskov, and Toropets. *SIRIO*, XIV, 253, 265–266, 291–292, 327, 329, 346–347, 351, 376–377, 401–402.

90. For example, the Senate's decree of Aug. 22, 1767, *PSZ* no. 12966, forbidding the submission of petitions directly to the empress, was to be read in all the churches of the empire. Catherine's decree on May 25, 1766, *PSZ* no. 12659, on the survey, stipulated that before the surveyors actually began

work in any area, an explanation of the rules and procedures by which the survey would be conducted was to be read in all the churches of the affected area.

91. In their nakazy the nobles of the following uezds cited the flight of serfs to Poland as a major problem: Vodskaia Piatina of Novgorod, Derevskaia Piatina of Novgorod, Opochka, Ostrov, Pustorzhev, Obonezhskaia Piatina of Novgorod, Shelonskaia Piatina of Novgorod, Velikie Luki, Pskov, and Toropets. *SIRIO*, XIV, 256, 261, 266–268, 277, 295–303, 332–333, 342–343, 365, 381, 401–402. The memorandum from the guberniia chancellery to the Legislative Commission is dated Sept. 16, 1768. The first section is entitled "On strengthening the borders and preventing flights to Poland and Livonia and on the return to their owners of those who have fled." The first sentence reads: "All landowners living in Novgorod Guberniia suffer great damage [*razorenie*] and danger from the flight of peasants to Poland and Livonia." TsGADA, f. 342 (Novoulozhennye komissii), d. 240, p. 5.

92. Sievers to Catherine, Oct. 19, 1770. TsGADA, f. 16, d. 785, p. 177.

93. Sievers to Catherine, Sept. 19, 1770, Oct. 19, 1770, and March 10, 1771. All quoted in Blum, *Ein russischer Staatsmann*, I, 309, 315, 331.

94. Sievers to Catherine, June 14, 1781. TsGADA, f. 16, d. 788, part 3, p. 238.

95. Sievers to Catherine, Nov. 4, 1770, April 25, 1771, May 6, 1771, and June 14, 1781. TsGADA, f. 16, d. 785, pp. 180 ob., 204 ob., and 211, and d. 788, part 3, p. 238. In December 1781, six months after Sievers left office, the government finally took his advice and created a separate guberniia of Olonets.

96. This petition was included in Sievers's report to the Senate on Nov. 16, 1767. TsGADA, f. 248, d. 3716, pp. 223–224.

97. Sievers to Catherine, June 14, 1781. TsGADA, f. 16, d. 788, part 3, p. 238.

98. Braudel, *Capitalism and Material Life*, p. xiv.

99. Sievers to Catherine, Dec. 9, 1764. TsGADA, f. 16, d. 785, pp. 17–17 ob.

100. Sievers to Catherine, Aug. 21, 1767. TsGADA, f. 168, d. 101, p. 17 ob.

101. Sievers to Catherine, Oct. 23, 1768. TsGADA, f. 16, d. 785, pp. 75–75 ob.

Chapter V. Reorganization of Provincial Russia

1. Dietrich Geyer, "Staatsbau und Socialverfassung—Problem des russischen Absolutismus am Ende des 18 Jahrhunderts," pp. 366–367.

2. V. M. Kabuzan, "Nekotorye materialy dlia izucheniia istoricheskoi geografii XVIII–nachala XIX v.," p. 154.

3. *PSZ* no. 11989.

4. As noted in Chapter IV, the documents in the Senate's archives illustrate the government's ignorance about the empire and its own essential affairs. Having informed Catherine that the Great Russian provinces of the empire contained 165 uezd chancelleries, the Shtats-Kontora then submitted to the Senate a doklad that enumerated 169 uezds and 41 provintsiias in the guberniias of Moscow, Novgorod, Voronezh, Kazan, Smolensk, Ufa, Belgorod, Nizhegorod, Astrakhan, and Orenburg. In that very same doklad, however, the Shtats-Kontora put the total number of uezds at 167, and an accompanying statement from Shtats-Komissar Ashitov put the total at 166. TsGADA, f. 248 d. 3588 (Komissiia o gorodakh), pp. 3–7 ob. After more

than a year of investigation the Senate concluded on the basis of information provided by the governors that in actuality those same 11 guberniias plus Kiev contained 34 provintsiias and 165 uezds. Ibid., d. 3716 (Pervyi Departament), p. 521.

5. *PSZ*, no. 12259.
6. TsGADA, f. 248, d. 3588, pp. 335–350. Although uezd chancelleries already existed in the towns of Novaia Ladoga and Porkhov, according to the report of the Shtats-Kontora, neither town had an uezd dependent on its chancellery—a higly unusual situation. See Chapter IV, note 100, and John P. Le Donne, "The Territorial Reform of the Russian Empire 1775–1796, I, Central Russia 1775–1784."
7. In addition to Sievers's memorandum on the towns and uezds of Novgorod Guberniia, the archive of the Commission on Towns contains comparable memoranda from the governors of Moscow, Voronezh, Arkhangel, Nizhegorod, Belgorod, Smolensk, Kazan, and Orenburg. TsGADA, f. 248, d. 3588, pp. 92–334.
8. Sievers's donoshenie of April 29, 1765. Ibid., pp. 335 ob.–336.
9. Sievers to Catherine, April 27, 1765. TsGADA, f. 16, d. 785, pp. 36–37.
10. Proposals for the reorganization of Moscow, Novgorod, Belgorod, and Voronezh guberniias were submitted to the Senate in 1766. Proposals on the reorganization of Smolensk, Arkhangel, Nizhnii Novgorod, Kazan, and Orenburg were submitted in 1767. TsGADA, f. 248, d. 3716, pp. 146–435.
11. Senate resolution on the reorganization of Novgorod Guberniia, dated Dec. 14, 1766. Ibid., pp. 439–441.
12. Sievers to the Senate, Jan. 15, 1767. Sievers's response indicates that the points contained in the Senate's resolution of Dec. 14, 1766, had been communicated to him on April 7, 1766. TsGADA, f. 248, d. 3588, pp. 359–373.
13. TsGADA, f. 248, d. 3716, pp. 480–521. Sievers was not satisfied with the Senate's proposal. In addition to the changes recommended by the Senate, he wanted uezds created around Tikhvin and Borovichi, and he wanted Valdai, Vyshnii Volochok, Ostashkov, and Borovichi recognized as towns. He continued to fight for those additional changes and finally succeeded in 1772.
14. TsGADA, f. 370 (Gosudarstvennoe Drevnekhranilishche. Dela kasaiushchiiasia do obrazovania razlichnykh gosudarstvennykh uchrezhdenii), d. 35 (Komissiia o sostavlenii proekta novago ulozheniia. Komissiia ob obshchem prave), pp. 1–3 ob.
15. TsGADA, f. 342 (Novoulozhennye Komissii), d. 123 (Dnevnye zapiski chastnoi komissii o portiatke [sic] gosudarstva v sile obshchago prava), books I–IV. The five members appointed to the Partial Commission were: Count Andrei Shuvalov, the deputy of the farmer-soldiers of Orlov Provintsiia; Fedotii Verigin, the deputy of the nobles of the Derevnaia Piatina of Novgorod; Count Ivan Golovin, the deputy of the nobles of Vyborg; Aleksei Naryshkin, the deputy of the nobles of Staritskii Uezd; and Baron Friedrich Levenwold, the deputy of the nobles of Estnitsk. Naryshkin and Verigin had to leave the Partial Commission before 1771 to take up other duties.
16. Ibid., book I, p. 61.
17. Ibid., book I, pp. 80–81; book II, pp. 1–4.
18. Ibid., book I, pp. 17, 27.
19. Ibid., book II, p. 18.

20. The Senate's response was noted in the journal of the Partial Commission on July 23, 1769. Ibid., book II, p. 46.
21. Ibid., book I, p. 61.
22. Ibid., book I, p. 5.
23. Ibid., book II, p. 50.
24. Ibid., book II, pp. 49–53.
25. Ibid., book II, p. 60.
26. Ibid., book III, p. 48; book IV, p. 28. More differences arose over the response to Catherine's third assignment. In that connection the journal entry for June 25, 1771, says that the Partial Commission had had trouble all along applying Catherine's assignments and its responses to Livonia and Estland and so had asked Baron Ungern and Professor Ursinus to meet with the members of the Partial Commission and advise them. Ibid., book IV, p. 19.
27. *PSZ* no. 13977 (May 8, 1773).
28. Senate report on the status of provincial administration before the reform of 1775, undated. LOII, f. 36 (Vorontsovykh), d. 401, pp. 296–298. Although a guberniia of Tver had been contemplated and possibly even authorized before 1775, I have found no evidence of such a guberniia actually being created prior to the implementation of the Fundamental Law.
29. Jones, *Emancipation of the Russian Nobility,* pp. 202–220, and the references cited therein.
30. *PSZ* no. 14392, articles 1 and 17. Sievers played a major role in persuading the empress to eliminate the provintsiia as a unit of administration. Jones, *Emancipation of the Russian Nobility,* p. 215n.
31. V. F. Zheludkov, "Vvedenie gubernskoi reformy 1775 goda," pp. 201–203.
32. *PSZ* no. 11989.
33. According to Paul Dukes, *Catherine the Great and the Russian Nobility,* p. 166, the governor of Smolensk and his assistants were prosecuted for accepting bribes, and the governor of Belgorod was prosecuted for corruption involving the alcohol monopoly. A. I. Glebov, the procurator-general of the Senate, was dismissed in December 1763 after being implicated in graft and corruption for which he was not prosecuted. In Novgorod Guberniia Sievers had the voevoda of Ustiuzhna and his assistants removed for corruption and the director of the Vyshnii Volochek Canal arrested for embezzlement. Sievers to Catherine, June 8, 1772, and Dec. 1772.TsGADA, f. 16, d. 785, pp. 234, 244. According to Got'e, *Istoriia oblastnogo upravleniia v Rossii,* I, 188, the number of prosecutions of officials for corruption reached a fifty-year high between 1762 and 1765.
34. Morrison, "Catherine II's Legislative Commission," pp. 472–473.
35. TsGADA, f. 370, d. 35, pp. 1–1 ob.
36. Ibid., p. 103 ob.
37. TsGADA, f. 342, d 123, book I, p. 13.
38. For specifics, see Jones, *Emancipation of the Russian Nobility,* pp. 80–85, and Augustine, "Economic Attitudes and Opinions," pp. 43–44.
39. TsGADA, f. 342, d. 123, book II, p. 61.
40. Ibid., p. 64.
41. *PSZ* no. 13977 (May 8, 1773). Figures on the size and costs of administrative staffs in 1763 are taken from the *Kniga Shtatov* (vol. XLIV of *PSZ*) no. 11991.

42. *PSZ* no. 14392, preamble.
43. Zheludkov, "Vvedenie gubernskoi reformy 1775 goda," pp. 201–203.
44. *PSZ* no. 14392, articles 1–14.
45. Ibid., articles 18–28.
46. *Kniga Shtatov* (vol. XLIV of *PSZ*) no. 14392.
47. My computation for 1781 is based on the staffing roster given in *Kniga Shtatov* no. 17494 and goes as follows: 1 governor-general + 4 x 92 guberniia officials + 35 x 37 uezd officials = 1,668. However, since the post-1775 shtat does not include clerks and other low-level positions, it becomes necessary for purposes of comparison to eliminate their counterparts from the shtat promulgated on December 15, 1763, given in *Kniga Shtatov* no. 11991. To do so, I have removed from my calculation the employees listed in that shtat below the rank of *pod kantseliarist*, although it could be argued that no one should be counted below the rank of *registrator*. If the latter standard were applied, the total number of officials, as opposed to clerks and laborers, in all of Novgorod Guberniia in 1764 would have been only 74. A second complication in calculating the figure for 1764 is that no town at that time was the seat of more than one level of administration. Higher levels superseded lower ones, so that Novgorod, the seat of the guberniia administration, did not have a separate provintsiia or uezd administration, and Tver, Pskov, Velikie Luki, and Beloozero, the seats of provintsiia administration, had no separate uezd administrations. With those adjustments, the computation for 1764 becomes 29 guberniia officials + 4 x 16 provintsiia officials + 15 x 10 uezd officials = 243. Even if everyone given in the roster of Dec. 15, 1763, were included in our calculation, the total for 1764 would come to only 367–412 officials. See Chapter IV, note 84.
48. The figure for 1781 was obtained by combining the staffing roster for each unit with the number of units established by 1781 (according to Zheludkov, "Vvedenie gubernskoi reformy 1775 goda," pp. 201–203). The figure for 1763 was obtained by combining the staffing roster for 1763, as interpreted in note 47 above, with the number of units given in the Senate's doklad of Jan. 19, 1768. See Table 1. The computation thus becomes 12 x 29 guberniia officials + 34 x 16 provintsiia officials + 165 x 10 uezd officials + 13 x 1 komissar = 2,555. Even if the shtat of Dec. 15, 1763, had been extended in the same proportion to all the territory covered by the Fundamental Law in 1781, it is impossible to imagine that the number of provincial officials could have exceeded 4,000.
49. The figure for 1763 is taken directly from the Senate's doklad of Jan. 19, 1768. See Table 1. The figure for 1785 is from V. F. Zheludkov, "Krest'ianskaia voina pod predvoditel'stvom E. I. Pugacheva i podgotovka gubernskoi reformy 1775 g.," p. 63. According to M. V. Klochkov, *Ocherki pravitel'stvennoi deiatel'nosti vremeni Pavla I*, p. 412, those expenses had risen to 10,921,388 by the end of Catherine's reign.
50. S. Frederick Starr, *Decentralization and Self-Government in Russia, 1830–1879* pp. 46–48. See also Richard Wortman, *The Development of a Russian Legal Consciousness*, p. 238.
51. See note 33 above. Although Catherine was more diligent than her predecessors in suppressing corruption, her efforts in that direction were never thorough, persistent, or exceptionally severe. Glebov, for example, was removed as

procurator-general in 1763 because of his involvement in corruption, but in 1775 Catherine appointed him governor-general of Smolensk. He soon had to forfeit that post because of his involvement in a new scandal, but he suffered little more than disgrace. Later in Catherine's reign Gavaril Derzhavin experienced great difficulties and frustration in his efforts to bring corrupt provincial officials to justice. The fact that Catherine sought to reduce corruption to tolerable levels rather than to eliminate it can be explained by the corresponding fact that bribery and extortion were deeply rooted in Russian tradition and may well have been "necessary" for the functioning of the system, as Yaney has claimed. Yaney, *Systematization of Russian Government*, pp. 33–34.

52. TsGADA, f. 10, d. 17, p. 525. These figures were appended to Catherine's own notes on law and local government. The document listing the number of officials is undated and is not in Catherine's hand. Under the circumstances, I assume it was compiled by a secretary for the purpose of allowing the empress to measure the results of the provisions on elective service introduced with the reform of 1775.

53. In January 1779, after admonishing the governors and governors-general to instill a desire for state service in noble youth, Catherine admitted that "for the present, the activities of our institutions still cause great difficulty in redressing very quickly the insufficiency of civil servants." *PSZ* no. 14831. Her decree then granted governors and governors-general permission to hire the sons of priests, the sons of merchants, and all graduates of Moscow University or the Vospitatel'nyi Dom on the same basis as nobles. In 1780 she even gave Governor-General Stupishin of Viatka permission to appoint free peasants to administrative duties, provided they were not assigned official ranks. *Stoletie Viatskoi Gubernii, 1780–1880*, p. 13.

54. The materials generated by that order are to be found in TsGADA, f. 370, d. 23. The files to be inspected by Nepliuev were compiled in accordance with Catherine's decree of Feb. 7, 1764. *PSZ*, no. 12030.

55. Catherine, *Memoirs*, p. 365.

56. Catherine, *Instruction*, article 545. Dukes, ed., *Russia under Catherine the Great*, II, 110.

57. V. I. Kolosov, *Proshloe i nastoiashchee g. Tveri*, p. 60. For details of their work, see V. I. Baldina et al., eds., *Arkhitektor Dmitrii Vasil'evich Ukhtomskii. Katalog*, pp. 26, 48.

58. *PSZ* no. 11883.

59. Ibid. no. 11727 (Dec. 11, 1762). Ivan Betskoi submitted his own rather grandiose plan for the reconstruction of Tver, but the plan actually used to rebuild the city was drafted by the architects on the scene. Maikov, *Ivan Ivanovich Betskoi*, p. 71, says that Catherine initially approved of Betskoi's plan and ordered the Senate to implement it.

60. In September 1781, for example, Governor-General R. I. Vorontsov informed the empress that the inhabitants of Kostroma "are to be found in extreme agitation. The town has received a plan in which the town square would occupy a great expanse, such that many houses, including stone ones, would have to be razed. On top of that, six other squares are prescribed, which ought to take up half the town. Convinced by the pleas of the residents, I reduced the size of the square somewhat, by means of which all of the stone houses could remain unrazed." TsGADA, f. 16, d. 638, p. 9.

61. V. Shikov, "Raboty A. V. Kvasova i I. E. Starova po planirovki russkikh goro-dov," p. 30. The confirmed plans of all towns were collected and published in a supplement to the *PSZ* entitled *Kniga chertezhei i risunkov* (St. Petersburg, 1839.)

62. Robert Jones, "Urban Planning and the Development of Provincial Towns in Russia during the Reign of Catherine II," pp. 338–339.

63. Ibid., pp. 339–340.

64. *PSZ* no. 12659. See also German, *Istoriia russkago mezhevaniia*, p. 213, and Iu. V. Klokman, *Sotsial'no-ekonomicheskaia istoriia russkogo goroda*, p. 60.

65. *PSZ* no. 13780.

66. Jones, "Urban Planning," p. 340.

67. *PSZ* no. 13780 (April 2, 1772). See also Coxe, *Travels into Poland, Russia, Sweden, and Denmark*, I, 421.

68. *PSZ* no. 13780.

69. K. N. Serbina, *Ocherki iz istorii sotsial'no-ekonomicheskoi istorii russkogo goroda. Tikhvin Posad XVI–XVIII vv.*, p. 425.

70. "Ustav Blagochiniia," *PSZ* no. 15379 (April 8, 1782), section A.

71. TsGADA, f. 16, d. 788, pt. 3, p. 367.

72. "Shtat Blagochiniia Tverskoi Gubernii, August 1782," TsGADA, f. 16, d. 974 (Donoseniia [sic] gubernatora Iakova Briusa o guberniiakh Novgorodskoi i Tverskoi 1782, 1783, 1784), pp. 31–67.

73. "Shtat Blagochiniia Tveri i drugikh gorodov Tverskoi gubernii, January 7, 1785," TsGADA, f. 16, d. 975 (Donoseniia [sic] gubernatora Nikolaia Ar-kharova o guberniiakh Novgorodskoi i Tverskoi 1784–1793), p. 41.

74. Ibid., p. 37. There is an obvious discrepancy between the appropriations for urban police in Novgorod Guberniia and those for Tver, but if the 9,440 ru-bles not spent in Novgorod is subtracted from its appropriation, the two fig-ures fall into line.

75. "Ustav Blagochiniia," *PSZ* no. 15379, section B.

76. On the intellectual antecedents of Catherine's Police Statute and its relation-ship to similar measures in Germany, see Raeff, "The Well-Ordered Police State," pp. 1221–1243.

77. In terms of speed and convenience, the courts created by the reform of 1775 were a significant improvement over their predecessors. See Jones, *Emancipa-tion of the Russian Nobility*, pp. 80–82, 258–259.

78. Several of the nobles' nakazy to the Legislative Commission asked the state to open institutions of credit in the provinces similar to the banks established in Moscow and St. Petersburg under Elizabeth. Ibid., p. 73; Wilson Augustine, "Notes toward a Portrait of the Eighteenth Century Russian Nobility," pp. 393–395.

79. See Jones, "Urban Planning," p. 334n.

80. Serbina, *Ocherki iz istorii sotsial'no-ekonomicheskoi istorii russkogo goroda. Tikhvin Posad XVI–XVIII vv.*, pp. 424–425.

81. David M. Griffiths, "Eighteenth Century Perceptions of Backwardness: Pro-jects for the Creation of a Third Estate in Catherinian Russia," pp. 452–472, and Daniel, "Russian Attitudes toward Modernization," pp. 71–84.

82. Daniel, "Russian Attitudes toward Modernization," p. 23; Coquin, *La grande commission legislative*, pp. 114–123. As late as 1760 the imperial government

issued a decree ordering the arrest of retailers who did not belong to a posad. *PSZ* no. 11145 (Nov. 20, 1760).

83. TsGADA, f. 248, d. 5588, pp. 335–350. See note 6 above.
84. TsGADA, f. 16, d. 785, p. 13.
85. Ibid., pp. 206–209 ob. These statements are contained in a memorandum in Sievers's hand preserved among his letters and dispatches to the empress, but this particular document bears no date and no address. Since the documents in this delo are in chronological order and were collected by the recipient rather than the sender, I surmise that this memorandum was delivered to Catherine between April 25 and May 6, 1771.
86. Jones, "Jacob Sievers," pp. 434–435. In Sievers's opinion the proper way to move the townsmen in the direction desired by the state was to "find some means intermediate between compulsion and free will."
87. Senate doklad on the reorganization of local administration, Jan. 19, 1768. TsGADA, f. 248, d. 3716, pp. 383–384.
88. *PSZ* no. 13468 (May 28, 1770).
89. Senate doklad on the establishment of four new towns in Novgorod Guberniia, June 7, 1770. TsGADA, f. 248, d. 3823, pp. 117–124.
90. Donoshenie of Sievers to the Senate, Sept. 6, 1770. TsGADA, f. 248, d. 3823, p. 142.
91. *PSZ* no. 12801 (Dec. 14, 1766).
92. Coquin, *La grande commission legislative*, pp. 36–38; M. A. Lipinskii, "Novye dannye dlia istorii ekaterininskoi komissii o sochinenii proekta novago ulozheniia," pp. 225–239.
93. Dukes, ed., *Russia under Catherine the Great*, II, 90–93. On Catherine's ambiguities on this issue, see Ditiatin, *Ustroistvo i upravlenie gorodov Rossii*, I, 405–406, and Daniel, "Russian Attitudes toward Modernization," p. 105.
94. Daniel, "Russian Attitudes toward Modernization, " pp. 107–110. The members of the Partial Commission on the Towns were: A. I. Glebov, the former procurator-general, elected by the nobles of Likhvin; Senator Adam Osuf'ev, serving as the "guardian" of the Samoeds; I. Pieteramarskii, elected by the townsmen of Astrakhan; Stepan Samoilov, elected by the townsmen of Eniseisk; and Lorens Stral'born, elected by the townsmen of Narva.
95. *SIRIO*, XXXVI, 179–232. The members of the Partial Commission on the Middle Sort of People were: Prince M. M. Shcherbatov, elected by the Iaroslavl nobility; Count Ernst Minnikh, also a member of the Commission on Commerce, serving as the deputy of the Chancellery for Tariff Collections; Prince Ivan Viazemskii, elected by the Dmitrov nobility; Stepan Narishkin, elected by the Mikhailov nobility; and Mikhail Stepanov, elected by the townsmen of Venev.
96. Viktor Krylov, "Ekaterininskaia komissiia v eё otnoshenii k dukhovenstvu kak sosloviiu," pp. 758–770.
97. Daniel, "Russian Attitudes toward Modernization," p. 120.
98. *PSZ* no. 13780.
99. Klokman, *Sotsial'no-ekonomicheskaia istoriia russkogo goroda*, p. 134. For examples see *PSZ* nos. 14792 (Kostroma), 14973 (Vologda), 15060 (Simbirsk), and 15061 (Penza).
100. *PSZ* no. 16188 (April 21, 1785), article 77.
101. *PSZ* no. 14275.

102. *PSZ* no. 14327 (May 25, 1775).
103. Klokman, *Sotsial'no-ekonomicheskaia istoriia russkogo goroda*, p. 91.
104. Ibid., p. 23.
105. *Letopis' o sobytiakh v g. Tveri tverskago kuptsa Mikhaila Tiul'pina*, ed. V. Kolosov, p. 13. Bruce to Catherine, Sept. 2, 1782. TsGADA, f. 16, d. 974, p. 17.
106. *PSZ* no. 16188 (April 21, 1785), articles 102–119.
107. Ibid., section D.
108. *PSZ* no. 15459 (July 2, 1780); Catherine II *Memoirs*, p. 365.
109. *PSZ* no. 15572 (Nov. 7, 1782).
110. Jones, "Jacob Sievers," p. 429. These laws antedated Catherine's accession.
111. Sievers to Catherine, Oct. 10, 1775. TsGADA, f. 168, d. 137, p. 5.
112. In the undated memorandum described in note 83 above Sievers proposed that the capital requirements should be 25, 50, and 100 rubles. TsGADA, f. 16, d. 785, p. 208 ob.
113. Ibid., p. 209 ob.
114. Sievers to Catherine, July 1, 1775. TsGADA, f. 168, d. 137, p. 8 ob.
115. Sievers to Catherine, March 12, 1780. TsGADA, f. 5, d. 130, p. 73 ob.
116. Ilovaiskii, "Graf Iakov Sivers," p. 545.
117. *PSZ* no. 16188, article 24.
118. *PSZ* no. 16914 (Oct. 26, 1790). On the issue of the nobility's role in commerce, see Victor Kamendrowsky and David Griffiths, "The Fate of the Trading Nobility Controversy in Russia: A Chapter in the Relationship between Catherine II and the Russian Nobility," 198–221.
119. *PSZ* no. 12801.
120. *PSZ* no. 14392, articles 72, 73.
121. *PSZ* no. 16188, articles 158–165.
122. J. Michael Hittle, *The Service City: State and Townsmen in Russia 1600–1800*, pp. 224–229.
123. *PSZ* no. 15379, chapter D. For a discussion of that section of the Statute on Police and its antecedents, see Vladimir Grigor'ev, "Zertsalo upravy blagochiniia," pp. 73–103, and Raeff, "The Well-Ordered Police State," pp. 1236–1237.
124. This work has been translated and published as an appendix to J. L. Black, *Citizens for the Fatherland: Education, Educators, and Pedagogical Ideas in Eighteenth Century Russia*, pp. 209–226. On p. 134 Black says that the Russian work was modeled on an Austrian school text by J. I. Felbiger.
125. Jones, *Emancipation of the Russian Nobility*, pp. 77–78.
126. Augustine, "Economic Attitudes and Opinions," pp. 64–73.
127. Sievers to Catherine, Dec. 9, 1764. TsGADA, f. 16, d. 785, pp. 9–9 ob.
128. Yaney, *Systematization of Russian Government*, pp. 116–118.
129. *PSZ* no. 10237 (May 13, 1754). See also P. I. Ivanov, *O general'nom mezhevanii zemel' v Rossii*, p. 5; Milov, *Issledovanie ob "ekonomicheskikh primechaniiakh" k general'nomu mezhevaniiu*, pp. 10–13; German, *Istoriia russkago mezhevaniia*, pp. 161–200.
130. N. V. Bochkov, *Istoriia zemelnykh otnoshenii i zemleustroistva*, p. 26.
131. German, *Istoriia russkago mezhevaniia*, pp. 201–202.
132. Ibid., pp. 217–218.
133. Ibid., p. 222.

134. Ibid., p. 211.
135. See Jones, *Emanicpation of the Russian Nobility*, pp. 254, 258–259.
136. *PSZ* no. 16187, articles 21–36.
137. Geyer, "Staatsbau und Sozialverfassung," p. 39.
138. J.O.C. Mackrell, *The Attack on Feudalism in Eighteenth Century France*, pp. 140–145. On the other hand, both the government of Louis XVI and Montesquieu took the view that such rights *were* a form of property. Could it be possible, therefore, that in her handling of the peasant question Catherine was acting on principle in accordance with Montesquieu's teaching that a lawful monarch should not deprive his subjects of their liberties or their property without their consent? If so, the implications are fascinating.
139. See Ransel, *Politics of Catherinian Russia*, pp. 150–153.
140. Sievers made this statement in the undated and unaddressed memorandum described in note 85 above. TsGADA, f. 16, d. 785, pp. 39 ob.–40.
141. Sievers to Catherine, July 1, 1775. TsGADA, f. 168, d. 137, pp. 8–8 ob. Sievers to Catherine, June 14, 1778. TsGADA, f. 16, d. 788, part 1, p. 91.
142. Sievers to Catherine, July 1, 1775. TsGADA, f. 168, d. 137, pp. 8–8 ob.
143. Blum, *Ein russischer Staatsmann*, II, 98–99.
144. Sievers to Catherine, Jan. 17, 1766. TsGADA, f. 168, d. 101, p. 1 ob.
145. Blum, *Ein russischer Staatsmann*, II 95. Sievers made this claim in the mémoire he wrote for the minister of the interior under Alexander I. I have discussed this source and my dependence on Blum's quotations from it in the introduction.
146. Jones, *Emancipation of the Russian Nobility*, pp. 133–134.
147. *Trudy vol'nago ekonomicheskago obshchestva k pooshchreniiu v Rossii zemledeliia i domostroitel'stva*, III, 51–52.
148. This argument is presented at length and in detail in Jones, *Emancipation of the Russian Nobility*. Since the subject of this book overlaps at this point with the subject of my earlier book, some repetition of argument and evidence is inevitable, but I have tried to keep it to a minimum.
149. Peter's remark about the Livonian nobility is recorded in a somewhat garbled entry in the Senate's journal for Jan. 17, 1762. TsGADA, f. 248, kniga 3426, p. 312.
150. *SIRIO*, XIV, 375–376.
151. *PSZ* no. 12801 (Dec. 14, 1766).
152. *PSZ* nos. 13651 (Sept. 2, 1771), 13662 (Sept. 25, 1771), and 13748 (Jan. 14, 1772).
153. Sievers to Catherine, March 1767. TsGADA, f. 16, d. 785, p. 67.
154. Sievers to Catherine, Jan. 25, 1769. Ibid., p. 161.
155. Sievers to Catherine, Oct. 13, 1769. Ibid., p. 165. The fate of these resolutions is uncertain. The Senate's records show no komissars in Novgorod Uezd in 1774, but since the Senate was concerned almost exclusively with the costs of administration, it may have ignored komissariats that were not funded by the state. The survey of Novgorod Uezd did not begin until 1778.
156. Sievers to Catherine, Dec. 9, 1764. Ibid., pp. 15 ob. 19 ob.
157. A. P. Bestuzhev-Riumin presented such a proposal in a written doklad to the commission, and Ia. P. Shakhovskoi had made a very similar proposal to the empress with respect to the reform of local administration. The other members of the Commission on the Freedom of the Nobility were K. G. Ra-

zumovskii, M. L. Vorontsov, Z. G. Chernyshev, M. N. Volkonskii, G. G. Orlov, and N. I. Panin. G. N. Teplov served as its secretary. Jones, *Emancipation of the Russian Nobility,* pp. 106–118, 190–191.

158. Ransel, *Politics of Catherinian Russia,* pp. 144–150, 160.

159. Ibid., pp. 186–190. On the other hand, many of the nobles' nakazy did call for the election of local officials by the nobility. See Jones, *Emancipation of the Russian Nobility,* pp. 85–88.

160. Jones, *Emancipation of the Russian Nobility,* pp. 195–196.

161. Ibid., pp. 194–195.

162. Ibid., p. 231.

163. These figures are taken from the undated document described in note 52 above. TsGADA, f. 10, d. 17, p. 525.

164. TsGADA, f. 16, d. 636, p. 16 ob. Earlier the members of the Partial Commission on the Order of the Realm had found their efforts to reorganize local administration complicated by the predominance of court peasants and economic peasants in some areas where there were "only one or two pomeshchiks." TsGADA, f. 342, d. 123, book II, p. 9.

165. Sievers to Catherine, March 1, 1781. TsGADA, f. 16, d. 788, part. 3, pp. 198–198 ob. Catherine's observation arose from her tour through Pskov Guberniia in 1780 on her way to meet Joseph II in Mogilev.

166. Quoted in N. D. Chechulin, *Russkoe provintsial'noe obshchestvo vo vtoroi polovine XVIII veka,* p. 70.

167. In 1781 Sievers asked that 3,000 rubles be appropriated on a regular basis to cover the costs of official entertaining during the meetings of the nobility, for which he had been paying out of his own pocket since 1776. Sievers to Catherine, March 1, 1781. TsGADA, f. 16, d. 788, part. 3, pp. 202–203.

168. Sievers to Catherine, undated. TsGADA, f. 16, d. 788, part. 2, p. 125.

169. Sievers to Catherine, Dec. 21, 1777. TsGADA, f. 16, d. 788, part. 1, p. 81.

170. Sievers to Catherine, April 21, 1777. TsGADA, f. 168, d. 153, p. 5.

171. *PSZ* no. 14861.

172. TsGADA, f. 370 (Gosudarstvennoe Drevnekharanilishche. Dela kasaiushchiiasia do obrazovaniia razlichnykh gosudarstvennykh uchrezhdenii), d. 39 (Komissiia o vol'nosti dvorianstva. Mnenie novogorodskago [sic] gubernatora Siversa o dvorianskoi gramote), pp. 3–5. The delo is an eight-page commentary on the specific articles of what was to become the Charter to the Nobility. Although it is undated, it mentions the law of March 17, 1775, and so it had to have been written sometime between then and April 21, 1785. On March 12, 1780, Sievers sent Catherine his comments on what was to become the Charter to the Towns. TsGADA, f. 5, d. 130, pp. 11–20. Although f. 370, d. 39, is ascribed to a Commission on the Freedom of the Nobility, the original commission with that title had ceased to function long before 1775. I find it suggestive that most of the dela in fond 370 are projects and proposals drafted by committees of the Legislative Commission. Was the Charter to the Nobility actually drafted by some sort of commission and not by Catherine, as is commonly supposed? And was that commission somehow connected to the Legislative Commission? This subject requires further investigation.

173. *PSZ* no. 16187, section B, articles 37–71.

174. Ibid., articles 38, 39, 41, 43, 44, 46.

175. Ibid., article 64.
176. Ibid., articles 74–89.

Chapter VI. Development of Northwestern Russia

1. Ilovaiskii, "Novgorodskaia guberniia," p. 481.
2. Sievers to Catherine, June 14, 1781. TsGADA, f. 16, d. 788, part 3, p. 238.
3. Blum, *Ein russischer Staatsmann,* II, 183.
4. In a memorandum written in February 1797 announcing Sievers's appointment as director of water communications, Procurator-General Kurakin ordered Sievers and Arkharov "to assist each other for the benefit of the state." Arkharov objected bitterly, and a second memorandum from Kurakin announced Arkharov's resignation and replacement. TsGIA, f. 156 (Departament vodianykh kommunikatsii), op. 1, d. 1, pp. 1–2. On Sievers's appointment as director of water communications for the Russian Empire, see *PSZ* no. 17848 (Feb. 27, 1797).
5. Sievers to Catherine, Dec. 9, 1764. TsGADA, f. 16, d. 785, pp. 10–10 ob.
6. Recounted in a Senate report of Oct. 9, 1774. TsGADA, f. 16, d. 299 (O novom vodianom soobshchenii cherez Lidskoe Ozero po proekty Senatora Mikhaila Dedeneva), p. 1.
7. TsGADA, f. 16, d. 290 (Predstavlenie Generala-Poruchika Dedeneva o kratchaitem vodianem puti mezhdu rr. Volgoiu i Volkhovym), pp. 1–20.
8. Sievers preferred the Seliger route and said so, but the Senate found it "too long, too difficult, and too costly." The senators termed Dedenev's project "most convenient and useful to the state and indispensably necessary for the city of St. Petersburg." TsGADA, f. 16, d. 299, 1 ob.–110 ob.
9. Sievers to Catherine, May 24, 1768. TsGADA, f. 16, d. 785, pp. 70–70 ob.
10. Sievers to Catherine, Oct. 23, 1768. Ibid., pp. 75–75 ob.
11. Blum, *Ein russischer Staatsmann,* I, 197, 390.
12. Ibid., pp. 269–270.
13. Sievers to Catherine, Nov. 19, 1772. TsGADA, f. 16, d. 785, p. 242.
14. *PSZ* no. 14070 (Nov. 22, 1773).
15. The Serdiukov concession contained seven mills, a distillery, a brewery, three smithies, eight houses, seventeen huts, and sixty commercial buildings. E. G. Istomina, "Vyshnevolotskii vodnyi put' vo vtoroi polovine XVIII–nachala XIX v.," p. 198.
16. *PSZ* no. 14809 (Oct. 9, 1778). See also the staffing chart published under that number in the *Kniga Shtatov.*
17. Blum, *Ein russischer Staatsmann,* II, 314.
18. Ibid., p. 428.
19. D. Dubenskii, *Razsuzhdenie o vodianykh soobshcheniakh v Rossii,* p. 29. The details of Gerhard's final project, to extend the system of aqueducts as far as Lake Vel'ia are recounted in Bruce's report of Nov. 25, 1783, and Arkharov's report of Jan. 7, 1785. TsGADA, f. 16, d. 974, pp. 132–133, and d. 975, pp. 34 ob.–35.
20. Bruce to Catherine, Jan. 23, 1785. TsGADA, f. 16, d. 974, p. 126.
21. Arkharov to Catherine, undated. TsGADA, f. 16, d. 975, p. 106.

22. Dubenskii, *Razsuzhdenie o vodianykh soobshcheniakh v Rossii*, p. 28. Bernshtein-Kogan, *Vyshnevolotskii vodnyi put'*, claims that the reconstruction lasted until 1797 and cost a total of 1,475,000 rubles, but he cites no source, and his figure seems incredibly high in comparison with Gerhard's original estimate of 75,000 rubles transmitted in Arkharov's report of Jan. 7, 1785. TsGADA, f. 16, d. 975, pp. 31–32.
23. Blum, *Ein russischer Staatsmann*, II, 428–430.
24. Ibid., pp. 236–237, 399.
25. Istomina, "Vyshnevolotskii vodnyi put'," p. 200.
26. Arkharov to Catherine, Nov. 6, 1786. TsGADA, f. 16, d. 975, pp. 190–190 ob. The total for the previous year was 3,217, given in Arkharov to Catherine, Nov. 28, 1785, ibid., p. 27.
27. Bernshtein-Kogan, *Vyshnevolotskii vodnyi put'*, p. 30.
28. Sievers to Catherine, Sept. 25, 1781, and Nov. 12, 1781. TsGADA, f. 16, d. 788, part 3, pp. 252–254 ob.
29. *PSZ* no. 17848 (Feb. 2, 1797) and no. 18403 (Feb. 28, 1798).
30. These achievements are recounted in a memorandum written by engineer François Devolant to the Department of Water Communications on April 29, 1809. Devolant, whom Sievers had hired in 1798, offered high praise for Sievers's work as director of water communications. TsGIA, f. 155 (Vodianye kommunikatsii), op. 1, d. 1, p. 68.
31. Paul to Kurakin, Jan. 20, 1798. TsGIA, f. 156 (Departament vodianykh kommunikatsii), op. 1, d. 1, p. 27.
32. Dubenskii, *Razsuzhdenie o vodianykh soobshcheniakh v Rossii*, p. 56.
33. TsGADA, f. 16, d. 785, pp. 9–9 ob.
34. Catherine's order is cited in Sievers's reply acknowledging receipt and promising compliance, dated Sept. 8, 1766. TsGADA, f. 16, d. 785, pp. 59–59 ob.
35. German, *Istoriia russkago mezhevaniia*, p. 213.
36. *PSZ* no. 14392, articles 270, 276.
37. V. F. Meien, *Rossiia v dorozhnom otnoshenii*, I, 19–20.
38. "Report de l'expédition des chemins de l'Empire et ses operations jusqu'à 1809." TsGIA, f. 155, op. 1, pp. 78–83. Paul's original appointees to this agency were the engineers DeWitt, Devolant, and Gerhard. The last two, and possibly all three, were employees of the Department of Water Communications. I have not been able to determine the relationship between this agency and that department.
39. Sievers to Catherine, Jan. 5, 1769, and Jan. 28, 1769. TsGADA, f. 168, d. 110, pp. 1–3, and f. 16, d. 785, pp. 192–193.
40. Reported to Catherine in Sievers's letter of Oct. 13, 1769. TsGADA, f. 16, d. 785, p. 161.
41. *PSZ* no. 13583 (March 15, 1771).
42. Sievers to Catherine, May 9, 1771. TsGADA, f. 16, d. 785, p. 213.
43. Quoted in Blum, *Ein russischer Staatsmann*, II, 360.
44. Sievers acknowledged receipt of that decree on Nov. 23, 1780. TsGADA, f. 16, d. 788, part 2, p. 250. Obviously, Blum erred in asserting that Sievers's appeal went unanswered. *Ein russischer Staatsmann*, II, 364.
45. *PSZ* no. 15087.
46. TsGADA, f. 16, d. 788, part. 2, pp. 271–272.

47. Bruce to Catherine, Aug. 21, 1782. TsGADA, f. 16, d. 974, pp. 15–16.
48. Ibid.
49. Arkharov to Catherine, undated but probably written early in 1785. TsGADA, f. 16, d. 975, p. 37.
50. Arkharov to Catherine, Dec. 15, 1786. Ibid., pp. 128–128 ob.
51. Arkharov to Catherine, undated but probably written in 1786 or early 1787. Ibid., p. 154.
52. Blum, *Ein russischer Staatsmann*, II, 294.
53. Sievers to Catherine, Nov. 12, 1779. TsGADA, f. 16, d. 788, part. 2, p. 20.
54. G. Maksimovich, *Deiatel'nost Rumiantseva-Zadunaiskago po upravleniiu Malorossii*, pp. 67–86.
55. Acknowledged in Sievers to Catherine, October 13, 1765. TsGADA, f. 16, d. 785, pp. 33–33 ob.
56. Acknowledged in Sievers to Catherine, Nov. 28, 1765. TsGADA f. 16, d. 264, p. 34.
57. Sievers to Catherine, with a covering letter to "Monsieur" (almost certainly Teplov), Sept. 10, 1766. Ibid., pp. 23–27.
58. Sievers to Catherine, May 24, 1768. TsGADA, f. 16, d. 785, p. 72.
59. Blum, *Ein russischer Staatsmann*, II, 239.
60. Sievers to Catherine, March 1, 1781. TsGADA, f. 16, d. 788, part. 3, pp. 199–199 ob.
61. Tutolmin to Catherine, Aug. 2, 1782. Ibid., pp. 372–375.
62. Karmanov, *Sobranie sochinenii*, pp. 108–115.
63. Sievers to Catherine, undated. TsGADA, f. 16, d. 788, part 3, pp. 353–354. The chronological sequence in which these reports are filed suggests that this report was written between January and August 1782.
64. TsGADA, f. 788, part 3, p. 353.
65. Pokrovskii, ed., *General'noe soobrazhenie po tverskoi gubernii*, p. 13. The total of 2,081 houses is reasonably close to the figure of 2,167 given by Bruce in his report of August 1782 on the introduction of the Statute on Police. See Chapter V, note 72.
66. Bruce to Catherine, Nov. 25, 1782. Quoted in Blum, *Ein russischer Staatsmann*, II, 434.
67. Coxe, *Travels into Poland, Russia, Sweden, and Denmark*, I, 421.
68. Quoted in Kolosov, *Proshloe i nastoiashchee g. Tveri*, p. 71. Catherine was sometimes guilty of exaggeration in her correspondence with foreigners, but in this instance her judgment is supported by the testimony of Academician P. S. Pallas, who passed through Tver in 1793 and later wrote that Tver "may now with propriety be ranked among the most elegant and regular provincial towns in Europe." *Travels through the Southern Provinces of the Russian Empire in the Years 1793 and 1794*, I, 7.
69. Sievers referred to these dikes, noting that they "have proven very useful," in his communication to Catherine dated Dec. 24, 1781. TsGADA, f. 16, d. 788, part 3, pp. 96–96 ob. The floods, caused by ice jams that prevented the Tvertsa from emptying into the Volga, are described by Karmanov in *Sobranie sochinenii*, pp. 106–107.
70. The details are recounted in Bruce to Catherine, March 22, 1784. TsGADA, f. 16, d. 974, p. 143. Bruce informed the empress that the statue had not been built because Sievers had spent the money on the nobles' school.

71. Kolosov, *Proshloe i nastoiashchee g. Tveri*, p. 62.
72. Blum, *Ein russischer Staatsmann*, I, 268–269.
73. Sievers to Catherine, June 11, 1780. TsGADA, f. 16, d. 788, part. 2, p. 31.
74. TsGADA, f. 16, d. 788, part. 3, p. 196 ob.
75. Sievers to Catherine, May 20, 1781. Ibid., p. 233.
76. Sievers to Catherine, 1781 (day and month not given). Ibid., pp. 153–184.
77. Sievers informed Catherine of this action in his letter of Dec. 24, 1781, from Bauenhof, his Livonian estate. Ibid., pp. 96–96 ob.
78. Bruce to Catherine, October 1782. TsGADA, f. 16, d. 794, p. 28. To appreciate the significance of Bruce's remark for Catherine, see her assessment of the differences between St. Petersburg and Moscow. Catherine II, *Memoirs*, p. 365.
79. Blum, *Ein russischer Staatsmann*, II, 434.
80. A. Shchekatov, ed., *Geograficheskii slovar' rossiiskago gosudarstva*, IV, 692.
81. The lower figure is from Istomina, dissertation, p. 225; the higher one is from Rozman, *Urban Networks*, p. 187.
82. Ilovaiskii, "Novgorodskaia guberniia," pp. 494–495.
83. The first figure is from Tutolmin's report of 1782 on the rebuilding of towns in Tver Guberniia. TsGADA, f. 16, d. 788, part. 3, pp. 353–354. The second is from Bruce's report of August 1783 on the implementation of the Statute on Police in Tver Guberniia. TsGADA, f. 16, d. 974, p. 67. The 83 stone houses would almost certainly have stood in the gradskaia section of the city, which, according to Bruce, contained 837 houses in all.
84. Blum, *Ein russischer Staatsmann*, I, 181.
85. Istomina, dissertation, p. 394.
86. Blum, *Ein russischer Staatsmann*, II, 355.
87. Rozman, *Urban Networks*, p. 188.
88. Sorina, "Ocherk sotsial'no-ekonomicheskoi istorii g. Vyshnego-Volochka vo vtoroi polovine XVIII veka i nachala XIX veka," p. 123.
89. Tutolmin to Catherine, TsGADA, f. 16, d. 788, part 3, pp. 353–354.
90. Sorina, "Ocherk sotsial'no-ekonomicheskoi istorii g. Vyshnego-Volochka vo vtoroi polovine XVIII veka i nachala XIX veka," p. 126.
91. V. A. Shkvarikov, *Ocherki istorii planirovki i zastroiki russkikh gorodov*, p. 176.
92. Sorina, "Ocherk sotsial'no-ekonomicheskoi istorii goroda ostashkova v kontse XVIII–pervoi chetverti XIX v.," p. 12.
93. The first figure is from a document in the Senate archives entitled "Report of the College of Economy on the Population and Revenue of Vyshnii Volochek, Ostashkov, and Valdai in 1770." TsGADA, f. 248, d. 3823, p. 163. The second and third figures, taken respectively from the economic observations of the General Survey and from the Fifth Revision, are given by Sorina in "Ocherk sotsial'no-ekonomicheskoi istorii goroda ostashkova v kontse XVIII–pervoi chetverti XIX v.," p. 10.
94. The first figure is from the report of the College of Economy cited in the preceding note. TsGADA, f. 248, d. 3823, p. 165. The second is from Istomina, dissertation, p. 413.
95. Bruce to Catherine, Jan. 5, 1783. TsGADA, f. 16, d. 974, p. 83.
96. Istomina, dissertation, p. 413.
97. TsGADA, f. 16, d. 974, p. 84.

98. Ibid.
99. Ilovaiskii, "Novgorodskaia guberniia," p. 486; Blum, *Ein russischer Staatsmann,* I, 354–356.
100. Sievers to Catherine, March 1776. TsGADA, f. 16, d. 788, part 1, p. 36.
101. Blum, *Ein russischer Staatsmann,* II, 238.
102. For examples, see Ditiatin, *Ustroistvo i upravlenie gorodov Rossii,* I, 379; Gitermann, *Geschichte Russlands,* II, 220; Miliukov, *Ocherki po istorii russkoi kultury,* I, 241; A. Korsakov, *O formakh promyshlennosti v zapadnoi Evropy i Rossii,* pp. 104–110.
103. Karmanov, *Sobranie sochinenii,* pp. 1–4, 13, 157.
104. Vladimir Kolosov, *Tver v tsarstvovanie imperatritsy Ekateriny II,* p. 24; TsGADA, f. 16, d. 787, p. 8.
105. Jones, *Emancipation of the Russian Nobility,* pp. 68–71; Daniel, "Russian Attitudes toward Modernization," pp. 141–146.
106. Daniel, "Russian Attitudes toward Modernization," pp. 68, 73, 80; Coquin, *La grande commission legislative,* pp. 168–169.
107. Sievers to Catherine, Dec. 9, 1764, and March 24, 1768. TsGADA, f. 16, d. 785, pp. 8–8 ob., 71.
108. Black, *Citizens for the Fatherland,* pp. 88–89.
109. TsGADA, f. 168, d. 137, p. 8.
110. Report of the board of public welfare of Tver Guberniia for 1776–1779, transmitted to the Senate sometime during the first six months of 1780. TsGADA, f. 16, d. 788, part 2, pp. 186–188 ob.
111. Kolosov, *Tver v tsarstvovanie imperatritsy Ekateriny II,* p. 10; TsGADA, f 16, d. 788, part 2, p. 9. Sievers would have known whether or not schools existed; if they did not exist, we would expect him to say so and to ask for money to create them.
112. TsGADA, f. 16, d. 794, pp. 17 ob., 26. Blum, *Ein russischer Staatsmann,* II, 234, says that in May 1778 Catherine appropriated 3,000 rubles for schools in Novgorod.
113. TsGADA, f. 16, d. 788, part 3, p. 211 ob.
114. TsGADA, f. 16, d. 975, p. 120.
115. Black, *Citizens for the Fatherland,* pp. 130–144.
116. Ibid., pp. 144, 155.
117. Ibid., p. 148.
118. Sievers to Catherine, Jan. 19, 1779. TsGADA, f. 16, d. 788, part 1, pp. 248–272.
119. Sievers to A. R. Vorontsov, January 1779. LOII, f. 36, d. 1188, pp. 110–111.
120. Sievers to Catherine, June 3, 1779. TsGADA, f. 16, d. 788, part 2, p. 10 ob.
121. Ilovaiskii, "Graf Iakov Sivers," pp. 578, 584.
122. Sievers to Catherine, July 11, 1779. TsGADA, f. 16, d. 788, part 2, p. 12.
123. Blum, *Ein russischer Staatsmann,* II, 360.
124. Ilovaiskii, "Graf Iakov Sivers," p. 578.
125. Sievers to Catherine, Feb. 28, 1781. TsGADA, f. 16, d. 788, part 3, p. 195.
126. Ibid., pp. 194–195.
127. Sievers to Catherine, March 11, 1781. Ibid., p. 216.
128. Bruce to Catherine, March 27, 1784. TsGADA, f. 16, d. 974, pp. 143–143 ob.

129. TsGIA, f. 1350 (Ekonomicheskoe primechanie tverskoi gubernii), op. 312, d. 175, p. 3 ob.
130. Blum, *Ein russischer Staatsmann,* II, 269.
131. V. Drashusov, ed., *Materialy dlia istorii imperatorskago moskovskago vospitatel'nago doma,* II, 47. According to Shpilevskii, "Politika narodonaseleniia v tsarstvovanie Ekateriny II," p. 77, the mortality rate of the Vospitatel'nyi Dom itself was 98.53% in 1768.
132. Sievers to Catherine, March 25, 1772. TsGADA, f. 16, d. 785, p. 241.
133. Drashusov, ed., *Materialy dlia istorii imperatorskago moskovskago vospitatel'nago doma,* II, 47–49.
134. TsGADA, f. 16, d. 788, part 2, p. 186 ob.
135. Ibid., p. 9.
136. Kolosov, *Tver v tsarstvovanie imperatritsy Ekateriny II,* p. 17.
137. Bruce to Catherine, Oct. 8, 1782. TsGADA, f. 16, d. 974, pp. 26–27.
138. L. Trefolev, "Aleksei Petrovich Mel'gunov, general-gubernator ekaterininskikh vremen," pp. 944–945.
139. TsGADA, f. 16, d. 788, part 2, pp. 186 ob., 9; Kolosov, *Tver v tsarstvovanie imperatritsy Ekateriny II,* p. 17.
140. Bruce to Catherine, Oct. 8, 1782. TsGADA, f. 16, d. 974, pp. 26–27.
141. Ibid.; Kolosov, *Tver v tsarstvovanie imperatritsy Ekateriny II,* p. 17.
142. Bruce to Catherine, Oct. 8, 1782. TsGADA, f. 16, d. 974, pp. 26–27. According to a Senate doklad of Oct. 6, 1771, one monastery in each guberniia was designated as an asylum for insane people who were not being cared for by their families. In Novgorod, the Zelcmetskoi monastery was designated for that purpose. TsGADA, f. 248, d. 2833, pp. 1–3.
143. A. Stog, *Ob obshchestvennom prizrenii v Rossii,* p. 91.
144. Kolosov, *Tver v tsarstvovanie imperatritsy Ekaterine II,* pp. 11–12.
145. Coquin, *La grande commission legislative,* pp. 95–96.
146. Stog, *Ob obshchestvennom prizrenii,* pp. 108–109. Stog says that their combined income in 1803 was 601,410 rubles of assignats and 33,970 rubles of silver, while their combined expenses totaled 392,670 rubles of assignats and 44,240 rubles of silver.
147. Reports of Inspectors-General Vorontsov and Naryshkin on the guberniias of St. Petersburg and Olonets in 1796. LOII, f. 36, d. 478, pp. 32, 143.
148. Catherine II, *Memoirs,* p. 381.
149. Ibid., p. 385. On Catherine's association of factories with the Moscow epidemic and the plague riot, see John T. Alexander, *Bubonic Plague in Early Modern Russia: Public Health and Urban Disaster,* pp. 265–267.
150. *Instruction,* articles 314–316.
151. Bartlett, *Human Capital,* p. 146.
152. S. G. Strumilin, *Istoriia chernoi metallurgii v SSSR,* I, 459–493.
153. Blum, *Ein russischer Staatsmann,* II, 237. See also Sorina, "K voprosu o protsese sotsial'nogo rassloeniia goroda," p. 293.
154. TsGADA, f. 16, d. 785, p. 7.
155. Istomina, dissertation, pp. 377–378, 382.
156. Ibid., p. 293.
157. E. G. Istomina, *Granitsy, naselenie i goroda novgorodskoi gubernii (1727–1917),* p. 81.
158. TsGADA, f. 16, d. 785, pp. 7–8.

159. Blum, *Ein russischer Staatsmann,* II, 15.
160. *Shtat* of the Staraia Russa saltworks. TsGADA, f. 16, d. 975, p. 253.
161. Iu. V. Klokman, *Ocherki sotsial'no-ekonomicheskoi istorii severo-zapada Rossii v seredine XVIII v.,* pp. 72–120.
162. Istomina, referat, p. 80.
163. Sorina, "K voprosu o protsese sotsial'nogo rassloeniia goroda," p. 289.
164. Sorina, "Ocherk sotsial'no-ekonomicheskoi istorii goroda ostashkova v kontse XVIII–pervoi chetverti XIX v.," p. 11.
165. Sorina, "K voprosu o protsese sotsial'nogo rassloeniia goroda," p. 289.
166. Istomina, dissertation, pp. 282–283.
167. Blum, *Ein russischer Staatsmann,* I, 268.
168. Heinrich Storch, *Historische-statistische Gemälde des russischen Reichs,* supplement V–VII, pp. 1–2, Table 1.
169. Blum, *Ein russischer Staatsmann,* I, 273.
170. Ibid., p. 267.
171. N. D. Chechulin, *Ocherki po istorii russkikh finansov v tsarstvovanie Ekateriny II,* pp. 320–323.
172. Sievers to Catherine, Nov. 19, 1772. TsGADA, f. 16, d. 785, p. 242 ob.
173. Ilovaiskii, "Graf Iakov Sivers," p. 505.
174. Sievers to Viazemskii, June 5, 1780. TsGADA, f. 788, part 2, p. 230.
175. Sievers to Catherine, June 7, 1780. Ibid., p. 33.
176. TsGADA, f. 168, d. 785, p. 20.
177. Blum, *Ein russischer Staatsmann,* II 212.
178. Sievers to Catherine, Dec. 9, 1764. TsGADA, f. 16, d. 785, pp. 20 ob.–21.
179. *PSZ* nos. 4060, 4379. See also Tsvetkov, *Izmenenie lesistosti evropeiskoi Rossii,* pp. 61–66.
180. *SIRIO,* IV, 315.
181. *PSZ* no. 15518.
182. *PSZ* no. 16364.
183. *PSZ* nos. 16162, 18429, 18534.
184. Blum, *Ein russischer Staatsmann,* II, 213–215.
185. Bruce to Catherine, undated. TsGADA, f. 16, d. 974, pp. 148–151 ob.
186. Istomina, dissertation, pp. 352–357; Dubenskii, *Razsuzhdenie o vodianykh soobshcheniakh v Rossii,* p. 55.
187. Bernshtein-Kogan, *Vyshnevolotskii vodnyi put',* p. 30.
188. TsGADA, f. 16, d. 974, pp. 134–135.
189. TsGADA, f. 16, d. 975, p. 112.
190. TsGADA, f. 16, d. 785, pp. 21–21 ob.
191. I. Kaplan, *Pervyi uglekopy na Valdae,* pp. 1–20.
192. Ibid., pp. 22–30.
193. Arkharov to Catherine, no date. TsGADA, f. 16, d. 975, pp. 170–180; Istomina, dissertation. See also Pallas, *Travels through the Southern Provinces of the Russian Empire,* 6.
194. TsGADA, f. 16, d. 785, p. 22.
195. Quoted in Blum, *Ein russischer Staatsmann,* I, 175.
196. Ilovaiskii, "Graf Iakov Sivers," p. 579.
197. Sievers to Catherine, TsGADA, f. 16, d. 788, part 2, p. 17.

198. Ibid., part 3, pp. 200 ob.–201.
199. Blum, *Ein russischer Staatsmann*, I, 206–207; Ilovaiskii, "Graf Iakov Sivers," p. 468.
200. Sievers made this claim in his autobiographical memorandum to Alexander's minister of the interior, according to Blum, *Ein russischer Staatsmann*, II, 468.
201. *SIRIO*, XXXII, 575–585; Jones, *Emancipation of the Russian Nobility*, pp. 145–148; Bartlett, *Human Capital*, pp. 93–94.
202. Report of Chancellor Gregory Erbatov of the College of Economy to Sievers, March 15, 1765. TsGADA, f. 16, d. 785, p. 44.
203. Blum *Ein russischer Staatsmann*, I, 194–195.
204. TsGADA, f. 168, d. 101, p. 11.
205. Blum, *Ein russischer Staatsmann*, II, 96.
206. Ibid., I, 195. Ilovaiskii, "Graf Iakov Sivers," p. 478, indicates that Volkersahm took over the administration of the estate while Engelhardt remained in charge of purely agricultural affairs.
207. Blum, *Ein russischer Staatsmann*, II, 96. On Eliagin's experiment at Iamburg, see Bartlett, *Human Capital*, pp. 173–174.
208. Sievers to Catherine, Feb. 26, 1775. TsGADA, f. 16, d. 785, p. 306 ob.
209. Blum, *Ein russischer Staatsmann*, II, 95.
210. Jones, *Emancipation of the Russian Nobility*, p. 162.
211. Ibid., pp. 144–163.
212. Blum, *Ein russischer Staatsmann*, II, 184.
213. Jones, *Emancipation of the Russian Nobility*, p. 86; *SIRIO*, IV, 249; VIII, 505.
214. Rubinshtein, *Sel'skoe khoziaistvo Rossii*, pp. 321, 322, and Rubinshtein, "Ulozhenaia komissiia," p. 343.
215. Ilovaiskii, "Graf Iakov Sivers," 480–481, quotes from Sievers's reply to the Senate. On Jan. 7, 1766, Sievers reported the matter to the empress. TsGADA, f. 168, d. 101, p. 2.
216. *PSZ* no. 12824.
217. Augustine, "Economic Attitudes and Opinions," pp. 131–137.
218. Sievers to Catherine, Jan. 9, 1766. TsGADA, f. 168, d. 101, pp. 3 ob.–5. On the growth of the population, Sievers noted that "the increase is greater where men remain at the plow and less where they are on passport." Quoted in Blum, *Ein russischer Staatsmann*, I, 203.
219. Blum, *Ein russischer Staatsmann*, I, 163.
220. *PSZ* no. 12406 (May 31, 1765).
221. Sievers to Catherine, July 25, 1766. TsGADA, f. 168, d. 101, p. 8.
222. Istomina, dissertation, pp. 275–276.

Chapter VII. Obstacles and Alternatives

1. Sievers to Catherine. TsGADA, f. 16, d. 788, part 3, pp. 234–234 ob.
2. Sievers to Catherine, Feb. 10, 1792. TsGADA, f. 5, d. 130, p. 9.
3. Quoted in Blum, *Ein russischer Staatsmann*, I, 364.
4. Quoted in ibid., II, 24.

5. Ibid., pp. 439–440.
6. Sievers to Catherine, Feb. 5, 1776. TsGADA, f. 16, d. 788, part 1, p. 10.
7. Quoted in Ilovaiskii, "Graf Iakov Sivers," p. 560.
8. Ibid.
9. Sievers to Catherine, March 1776. Quoted in Blum, *Ein russischer Staats-mann*, II, 167.
10. Sievers to Catherine, April 1776. TsGADA, f. 16, d. 788, part 1, p. 49.
11. Blum, *Ein russischer Staatsmann*, I, 322.
12. Ibid., p. 367.
13. Ibid., II, 10.
14. In his memorandum to Alexander's minister, Sievers wrote that Catherine had completed a reform of the central administration, including the Senate, before she left Moscow in December 1775 but that Viazemskii and Potemkin had persuaded her not to implement it. Ibid., pp. 150–156. Logically, the reform of provincial administration would have made some reform of the central administration necessary. Unfortunately, Sievers supplies few details beyond the implication that the role of the Senate would have been significantly diminished in the reform he expected.
15. Sievers to Catherine, Feb. 26, 1776. TsGADA, f. 16, d. 788, part 1, p. 28 ob.
16. Blum, *Ein russischer Staatsmann*, II, 167–168.
17. Sievers to Catherine, March 15, 1776. Quoted in ibid., pp. 168–169.
18. On Viazemskii's subsequent use of the provincial procurators to control provincial officials, see M. I. Lazarevskii, *Leksii po russkomu gosudarstvennomu pravu*, I, 451–452.
19. *PSZ* no. 13962. On Viazemskii's multiple offices and the extraordinary power they conferred in combination, see *Istoriia Pravitel'stvuiushchego Senata*, II, 377–379, and Klochkov, *Ocherki pravitel'stvennoi deiatel'nosti*, pp. 384–385.
20. *PSZ* nos. 15075 and 15076 (Oct. 24, 1780).
21. Quoted in Blum, *Ein russischer Staatsmann*, II, 435.
22. Ibid., I, 363.
23. V. Semennikov, "Literaturnaia i knigopechatnaia deiatel'nosti v provintsii v kontse XVIII i nachale XIX vekov," p. 17.
24. Sievers to Catherine, Nov. 28, 1778. TsGADA, f. 16, d. 788, part 1, pp. 133–133 ob.
25. *PSZ* no. 14927 (Oct. 3, 1779).
26. Semennikov, "Literaturnaia i knigopechatnaia deiatel'nosti," p. 19. A print shop opened in Novgorod in 1796, but none had been established in Tver by 1805. *Tverskoi Vestnik* would have been the first journal published in the provinces.
27. Quoted in Blum, *Ein russischer Staatsmann*, II, 354.
28. Quoted in ibid., pp. 156–157.
29. Quoted in ibid., pp. 136–137.
30. According to V. A. Bil'basov, *Istoriia Ekateriny Vtoroi*, II, 99, Catherine spoke those words to Z. G. Chernyshev on the day of the coup. For expressions of antiwar sentiment by Russian statesmen and intellectuals during the 1760s and 1770s, see Gleason, *Moral Idealists*.
31. Blum, *Ein russischer Staatsmann*, I, 352–353.

32. Sievers to Catherine, Oct. 29, 1769. TsGADA, f. 168, d. 110, p. 1.
33. Quoted in Blum, *Ein russischer Staatsmann,* I, 352–353.
34. Ibid., p. 371.
35. Ilovaiskii, "Graf Iakov Sivers," p. 206.
36. Quoted in Blum, *Ein russischer Staatsmann,* II, 482.
37. Sievers to Gunsel, August 1790. Quoted in ibid, p. 518.
38. Quoted in ibid., p. 128.
39. Ibid.
40. On Nov. 12, 1779, Sievers wrote to Catherine about a dispute between the town of Tikhvin and the commandant of its garrison: "I have written to General Potemkin about this, but as Your Majesty knows well enough and as I have learned to my misfortune, he is no friend of mine. I ask Your Majesty to say a few words so that an entire town does not suffer because of my personal and private animosities." TsGADA, f. 16. d. 788, part 3, p. 20.
41. In a letter dated Jan. 26, 1775, Sievers told Catherine that his expenses for a year never came to less than 4,000 rubles. TsGADA, f. 16, d. 137, pp. 1–2.
42. Ilovaiskii, "Graf Iakov Sivers," p. 567.
43. Ibid., pp. 567–568; Blum, *Ein russischer Staatsmann,* I, 177–185.
44. Sievers to Catherine, Nov. 25, 1778. Quoted in Blum, *Ein russischer Staatsmann,* II, 284–285.
45. Sievers to Catherine, Oct. 6, 1778. TsGADA, f. 5, d. 130, p. 2.
46. Blum, *Ein russischer Staatsmann,* II, 277.
47. Sievers to Catherine, Nov. 29, 1778. Quoted in ibid., pp. 283–284. Blum quotes the full text of this letter and of Catherine's rebuke, written on Nov. 25, 1778.
48. Ibid., pp. 282–283.
49. Ibid., pp. 295–296.
50. Sievers to Catherine, March 11, 1781. TsGADA, f. 16, d. 788, part 3, p. 216.
51. In his letter of explanation Sievers offered his own account of the entire episode and insisted that it was he who should complain about the War College rather than the other way around. Sievers to Catherine, March 3, 1781. TsGADA, f. 16, d. 788, part 3, p. 212.
52. In 1790, when his son-in-law needed additional influence in the capital and Sievers's daughter suggested the possibility of an appeal to Potemkin, he responded: "He has friendship with your husband and has paid attention to me even though he was my enemy and helped to humiliate me." Quoted in Blum, *Ein russischer Staatsmann,* II, 529.
53. Ibid., p. 366.
54. Sievers to Catherine, Oct. 13, 1779. TsGADA, f. 16, d. 788, part 2, pp. 16 ob.–17.
55. Catherine to Sievers, Oct. 23, 1779. Quoted in Blum, *Ein russischer Staatsmann,* II, 318.
56. Augustine, "Economic Attitudes and Opinions," p. 145.
57. TsGADA, f. 248, d. 6444, pp. 705–766.
58. Heinrich Storch, *Tableau historique et statistique de l'empire de la Russie,* II, 222.
59. Mironov, "Eksport russkago khleba," pp. 174–175.
60. Itzkowitz and Mote, comps., *Mubadele,* p. 81.

61. Quoted in Parker, *Historical Geography of Russia*, p. 193.
62. E. S. Kogan, *Ocherki istorii krepostnogo khoziaistva po materialam votchinii Kurakinykh*, p. 18. See also the nakaz of the nobles of Livna, which states that newly cultivated steppe land yielded five times more than regular steppe land. *SIRIO*, LXVII, 401.
63. Braudel, *Capitalism and Material Life*, p. 75.
64. Ransel, *Politics of Catherinian Russia*, pp. 231–246.
65. Catherine to Rumiantsev, Nov. 23, 1770. *SIRIO*, XCVII, 183.
66. Bartlett, *Human Capital*, p. 75.
67. Ibid., pp. 115–116.
68. J. A. Guldenstadt, *Reise durch Russland und im Caucasischen Gebirge*, provides an account of the southern expedition and its findings.
69. E. I. Druzhinina, "Znachenie russko-nemetskikh nauchnykh sviazei dlia khoziaistvennogo razvitiia iuzhnoi ukrainy v kontsa XVIII v.," pp. 225–232.
70. One, under Zuev, left for the Pontic Steppe in May 1781 and returned at the end of September 1782. After the Russian annexation of the Crimea, Potemkin persuaded the Academy to send Gablits into the new province to observe and describe its natural resources "according to the three kingdoms of nature." Pallas headed a second expedition to the Crimea in 1793–1794 and published his findings in 1795. Ibid., pp. 233–239, 250.
71. For details, see Alan P. Fisher, "Moscovy and the Black Sea Slave Trade."
72. Ibid., p. 393.
73. For details of Potemkin's activities in the south, see Theresa Adamczyk, *Furst G. A. Potemkin. Untersuchungen zu einer Legensgeschichte*; E. I. Druzhinina, *Severnoe prichernomor'e v 1775–1800*; Marc Raeff, "In the Imperial Manner"; Bartlett, *Human Capital*, pp. 109–142.
74. Bartlett, *Human Capital*, pp. 126–128.
75. Druzhinina, *Severnoe prichernomor'e*, p. 261.
76. Ransel, *Politics of Catherinian Russia*, pp. 224–226.
77. According to V. Z. Dzhincharadze, "Iz istorii tainoi ekspeditsii pri Senate (1762–1801 gg.)," p. 98, The conspirators cited the selection of Orlov to be Russia's chief negotiator at the peace conference at Fokshani and his intention to prolong the war for his own selfish interests as reasons for wanting to overthrow Catherine's government.
78. Ransel, *Politics of Catherinian Russia*, p. 227.
79. In one of his letters to Catherine Sievers commented on the arrival in Tver of some panicked noblemen from Moscow. TsGADA, f. 168, d. 131, pp. 4–4 ob.
80. Blum, *Ein russischer Staatsmann*, II, 128.
81. Ibid., p. 128.
82. Quoted in David Marshal Lang, "Radishchev and Catherine II: New Gleanings from Old Archives," p. 57.
83. Giterman, *Geschichte Russlands*, II, 296–297. Von Tauenzein's description of Russia in 1796 sounds remarkably like Catherine's description of Russia in 1762.
84. Druzhinina, "Znachenie russko-nemetskikh nauchnykh sviazei," p. 250, and Patricia Herlihy, "Russian Grain and Mediterranean Markets 1774–1861," p. 83. In contrast to their assertions of deliberate neglect, Bartlett asserts that Paul favored the settlement and development of the south but failed to accom-

plish anything significant there; *Human Capital,* pp. 181–184. None of the three authors cited here provides adequate documentation on this point.

85. Although I reject the main thesis of Tarle's article, "Byla li ekaterininskaia Rossiia ekonomicheskoi otstaloi stranoi?" I concur with his judgment that the level of Russia's development declined *relative to that of western Europe* between 1796 and 1856.

86. Kabuzan, *Izmeneniia v razmeshchenii naseleniia,* pp. 107, 155. The guberniias of the Lower Volga region were Saratov, Astrakhan, and those of the Caucasus; those of Novorossiia were Ekaterinoslav, Kherson, Taurus, the Don Host, and the Black Sea Host. The guberniias of the northern lake region were St. Petersburg, Novgorod, Pskov and Olonets. Those of the central industrial region were Tver, Kaluga, Moscow, Vladimir, Iaroslav, Nizhnii Novgorod, and Kostroma. As might be expected, the growth of population in the central agricultural region (Voronezh, Riazan, Tambov, Orlov, Kursk, and Tula) was intermediate between those of the north and the south.

87. Herlihy, "Russian Grain and Mediterranean Markets," pp. 1, 239–240.

88. William McNeil, *Europe's Steppe Frontier,* pp. 200–202.

89. Holldack, "Der Physiocratismus und die Absolute Monarchie," pp. 531–533.

90. On the use of the Petrine myth by the Panin faction and especially by Fonvizin, see Ransel, *Politics of Catherinian Russia,* pp. 267–268. In public Catherine asserted her own claim to Peter's legacy with words and symbols that included the "Bronze Horseman," the famous equestrian statue of Peter I that bears the incription: "To Peter the First from Catherine the Second." In private, however, she repeatedly suggested that St. Petersburg had been built in the wrong place and that Rusia's capital should have been located at Taganrog or some other site on the coast of the Black Sea. Karen Rasmussen, "Catherine II and the Image of Peter I," p. 56n. In fact, Peter's own preference had been to expand southward rather than northward; but for circumstances beyond his control, Azov might have become Russia's new capital.

Glossary

BARSHCHINA. Labor dues owed by a serf to his master

DVORIANSTVO. The Russian nobility

EKSPEDITSIIA (pl. EKSPEDITSII). A special office or agency of the imperial government

GOROD (pl. GORODA). An official town; a seat of local administration

GORODNICHII. After 1775 the appointed chief of the urban police

GUBERNIIA. The highest unit of provincial administration

IAM (pl. IAMY). A settlement along a major highway providing coach and messenger service; a station

IAMSHCHIK. A state coachman-messenger

ISPRAVNIK. After 1775, the chief of the rural police elected by the local nobles

KUPECHESTVO. The merchantry; after 1775, the class of wealthier townsmen

MESHCHANE. The members of the meshchanstvo

MESHCHANSTVO. A legal category of urban residents; after 1785 the class of poorer townsmen

NAKAZ (pl. NAKAZY). An instruction or cahier presented to the Legislative Commission of 1767

OBROK. Money dues owed by a serf to his master

POMESHCHIK. A noble landowner

POMESTIE. A nobleman's estate

POSAD. (pl. POSADY). An urban commune; also an urban settlement not registered as a *gorod*

POSADSKII CHELOVEK (pl. POSADSKIE LIUDI). A legally registered member of a *posad*

PRIKAZ. An office or agency

PROVINTSIIA. Before 1775, the intermediate unit of provincial administration

RAZNOCHINITS (pl. RAZNOCHINTSY). Someone not registered in one of the major legal-administrative categories

SELO (pl. SELA). A village

SHTAT. A staffing roster or register of the positions in a government agency

SLOBODA. A suburb; a division of a POSAD

SOTSKIE. Literally, "hundreds"; a legal administrative unit, especially of peasants, charged with keeping order and performing services for the state

TRAKT. A major highway having coach and messenger service

UEZD. The basic level of provincial administration; a district or county

Bibliography

THE FOLLOWING IS A CONSOLIDATED LIST of all the primary and secondary sources cited in this book. Descriptions and discussions of the sources are given in appropriate locations in the text and notes.

Archives

Archival citations are given in the following form: f. (*fond*, meaning category or collection), op. (*opis'*, list or inventory, used as needed), d. (*delo*, dossier or file), p. (page or paper). The English p. has been substituted for the Russian l. (*list*, page or sheet) to avoid confusion with numerals. The abbreviation ob. (*oborot*) has been used when necessary to indicate the verso of a numbered page.

Leningradskoe otdelenie instituta istorii akademii nauk SSR (LOII)
  f. 36 Vorontsovykh
      d. 398 Projects and correspondence on public affairs
      d. 399 A. R. Vorontsov's reports on provincial inspections
      d. 478 A. R. Vorontsov's reports on provincial inspections
Tsentral'nyi gosudarstvennyi arkhiv derevnikh aktov (TsGADA).
  f. 5 (razriad 5) Gosarkhiv. Perepiska vysochaishikh osob s chastnymi litsami
      d. 130 Correspondence between Catherine II and Sievers
  f. 10 (razriad 10) Gosarkhiv. Kabinet Ekateriny II i ego prodolzhenie
      d. 17 Catherine's notes on law and government
  f. 11 (razriad 11) Gosarkhiv
      d. 1312 Letters from Sievers to Count A. K. Razumovskii from Grodno, 1793
  f. 16 (razriad 16) Gosarkhiv. Vnutrennee Upravlenie
      d. 264 Materials on the postal service
      d. 280 Materials on the waterways

d. 284   Materials on waterways
d. 290   Materials on waterways
d. 292   Materials on waterways
d. 299   Materials on waterways
d. 481   Reports of General Politsmeistr Chicherin
d. 785   Reports of Governor Sievers
d. 786   Reports of Governor Sievers
d. 787   Reports of Governor Sievers
d. 788   Reports of Governor-General Sievers and Governor Tutol-
         min
d. 974   Reports of Governor-General Bruce
d. 975   Reports of Governor-General Arkharov
f. 168   Snosheniia russkikh gosudarei s pravitel'stvennymi i s dolzhno-
         stnymi po vnutrennim delam
    d. 101   Letters and reports of Sievers to the empress and the Senate
    d. 110   Letters and reports of Sievers to the empress
    d. 131   Letters and reports of Sievers to the empress
    d. 137   Letters and reports of Sievers to the empress
    d. 153   Letters and reports of Sievers to the empress
f. 248   Dela Senata
    d. 2833   Materials relating to the treatment of the insane
    d. 3426   Minutes and proceedings of the Senate
    d. 3588   Papers of the Commission on Towns
    d. 3716   Papers of the First Department of the Senate for 1765 and
              1766.
    d. 3823   Papers of the central iam administration
    d. 4799   Correspondence of the Senate with provincial agencies
    d. 6444   Reports of government agencies to the Senate
f. 291   Glavnyi Magistrat
    d. 13066   Materials relevant to the merchants of Novgorod Gu-
               berniia
    d. 15127   Materials relevant to the merchants of Novgorod Gu-
               berniia
f. 342   Novoulozhenye komissii
    d.   111   Determinations   of   the   Legislative   Commission,
               1767–1796
    d. 123   Journal of the Partial Commission on the Order of the
             Realm
    d. 240   Nakaz of the Novgorod Guberniia Chancellery to the Leg-
             islative Commission.
f. 370   Gosudarstvennoe Drevnekhranilishche. Dela kasaiushchiesia do
         obrazovaniia razlichnykh gosudarstvennykh uchrezhdenii
    d. 33   Senate doklad on the reorganization of local administration,
            1766

d. 35 Legislative Commission: Catherine's assignments to the Partial Commission on the Order of the Realm
d. 37 Legislative Commission: Directing Commission
d. 39 Commission on the Liberty of the Nobility: Memorandum from Governor-General Sievers
f. 397 Komissiia o kommertsii
d. 445/32 Petition from the merchants of Novgorod Guberniia
d. 445/55 Materials on the merchants of Novgorod Guberniia

Tsentral'nyi gosudarstvennyi istoricheskii arkhiv (TsGIA)
f. 155 Vodianye kommunikatsii
op. 1, d. 1 Materials on waterways and roads, 1796–1825
f. 156 Departament vodianykh kommunikatsii
op. 1, d. 1 Materials on the creation and operations of this agency
f. 1350 Ekonomicheskoe primechanie tverskoi gubernii 1825
op. 312 d. 42 Atlas tverskoi gubernii 1825
dd. 164–175 Economic description of the eleven uezds of Tver Guberniia
f. 1487 Kolektsiia plany i chertezhi shosseikh i vodianykh soobshchenii
d. 6 Three maps of the Vyshnii Volochek System, 1778–1779.
d. 658 Undated map of the Tvertsa River and the works at Vyshnii Volochek

Tsentral'nyi gosudarstvennyi voenno-istoricheskii arkhiv (TsGVIA)
f. VUA
d. 20875 General map of Novgorod Guberniia, 1765
d. 20876 Geometric map of Novgorod Guberniia, 1785
d. 20878 Two general maps of Novgorod Guberniia, 1798

Published Primary Sources

Bartenev, P. I., ed. *Os'mnadsatyi vek: istoricheskii sbornik*. 4 vols. Moscow, 1868–1869.

Catherine II. *Instruction (Nakaz) to the Legislative Commission*. Published as volume II of Paul Dukes, ed., *Russia under Catherine the Great*. Newtonville, Mass., 1967.

———. *Memoirs of Catherine the Great*. Edited by D. Maroger. New York, 1955.

———. "Razskaz imperatritsy Ekateriny II o pervykh piati godakh eë tsarstvovaniia." *RA*, 1865, pp. 468–490.

COXE, WILLIAM. *Travels into Poland, Russia, Sweden, and Denmark*. 2 vols. London, 1784.

Drashusov, V., ed. *Materialy dlia istorii imperatorskago moskovskago vospitatel'nago doma*. 2 vols. Moscow, 1863–1868.

Du Pont de Nemours, Pierre Samuel. *De l'origine et progrès d'une science nouvelle*. London, 1768.

Gmelin, S. G. *Reise durch Russland zur Untersuchung der drei Naturreiche*. 4 vols. St. Petersburg, 1770–1774.

Guldenstadt, J. A. *Reisen durch Russland und im Caucasischen Gebirge*. 2 vols. St. Petersburg, 1787–1791.

Itzkowitz, Norman, and Mote, Max E., comps. *Mubadele: An Ottoman-Russian Exchange of Ambassadors*. Chicago, 1970.

Justi, Johann Heinrich von. *Gesammelte politische und finanz Schriften*. 3 vols. Copenhagen, 1761.

Karmanov, D. I. *Sobranie sochinenii otnosiashchikhsia k istorii tverskago kraia*. Edited and introduced by Vladimir Kolosov. Tver, 1873.

Kniga Shtatov. This is vol. 43 of *Polnoe sobranie zakonov rossiiskoi imperii*.

Le Thrône, Z. B. *De l'administration provinciale*. 2 vols. Basel, 1788.

Mirabeau, Honoré Gabriel Victor Riqueti, comte de. *Die preussische Monarchie*. 4 vols. Leipzig, 1793. First pub. London, 1788.

Pallas, P. S. *Travels through the Southern Provinces of the Russian Empire in the Years 1793 and 1794*. 2 vols. London, 1812.

Polnoe sobranie zakonov rossiiskoi imperii. 1st ser. 45 vols. St. Petersburg, 1830.

Putnam, Peter, ed. *Seven Britons in Imperial Russia 1698–1802*. Princeton, 1952.

Russkaia Starina. 1870–1918. Volume 12 (1875) contains Catherine's letter to Teplov on grain usage and the production of alcohol.

Russkii Arkhiv. 1863–1917. The volume for 1865 contains Catherine's account of her first five years in power, listed above as Catherine, "Razskaz." The volumes for 1865 and 1866 contain letters from Catherine to Teplov and other statesmen. The volume for 1891 contains Popov's letter to Alexander I, quoting Catherine on her method of preparing legislation. The volume for 1892 contains paraphrased excerpts from Sievers's accounts of some of his travels through Novgorod Guberniia.

Sbornik imperatorskago russkago istoricheskago obshchestva. 148 vols. St. Petersburg, 1867–1916. Volume 1 contains Catherine's letter to M.T.R. Jeoffrin and an account of Catherine's journey from St. Petersburg to Mogilev and back in 1780. Volumes 1, 4, 8, 68, and 93 contain the nobles' nakazy to the Legislative Commission of 1767. Volume 107 contains the nakaz of the merchants of Novgorod to the Legislative Commission.

Schlözer, August Ludwig von. *Allgemeines Staats Recht*. Göttingen, 1793.

Shcherbatov, M. M. *Sochineniia kniazia M. M. Shcherbatov*. Edited by I. P. Krushchov and A. G. Voronov. 2 vols. St. Petersburg, 1896–1898.

Sonnenfels, Joseph. *Grundsätze der Policey, Handlung und Finanz*. 8th ed. 3 vols. Vienna, 1918.

Tiul'pina, M. *Letopis' o sobytiakh v g. Tver' tverskago kuptsa Mikhaila Tiul'pina 1762–1823*. Edited by Vladimir Kolosov. Tver, 1902.

Tolchenov, I. A. *Zhurnal ili zapiski i prikliuchenii I. A. Tolchenova*. Edited by N. I. Pavlenko. Moscow, 1974.

Trudy vol'nago ekonomicheskago obshchestva k pooshchreniiu v Rossii zemledeliia i domostroitel'stva. 1st ser. 30 vols. St. Petersburg, 1765–1776.

Secondary Sources

Adamczyk, Theresa. *Furst G. A. Potemkin. Untersuchungen zu einer Lebensgeschichte*. Osnabruck, 1966. Orig. pub. 1936.

Alexander, John T. *Bubonic Plague in Early Modern Russia: Public Health in Early Modern Russia*. Baltimore and London, 1980.

Augustine, Wilson. "The Economic Attitudes and Opinions Expressed by the Russian Nobility in the Great Commission of 1767." Ph.D. diss. Columbia University, 1969.

———. "Notes toward a Portrait of the Eighteenth Century Russian Nobility." *CSS* 4 (1970): 373–425.

Bakmeister, L. B. *Topograficheskie izvestiia sluzhashchie dlia polnago-geograficheskago opisanii Rossiiskoi Imperii*. St. Petersburg, 1771.

Baldina, V. I., et al., eds. *Arkhitektor Dmitrii Vasil'evich Ukhtomskii. Katalog*. Moscow, 1973.

Bartlett, Roger. *Human Capital: The Settlement of Foreigners in Russia 1762–1804*. Cambridge, 1979.

Battersby, W. J. *De La Salle: A Pioneer of Modern Education*. London, 1949.

Beliavskii, M. T. *Krest'ianskii vopros v Rossii nakanune vosstaniia E. I. Pugacheva*. Moscow, 1965.

———. "Trebovaniia dvorian: perestroika organov upravleniia i suda na mestakh." *Nauchnye doklady vysshei shkoly istoricheskie nauki* 4 (1960): 125–143.

Berkov, P. N. "Histoire de l'*Encyclopédie* dans la Russie du XVIII siècle." *RES* (1965): 47–58.

Bernshtein-Kogan, S. V. *Vyshnevolotskii vodnyi put'*. Moscow, 1946.

Bil'basov, V. A. *Istoriia Ekateriny Vtoroi*. 2 vols. Berlin, 1910.

Black, J. L. *Citizens for the Fatherland: Education, Educators, and Pedagogical Ideals in Eighteenth Century Russia*. Boulder, Colo., 1979.

Blanning, T.W.C. *Joseph II and Enlightened Despotism*. London, 1979.

Blum, Karl. *Ein russischer Staatsmann. Des Grafen Jakob Johann Sievers Denkwürdigkeiten zur Geschichte Russlands.* 4 vols. Leipzig and Heidelberg, 1857.

Bochkov, N. V. *Istoriia zemelnykh otnoshenii i zemleustroistva.* Moscow, 1956.

Bogoslavskii, M. M. *Oblastnaia reforma Petra Velikago: provintsiia 1719–1727.* Moscow, 1902.

Braudel, Fernand. *Capitalism and Material Life.* New York, 1967.

Brown, John H. "The Publication and Distribution of the *Trudy* of the Free Economic Society, 1765–1796." *RR* 36 (1977): 341–350.

Bulygin, I. A. *Polozhenie krest'ian i tovarnoe proizvodstvo v Rossii, vtoraia polovina XVIII veka.* Moscow, 1966.

Chechulin, N. D. *Nakaz imperatritsy Ekateriny II dannyi komissii o sochinenii proekta novago ulozheniia.* St. Petersburg, 1907.

———. *Ocherki po istorii russkikh finansov v tsarstvovanie Ekateriny II.* St. Petersburg, 1906.

———. "Predposlednee slovo ob istochnikakh 'Nakaza.' " In *Sbornik statei v chest' Dmitriia Aleksandrovicha Korsakova, po povodu sorokoletiia ego uchenoi i piatidesiatiletiia uchenoi-literaturnoi deiatel'nosti.* Kazan, 1913.

———. *Russkoe provintsial'noe obshchestvo vo vtoroi polovine XVIII veka.* St. Petersburg, 1889.

Chulkov, M. D. *Istoricheskoe opisanie rossiiskoi kommertsii pri vsekh ee portakh i granitsakh ot drevnikh vremen.* 7 vols. St. Petersburg, 1781–1788.

Clendenning, P. H. "Eighteenth Century Russian Translations of Western Economic Works," *Journal of European Economic History* 1 (1972): 745–753.

Confino, Michael. *Domaines et seigneurs en Russie vers la fin du XVIII siecle.* Paris, 1963.

Coquin, François-Xavier. *La grande commission legislative, 1767–1768. Les cahiers de doléance urbaines (Province de Moscou).* Paris and Louvain, 1972.

Daniel, Wallace. "Russian Attitudes Toward Modernization: The Merchant-Nobility Conflict in the Legislative Commission, 1767–1774." Ph.D. diss., University of North Carolina, Chapel Hill, 1973.

Daniels, Rudolph. "V. N. Tatishchev: A Rationalist Historian and Theorist of the Petrine Service Nobility." Ph.D. diss., Pennsylvania State University, 1971.

Den, V. E. *Naselenie Rossii po piatoi revisii.* 2 vols. Moscow, 1902.

Derathe, Robert. "Les philosophes et le despotisme." In *Utopie et institutions au XVIII siècle: Le pragmatisme des lumières,* pp. 58–73. Paris and The Hague: 1963.

Ditiatin, I. I. *Ustroistvo i upravlenie gorodov Rossii.* 2 vols. St. Petersburg, 1875.

Dorn, Walter L. "The Prussian Bureaucracy in the Eighteenth Century." *Political Science Quarterly* 46 (1931): 403–423; 47 (1932): 259–273.

Druzhinina, E. I. *Severnoe prichernomor'e v 1775–1800.* Moscow, 1959.

―――. "Znachenie russko-nemetskikh nauchnykh sviazei dlia khoziaistvennogo razvitiia iuzhnoi ukrainy v kontsa XVIII v." In *Mezhdunarodnye sviazi Rossii v XVII-XVIII vv.* Moscow, 1966.

Dubenskii, D. *Razsuzhdenie o vodianykh soobshcheniakh v Rossii.* Moscow, 1825.

Dukes, Paul. *Catherine the Great and the Russian Nobility.* Cambridge, 1967.

―――. ed. *Russia under Catherine the Great.* 2 vols. Newtonville, Mass., 1977.

Dzhincharadze, V. Z. "Iz istorii tainoi ekspeditsii pri Senate (1762–1801 gg.)." *Uchenye zapiski novgorodskogo gosudarstvennogo pedagogicheskogo instituta, istoriko-filologicheskii fakultet* 2 (1957): 83–117.

Eckaute, Denise. "La legislation des forêts au XVIII siècle." *CMRS* 9 (1968): 194–208.

Firsov, N. N. *Pravitel'stvo i obshchestvo v ikh otnosheniiakh k vneshnei torgovli Rossii v tsarstvovanie imperatritsy Ekateriny II.* Kazan, 1902.

Fisher, Alan P. "Moscovy and the Black Sea Slave Trade." *CASS* 6 (1972): 575–594.

Florovskii, Georges. *Puti russkago bogosloviia.* Paris, 1937.

Garrard, John G. "The Emergence of Modern Russian Literature and Thought." In John G. Garrard, ed., *The Eighteenth Century in Russia,* pp. 1–21. Oxford, 1973.

Gay, Peter. *The Enlightenment: An Interpretation.* New York, 1966.

German, I. E. *Istoriia russkago mezhevaniia.* Moscow, 1907.

German, Karl. *Statisticheskie izsledovaniia otnositel'no Rossiiskoi Imperii.* St. Petersburg, 1819.

Geyer, Dietrich. "Gesellschaft als staatliche Veranstaltung. Bemerkungen zur Sozialgeschichte der russischen Staatsverwaltung im 18 Jahrhundert." *JGO* 14 (1966): 21–50.

―――. "Staatsbau und Sozialverfassung—Problem des russischen Absolutismus am Ende des 18 Jahrhunderts." *CMRS* 7 (1966): 366–377.

Gitermann, Valentin. *Geschichte Russlands.* 3 vols. Zurich and Hamburg, 1946.

Gleason, Walter. *Moral Idealists, Bureaucracy, and Catherine the Great.* New Brunswick, N. J., 1981.

―――. "Political Ideals and Loyalties of Some Russian Writers of the Early 1760s." *SR* 34 (1975): 560–575.

Got'e, Iu. V. *Istoriia oblastnogo upravleniia v Rossii ot Petra Velikago do Ekateriny II.* 2 vols. Moscow and Leningrad, 1913 and 1941.

Griffiths, David. "Catherine II: The Republican Empress." *JGO* 11 (1973): 323–344.

————. "Eighteenth Century Perceptions of Backwardness: Projects for the Creation of a Third Estate in Catherinian Russia." *CASS* 13 (1979): 452–472.

Grigor'ev, Vladimir. "Zertsalo upravy blagochiniia." *Russkii istoricheskii Zhurnal* 1 (1917): 73–103.

Hassell, James. "Catherine II and Procurator-General Viazemskii." *JGO* 24 (1976): 23–30.

Haumant, Emile. *La culture française en Russie 1700–1900.* Paris, 1931.

Herlihy, Patricia. "Russian Grain and Mediterranean Markets 1774–1861." Ph.D. diss., University of Pennsylvania, 1963.

Herzen, Alexander. *Kniaz Shcherbatov i A. Radishchev.* London, 1858.

Hinrichs, Karl. *Preussentum und Pietismus in Brandenburg-Preussen als religios-soziale Reformbewegung.* Göttingen, 1971.

Hittle, J. Michael. *The Service City: State and Townsmen in Russia 1600–1800.* Cambridge, Mass., 1979.

Holldack, Heinz. "Der Physiocratismus und die Absolute Monarchie." *Historische Zeitschrift* 145 (1932): 517–549.

Ilovaiskii, D. I. "Graf Iakov Sivers." In *Sochineniia D. I. Ilovaiskago.* Moscow, 1884.

————. "Novgorodskaia guberniia sto let tomu nazad." *RV* 48 (1867): 480–502.

Istomina, E. G. *Granitsy, naselenie i goroda novgorodskoi gubernii (1727–1917).* Leningrad, 1972.

————. "Novgorodskaia guberniia vo vtoroi polovine XVIII veka. Opyt istoriko-geograficheskogo issledovaniia." Kandidat's dissertation, Moscow State University, 1969. This entry is referred to in the notes as Istomina, dissertation.

————. *Novgorodskaia guberniia vo vtoroi polovine XVIII v (opyt istoriko-geograficheskogo issledovaniia).* Moscow, 1969. This is the published summary or *referat* of the dissertation listed immediately above. This entry is referred to in the notes as Istomina, referat.

————. "Vyshnevolotskii vodnyi put' vo vtoroi polovine XVIII–nachala XIX v." In A. L. Narochnitskii et al., eds., *Istoricheskaia geografiia Rossii VII–nachalo XIX v. Sbornik statei k 70-letiiu Professora Liubomira Grigorèvicha Beskrovnogo.* Moscow, 1975.

Istoriia Pravitel'stvuiushchego Senata. 5 vols. St. Petersburg, 1911.

Ivanov, P. I. *O general'nom mezhevanii zemel' v Rossii* St. Petersburg, n.d.

————. *Opyt biografii general-prokurorov i ministrov iustitsii.* St. Petersburg, 1863.

Johnson, Hubert C. *Frederick the Great and His Officials.* New Haven, 1975.

Johnson, William H. E. *Russia's Educational Heritage.* New York, 1969. Orig. pub. 1950.

Jones, Robert E. *The Emancipation of the Russian Nobility.* Princeton, 1973.

————. "Jacob Sievers, Enlightened Reform, and the Development of a 'Third Estate' in Russia." *RR* 36 (1977): 424–437.

————. "Urban Planning and the Development of Provincial Towns in Russia during the Reign of Catherine II." In John G. Garrard, ed., *The Eighteenth Century in Russia*. pp. 321–344. Oxford, 1973.

Kabuzan, V. M. *Izmeneniia v razmeshchenii naseleniia Rossii v XVIII—pervoi polovine XIX v.* Moscow, 1971.

————. "Nekotorye materialy dlia izucheniia istoricheskoi geografii XVIII–nachala XIX v." *Problemy istochnikovedeniia* 11 (1936).

Kahan, Arcadius. "Continuity in Economic Activity and Policy during the Post-Petrine Period in Russia." *Journal of Economic History* 25 (1965): 61–85.

————. "The Costs of Westernization in Russia: The Gentry and the Economy in the Eighteenth Century." *SR* 25 (1966): 40–56.

Kaiser, Friedhelm. *Der europäische Anteil an der russischen Rechtsterminologie der petrinischen Zeit. Forschungen zur osteuropäischen Geschichte* 10 (1965).

Kamendrowsky, Victor, and Griffiths, David. "The Fate of the Trading Nobility Controversy in Russia: A Chapter in the Relationship between Catherine II and the Russian Nobility." *JGO* 26 (1978): 198–221.

Kaplan, I. *Pervyi uglekopy na Valdae.* Moscow, 1949.

Khodnev, A. I. *Istoriia imperatorskago vol'nago ekonomicheskago obshchestva.* St. Petersburg, 1865.

Kirchner, Walter. *Commercial Relations between Russia and Europe 1400–1800.* Bloomington, 1966.

Kizevetter, A. A. *Istoricheskie siluety. Liudy i sobytiia.* Berlin, 1931.

————. *Posadskaia obshchina v Rossii XVIII st.* Moscow, 1903.

Kliuchevskii, V. O. *Kurs russkoi istorii.* Vols. 4 and 5. Moscow, 1937.

Klochkov, M. V. *Ocherki pravitel'stvennoi deiatel'nosti vremeni Pavla I.* St. Petersburg, 1916.

Klokman, Iu. V. *Ocherki sotsial'no-ekonomicheskoi istorii severo-zapada Rossii v seredine XVIII v.* Moscow, 1960.

————. *Sotsial'no-ekonomicheskaia istoriia russkogo goroda.* Moscow, 1967.

Knabe, Bernd. *Die Struktur der russischen Posadgemeinden und der Katalog der Beschwerder und Forderungen der Kaufmannschaft (1762–1767). Forschungen zur osteuropäischen Geschichte* 22 (1975).

Knoppers, Jake V. T. *Dutch Trade with Russia from the Time of Peter I to Alexander I: A Quantative Study in Eighteenth Century Shipping.* 3 vols. Montreal, 1976.

Kogan, E. S. *Ocherki istorii krepostnogo khoziaistva po materialam votchinii Kurakinykh.* Moscow, 1960.

Kolosov, Vladimir. *Istoriia tverskoi dukhovnoi seminarii.* Tver, 1889.

————. *Proshloe i nastoiashchee g. Tveri*. Tver, 1917.

————. *Tver v tsarstvovanie imperatritsy Ekateriny II*. Tver, 1896.

Korf, S. A. "Ocherk istoricheskago razvitiia gubernatorskoi dolzhnosti v Rossii." *Vestnik Prava* 31 (1901): 130–147.

Korsakov, A. *O formakh promyshlennosti v zapadnoi Evropy i Rossii*. Moscow, 1861.

Krylov, Viktor. "Ekaterininskaia komissiia v eë otnoshenii k dukhovenstvu kak sosloviiu." *Vera i razum*, 1903, pp. 467–483, 553–584, 622–639, 695–723, 758–771.

Labriolle, Françoise de. "Le prosveščenie russe et les lumières en France 1760–1789." *RES* 45 (1966): 75–92.

Lang, David Marshal. "Radishchev and Catherine II: New Gleanings from Old Archives." In John S. Curtiss, ed., *Essays in Russian and Soviet History in Honor of Geroid Tanquary Robinson*. New York, 1962.

Lazarevskii, M. I. *Leksii po russkomu gosudarstvennomu pravu*. 2 vols. St. Petersburg, 1910.

Le Donne, John P. "Appointments to the Russian Senate 1762–1796." *CMRS* 14 (1975): 27–56.

————. "The Territorial Reform of the Russian Empire 1775–1796. I. Central Russia 1775–1784." *CMRS* 23 (1982): 147–185.

Lipinskii, M. A. "Novye dannye dlia istorii ekaterininskoi komissii o sochinenii proekta novago ulozheniia." *ZMNP* 251 (June 1887).

Lodyzhenskii, K. N. *Istoriia russkago tamozhnago tarifa*. St. Petersburg, 1886.

Luppol, Ivan. "The Empress and the Philosophe." In Marc Raeff, ed., *Catherine the Great: A Profile*, pp. 41–63. London, 1972.

McConnell, Allen. "The Autocrat and the Open Critic." In Marc Raeff, ed., *Catherine the Great: A Profile*, pp. 156–178. London, 1972.

————. *A Russian Philosophe: Alexander Radishchev 1749–1802*. The Hague, 1964.

Mackrell, J.O.C. *The Attack on "Feudalism" in Eighteenth Century France*. London and Toronto, 1973.

McNeil, William. *Europe's Steppe Frontier*. Chicago and London, 1964.

Madariaga, Isabel de. *Russia in the Age of Catherine the Great*. New Haven and London, 1981.

Maikov, P. M. *Ivan Ivanovich Betskoi*. St. Petersburg, 1902.

Maksimovich, G. *Deiatel'nost Rumiantseva-Zadunaiskago po upravleniiu Malorossii*. Nizhin, 1913.

Marcum, Janet. "Simeon R. Vorontsov: Minister to the Court of St. James." Ph.D. diss., University of North Carolina, Chapel Hill, 1970.

Masson, Henri. *Secret Memoirs of the Court of St. Petersburg*. New York, 1970.

Meien, V. F. *Rossiia v dorozhnom otnoshenii*. 3 vols. St. Petersburg, 1902.

Melton, Edgar. "The Peasant Economy and the World Market 1785–1860." Paper read at the New England Slavic Association Conference, April 1978.

Miliukov, P. N. *Ocherki po istorii russkoi kultury.* Vol. III. Paris, 1930.

Milov, L. V. *Issledovanie ob "ekonomicheskikh primechaniiakh" k general'nomu mezhevaniiu.* Moscow, 1965.

Mironov, B. N. "Eksport russkogo khleba vo vtoroi polovine XVIII–nachale XIX v." *IZ* 93 (1974): 149–188.

Morrison, Kerry. "Catherine II's Legislative Commission: An Administrative Interpretation." *CSS* 4 (1970): 464–484.

Ocherki istorii Leningrada, I. Period feodalisma 1703–1861. Leningrad and Moscow, 1955.

Ogg, David. *Europe of the Ancien Régime 1715–1783.* New York, 1965.

Oreshkin, V. V. *Vol'noe ekonomicheskoe obshchestvo v Rossii 1765–1917.* Moscow, 1963.

Parker, W. H. *An Historical Geography of Russia.* London, 1968.

Parry, G. "Enlightened Government and Its Critics in Germany." *Historical Journal* 6 (1963): 180–192.

Pavlenko, N. I. *Dvorianstvo i krepostnogo stroi Rossii XVI–XVIII vv.* Moscow, 1975.

————. "Monastyrskoe khoziaistvo XVIII v. po votchinnym instruktsiiam." In N. M. Druzhinin et al., eds., *Problemy obshchestvenno-politicheskoi istorii Rossii i slavianskikh stran, sbornik statei k 70 letiiu Akademkia M. N. Tikhomirova,* pp. 313–321. Moscow, 1963.

Petrova, A. I. "Antifeodal'naia bor'ba monastyrskikh krest'ian tverskogo kraia v pervoi polovine XVIII veka." In *Krest'ianskoe i revoliutsionno-demokraticheskoe dvizhenie v XVIII–XIX vv.* Kalinin, 1969.

Pintner, Walter M. "Russia as a Great Power, 1709–1856: Reflections on the Problem of Relative Backwardness, with Special Reference to the Russian Army and Russian Society." Kennan Institute for Advanced Russian Studies, Occasional Paper no. 33.

————. *Russian Economic Policy under Nicholas I.* Ithaca, 1967.

Pipes, Richard. *Karamzin's Memoir on Ancient and Modern Russia.* Cambridge, Mass., 1959.

————. *Russia under the Old Regime.* New York, 1974.

Pisarevskii, G. G. *Iz istorii inostrannoi kolonizatsii v Rossii v XVIII v.* Moscow, 1909.

Pokrovskii, I. "Ekaterininskaia komissiia o sostavlenii proekta novago ulozheniia i tserkovnye voprosy v nei 1766–1771." In *Pravoslavnyi sobesednik,* pp. 3–52, 139–168, 285–340. Kazan, 1910.

Pokrovskii, V. I. *General'noe soobrazhenie po tverskoi gubernii izvlechennoe iz podrobnago topograficheskago i kameral'nago po gorodam i uezdam opisaniia.* Tver, 1873.

————. *Istoriko-statisticheskoe opisanie tverskoi gubernii.* 2 vols. Tver, 1879.

Pushkarev, L. N. "Akademiia Nauk i russkaia kul'tura XVIII veka." *Voprosy istorii,* 1974, pp. 28–38.

Raeff, Marc. "The Domestic Policies of Peter III and His Overthrow." *AHR* 75 (1970): 1289–1310.

————. "The Empress and the Vinerian Professor: Catherine II's Projects of Government Reforms and Blackstone's *Commentaries.*" *Oxford Slavonic Papers* 7 (1974): 18–40.

————. "The Enlightenment in Russia and Russian Thought in the Enlightenment." In John G. Garrard, ed., *The Eighteenth Century in Russia,* pp. 25–47. Oxford, 1973.

————. "In the Imperial Manner." In Raeff, ed., *Catherine the Great: A Profile,* pp. 197–246. London, 1972.

————. "Pugachev's Rebellion." In Robert Forster and Jack Greene, eds., *Preconditions of Revolution in Early Modern Europe.* Baltimore and London, 1970.

————. "Random Notes on the Reign of Catherine II in the Light of Recent Literature." *JGO* 19 (1971): 541–556.

————. "Les Slaves, les Allemands, et les 'Lumières.'" *CSS* 1 (1967): 521–551.

————. "The Well-Ordered Police State and the Development of Modernity in Seventeenth and Eighteenth Century Europe: An Attempt at a Comparative Approach." *AHR* 80 (1975): 1221–1243.

Rahbek-Schmidt, Knud. "The Treaty of Commerce between Great Britain and Russia 1765: A Study on the Development of Count Panin's Northern System." *Scandoslavica* 1 (1954): 115–134.

Ransel, David L. *The Politics of Catherinian Russia: The Panin Party.* New Haven, 1975.

Rasmussen, Karen. "Catherine II and the Image of Peter I." *SR* 37 (1978): 51–69.

Riazhskii, G. A., ed. *Topograficheskoe opisanie vladimirskoi gubernii sostavlennoe v 1784 godu.* Vladimir, 1906.

Rosenberg, Hans. *Bureaucracy, Aristocracy, and Autocracy: The Prussian Experience 1660–1815.* Cambridge, Mass., 1958.

Rothkrug, Lionel. *Opposition to Louis XIV: The Political and Social Origins of the French Enlightenment.* Princeton, 1970.

Rozman, Gilbert. *Urban Networks in Russia 1750–1800 and Premodern Periodization.* Princeton, 1976.

Rubinshtein, N. L. *Sel'skoe khoziaistvo Rossii vo vtoroi polovine XVIII v.* Moscow, 1957.

————. "Topograficheskie opisaniia namestnichestva i gubernii XVIII v.—pamiatniki geograficheskogo i ekonomicheskogo izucheniia Rossii." *Voprosy geografii* 31 (1953): 39–89.

————. "Ulozhenaia komissiia 1754–1766 gg. i ee proekt novogo ulozheniia 'O sostoiannii poddannykh voobshche.'" *IZ* 38 (1951): 208–251.

Russkii biograficheskii slovar'. 25 vols. St. Petersburg, 1896–1918.

Semennikov, V. "Literaturnaia i knigopechatnaia deiatel'nosti v provintsii v kontse XVIII i nachale XIX vekov." *Russkii bibliofil*, 1911, pp. 14–41.

Semevskii, V. I. *Krest'iane v tsarstvovanie Ekateriny II*. 2 vols. St. Petersburg, 1901, 1903.

Serbina, K. N. *Ocherki iz istorii sotsial'no-ekonomicheskoi istorii russkogo goroda. Tikhvin Posad XVI–XVIII vv.* Moscow and Leningrad, 1951.

Serpukov, N. M. "Ob izmenenii razmerov dushevladeniia pomeshchikov evropeiskoi Rossii v pervoi chetverti XVIII–pervoi polovine XIX v." In *Ezhegodnik po agrarnoi istorii vostochnoi evropy 1963*. Vilnius, 1964.

Shchekatov, A., ed. *Geograficheskii slovar' rossiiskago gosudarstva*. 7 vols. Moscow, 1801–1808.

Shikov, V. "Raboty A. V. Kvasova i I. E. Starova po planirovki russkikh gorodov." In *Arkhitekturnoe nasledstvo*. Moscow, 1953.

Shkvarikov, V. A. *Ocherki istorii planirovki i zastroiki russkikh gorodov*. Moscow, 1954.

Shpilevskii, M. "Politika narodonaseleniia v tsarstvovanie Ekateriny II." *Zapiski imperatorskago novorossiiskago universiteta* 4 (1871): 1–178.

Sivkov, K. V. "Voprosy sel'skogo khoziaistva v russkikh zhurnalakh poslednei tretei XVIII v." In *Materialy po istorii zemledeliia SSSR*. Moscow, 1952.

Small, Albion. *The Cameralists, Pioneers of German Social Policy*. New York, 1905.

Sorina, Kh. D. "K voprosu o protsese sotsial'nogo rassloeniia goroda v sviazii s formirovaniem kapitalisticheskikh otnoshenii v Rossii v XVIII v. (g. Tver')." *Uchenyi zapiski kalininskogo gosudarstvennogo pedagogicheskogo instituta* 38 (1964): 281–300.

————. "Ocherk sotsial'no-ekonomicheskoi istorii goroda ostashkova v kontse XVIII–pervoi chetverti XIX v." In *Iz proshlogo i nastoiashchego kalininskoi oblasti*. Moscow, 1965.

————. "Ocherk sotsial'no-ekonomicheskoi istorii g. Vyshnego-Volochka vo vtoroi polovine XVIII veka i nachala XIX veka." *Uchenyi zapiski kalininskogo gosudarstvennogo pedagogicheskogo instituta* 35 (1961): 122–136.

Starr, S. Frederick. *Decentralization and Self-Government in Russia, 1830–1879*. Princeton, 1972.

Stog, A. *Ob obshchestvennom prizrenii v Rossii*. Moscow, 1818.

Stoletie Viatskoi Gubernii, 1780–1880. Viatka, 1880.

Storch, Heinrich. *Historische-statistische Gemälde des russischen Reichs.* Leipzig, 1803.

————. *Tableau historique et statistique de l'empire de la Russie.* 2 vols. Paris and Basel, 1801.

Strumilin, S. G. *Istoriia chernoi metallurgii v SSSR.* Vol. I. Moscow, 1954.

Svodnyi katalog russkoi knigi XVIII veka 1725–1800. 3 vols. Moscow, 1963.

Taranovskii, F. V. "Politicheskaia doktrina v nakaze imperatritsy Ekateriny II." In *Sbornik statei posviashchennyi M. F. Vladimirskomu-Budanovu.* Kiev, 1904.

Tarle, E. V. "Byla li ekaterininskaia Rossiia ekonomicheskoi otstaloi stranoi?" In Tarle, *Sochineniia,* vol. 4. Moscow, 1958.

Treadgold, Donald. *The West in Russia and China: Russia 1472–1917.* Cambridge, 1973.

Trefolev, L. "Aleksei Petrovich Mel'gunov, general-gubernator ekaterininskikh vremen." *RA,* 1865, pp. 932–978.

Troitskii, S. M. "Finansovaia politika russkogo absoliutizma vo vtoroi polovine XVII–XVIII vv." In N. M. Druzhinin et al., eds., *Absoliutizm v Rossii XVII–XVIII vv. Sbornik statei k semidesiatiletiiu so dna rozhdeniia i sorokaniatiletiiu nauchnoi i pedagogicheskoi deiatel'nosti B.B. Kafengauza.* Moscow, 1964.

————. "Obsuzhdenie voprosa o krest'ianskoi torgovle v komissii o kommertsii v seredine 60x godov XVIII v." In N. I. Pavlenko, ed., *Dvorianstvo i krepostnoi stroi Rossii XVI–XVIII vv.,* pp. 227–239. Moscow, 1975.

————. *Russkii absoliutizm i dvorianstvo.* Moscow, 1974.

Tsvetkov, M. A. *Izmenenie lesistosti evropeiskoi Rossii s kontsa XVII stoletiia po 1914 g.* Moscow, 1957.

————. "Kartograficheskie materialy general'nogo mezhevaniia," *Voprosy geografii* 31 (1953): 90–121.

Volkov, S. I. *Krest'iane dvortsovykh vladenii podmoskov'ia v seredine XVIII veka.* Moscow, 1959.

Von Laue, Theodore. *Sergei Witte and the Industrialization of Russia.* New York, 1963.

Wangermann, Ernst. *The Austrian Achievement 1700–1800.* London, 1973.

White, R. J. *Europe in the Eighteenth Century.* New York, 1965.

Wilson, Arthur. "Diderot in Russia 1773–1774." In John G. Garrard, ed., *The Eighteenth Century in Russia,* pp. 166–197. Oxford, 1973.

Winter, Eduard, ed. *August Ludwig Schlözer und Russland.* Berlin, 1961.

————. *Halle als Ausgangspunkt der deutschen Russlandkunde in 18 Jahrhundert.* Berlin, 1953.

Wortman, Richard. *The Development of a Russian Legal Consciousness.* Chicago, 1976.

Yaney, George. *The Systematization of Russian Government.* Urbana, Chicago, and London, 1973.

Zheludkov, V. F. "Krest'ianskaia voina pod predvoditel'stvom E. I. Pugacheva i podgotovka gubernskoi reformy 1775 g." *Vestnik Leningradskogo Universiteta* 8 (1963): 56–65.

———. "Vvedenie gubernskoi reformy 1775 goda." In V. N. Bernadskii, ed., *Ocherki po istorii klassovoi bor'by i obshchestvenno-politicheskoi mysli Rossii tret'ei chetverti XVIII v.* Leningrad, 1962.

Index

(Italic page numbers indicate figures or tables.)

243